ELVIS' FAVORITE DIRECTOR

TO AL –
A GREAT LUNCH COMPANION!
BEST WISHES!
MIKE

2013

Other Titles by Michael A. Hoey

*Elvis, Sherlock and Me: How I Survived Growing Up in Hollywood**

Inside Fame on Television: A Behind the Scenes History

*Sherlock Holmes & the Fabulous Faces: The Universal Pictures Repertory Company**

The Drury Lane Theatre Mystery

*Published by BearManor Media

ELVIS' FAVORITE DIRECTOR

The Amazing 52-Year Career of Norman Taurog

by
Michael A. Hoey

BearManor Media
2013

Elvis' Favorite Director: The Amazing 52-Year Career of Norman Taurog

For information, address:

BearManor Media
P. O. Box 71426
Albany, GA 31708

bearmanormedia.com

Typesetting and layout by John Teehan

Published in the USA by BearManor Media

ISBN—1-59393-755-5
978-1-59393-755-3

To my daughters Lauren and Karin
and my son Dennis,
for their love and support
during a very difficult
time in my life.

I love them very much.

Contents

Introduction

Norman Taurog is unjustly accused of directing most of Elvis Presley's bad movies, but his detractors forget such other directors' mind-numbing Elvis vehicles as *Clambake*, *Easy Come, Easy Go*, *Harum Scarum*, *Frankie and Johnny* and *Kissin' Cousins*. Directorially speaking, all of Taurog's Elvis films retain the same professional style as his earlier award-winning films. He wasn't a celebrated director in the manner of a Hitchcock, Ford, or Wilder, but he was a top craftsman in his field. To this day Taurog remains the youngest director ever to win an Academy Award for his directing of 1931's *Skippy* (which was also nominated for Best Picture), and he was nominated again for *Boys Town* in 1938 (which was also nominated for Best Picture), and in which Spencer Tracy won his second consecutive Oscar for his performance as Father Flanagan. To really appreciate Norman Taurog's work you need to go back and examine the more than one hundred silent and sound two-reel comedy shorts, as well as the 78 feature films that represent his total handiwork over the length and breadth of his professional life.

Norman Taurog's career spans virtually the entire history of films from the silent era to the Elvis Presley era. In less than eleven years, before celebrating his 32nd birthday, Taurog wrote and directed 102 two-reel comedies starring comedians Larry Semon, Lloyd Hamilton, Oliver Hardy, Lupino Lane, Bobby Clark, Jack Benny and W.C. Fields. Over the next 38 years he would direct such stars as Fred Astaire, Bing Crosby, Maurice Chevalier, Ethel Merman, Deanna Durbin, Alice Faye, Cary Grant, Kathryn Grayson, Van Johnson, Deborah Kerr, David Niven, Eleanor Powell, Jane Powell and Spencer Tracy.

Norman Taurog and Elvis Presley on the set of their final film together *Live a Little, Love a Little* (1968).

He did six films with Mickey Rooney, four with Judy Garland, two with Mario Lanza, six with Dean Martin and Jerry Lewis, two more with Jerry Lewis alone, and nine films with Elvis Presley.

He directed elaborate musicals such as *The Big Broadcast of 1936* (1935), *Broadway Melody of 1940* (1940), *Girl Crazy* (1943) and *Words and Music* (1948); serious dramas including *Skippy* (1931) and its sequel *Sooky* (1931), *The Adventures of Tom Sawyer* (1938), *Boys Town* (1938) and its sequel *Men of Boys Town* (1941), *Young Tom Edison* (1940), and the story of the development of the first Atomic bomb, *The Beginning or the End* (1947); and contemporary comedies like *A Bedtime Story* (1933) with Maurice Chevalier, *We're Not Dressing* (1934) with Bing Crosby and Carole Lombard, *You Can't Have Everything* (1937) with Alice Faye and Don Ameche, *The Bride Goes Wild* (1948) with Van Johnson and June Allyson, *Room For One More* (1952) with Cary Grant and Betsy Drake, *Bundle of Joy* (1956) with Debbie Reynolds and Eddie Fisher and *Onionhead* (1958) with Andy Griffith. And he did the majority of these films without the benefit of sight in his left eye.

There's an old adage in the film business, "You're only as good as your last picture," and fortunately or unfortunately, depending on your taste in Elvis Presley movies, I wrote the screenplay for Norman Taurog's last picture, *Live a Little, Love a Little* (1968), but we'll talk more about that later. Norman was my friend and mentor and I worked beside him on each of his last eight films. We met just as my career was getting started and his was entering his final decade. I was a young producer at Warner Bros. Studios in 1962 when he directed my first film *Palm Springs Weekend* (1963). For the next six years I worked side by side with him as a writer and idea man on every one of those eight films (five of them starred Elvis Presley) until his retirement in 1968. There were actually ten films, if you count the two short films that we made to raise funds for the building program at Harvard School for Boys, the semi-military prep school on Coldwater Canyon in Studio City, California, where his teenage son Jonathan was a student. I remained Norman Taurog's friend until his death from cancer in 1981.

Elvis Presley in *G.I. Blues.*

Juliet Prowse in *G. I. Blues.*

G.I. Blues – The Beginning

It was 1960; Elvis Presley was back from Germany and his two-year tour of duty in the U.S. Army and looking forward to resuming his film career. His hopes were for a juicy dramatic role along the lines of the ones he played in *Love Me Tender* (1956), *Jailhouse Rock* (1957) and *King Creole* (1958), three of the four films he made before entering the Army in 1958. What he got instead was *G.I. Blues* (1960), a romanticized, song-filled version of his time in the Army in Germany.

In 1956, having seen Elvis Presley on a half-hour television program called *Stage Show*, hosted by Tommy and Jimmy Dorsey, Producer Hal Wallis decided to give Presley a screen test, with the idea of having him play the third lead in his upcoming production of Tennessee Williams *The Rainmaker* (1957). The test revealed that the young singer could indeed act, although he was still a little rough around the edges, and Wallis signed Elvis to a one-picture commitment with an option for six more films for an initial fee of $15,000. He soon realized that *The Rainmaker* wasn't the appropriate vehicle for Elvis, and when Twentieth Century-Fox wanted him for a co-starring role in *Love Me Tender* (1957) he agreed to loan him out. When *Love Me Tender* turned out to be a big success, Wallis wrote a new non-exclusive contract for Elvis at $2,500 a week and proposed to give him and his manager, Colonel Tom Parker, a $25,000 bonus. The Colonel balked at that, insisting that he be paid a separate fee for his services and a separate bonus. With the intersession of Abe Lastfogel of the William Morris Office, an arrangement was reached whereby the Colonel would receive a separate bonus of $25,000 and would be credited and paid on every Elvis film as a "Technical Advisor." At this point the Colonel effectively moved from his original 25% commission to a 50-50 split on everything Elvis made from that time onward.

Hal Wallis had promised Elvis he would find dramatic roles for him, but had changed his mind and decided that the proper way to feature the hottest star in Hollywood at the time was to play up his natural appeal as a singer. Elvis wasn't happy; he'd known for months that his next film wouldn't compare to his earlier ones and he was angry with Wallis for not keeping his promise. Elvis idolized both James Dean and Marlon Brando and felt, if given the right roles to play, he could emulate their success. He ordered the Colonel to find projects that would give him that opportunity. Nicholas Ray, who had directed James Dean in *Rebel Without a Cause* (1955), claimed that he once ran into Elvis in the MGM Commissary and Elvis had got down on his knees and recited whole passages of dialogue from the script of *Rebel.* "Elvis must have seen *Rebel* a dozen times by then," Ray recalled, "and remembered every one of Jimmy's lines."

Since Elvis' contract with Wallis was non-exclusive and allowed him to make films with other studios, he would ultimately play several quasi-dramatic roles over the next few years in films such as *Flaming Star* (1960) and *Wild in the Country* (1961). But with the public failing to respond to them, Colonel Parker, ever the showman, soon convinced Elvis that his career was safer in lightweight films. In spite of his disappointment, Elvis had to admit that the Colonel's formula seemed to be working; his films would show up in the list of top ten money-makers over the next four years, and Elvis was soon earning a salary of a million dollars per picture and 50 percent of the profits—and of course the Colonel took 50 per cent of all of Elvis' earnings. However, that same formula would lead to his eventual downfall in Hollywood.

Norman Taurog and Elvis Presley met for the first time in Hal Wallis' office at Paramount studios on Thursday, April 21, 1960. Taurog, who was to direct Elvis in *G.I. Blues*, had watched *Loving You* (1957) and *King Creole* in a studio projection room and was impressed with Elvis' acting talent. He would later tell an interviewer, "This may surprise you, but I think Elvis, if we gave him serious roles to play, would be recognized as one of the best actors." Well practiced at dealing with stars that had grandiose opinions of themselves, Taurog was pleasantly surprised to find a polite young man who quietly shook his hand when they met and called him "Mr. Taurog." Elvis in turn was impressed with Taurog's friendly, open manner and genuine warmth. It was the beginning of a relationship that lasted until Elvis' death in 1977; they would become good friends, make nine films together, and Taurog's son Jonathan would tour with Elvis in the 70s.

Elvis went directly from that brief meeting in Wallis' office to the "new" RCA Victor Studios in Hollywood to begin rehearsing and recording the songs for *G.I. Blues* with his musicians and the Jordanaires vocal group. He was happy that he wasn't being forced to use the big recording stage at Paramount Studios, which he found "unfriendly and impersonal," but he wasn't happy with the selection of songs, or the fact that there were so many of them. Once again his judgment would prove faulty, as the *G.I. Blues* soundtrack album of eleven songs, including a new version of his previous hit "Blue Suede Shoes," sold over 400,000 copies by the end of 1960, was nominated for a Grammy and was certified Gold three years later. Still one of Elvis' most popular soundtrack albums, it went Platinum in 1992.

The writing team of Edmund Beloin and Henry Garson, who had done the final revisions for Hal Wallis on the screenplay of the Taurog-directed *Don't Give up the Ship* in 1958, had come up with an original idea for an Elvis Presley film called *Christmas in Berlin*. Wallis bought the treatment and put them to work on developing a screenplay while Elvis was still serving as a tank gunner with the Third Armored "Spearhead" Division in Friedberg, West Germany. That screenplay would initially be called *Café Europa*, but by July 21, 1959 it had become known as *G.I. Blues*.

Wallis decided that he wanted to shoot *G.I. Blues* in color with VistaVision cameras, and on July 22, assistant director Michael "Micky" Moore shot some nighttime VistaVision color film tests at the corner of Hollywood Boulevard and La Brea Avenue. Micky Moore and his brother Pat had been at Paramount most of their lives. Both had been child actors in silent films, starring in films with Mary Pickford, Gloria Swanson, Mary Miles Minter and Blanche Sweet. Pat, two years older than Micky, had played the Pharaoh's son in Cecil B. DeMille's 1923 production *The Ten Commandments*, and Micky

(L-R) Cameraman Loyal Griggs, Producer Hal Wallis and Second Unit Director Micky Moore on location in Germany.

had played the boy Apostle Mark in DeMille's *The King of Kings* (1927). After they grew up, Micky went back to Paramount as a prop man and eventually worked his way up to first assistant director, and Pat became a music editor.

On Monday, August 10, 1959, Hal Wallis and Micky Moore along with cameraman Loyal Griggs and his crew and equipment, arrived in Frankfurt, Germany, to pick locations and film Second Unit footage with Moore directing. They planned three weeks of filming with a double for Elvis, who, since he was still in the Army at that time, was forbidden from appearing in front of a camera. Elvis' double, Private First Class Tom Creel, looked so much like Elvis that Moore was able to use him to great advantage during the shoot. The studio was granted full cooperation from the U.S. Army and in particular the Third Armored Division, to which Presley was attached. On August 16, 1959, Micky Moore sent a hand-written letter to Jack Saper, Wallis' personal assistant, in which he spoke of the filming going well and on schedule. Moore filmed armored maneuvers with two platoons of tanks and some armored carriers, and also filmed long shots on the Rhine River of an excursion boat sailing past villages and castles. According to Moore, Tom Creel was so convincing a double for Elvis that when they shot the exterior of a nightclub in Friedberg, word got out that Elvis was there and a huge crowd gathered, wanting to see him. Moore had to call out the German police to restore order so they could continue filming. The company finished on schedule and Moore and his wife took a brief vacation to Rome and Paris, before returning to Hollywood and taking up his duties as Norman Taurog's assistant director on the First Unit.

Hal Wallis had originally intended for Michael Curtiz, who had directed Elvis in *King Creole*, to direct *G.I. Blues*, and had sent him the *Christmas in Berlin* treatment. Curtiz loved it and sent Wallis a memo to that effect on January 21, 1959, in which he said that he felt that it would make an "excellent Presley picture." At some point, Wallis decided that Norman Taurog, who had recently directed Jerry Lewis in Wallis' *Don't Give Up the Ship* (1959) and *Visit to a Small Planet* (1960) and before that had directed the team of Martin and Lewis in six other Paramount films, would be a better choice to handle the comedy. Taurog signed his contract on December 29, 1959, for a salary of $75,000 for 15 weeks plus five free weeks if needed. His start date was March 15, 1960.

Both the Screen Actors Guild and the Writers Guild went on strike in early 1960 over residual payments for movies sold to television and increases in their pensions and health plans. The actors went out in March and settled with the producers in six weeks, but the writers, who went on strike in January, stayed out for 21 weeks and didn't settle until the middle of June. Taurog wasn't able to work with Eddie Beloin and Hank Garson because of the strike, but he had his right-hand-man Jack Mintz with him to make whatever changes he needed to accommodate casting and location requirements, which was allowed in the WGA contract. Casting for the female lead had been going on for some time; in October of 1959, talent test were shot with Dolores Hart, who had appeared with Elvis in *Loving You* (1957) and *King Creole* (1958), for roles in both *Summer and Smoke* (1961) and *G.I. Blues*. Additional tests were made the next day with Ursula Andress, Joan Blackman and Dolores Hart once again. In March of 1960 the talent search was still on and Paul Nathan, Wallis' associate producer, sent Wallis a memo in which he jokingly suggested that he and Taurog go to Europe on a search. He finished by saying, "Only solution we all go to Europe hunting broads. Taurog already packed and has license and I feel I can pass for white with new nose." (Apparently Nathan had recently had an operation on his nose).Wallis answered, "Don't know what good your new nose would be talent hunting. You're supposed to see them not smell them." Nathan had begun at Paramount in the casting department shortly after returning from service in World War II, and his first film with Hal Wallis was *Rope of Sand* (1949), for which he was one of two casting directors. He became Wallis' personal casting director and eventually his story editor. In 1955 he became Wallis' associate producer and remained in that capacity on every film that Wallis made at Paramount and later at Universal.

On April 22, Norman Taurog directed Juliet Prowse in a test scene with Frank Gorshin, and four days later he directed Elvis and Prowse in another test scene. A memo from Paul Nathan regarding Juliet Prowse describes Taurog as not caring for her. "He feels she is terribly tall, gawky and only nice looking rather than sexy." There was a flurry of interest in Elke Sommer around the end of April, but ultimately the decision was made to go with Juliet Prowse, who was borrowed from Twentieth Century-Fox for the film at a $1,000 a week, with a ten week guarantee for $10,000.

The baby that Elvis' character supposedly babysits while wooing Juliet Prowse was in fact six babies (actually three sets of twins) each with a specific job. California State law required that an infant could not work under the lights and before the camera for more than two hours each day, so the twins would alternate and the baby that reacted best would be given the close-ups and the others would be used in long shots.

On April 25 Taurog and his crew went to the Reserve Tank Maintenance Depot in Burbank on a location survey. Taurog then spent Friday, April 29, on Paramount's Stage 8 in the *Int. Rathskeller* set, rehearsing scenes 40-46 with Elvis, Arch Johnson, James Douglas and Robert Ivers, who played fellow G.I.'s, and Fred Essler, who played Papa Mueller, the owner of the Rathskeller. Taurog blocked the scenes and set the camera positions with head cameraman Loyal Griggs and his crew and then had Micky Moore dismiss everyone, after giving them their calls for Monday morning.

Filming officially began on Monday, May 2, 1960, and about mid-way through production, Elvis was scheduled to film the song "Wooden Heart," which was based on an old German folk song that was adapted with new lyrics by Fred Wise, Ben Weisman, Kay Twomey and the German orchestra leader, Bert Kaempfert. It was staged by choreographer Jack Baker so that Elvis would sing the song to some wooden puppets of a little girl and her father on a miniature stage in front of an audience of children. Bob Baker and his two helpers, Donald G. Sahlin and F. Alton Wood, created the puppets and handled them for the shoot. Baker, who had been giving shows for years at a puppet theater he had built in downtown Los Angeles, had been in the business since he was a child. He had even appeared as an actor in several films directed by Taurog, including *Skippy* and *Are Husbands Necessary?* When I interviewed him, Baker, who is in his late eighties, couldn't remember too much about working with Taurog, but in an earlier interview he had given to film researcher Bill Bram he described filming the "Wooden Heart" number with Elvis.

"Presley came out onto the stage and saw the puppets and started to work with them," Baker recalled. "He worked for about three minutes and he asked to stop. He worked a few more minutes and again he had to stop. Finally, he worked five minutes and he had to stop and he told the director, 'I can't take it, I've got to go back to my dressing room.' He added, 'I don't know

(L-R) puppeteer Donald G. Sahlin, Juliet Prowse, Elvis and head puppeteer Bob Baker.

if any of you people have ever been up here to sing to a puppet.' He couldn't get any reaction from the puppets of course and that threw him. He said, 'I can't do it! I literally can't do it. This is the hardest thing I've ever had to do.' So he went to his dressing room and was there for over an hour. Norman Taurog started pacing up and down, and finally Elvis came and just had a hell of a time singing to the puppets. We were also instructed 'do not, under any circumstances, touch his hair. No way. Do not touch his hair with any one of the puppets.' And finally at the very end, I guess it was Norman that came over, and he took the father puppet, the older man, and he pinched Presley's hair. Elvis could've killed him on the spot, but I guess Taurog was the only one that could get away with it. It took about three days to rehearse and film the entire sequence. And they did a very big spread in Life Magazine—a five-page spread, but it was preempted by some sort of a conflict. Whatever war we were fighting that year preempted it. Over the years I've had lots of people tell me they love that sequence, and it is a cute sequence."

Filming was completed on June 24, 1960. The production report for the final day of shooting shows that the company finished principal photography at 2:50 PM, with Elvis singing "Didja Ever" at the Armed Forces Show on Paramount's Stage A, which was dressed to look like an Army hangar. The company then moved to Stage 2 where they filmed a special trailer for the film. At the wrap party, Colonel Parker showed up, accompanied by his wife Marie, dressed as a Confederate Colonel, complete with saber and flowing moustache, courtesy of Paramount's wardrobe and makeup departments.

On September 12, 1960, a special screening of *G. I. Blues* was held at Paramount Studios for members of the Theater Owners of America, who were in Hollywood for their annual convention. Elvis and Juliet Prowse attended, and the next day Paul Nathan sent Wallis, who was in Tokyo, a telegram stating, "Screening last night howling success unanimous exhibitor praise Presley Prowse who personally attended friendly gay party." Nathan followed this up with a more detailed letter to Wallis, who was staying at the Imperial Hotel in Tokyo, scouting locations for his upcoming production *A Girl Named Tamiko* (1962). Nathan described the evening in the following manner: "The Theatre was packed," he wrote, "Even the front row was taken and many people were standing.

"There was applause after all of the numbers and even after Juliet's two dance numbers. Many of the exhibitors came up and said they thought this was the best and most commercial picture we had ever made or that they had ever seen. Hedda Hopper sat with me and said she had never seen Elvis, and when it was over she told me she thought he was fantastic and so was the movie. She kept laughing and even applauding during it. The Party was really something. They turned the whole Commissary into the Club Europa…

Elvis couldn't have been more gracious in signing autographs for everybody, as did Juliet Prowse." Two days later, Hedda Hopper wrote in her syndicated column: "Elvis Presley's *G.I. Blues* with Juliet Prowse is a humdinger of a picture. It'll make a mint. Scenes of him in uniform in and under tanks and Jeeps in Germany with his pals are mighty good. And a babysitting scene with Juliet Prowse is hilarious. Elvis had many fans before—he'll have more after this. Norman Taurog has done a sensitive bit of directing."

The film's reviewers apparently saw it differently, with James Powers in *The Hollywood Reporter* describing the star as a "subdued and changed Elvis Presley... The ex-GI-rating singing star is likely to disappoint old fans in this new Paramount release... Presley is personable although he is never convincing. He gives the impression he is about to break up, hardly a help in a film where the remaining players are going about their business as if it mattered." *Variety* echoed the same concern, declaring, "*G.I. Blues* restores Elvis Presley to the screen in a picture that seems to have been left over from the frivolous filmusicals of World War II. On the logical assumption that the teenage following that vaulted Presley to the top a few years back has grown older, wiser and more sophisticated in its tastes, the rather juvenile Hal Wallis production may have to depend on younger, pre-teen age groups for its chief response... Norman Taurog's direction has that made-in-Hollywood look about it, with the exception of a few genuine West German views. It's a long picture and the pace engineered by Taurog gets pretty sluggish." Bosley Crowther in the *New York Times*, who obviously disliked the original Elvis, crowed over the changes: "Whatever else the Army has done for Elvis Presley," he wrote. "It has taken that indecent swivel out of his hips and turned him into a good, clean, trustworthy, upstanding American young man. At least, that's the cinematic image projected in the first post-service picture of 1958's most celebrated draftee... Gone is that rock' n' roll wriggle, that ludicrously lecherous leer, that precocious country-bumpkin swagger, that unruly mop of oily hair. Almost gone are the droopy eyelids and that hillbilly manner of speech. He's a man of the world—almost." Of course Crowther didn't see these changes as a guarantee of a successful film, adding, "Well, it's not a question of how you like it—you older, quieter, people, that is... It's a question of how those squealing youngsters, Elvis' erstwhile fans, are going to take to a rock' n' roll singer with honey in his veins instead of blood."

Despite these tepid reviews, it was Hedda Hopper who called it correctly; *G.I. Blues* earned over $4.3 million at the box office and was the fourteenth highest grossing film of the year, and Edmund Beloin and Henry Garson received a nomination in 1961 from the Writers Guild of America for "Best Written American Musical." A charity premiere at Beverly Hills' Fox Wilshire Theater drew a crowd of over 1,500, mostly teenage on-lookers. Norman Taurog's wife Sue, who chaired the women's auxiliary of the Hemophilia Foundation, arranged for the star-studded event, complete with huge searchlights crisscrossing the night sky and a platoon from the Army's Armored Desert Training Center in Barstow, California. The only person missing was Elvis Presley, who was on location filming *Wild in the Country* in Napa, California.

Elvis was definitely back in a big way, and shortly after the successful exhibitors screening at Paramount, Hal Wallis announced to the press that he had signed Norman Taurog to direct Elvis' next picture. Taurog's journey with Elvis would continue; over the next eight years they would eventually make eight more films, and Elvis would refer to him as his favorite director. At this point, Norman Taurog had been directing films for over 40 years—how did it all begin?

The Early Years

He was an only child, born Norman Rae Taurog on his parents' second wedding anniversary, February 23, 1898, in Chicago, Illinois. His father, a wholesale fur dealer originally named Jacob Taurog, was a Russian Jew from Riga who had escaped the pogroms that had spread though Russia in the late 1800s and traveled by way of Hamburg, Germany, and Glasgow, Scotland, to the United States, arriving in New York on the S.S. *Ethiopia* on November 17, 1891. His mother was the former Anita "Annie" Goldsmith, whose father and mother had migrated to the United States from England and settled in New York City, where Anita had been born in 1872.

By 1896, Jacob Taurog had changed his first name to Arthur, met and married young Annie Goldsmith and moved to Chicago, where he established himself in the fur business. According to a November 18, 1934 *New York Times* interview that Norman Taurog gave to future John Ford screenwriter Frank S. Nugent, Taurog's mother, the daughter of artist David Goldsmith and the former Rachel Woolf, once wanted to become an actress, but her family had said no. "In those days," Taurog explained, "no nice girl would consider going on the stage.

"My parents brought me to New York when I was about a year old," Taurog continued. "We lived first on Ninety-Fourth Street between Amsterdam and Broadway." Displaying a photographic memory and talent as a mimic, Taurog began acting at the age of nine in stock companies in Bridgeport, Connecticut, and Union City, New Jersey, playing old men with beards and whiskers. His father didn't approve of his acting ambitions, wanting his son to carry on in the fur business, but when his mother read about tryouts for *A Good Little Devil,* a play that David Belasco was producing with Mary Pickford, Lillian Gish and Ernest Truex, she brought her son downtown to the Theatre Republic for an interview. Taurog's audition went well and he was given the role of Alan, as well as the job of understudying Ernest Truex.

The play opened on January 8, 1913, a month before Taurog's15th birthday, and ran for 133 performances. Soon after the play closed, Taurog was signed to appear as an office boy with Barney Bernard, Alexander Carr and Louise Dresser at the George M. Cohan Theatre in the comedy *Potash and Perlmutter*, which had a healthy 63-week run.

Fascinated by the nascent motion picture industry, Taurog first tried his hand at film acting, becoming one of the IMP kids at the Independent Moving Pictures Studios at Eleventh and Forty-Third Street. He made his film debut in a silent comedy short starring Florence Turner and King Baggott When the studio moved to Fort Lee, New Jersey, Taurog went to work there as one of the stock extras, earning $15 a week. He was given a small role in an Edith Roberts film, which Taurog spoke about to Frank Nugent. 'I remember that picture,' said Mr. Taurog with a woebegone look. 'It was called *Her Lover's Return*, a three-reeler. I worked one day and went to see myself in the rushes. I smelled up the whole projection room. It was terrific. I never saw such bad acting. So I asked to become a property boy. No one had the least objection.' " In an article that appeared 11 years later in the 15th Anniversary issue of *The Hollywood Reporter* under Taurog's name, he elaborated on that moment. "I can still see Julius Stern, head of the studio, when I stalked into his office and asked to be transferred to the Coast in the capacity of property man," Taurog wrote. "'You're crazy if you go,' he said. 'I'm crazy if I stay,' I answered."

Early in 1916, still trying to pursue the elusive goal of success in the film business, Taurog moved to California and took an apartment at 1763 Ivar Ave just off Hollywood Boulevard. His mother, whose marriage to Arthur Taurog was not going well, accompanied him. His father, not happy that his barely 17 year-old son had surrendered to the allure of Hollywood and still certain that his son and Anita would return in defeat, remained in New York and continued working as a travelling salesman in the fur business. Armed with several letters of recommendation, Taurog quickly found a job working for Henry (Pathé) Lehrman as a third assistant prop man, earning $35 a week on his Sunshine Comedies at Fox Film Studios. Years later, Taurog spoke about his time as a prop man: "In those days a studio property man could rent practically anything for a dollar. If we needed anything, from a Persian rug to a pet dog, all we had to do was ring a doorbell and peel off a greenback." Henry Lehrman was born in Vienna, Austria, attended Vienna Commercial University and served in the Austrian Army as a lieutenant. When he arrived in New York at the age of 24 he supposedly wrangled a job as an actor with D.W. Griffith at Biograph by passing himself off as a highly regarded employee of France's Pathé Films. When the ruse was discovered it earned him the derisive nickname "Pathé." Lehrman quickly established himself as a top comedy director for Mack Sennett, directing Charlie Chaplin in some of his earliest comedies. In his autobiography Chaplin described Lehrman as "a vain man and very conscious of the fact that he had made some successful comedies of a mechanical nature; he used to say that he didn't need personalities, that he got all his laughs from mechanical effects and cutting." Chaplin and Lehrman didn't get along, primarily due to their different concepts of comedy. According to Chaplin, Lehrman refused any suggestions that Chaplin would make, saying, "That might be funny in the theater, but in pictures we have no time for it. We must be on the go—comedy is an excuse for a chase."

Lehrman left Sennett in 1914 and formed the L-KO Kompany as a separate unit within the Universal Film and Manufacturing Company. L-KO, which stood for Lehrman Knock Out, had experienced some success with a comedian named Billie Ritchie. Lehrman, who was jealous of Sennett's success, had used Ritchie to create a character similar to Chaplin's the "Little Tramp" and Chaplin had sued him. Ironically, Ritchie had been a member of Fred Karno's Comedy Troupe in England and had appeared in the stage production, *A Night in the English Music Hall,* in a role that Chaplin would later take over. Lehrman left L-KO in 1916, after a dispute with Universal executives, and took over the Sunshine Comedies Unit at Fox.

Working for Lehrman as a prop man wasn't an easy job. "We never had sets," Taurog wrote in the *Reporter* article. "Starting to work in the morning it would take a fortune-teller to inform any of us of the props we might need during the course of the day. If we suddenly needed anything from a rug to a grand piano, it was up to the property man to scuttle forth and borrow it. This was never much of a trick, and the lady of the house was given a dollar for any inconvenience we might have caused." Taurog told me on several occasions that Henry Lehrman was an unpleasant man: "Some people called him an egomaniac," he added, and Lehrman's lack of concern for the safety of his actors had earned him the second nickname of "Mr. Suicide." Jack White, who was only two years older than Taurog, was directing Lloyd Hamilton comedies for Educational Pictures. "One day I saw this fat little prop boy running all over the place, taking care of all kinds of business," White said in an interview. "His energy was amazing and I asked him if he wanted to be an assistant director." Taurog was delighted to take White's offer and escape from Lehrman's dominating presence.

In 1917, after the United States had finally entered the War in Europe, Congress enacted the Selective Service Act and all men between the ages of 18 and 64 were required to register for the draft. Taurog duly registered, but because his weight was probably over the limit, he was never called into service. His registration form shows that he was working as an assistant director for the "Sunshine Comedies Co." He was now 18 years old, making $75 a week and learning his craft. But as the war in Europe was winding down, another killer suddenly materialized. The Influenza Pandemic of 1918-1919 spread around the world, even to the outer reaches of Alaska and remote islands in the Pacific. In America, over 675,000 died, ten times as many as in the war, but by late autumn of 1918 there were fewer new cases and by November influenza had almost completely disappeared from Southern California. The Los Angeles Health Department, as a precautionary measure, ordered the closure of all public areas including schools, churches, theaters, and all other recreational sites. Schools did not reopen for the next four months. Vitagraph Studios had shut down from September to November of 1918 and Taurog found himself with nothing to do but worry about his mother's health.

However, unlike typical flu epidemics of the past, in this case the most vulnerable people were the young and otherwise healthy adults, and in the end both mother and son survived without serious illness. Although it is quite possible that his father did not; Arthur Taurog died in 1919 in New York, conceivably a victim of the flu epidemic and before learning that his son had been given the chance to become a full-fledged director. Taurog, who had been assisting on some of Larry Semon's comedies, spoke of this promotion to Frank Nugent: "When I was a $75-a-week assistant director I got a call one day to see Larry Semon. He said, 'Taurog, how would you like to direct me?' and I said, 'Fine, Mr. Semon.' So he asked me how much I was getting. 'Seven hundred and fifty dollars a week,' I said. 'Whew! That's a bit high. How about $500?' he said. 'Nice to have seen you. Goodbye Mr. Semon,' I said. 'Wait!' he said, and he hurried into his office to talk to his production manager. He was smiling when he came out. 'I have arranged everything,' he said. 'Here's a three-year contract—$750 a week for the first year. $1,000 a week for the second and $1,250 a week for the third. Satisfactory?' So I said 'Yes,' and my knees were shaking like this. When I told my mother about the contract she thought I was crazy. She didn't believe it even when she signed it for me—she had to sign it, I was still under age. That was some raise, wasn't it?" As it turned out, Taurog and Semon's business relationship would last two years, and Taurog would share writing and directing credits with Semon on thirteen two-reel comedies, eventually becoming his business manager as well. Semon loved elaborate gags, such as collapsing buildings, auto wrecks and explosions, and Taurog would learn a great deal about comedy timing and the mechanics of sight gags from this experience.

Around the time that Taurog joined him, Semon had just signed a new three-year contract with the Vitagraph Company of America for $3,600,000 as producer, director and star, giving him $5,000 a week and full control of his films. Although today few people remember Larry Semon, he was considered one of the top film comedians during the early twenties, ranked just below Charlie Chaplin. Semon was born in West Point, Mississippi, the son of a Vaudeville magician, and as a young boy joined his father's act on the road. He eventually traveled to New York, where he worked in Vaudeville as a monologist in between jobs as a cartoonist for several New York newspapers. Semon started working in films in 1914 for the Vitagraph Company as a comedy writer and director and in 1917, after Hughie Mack the comedian he'd been directing left Vitagraph, he began playing the lead role in his films. Semon was only ten years older than Taurog—one of the wonderful things about Hollywood at that time was its youth; it was a young industry filled with young people bursting with enthusiasm and anxious to try innovative ideas.

In Taurog and Semon's first collaboration *The Fly Cop,* Taurog appeared briefly in the film, besides sharing his directing credit with both Semon and a part-time actor named Mort Peebles. Peebles worked again with Semon and Taurog on their next film, *School Days,* and would go on to direct a half-dozen two-reelers for Chester Films and Vitagraph before returning, after Taurog had left in 1922 to begin directing shorts on his own, to co-direct with Semon on two more films. Peebles' film career apparently came to an end in 1923, even though he lived until March of 1949, dying in Los Angeles just twelve days before his sixty- fifth birthday.

The team of Semon and Taurog was very successful, and over the next two years and thirteen films Semon's comedies continued to make big money. Although a much pleasanter man than Henry Lehrman, Semon had his problems as well, including his turbulent romance with his leading lady, Lucille Carlisle (who appeared in several of the Semon-Taurog films including *The Fly Cop, School Days* and *The Stage Hand*) and his acrimonious relationship with Vitagraph; they were frequently in court suing one another. In May of 1920 Vitagraph took Semon to court, demanding $407,388.22 in damages. An article that appeared in the *Motion Picture News* at that time reported on Vitagraph's claim that the defendant "deliberately increased the costs of his productions through delays, carelessness and waste to an unreasonable figure, with the aim of forcing the Vitagraph Company to release him from his contract. The suit is unique in that Vitagraph does not ask that it be released from its contract, but insists the star makes good the damages and continues his employment." According to the terms of the contract, Semon was contracted to make twelve two-reel comedies a year for three years. However, his schedules on films were such that he had only delivered six pictures so far that year and, as the article went on to state, "Vitagraph declares it is practically impossible for Semon to deliver more than a total of seven pictures during the first year." The parties apparently reached an agreement and Semon and Taurog went back to work for Vitagraph, with Semon still encouraging Taurog to come up with ideas for more extravagant sight gags.

Early on the morning of September 16, 1921, Norman Taurog received a long distance phone call from his old boss, Henry Lehrman in New York City, asking him to please meet the southbound Southern Pacific train from San Francisco that morning and take possession of the casket containing the body of Virginia Rappe.

He was to accompany the body to the undertaking rooms of Strother and Dayton, where it would lie in state until Monday morning. Rappe was an actress who had starred in several Lloyd Hamilton Sunshine Comedies for Lehrman before slipping back to playing uncredited bit parts. She had been Lehrman's girlfriend for several years, although their relationship had been somewhat volatile and they had split up several times before permanently calling it quits. The rumors around town were that Rappe, who was notoriously promiscuous and had relationships with many men, was pregnant with Lehrman's child and had traveled to San Francisco seeking an abortion, something she had reportedly done several times before. Over the Labor Day weekend Rappe, her manager Al Schemnacher and a woman named Bambina Maude Belmont had, whether by invitation or not, joined a party being hosted by Roscoe "Fatty" Arbuckle, actor Lowell Sherman and director Fred Fischbach held in several connecting rooms at the St. Francis Hotel. What happened on the night of September 5 in those hotel rooms has become a legendary Hollywood tragedy.

After several hours of partying and much consumption of bootleg liquor, Virginia Rappe became violently ill and began vomiting in the bathroom. According to testimony that Arbuckle later gave at trial, he entered the bathroom and found Rappe lying unconscious on the floor. Picking her up, he carried her into his bedroom and placed her on the bed, where she pleaded for a drink of water. By the time Arbuckle returned with the water, Rappe had rolled off the bed and was lying on the floor moaning and thrashing about. Believing she was faking, Arbuckle returned her to the bed where she continued to cry and moan. Soon she began screaming and tearing off her clothes. When Maude Belmont entered the room, Rappe cried out to her, "What did he do to me, Maudie? Roscoe did this to me." A doctor was called and administered a shot of morphine to Rappe, which quieted her down. Eventually Rappe, who had developed a fever, was transferred to a local hospital, where she died on September 9 of peritonitis and a ruptured bladder. A Grand Jury indicted Arbuckle for first-degree murder, based primarily on the testimony of Belmont, who quoted Rappe's words to her in the hotel room. He was eventually charged with manslaughter. The newspapers, particularly William Randolph Hearst's *San Francisco Examiner*, played up the story, printing a wild rumor that Arbuckle had raped Virginia with a champagne bottle or a coke bottle, a detail never mentioned in any of Arbuckle's three trials. Experts theorize that Rappe most likely had an internal infection (she had for some time suffered from cystitis, and witnesses testified that she'd previously contracted a venereal disease) which may have caused the bladder to rupture and after several days caused the peritonitis to set in.

Virginia Rappe's funeral, held in the small chapel at the Strother and Dayton Mortuary, drew crowds of curiosity seekers. Norman Taurog and another director, Al Herman, stood at the chapel door and turned back all but the closest friends of the dead girl. The burial was held at the Hollywood Cemetery on Santa Monica Boulevard behind the Paramount Studios and today is known as the Hollywood Forever Cemetery. Huge crowds had gathered and had to be controlled by police as they surged forward to catch a glimpse of the flower-covered casket. The large blanket of tiger lilies that covered the casket had been sent by Henry Lehrman, who was still in New York directing an Owen Moore comedy for Lewis and Myron Selznick. The pallbearers, besides Taurog and Herman, included Larry Semon and Oliver Hardy. Virginia Rappe was laid to rest in a plot purchased by Lehrman overlooking a small lake and beside the grave of Lehrman's former secretary who had died of pneumonia two years before. When Henry Lehrman died in 1946, he was buried beside Virginia Rappe.

A few months later, Taurog was subpoenaed to testify at Roscoe Arbuckle's trial in San Francisco. Taurog had little he could tell; he had worked with both Arbuckle and Rappe, but was not close with either of them and had never seen them together socially. His connection with Rappe was primarily through Henry Lehrman. By the time Arbuckle was acquitted in his third trial (the fist two ended in hung juries), the public had turned against him and his career was virtually over. The jury in the third trial took only five minutes to return with their "not guilty" verdict and a statement: "Acquittal is not enough for Roscoe Arbuckle. We feel that a great injustice had been done to him. We feel also that it was only our plain duty to give him this exoneration, under the evidence, for there was not the slightest proof adduced to connect him in any way with the commission of a crime. The happening at the hotel was an unfortunate affair for which Arbuckle, so the evidence shows, was in no way responsible. Roscoe Arbuckle is entirely innocent and free from all blame. We wish him success." Unfortunately, success would be denied "Fatty" Arbuckle. His career never returned to its previous heights and he spent the rest of his life trying to live down the false accusations. He died at the age of 46 on June 29, 1933.

Taurog and Larry Semon continued working together throughout 1921 and part of 1922 and Semon persisted in flouting Vitagraph's financial restrictions. A good example of Semon's extravagance was the filming of *The Sawmill* in late 1922, which would result in Vitagraph firing Taurog and all of Semon's staff. According to Richard M. Roberts, who wrote an extensive article about Semon in a 1999 issue of *Classic Images* magazine, Semon took his entire cast and crew of 75, including Taurog, Oliver "Babe" Hardy and Frank Alexander, on location to Hume Lake in Northern California and was gone for three months. One incident that contributed to the lengthy shooting schedule was a forest fire that broke out near the extensive lumber camp location that Semon had built for the picture. Semon and his company helped to extinguish the fire, but it then took several weeks for the smoke to clear so that filming could resume. Instead of returning to the studio to complete the picture, Semon gave his cast and crew a long vacation at Vitagraph's expense, while he and Taurog continued working on the script, letting them relax in the log cabins he'd had specially built to house everyone. The finished project contains some ambitious sight gags, including a chase atop giant logs on their way to a sawmill, numerous characters being doused in paint, sand and cement, and buildings being destroyed by falling trees and massive explosions. The stunts are truly spectacular, with stuntman Bill Hauber doubling Semon leaping across wide spaces, swinging on a rope like Tarzan, and diving from a tall building into the lake. However, for a film that supposedly holds the distinction of being the most expensive two-reel comedy ever filmed, *The Sawmill* has surprisingly few laughs. In his role as a foreman, "Babe Hardy," much thinner than we are used to seeing him, is actually quite vicious, even using a bullwhip on his workers. None-the-less, *The Sawmill* was hugely popular at the time, even if Vitagraph saw little profit.

Even before *The Sawmill*, Semon's erratic behavior and his ongoing legal skirmishes with Vitagraph had begun to wear on Taurog. On several occasions he was forced to use Bill Hauber to double Semon in scenes, while Semon was off somewhere with his lawyers dealing with legal matters. This was not all that difficult, as Taurog once admitted in an interview: "Since Hauber looked so much like Semon, I could shoot everything I needed with him and then film Semon's close-up at another time." Still, it was becoming more and more frustrating, with the final blow coming with Vitagraph's ignominious manner of terminating his employment. A *Variety* article on May 5, 1922, reported, "Norman Taurog, business manager and director for Larry Semon, is no longer with Vitagraph. According to information, Mr. Taurog was dismissed along with every member of Semon's company with the exception of Semon himself. It is said Vitagraph mailed Taurog his notice in the same style as those given extras, and that all Taurog read was 'Your services are no longer required with Vitagraph.'"

Taurog used this opportunity to move on to greener pastures, directing several short films for Universal Film Manufacturing Company and Fox Films with lesser known comics Johnny Fox and Joe Rock before signing a contract to return to his friend and former boss Jack White at Educational Films.

The Educational Years

Norman Taurog's association with Educational Films would last almost seven years. These years were probably the most formative of his professional life. It was during this time that Taurog, drawing on the knowledge gained from working with Larry Semon and Henry Lehrman, perfected his comedy timing and technique, while writing and directing two-reel comedies with some of the industry's top comedians, such as Lloyd Hamilton and Lupino Lane.

During his first three years with Educational, Taurog concentrated exclusively on directing and for the first, but far from the last time in his career, he found himself working with youngsters: A comedy called *Yankee Spirit*, the first of six films in Educational's Juvenile Comedy series, starring child actor named Bennie Alexander. An Educational Films press release in September of 1923 touted the series in these words: "For the first time a serious attempt is being made to produce juvenile pictures which will indirectly be of material aid in boosting the good work being done by the Boy Scouts and similar organizations. Heading the cast of the first picture will be Bennie Alexander, one of the best known juvenile actors on the screen, and who lately portrayed the leading role in the screen version of Booth Tarkington's *Penrod and Sam*. In the big cast supporting Bennie will be Ernest Butterworth, Roger Keene and several other well known boy actors. George Ovey, who has had the starring part in over two hundred comedies, has a prominent part in the picture. The director is Norman Taurog, one of the screen's most capable comedy directors, who has directed Larry Semon in a number of his comedy successes." Bennie Alexander, who would grow up to become Ben Alexander and co-star seven years later with Lew Ayres and Louis Wolheim in *All Quiet on the Western Front* and then in the 1950s appear with Jack Webb in television's iconic series, *Dragnet*.

Taurog's contract with Educational Films allowed him time to make a couple of films for Educational's landlord, the Universal Film Manufacturing Company, who also released Educational's product. It was an easy matter for Taurog, who simply walked across the studio lot, picked up his megaphone and went to work for producer Samuel Van Ronkel. Today the studio, founded by Carl Laemmle and situated at the entrance to the San Fernando Valley, is the site of NBC Universal and the Universal Studios Tours. Taurog's assignment, *Uncle Bim's Gifts*, kicked off a very successful series of shorts starring Joe Murphy as the popular comic strip character Andy Gump, created by Sidney Smith in 1917. Taurog directed two Andy Gump shorts in quick succession before returning to Educational. Universal released the shorts back to back on September 11and October 15, 1923, and Andy Gump turned out to be so popular that Taurog was quickly contracted to return and direct six more of the two-reelers over the next year and a half, before turning over the director's chair to Erle C. Kenton in May of 1925. Taurog obviously set the pattern for the series along with its star Joe Murphy, who bore a striking resemblance to his comic strip namesake, and the character became so popular that the final Andy Gump short, released in February of 1928, was the forty-ninth in the series.

Immediately after completing the first two Andy Gumps, Taurog was assigned by Jack White to work with a young comedian named Lige Conley who, because of the way he styled his hair, looked quite a bit like Charlie Chaplin when not in costume. Conley had been a supporting player for Mack Sennett and Hal Roach and had finally achieved stardom in Educational Films' Mermaid Comedies. The speed with which these two-reel comedies were turned out was quite amazing considering some of the complicated gags and spectacular automobile chases that were featured in most of them. Taurog once commented, "When I think of the hit and miss methods of those early days compared with the skill and planning that go into pictures today, I marvel that we turned out anything even vaguely resembling a motion picture." One of Conley's best comedies, which Taurog directed, was called *Fast and Furious* and featured Conley demonstrating pancake batter at a general store. A bag of cement gets mistakenly mixed into the batter instead of flour and some very amusing gags occur when customers try to eat the cement cakes. The second half is an elaborate chase involving cars, motorcycles, trains and some spectacular stunts that Taurog staged with an eye for thrills as well as laughs. There's also some clever stop-motion photography with eggs dancing on tiny chicken legs and some amusing double takes by Conley's co-star Spencer Bell, probably one of the first black actors to appear in films. Bell, who sometimes used the unfortunate *nom de screen* G. Howe Black, had previously appeared in several Larry Semon comedies during the early 20s and Taurog was familiar with his work. He would use Bell again when he briefly rejoined Semon as a personal favor for 1925's *The Cloudhopper* and again the following year with Lou Archer in *Creeps*. Taurog's nickname for Bell was "Holy" Spencer, because he was constantly quoting from the Scriptures, but Bell had a sense of humor as well. About to film a stunt that would require him to be suspended beneath an airplane, Bell asked the director Fred Hibbard to first test the wire with a dummy. When Hibbard assured him the wire was safe, he then requested a parachute. "But," argued Hibbard, "that would make a hump on your back and everyone could see it." "Boss," said Spencer firmly, "a small hump on my back today is better than a big hump in the graveyard next week." They compromised on a rehearsal with the dummy.

Bell's greatest claim to fame was his portrayal of the Cowardly Lion in Larry Semon's disastrous version of *The Wizard of Oz*. Semon had wanted to make this film for several years and Taurog had tried on several occasions to argue him out of the idea. The public proved Taurog correct by staying away in droves. Because of Semon's penchant for spending too much money, the film, which he produced and directed as well as starring in, practically bankrupted him.

The ambitious stunts that Taurog staged for the Lige Conley two-reelers sometimes took their toll on the cast. An article in the February 10, 1924, *Los Angeles Times* detailed the list of injuries that took place in just one day of filming of a burlesque football game for a Conley two-reeler called *Pigskin* that Taurog directed for Jack White: Otto Fries received a sprained knee while dragging five men the length of a football field, Jack Lloyd suffered a cut nose and a scraped wrist when a break-away scoreboard fell on him, and the star, Conley, skinned his wrists while hanging from the cross-bar of a goalpost. Taurog went on to direct Conley in eighteen shorts before leaving to take over the Lloyd Hamilton comedies in 1926. By this point in time he had personally directed over forty two-reel comedies and had firmly established himself as one of Hollywood's top comedy directors.

Taurog, who had continued to share an apartment with his mother, finally felt the need to be on his own and moved downtown to the Los Angeles Athletic Club on West 7th Street to begin enjoying life in the Hollywood scene as a single man. Taurog knew that he was not handsome—he was overweight, his hairline was receding and he wore glasses—but on the plus side, he had a terrific sense of humor, he was a successful director making big money, was friends with many of Hollywood's top stars, and his name was appearing in the newspapers quite regularly. Edwin Schallert devoted half a column to him in his *Los Angeles Times* piece of August 5, 1923, under the headline: "Director Returns to White Company." The column went on to say, Than Taurog, "one of the leading comedy directors in pictures today, made his start with Jack White several years ago when the latter rose to screen fame overnight as the director of the first 'lion' comedy. Today Taurog has rejoined Jack White to direct comedies under his supervision. For three years he was responsible for the direction of many of Larry Semon's greatest film successes, and more recently he directed a series of Universal comedies which bring to the screen Andy Gump and the Gump family, of cartoon fame. He is now directing the second Mermaid comedy featuring Lige Conley." Enjoying his new fame, Taurog would escort the young actresses he'd meet at the studio to dinner and dancing at all of the hot new clubs and restaurants.

Prohibition had become the law in 1920, when thirty-six states approved the 18th Amendment, one of the most unpopular laws in the history of the country, and with it came the speakeasies and bootleg liquor. Never was any law so flagrantly violated; some of the popular clubs in Los Angeles that surreptitiously served liquor at that time were the Vernon Country Club and a number of clubs along Washington Boulevard near the Samuel Goldwyn Studios, soon to become MGM, including the Kit Kat Club, Harlow's Café, Monkey Farm and Fatty Arbuckle's The Plantation Club. One of the largest sat on the corner of Washington and National Boulevards, the Green Mill. A huge Normandy—style farmhouse that occupied a block-wide lot, the Green Mill was one of the most popular night spots in town, and it was there that Norman Taurog, with his friend and fellow director Al Santell and two young ladies, drove up to the entrance at 11:30 one evening in December of 1923, only to be confronted by Federal Prohibition agents conducting a raid. One of the agents discovered a small flask in a side pocket of Taurog's fancy Cunningham V3 touring car and Taurog tried unsuccessfully to claim the flask wasn't his. The group was arrested and carted off to the County Jail, and Taurog's Cunningham was impounded. The story hit the papers the following morning, giving names and details of the arrest: "Under the law, a car in which liquor is being transported is liable to confiscation, so Norman Taurog prepared yesterday to battle for the possession of his $7,000 worth of automobile." With the aid of an attorney, Taurog was able to finally retrieve his car, but he undoubtedly paid a lot of money, received a ribbing from his friends and a motherly lecture from Anita Taurog, before he was permitted to put the incident behind him.

The most popular of Taurog's shorts were probably the Lloyd Hamilton comedies, (he wrote and directed nineteen). Lloyd Vernon Hamilton, a husky, wide-eyed comedian with fussy manners and a soft cap, had made a name for himself co-starring in the *Ham and Bud Series,* with Hamilton as the bulky member of the team, opposite the pocket-sized Bud Duncan. The duo made a total of 98 shorts between 1914 and 1917, after which Hamilton went off on his own and started working for Henry Lehrman and Jack White at William Fox's company. By the time Taurog rejoined him in 1926,

Hamilton had become so popular that he had left Fox, set up his own production company with Educational Films and produced and starred in 25 two-reelers, some directed by Roscoe Arbuckle who was struggling to revive his career. Taurog's first film for Hamilton, which he wrote and directed, was called *Careful Please* and featured Hamilton as a bill collector working a tough neighborhood rescuing the heroine (Marcella Daly) from the heavy (Dick Sutherland). Taurog manages to work in some good sight gags with Hamilton in a car being lifted into the air. In *Breezing Along*, which Taurog wrote and directed in 1927, there's a wonderful sequence in an employment office with Hamilton purloining a giant sausage from the sandwich of the man seated next to him and replacing it with a piece of rubber hose. Later, an extended sequence involving automobiles includes what might be the first version of process photography with a painted background on a rotating wheel behind the figures in the auto. In *Move Along*, Hamilton and Taurog developed a wonderful series of gags built around Hamilton trying to tie the laces on one of his shoes. The sequence culminates with Hamilton hailing a streetcar and using the entrance steps to tie his shoelaces before walking away. Many of his fellow comedians admired Hamilton's work; Buster Keaton once said that Hamilton was "one of the funniest men in pictures." Unfortunately, Hamilton, like so many of the screen personalities of that era, suffered from alcoholism, which affected both his health and his career. In the late 1920s, Hamilton was present at the scene of a murder at a speakeasy prompting Will Hays, the president of the Motion Picture Producers and Distributers of America (the film industry's censor board), to ban Hamilton from appearing in films. He did manage to return briefly to films after the advent of sound, but his drinking grew worse and he died at the age of 44 in 1935.

Also on the Universal Studios lot, where Taurog was directing the Lloyd Hamilton comedies, was a lesser known comic by the name of Eddie Boland. Boland, who with his slim physique and dark hair would have looked more like a leading man if not for the definitive Charlie Chaplin moustache he wore, had been working in films since 1912. He had gradually worked his way up, playing small roles in two-reel comedies and the occasional dramas, to starring in a series of silent comedies starting in 1915. One day while Norman Taurog was returning to his stage after the lunch break, he noticed two very attractive young women, one blonde and the other brunette and both dressed in fancy costumes, entering the stage where the Boland comedy *His First Job* was filming. Taurog recognized the blonde to be Dagmar Dahlgren; a onetime dance pupil of Isadora Duncan's who frequently worked in Boland's comedies. He didn't recognize the other girl and she was the one he was interested in meeting. Asking around, he learned that her name was Julie Leonard and that she often teamed with Dagmar in the Boland comedies as one of the "Vanity Girls." Dagmar was a popular figure in Hollywood's party crowd. She would ultimately marry four times, with one very brief liaison as the eighth of ten wives of Norman Selby, a boxer with a record of 81 wins (51 by knockout) who fought under the name Kid McCoy. Selby-McCoy was charged with first-degree murder in the death of wealthy socialite Teresa Mora, with whom he had been living. At the trial, Dagmar disputed one of Selby's alibis and he was convicted of manslaughter and sent to San Quentin.

Julie Leonard's family was Italian; her real name was Pohto, which was apparently changed to Polito by immigration officers when her grandparents arrived from Italy. The family settled originally in San Francisco, where her father, a second generation Italian-American named John (Pohto) Polito, was an attorney. John had married Mary Babbino when she was seventeen and he was studying for his bar exam, and they began having children almost immediately. Three daughters arrived over the next three years, Florence in March of 1900, Mabel in August of 1901, and Julie in November of 1902. They were followed eleven years later by a son, Jack in January of 1913. Once John Polito began practicing law he Anglicized his surname to Leonard and moved the family to Los Angeles, where he hoped to succeed as an attorney. When his career in law proved unsatisfactory, John tried his hand at real estate. Eventually even the marriage failed and John left Mary for a younger woman. Like her sisters, Julie never finished school but, taking advantage of her dark beauty, found work in movies as an extra. She soon caught the eye of casting directors and began playing small bit parts under the name of Julie Leonard.

Taurog didn't see Julie again for several years and during that time her roles continued to improve, even co-starring with Stan Laurel in a couple of two-reelers. One day their paths crossed once again and Norman wasted no time in asking her out to dinner. Soon they were dating on a regular basis, making the rounds of their favorite nightclubs. It wasn't long before their relationship grew more serious and Norman, being the dutiful son, took Julie to meet Anita and receive her blessing. It's a good bet that Anita didn't approve of this relationship, since Julie was Catholic and her parents were divorced, but never the less Norman and Julie were soon announcing their forthcoming marriage.

The wedding party, including E.R. Allen, the general manager of Educational-Mermaid Comedies, and his wife, who would stand up with them, and fellow director Stephen Roberts and his girlfriend Violet Wolfe, who were witnesses, took the train to San Francisco, where Julie and Norman were married at City Hall by Judge James Trout on May 23, 1925. After a brief honeymoon the Taurogs returned to Los Angeles and settled into a home at 1019 Roxbury Drive in Beverly Hills. Julie retired from films and happily became a member of the Beverly Hills social circle, hosting teas and dinner parties at her attractive mansion in the hills above Sunset Boulevard, or lunching at Vendome, Victor Hugo's, or the Brown Derby, the distinctive restaurant in the shape of a derby hat that Bob Cobb had opened on Wilshire Boulevard. Norman went back to directing Lloyd Hamilton and also Lupino Lane, a former British vaudevillian famous for his athletic ability and for being the master of the pratfall.

Lupino Lane made a whole series of two-reelers for Educational Films during the mid-twenties; William K. Everson, a professor of Cinema Studies at New York University, described *Movieland* (1926), one of the Lane two-reelers that Taurog both wrote and directed, as a "fast, non-stop slapstick which moves along at a breathless pace and is notable (a) for affording a free rein to Lupino for all of his acrobatic stunts, and (b) for providing always fascinating shots of the interior of a studio in the silent period." Lane was the cousin of actor Stanley Lupino, who was future movie star Ida Lupino's father. I never told Norman, probably because I didn't know at the time of his connection with Lupino Lane, that my father had appeared in several films that Lane directed when he returned to England from Hollywood in the 30s. Lupino and my father became good friends, and Lupino Lane was my godfather.

Did You Hear That?

On October 6, 1927 an event occurred that reverberated throughout the film industry: the introduction of sound. At the Warner Theatre in lower Manhattan, the brothers Warner premiered their film *The Jazz Singer*, starring Al Jolson. Actually, Hollywood had been aware of Warners, sound experiments with their Vitaphone shorts since the previous year, particularly John Barrymore's *Don Juan,* released in February of 1927, with a musical score and sound effects. Initial reaction had been mostly skepticism; nobody thought it was anything but a gimmick. However, *The Jazz Singer*, based on a play by Samuel Raphaelson that had a successful run of 303 performances at Broadway's Fulton Theatre in 1925, was a phenomenon. Audiences flocked to see and hear Jolson sing "Toot, Toot, Tootsie," often standing in lines that stretched around the block. The reviews heralded the arrival of the "talkies" and the demise of silent pictures. *The New York Times* declared: "Not since the first presentation of Vitaphone features, more than a year ago, has anything like the ovation been heard in a motion-picture theatre." *Variety* called it "undoubtedly the best thing Vitaphone has ever put on the screen." The boxoffice returns were indicative of its popularity and the film quickly became the biggest moneymaker in Warners' history, until the following year when Warners released a follow—up Jolson feature called *The Singing Fool* that racked up even larger profits.

The transition to sound didn't happen overnight; expensive new equipment had to be purchased and filming stages had to be completely soundproofed. The studios began experimenting with various sound systems; Warners' sound system, known as Vitaphone, didn't last. It was a cumbersome process that recorded the sound on phonograph discs that were synchronized with the picture as it was projected, and sometimes the synchronization slipped. Fox Film Corporation, in conjunction with General Electric, developed the Movietone system that utilized sound recorded directly onto film. RCA developed a similar system that they called the Photophone System. Eventually the studios realized that competing systems were impractical and signed an agreement with Western Electric to come up with a single, standardized sound system. Western Electric called their system Western Electric Noiseless Recording; later they called it Western Electric Sound System, and eventually Westrex Recording System. Since the RCA Sound System and the Westrex System were compatible, studios continued using both for their films. This lasted until the early 1950s, when Stereophonic sound arrived and studios and theaters had to change the systems all over again. The advent of sound caused the process of filmmaking to change dramatically for everyone. Actors began taking elocution lessons, cameramen had to relinquish their power on the set to the sound technician, and Norman Taurog, like every other director who was used to talking his actors through a scene while the camera was rolling, also had to adjust to the new medium—and adjust he did. His first feature effort not only had dialogue, but musical numbers as well.

George Jessel, who had originally starred in the Broadway production of *The Jazz Singer* and had, much to his regret, chosen to continue touring in the play rather than star in the film, was finding the play's boxoffice receipts dwindling now that the Jolson movie had become such a big success. Jessel hurriedly ended the tour and signed a contract with an independent company called Tiffany-Stahl Productions to star in a sound feature called *Lucky Boy* that was unashamedly a rip-off of *The Jazz Singer*. Jessel played a Jewish jeweler's son who, against his father's wishes, wants to break into show business and after several setbacks makes it as a singer in San Francisco. When his mother becomes ill, he is forced to give up his job and return to New York to help his father care for her. The mother eventually recovers and Jessel becomes a star on Broadway, with his proud parents in the audience.

Tiffany Productions was founded in 1921 by actress Mae Murray, her then- husband director Robert Z. Leonard and producer Maurice H. Hoffman, to produce a series of films starring Murray and directed by Leonard. When Murray and Leonard divorced in 1925, John H. Stahl took over as head of production, renaming the company Tiffany-Stahl Productions and moving the operation onto the former Reliance-Majestic Studios on Sunset Boulevard. By 1929, when Stahl hired Norman Taurog to direct *Lucky Boy*, the company had produced and distributed over 40 films. Since this would be Taurog's first experience at directing actors in speaking roles, he was paired with a New York stage actor named Charles C. Wilson. Wilson was there to make sure Taurog knew what to do with the dialogue, but quickly found that he wasn't needed. Having once been an actor himself, Taurog was more than capable of staging the dialogue scenes, even if they were somewhat overwritten by Jessel. The musical numbers were not complicated, as many of the songs were pre-tested successes; Jessel had been singing "My Mother's Eyes" for years in his vaudeville act. *Lucky Boy* was released in February of 1929 and was reasonably successful, due primarily to the public's continued curiosity about sound movies, but the reviews were nothing like *The Jazz Singer*'s, and Jessel took the brunt of their criticism. *The New York Times*' review complained of the excessive sentimentality in the plot, saying, "Jessel has such a troublesome time in his efforts to attain Broadway stardom that it takes a hard heart to point out the very evident sentimentality of his course. In each step of his career he appeals to the sentimental side of those who are in a position to help him, and he does it so often that the spectator with the aforementioned hard heart comes to sympathize with the Mr. Jed (or is it Lee) Ziegbert of the picture, who indicates that Georgie had better decamp the producer's office and set out for the subway circuit." Other reviews echoed the *Times*' sentiments, with one saying, "Lest you run the least chance of forgetting that George Jessel is the star of *Lucky Boy*, he calls the role he plays *George Jessel*. Not that there is much chance to overlook him, for the picture is a collection of songs—all of them sentimentalizing his mother --which he sings for all there [sic] worth. The acting of the other characters consists of asking *George* to sing. Sometimes he does so without being asked." Another was even more to the point: "'My Mother's Eyes' is the theme song which recurs whenever the action threatens to reach a point of complete, so to speak, immovability." There is vague evidence that Norman Taurog may have made a second film with Jessel entitled *The Ghetto*, but other than a few lobby cards that look suspiciously like the stills from *Lucky Boy* with several of the same cast members, I could find no references to it in any film sources. It is possible that the producer, John Stahl, may have later re-released *Lucky Boy* under a different title in an attempt to get around the bad reviews.

Not having set the screen on fire with his first sound film, Taurog returned to directing two-reel silent comedies and found himself back at Educational Films, writing and directing for his old friend Lloyd Hamilton. Taurog could see the handwriting on the wall: Two-reelers were on the way out, to be replaced by sound shorts with Broadway comedians and singing stars. The comedy team of Bobby Clark and Paul McCullough were just such an attraction. The two were childhood friends from Springfield, Ohio, who had become stars in vaudeville. McCullough, four years older than Clark, was the chubby straight man of the pair, and Clark's trademark of painted-on eyeglasses, a cigar and a bamboo cane were conceived while he and McCullough were working as clowns in the circus. One of Clark's favorite gags was to spit out the cigar, catch it a few feet in front of him and, putting it back in his mouth, continue to smoke it. After several successes on Broadway, the pair was signed by William Fox to appear in a series of comedy subjects for his company.

Taurog would eventually direct seven of these sound featurettes throughout the spring and summer of 1929 and they would come to be considered some of the best comedies of the year. After making some films for RKO, the team would break up in 1935, and McCullough, after suffering a nervous breakdown, would commit suicide by slitting his throat while seated in a barber's chair about to have a shave. Bobby Clark would eventually recover from the tragedy, return to Broadway and become a major star, appearing in several shows for impresario Mike Todd. He even hosted some segments of NBC's *Colgate Comedy Hour* in the 1950s, before his death of a heart attack in February of 1960.

1929 did produce some memorable sound films, mostly musicals like *Gold Diggers of Broadway, The Desert Song, Rio Rita, The Broadway Melody* and comedies like the Marx Brothers in *The Cocoanuts.* A few dramatic features, such as George Arliss in *Disraeli* and Mary Pickford in *Coquette,* were also well received. By 1930 the list of films was even more impressive with *All Quiet on the Western Front* from Universal, *Hell's Angels* from Howard Hughes and *The Green Goddess*, again starring Arliss. The Marx Brothers returned in *Animal Crackers*, and were joined by Harold Lloyd in *Feet First* and Eddie Cantor in *Whoopee.* Taurog, having proved his ability at directing sound films, his agents arranged a new contract with Tiffany-Stahl for him to direct a series of films with one of their top stars, handsome cowboy actor Rex Lease. For the first film, Taurog would again share the director's chores with B. Reeves Eason, who also had a hand in developing the story. William Reeves Eason, nicknamed "Breezy," was an experienced director and actor whose career in films went all the way back to 1915. In addition to having directed over fifty features and shorts, mainly westerns, he was famous for having directed the second unit and utilized 40 cameras to film the chariot race for *Ben-Hur* (1925). He would later direct the second unit for both *The Charge of the Light Brigade* and *They Died with Their Boots On* at Warner Bros. His nickname "Breezy" came from his laissez faire habit of printing the first take of a scene, no matter if the actors had flubbed lines or the camera had missed its mark.

No known print exists of *Troopers Three*, the first film that Norman Taurog co-directed for Tiffany-Stahl, but I have examined the screenplay that is on file in the Special Collections of the Academy of Motion Picture Arts and Sciences Margaret Herrick Library. The title page reads:

AN ORIGINAL SOUND AND DIALOGUE PHOTOPLAY OF
THE U.S. CAVALRY

STORY, DIALOGUE AND TITLES

By

ARTHUR GUY EMPEY

CONTINUITY

By

ARTHUR GUY EMPEY

and

REAVES REASON

There are four pages of character names and descriptions, followed by two pages of what is called a "location plot" that describes the various settings in the film. This is followed by a page with detailed instructions for titles, and then two and half pages titled "OPENING OF PICTURE," which is a detailed description of the action to serve as a background for the titles. The script then calls for screenwriter Arthur Guy Empey to ride up on a horse and speak, directly to the camera, what is described in the script as a "cleverly worded FOREWORD, eulogizing the cavalry and its achievements, stressing that since the inception of our independence it has always done its duty in its dashing, fearless and efficient way."

The story itself isn't quite so inspiring. It involves three ex-vaudevillians, (Rex Lease, Roscoe Karns and Slim Summerville), who find themselves out of a job and come up with the idea of joining the CMTC (Citizens Military Training Camp). The CMTC was a program maintained by the Federal Government, prior to World War I, as a series of summer camps for youths interested in military service, but with no permanent enlistment obligation required. Unfortunately for the three young men, they mistake a Corporal of the Cavalry for a civilian representative of the CMTC and wind up enlisted in the Army for three years. The rest of the film, according to the AFI catalogue of Feature Films, finds the boys trying to impress the troopers with their own importance, and Eddie starting a flirtation with Dorothy Clark, (Dorothy Gulliver) a Sgt's daughter. This incurs the wrath of Hank Darby

(Tom London), her escort. Later Eddie is rescued by Dorothy and sings a song he has written for her. Darby thrashes the winsome recruit; and though Eddie claims to have been thrown from a horse, Darby admits his guilt and is punished. Eddie is cold-shouldered by everyone, but proves his courage in battle maneuvers, rescuing Darby from a stable fire. Before he dies, Darby asks Eddie to take care of Dorothy. Thus, Eddie wins back the respect of his fellows and the girl.

The company filmed on several California locations, including Fort MacArthur, San Pedro; Fort Rosencrans National Cemetery, San Diego; and the United States Army Garrison at the Presidio of Monterey, where they filmed troopers of the 11th Cavalry Regiment on parade. It was clear how the duties were divided, with Easton directing the action sequences and Taurog handling the comedy scenes with Roscoe Karns and Slim Summerville, as well as the love scenes between Rex Lease and Dorothy Gulliver. *Troopers Three* was released on February 15, 1930, and was well received in larger cities. A shorter, silent version with titles was released soon thereafter to the smaller communities, where theaters, still hard-hit by the Depression, had yet to convert to sound. By the following year, theaters either installed sound systems or went out of business.

Taurog's next two Tiffany-Stahl films, again starred Rex Lease, who had entered silent films as an extra and, because of his good looks, quickly moved into starring roles, continuing in sound films frequently playing the hero of western adventures. By the end of the thirties, however, Lease found his popularity fading and was reduced to playing uncredited bit roles in films. He continued playing small roles in films and later in television series until he retired in 1960. In the Taurog films, Lease's co-star was a Jewish vaudeville comedian named Benny Rubin.

Rubin's antics in *Sunny Skies* and *Hot Curves (both 1930)* reminded one of another comedian who would come along some 20 years later named Jerry Lewis. Taurog would later direct Lewis in eight of his films and Lewis would in turn cast Rubin in six of *his* films. Rubin was a noted dialectician, and his characters of Benny Krantz and Benny Goldberg in *Sunny Skies* and *Hot Curves*, although given different surnames, was in effect the same fast-talking, extremely nervous, heavily accented young Jewish boy from the Upper East Side of New York. Rubin was in fact born in Boston, Massachusetts, on February 2, 1899, and began in show business as a tap dancer when he was 14 years old. Like his co-star Rex Lease, his career as a star in films was short-lived, but he went on to become a very successful character actor, appearing in over 200 films and television programs. He was a regular on Jack Benny's radio and television shows, often playing a supercilious information clerk who could never answer Benny's inquiries. Taurog's direction of both films is still heavily influenced by his experience in silent films, and he shows little desire to move the camera or worry particularly about matching action from the close shots to the wide-angle shots. Effervescent actress Patsy "Babe" Kane sings several songs in *Sunny Skies* and Taurog simply covers them with a wide and close angle and has his editor, Clarence Kolster, cut back and forth between the two. Kolster, a tall, thin, taciturn man with steel-rimmed glasses, began his editing career at Warners' in 1922 and spent most of his career there, except for short periods away, during which time he would edit five films for Tiffany-Stahl, James Whale's first-rate Universal films *Waterloo Bridge* (1931), *Frankenstein* (1931) and *The Old Dark House* (1932), and Ray Enright's *The Spoilers* (1942). By the time that I arrived at Warners' in 1959 as a young assistant film editor, Clarence Kolster, having edited over 100 features in 36 years, had moved over to the television department, where he was editing all of the studios hit series for ABC. Clarence was well-liked by his fellow editors, but he had little time for a young assistant who pestered him with questions.

Sunny Skies is set at a college where Benny shares a room with classmate, handsome Rex Lease. The thin plot centers on the antics of the roommates and their fellow students, with lots of sight gags and a few songs, but suddenly turns serious when Lease, in a drunken stupor, humiliates his girlfriend and Rubin accidentally falls out of a second-story window and lies near death in a hospital bed. The plot, partially written by Rubin, stretches medical science a bit when it has Lease secretly give a pint of his blood to save Rubin's life and then go out and play a few minutes of a football game, collapsing after carrying the ball to a game-winning touchdown. All ends well with both boys reunited with their respective girlfriends. Judging by the reviews of the second film, *Hot Curves*, which had a baseball background and was much lighter in tone, Rubin was well received as a film comedian. One reviewer enthused, "Benny Rubin, the Jewish gentleman who used to frolic about on the stage of a local theater, and who later decided to seek the larger confines of the film studios, blossoms out as a comedy star in *Hot Curves* a rambunctious vehicle built for laughing purposes." Directors were infrequently mentioned in film reviews and such was the case for Norman Taurog, who remained anonymous to the public, while his stock grew with the studios and his agents went to work on his behalf. It wasn't long before they'd succeeded in getting Paramount Pictures to offer an exclusive contract with yearly options.

On Top of the Paramount Mountain

Norman Taurog's career at Paramount Pictures began somewhat modestly: after signing his director's contract, he and Julie moved to New York, where Taurog spent the summer and winter of 1930 and the beginning of 1931 filming a series of sound shorts at Paramount's Astoria Studios in Queens. The shorts featured a mixture of comedy, music and specialty acts, highlighting stars Jack Benny, Smith and Dale, George Jessel (now trying his hand at comedy), Lillian Roth (singing songs to her boyfriend at a picnic), Willie and Eugene Howard, German born brothers who did songs and patter, and the juggling of The Three Swifts. Fearing he was destined to remain a shorts director forever, Taurog soldiered on until finally studio bigwigs Adolph Zukor and Jesse Lasky decided to give him a feature to direct.

The film's working title was *Manhattan Mary*, which was the title of the musical comedy that had inspired it. The stage version of *Manhattan Mary* had a very successful Broadway run of almost a year at the Apollo Theatre and starred Ed Wynn (known as "The Perfect Fool"). With music and lyrics by B.G. DeSylva and Lew Brown and based loosely on the play, the film, using Broadway actors, tells the story of a meek little waiter, a former vaudeville comedian (Wynn recreating his Broadway role) who works at a neighborhood restaurant. The owner's daughter (played by Ginger Rogers) also works there and dreams of making it in show business. Through an accident, Wynn knocks out the leader of a local gang (Preston Foster) and is chosen to head up a rival gang. With his new position and power, Wynn succeeds in forcing the manager (Lou Holtz, recreating his Broadway role) to give Rogers the job of understudy to Ethel Merman in *George White's Scandals*. (Merman and Rogers were both about to go into rehearsals for George Gershwin's Broadway production of *Girl Crazy).*Wynn then kidnaps Merman and holds her captive so that Rogers can take her place and of course then goes on and wows the critics.

Norman Taurog began filming in mid-August of 1930 at the Astoria Studios and the film, now titled *Follow the Leader,* was released in December. Most of the songs from the Broadway production were cut from the film; only one song, "Satan's Holiday" sung by Ethel Merman remained. But the critics still raved over the finished product. One said: "Ed Wynn, a top-notch comedian in musical comedy, makes his talkie debut in *Follow the Leader*, which served him a couple of years ago on the stage as *Manhattan Mary*. And right good it was too and, for that matter still is…[H]e delivers it all in good measure, including even that greatest of all his inventions that has stood the test of laughter for almost ten years, a contrivance for eating corn on the ear in the manner of a typewriter carriage." *Follow the Leader* opened in New York on December 5, 1930, and went into general release a week later. Its success prompted the Paramount brass to bring Taurog back to the West Coast for future assignments and a new contract paying him $1,000 a week.

The Hollywood lot of Paramount Pictures, one block from Melrose Boulevard between Marathon Street and Van Ness Avenue, was vastly different than the Astoria Studios in New York. Its main entrance, framed by a massive, gated archway, opened onto the 65 acres of land that Paramount shared with its neighbor, RKO Studios, The film factory contained 18 sound stages, several large office buildings, a commissary, a hospital, prop, wardrobe and makeup departments and editing and sound facilities. The studio's list of stars included such luminaries as Maurice Chevalier, Clara Bow, Gary Cooper, Marlene Dietrich, Jack Oakie, Mae West and the Marx Brothers.

The Taurogs moved into a new home at 1137 San Ysidro Drive in the canyons above Beverly Hills, and Norman's mother, Anita eventually came to live with them. Anita had married a wealthy retired merchant named Max E. Pollasky, but the union lasted only three years and Anita had separated from Pollasky in July of 1930. Two years later she would lose a divorce proceeding, in which she claimed that Pollasky refused to get her a decent home and spent too much money on his children by a prior marriage and not enough on her. According to an article that appeared in the *Los Angeles Herald* on April 20, 1932, after a two-week trial, the judge ruled in Pollasky's favor, saying, "The husband's choice of residence and mode of living implies a choice according to his, not the wife's, standard and mode of living." The judge did order Pollasky to pay Anita "within six months, $3,250 due on a previous court order, $1,500 additional attorney's fees, and $609 to pay doctor's bills and expenses."

Taurog reported to the Paramount lot to begin preparing a film to star Australian comedian Leon Errol, ZaSu Pitts, and child actors Mitzi Green and Jackie Searl. The film was based on two novels by Donald Ogden Stewart, *Mr. and Mrs. Haddock Abroad* and *Mr. and Mrs. Haddock in Paris*. It was initially to be called *Finn and Hattie Abroad*, and was first adapted for the screen by Sam Mintz. Mintz was a Russian émigré comedy writer, born in Belarus in 1897, who came to this country with his family in 1904. His previous screenplays included *Fools for Luck* (1928) with W. C. Fields and *Tom Sawyer* (1930) with Jackie Coogan and Mitzi Green. A 21-year-old contract writer by the name of Joseph L. Mankiewicz, whose older brother Herman J. Mankiewicz was a well-established writer at Paramount, was then assigned to write the screenplay. Joe Mankiewicz would later build his reputation as a writer-producer at MGM, and then win four Oscars in rapid succession for writing and directing *A Letter to Three Wives* (1949) and *All About Eve* (1950). Mankiewicz would direct the popular films *The Barefoot Contessa* (1954) and *Suddenly Last Summer* (1959) before sabotaging both his career and Twentieth Century-Fox Studios with the monstrously expensive *Cleopatra* (1963).

Taurog, still serving his apprenticeship with Paramount, was teamed with another new director, Norman Z. McLeod, to co-direct *Finn and Hattie*. Paramount, since first beginning to produce sound films, had frequently paired one inexperienced director with another inexperienced film director to test their abilities. A number of films, including the 1930 versions of *The Spoilers* and *The Royal Family of Broadway*, co-directed by newcomer George Cukor, were examples of this procedure. McLeod had started in 1922 as a cartoonist for Al Christie's *Christie Comedies*, working on over forty of Christie's half live-action and half animated shorts. He had recently signed with Paramount and, as was their routine, had co-directed with Lloyd Corrigan the Buddy Rogers-Frances Dee comedy *Along Came Youth* (1930). *Finn and Hattie* had a three-week shooting schedule and was budgeted at $250,000. Filming began on November 28, 1930, on location at the rural Southern Pacific railroad station in Chatsworth, California, where 250 box lunches were served to the film crew and a large compliment of extras. After seven days of filming at the First National Studios on Sunset Boulevard, the company wrapped production at Paramount Studios on December 16, 1930.

A lightweight affair about the Haddock family's ocean voyage to Europe and their misadventures with a pair of con artists, *Finn and Hattie* (the final title) was filled with numerous opportunities for Leon Errol and ZaSu Pitts to display their unique style of comedy. The film turned out to be a moderate success for Paramount, one of sixty films they released that year, with Mordaunt Hall of *The New York Times* happily reporting, "With Maurice Chevalier appearing in person on the stage, rendering in his inimitable fashion songs in French and English, and Donald Ogden Stewart's farce, *Finn and Hattie*, on the screen, the Paramount now is the house of laughter. M. Chevalier won hearty applause and soon after he had disappeared through the curtains the spectators were bubbling with merriment over the actions of Leon Errol, Mitzi Green, ZaSu Pitts, Jackie Searl and Lilyan Tashman in the talking picture which was directed by Norman Taurog and Norman McLeod." Both Taurog and McLeod would have major hits in their next films as solo directors, with Taurog directing his nephew, Jackie Cooper, in *Skippy* and McLeod directing the Marx Brothers in *Monkey Business*.

Julie Taurog's sister Mabel had been briefly married to a young musician named John Cooper and had given birth to a son, John Cooper, Jr. in September of 1922. John, Sr. had deserted the family before his son was born and Jackie, as he became known, was raised by his grandmother, and later by his mother when she married C.J. Bigelow, a studio production manager. In his autobiography, Jackie Cooper describes his grandmother in most unflattering terms:"I don't really have fond memories of my grandmother. It's a sad thing to have to say, but it's true. Yelling, pinching, slapping, hitting, pulling me from one place to the other by the ear—that's what I remember." It was Mary Polito, now divorced from her husband and a bitter, bigoted woman, who took care of Jackie while Mabel was trying to earn a living by travelling with singer Edith Clifford as her piano accompanist. Mary Polito lived in Hollywood, near some of the studios, and she would often join her neighbors in walking to the studio gates in the morning to see if they could be hired as extras in one of the productions that were filming that day. The routine would be for the director and his assistant to come out and select people he wanted from the waiting crowd. Frequently Mary would bring little Jackie with her, and one day, as Cooper described it in his book, a director picked her because "she had a little tow-headed kid with her—me. That's how I began a movie career, as a kid with his grandmother, working as an extra in dozens of films." Cooper's Wikipedia biography states that he appeared in Lloyd Hamilton two-reelers when he was three years old, using the last name of Leonard, but there are no credits that support that premise. It is entirely possible that he did, and quite possibly worked for his uncle by marriage, Norman Taurog, who was directing Hamilton shorts from 1926 to 1928. The youngster is also credited as appearing in a musical number in *Fox Movietone Follies of 1929*. Later in 1929, Cooper was signed by Hal Roach for his *Our Gang* comedies at MGM and by 1930 he had made his first feature, co-starring with Janet Gaynor in *Sunny Side Up*. In 1931, Paramount Pictures borrowed Cooper from Hal Roach to star in their production of *Skippy*. According to Cooper, Paramount paid Roach $25,000 for his services and Jackie got his regular salary of $50 a week.

Skippy was based on a popular comic strip character created by Percy Crosby that debuted as a cartoon in *Life* magazine in 1923, and then began

The original cartoon Skippy.

in weekly newspapers in 1925 and in the Sunday comics the following year. Considered by many to be one of the classics of the form, Skippy Skinner, the rambunctious fifth-grader, and his pals grew rapidly in popularity and was soon appearing in newspapers in 28 countries and in 14 languages. Skippy was the subject of a 1929 novel, and in 1930, Paramount purchased the rights and gave Louis D. "Bud" Lighton the job of producing the screen version. Lighton hired former newspaper columnist and playwright Don Marquis to develop a screen treatment based on Crosby's characters. Marquis had never written for the screen, but was famous for his newspaper column *archy and mehitabel,* about a fictional alley cat and a cockroach who left poems on his typewriter. Norman McLeod then spent some time shaping Marquis' material into screenplay form, before going off to join Lloyd Corrigan on *Along*

Came Youth. Sam Mintz was then assigned to do a rewrite and Edward Sloman, who had recently helmed a series of Richard Arlen adventure films for Paramount's "B" unit, was given the directing assignment. That arrangement lasted only a short while before Joe Mankiewicz replaced Sam Mintz and Norman Taurog was handed the director's chore.

As casting progressed, Taurog's nephew by marriage, Jackie Cooper, was joined by child actors and studio contractees Mitzy Green and Jackie Searl to play Skippy's friends, Eloise and Sidney, and Jackie Coogan's five year-

Norman Taurog and Jackie Cooper in 1931.

old brother, Robert, was signed for the role of Sooky, Skippy's pal in Shanty Town. The plot was clearly designed to subject the viewer to every emotion imaginable; from laughter as Skippy pretends to be dressing in the morning, or tries to break into his savings bank without touching it, to outright heartbreak as Skippy tearfully prays for Sooky's dog. There is a legend, perpetuated by Jackie Cooper's autobiography appropriately titled *Please Don't Shoot My Dog* that "Uncle Norman" resorted to the sadistic device of threatening to shoot Jackie's real dog if he didn't cry for the camera. Taurog was already well known for his ability to work with child actors and undoubtedly resorted to a number of tricks to get the desired results, including rewarding a good performance with chocolate bars or quarters (I saw him hand out quarters to children in several films that I worked on with him). Whether Cooper's version is apocryphal is a matter of conjecture, but when I asked former child actor and well-known producer-director Gene Reynolds about it, he recounted a different version. Reynolds was President of the Directors Guild of America from 1993 to 1997 and Joseph C. Youngerman was at that time the National Executive Director. Youngerman had started in the business as a prop man before becoming an assistant director and had been Taurog's prop man on *Skippy*. Here's his version of what happened, as told to me by Gene Reynolds: "They were at Paramount and Joe was a prop man and what they would do with Jackie, according to Youngerman, they would turn to Jackie and Taurog would say 'Joe, you're fired! You didn't get that prop here on time! You're fired!' And Jackie would holler, 'Don't fire Joe, I love Joe!' He would cry and they would say, "Roll." Vincente Minnelli once admitted to using the same approach to secure a crying scene with little Margaret O'Brien in *Meet Me in St. Louis* (1944). Reynolds, who played the crippled boy Tony Ponessa for Taurog in *Boys Town* (1938), then appeared with Cooper in *The Spirit of Culver* (1939), had another story to tell about crying:

"Jackie Cooper, Freddie Bartholomew and I are working on a movie called *The Spirit of Culver* at Universal," he continued. "And I play a guy called Carruthers, one of the cadets. And Jackie's a cadet and Freddie's a cadet and we all had our kind of clichéd characters. My clichéd character was the boy who was always writing home to his mother. So in the script the mother dies and there's the big scene of course where Jackie comes in and says, 'What's the matter?' And I'm sitting at my desk and I can't write because my mother has died and I'm crying. So they shoot the master between Jackie and me I and I'm crying. And then, the guy that was Deanna Durbin's first husband [Vaughn Paul, married to Durbin from 1941 to 1943], he was the first assistant director. I cried, they get the master and he calls lunch." With a laugh, Gene explained, "Now of course, a dollar is a dollar. If you work into lunch they're going to get nailed meal penalties. So we go to lunch and after lunch we throw the football around for fifteen minutes and then, 'Okay, let's go back to work.' So we go to makeup, I go back and I'm sitting in that chair. 'Okay, let's go', and I can't cry. I've had lunch, I've played football, and I've laughed a lot, so naturally I couldn't cry. I'm sitting there working on it, trying like hell to cry. So finally the director, Joseph Santley, says 'spritz him in the eyes with the camphor,' and I said no, no, I'll do it... but I couldn't do it. Finally, fifteen minutes, standing around waiting for this kid to cry and there's a lot of tension I can feel, and Jackie Cooper says to me, 'What did Uncle Norman say about using camphor for your eyes?' He called him Uncle Norman. And I said, 'Uncle Norman? He said, 'A good actor doesn't need it,' and as I said that I broke into tears and they got the shot."

In an interview in a Motion Picture Association of America publication in March of 1947, Taurog spoke about directing children: "To begin with, I look for two qualities, intelligence and personality. Nothing more is necessary. Children have one-track minds, so there is never anything to distract them from what they are doing at the moment. Another thing about them is that they have no phobias, no fixed fears. For this reason it is both foolish and dangerous to frighten them into a required mood. They must be persuaded into it by an appeal to their natural sympathies. Acting is creating, and a child can create as completely as an adult."

When *Skippy* opened in New York on April 4, 1931, Mordaunt Hall of *The New York Times* opened his review with the following praise: "Percy Crosby's wily little comic strip character, Skippy, is to be seen on the Paramount screen in a talking picture bearing his widely known name. He is impersonated by Jackie Cooper, an unusually clever child actor who was recruited from Hal Roach's *Our Gang* comedies. This youthful player gives a truly remarkable portrayal in a film that is endowed with wholesome amusement and affecting tenderness." Other reviews echoed the praise: "Tiny Master Cooper is a mighty actor. Barrymore himself might profit by the study of the kid's technique...All the kids do valiant work—but Jackie Cooper is the kid you can't forget." Some reviewers included acclaim for the creative team: "Jackie Cooper and Bobby Coogan as Skippy and Sooky are amazing. No taint of that painful precociousness of child actors mars their work; they're just kids. How much of this is due to their own ability is a question. The dialogue, which doesn't try to fit adult words to kid's tongues, is splendid, and Norman Taurog has certainly shown high talent in transferring to the screen what goes on in the minds and hearts of children." Added another reviewer, "Unlimited praise is due Taurog, whose skill in handling the child actors has enabled them to play their roles in a manner worthy of veterans. Taurog has injected into the talker the human and appealing tenderness of children. His young players act at all times like the children they are."

Whatever Taurog did to pull off Cooper's performance, it worked and the film became a break-out hit for Paramount, Cooper became a star, and

Publicity shot for the film with (L-R) Robert Coogan, Jackie Searl and Jackie Cooper.

Please Don't Shoot My Dog was certainly a catchy title to sell books. In spite of the success he owed to Taurog's guidance of his performance in *Skippy*, and the fact that after Cooper's mother died, Taurog became his guardian, Jackie Cooper, according to what he has written in his autobiography, grew to loathe Taurog and wrote some very unkind things about him. Undoubtedly influenced by his maternal grandmother, Mary Polito, who referred to Taurog as "That fat Jew bastard," Cooper found many things to dislike about his uncle: "Taurog was a good director," Cooper wrote in his book. "I discovered later, when I began having a basis for comparison that he was one of the best—but from the first he frightened me and confused me." Cooper grudgingly admitted that Uncle Norman took a paternal interest in his well-being, and at one point he even harbored the fantasy that Taurog might have been his father. When his mother died and Cooper, still underage, was afraid that her husband, C.J. Bigelow, a man he also despised, would become his guardian, Taurog and Mabel's brother Jack Leonard arranged for Taurog to take over the guardianship. For years, Cooper would rely on Taurog for advice, while at the same time growing to resent him, and after he reached maturity they drifted apart. In 1960, when Taurog was casting his first film with Elvis Presley, *G.I. Blues*, he suggested that Cooper be cast as Elvis' buddy, a part ultimately played by Robert Ivers. From the tone of Cooper's writings it was clear that he was a very bitter man. Gene Reynolds remembered an incident involving a tribute that the Directors Guild held for Taurog: "They put me on the panel because I had worked with Taurog," Gene recalled, "Jackie was not there. Afterwards I ran into Jackie and I said, 'they had a nice tribute for Norman Taurog at the Guild. Why weren't you there?' And Jackie said, 'I never heard from him during the war.' Which I thought was very childish." Cooper's wartime duties didn't even begin until mid-1944 when he was drafted and joined the Navy's V-12 educational program, which was designed to supply commissioned officers for duty during World War II. Norman Taurog, still Cooper's guardian when he was drafted, arranged for him to attend Loyola University in Los Angeles for his continued schooling under the V-12 program. When Cooper, who had received only a small amount of formal schooling when not being tutored on movie sets, had trouble with his studies, Taurog hired a private tutor for him. After Cooper completed his undergraduate courses at Loyola, Taurog arranged for him to be transferred to Notre Dame in South Bend, Indiana, for further instruction. While there, Cooper, somewhat innocently, was arrested for contributing to the delinquency of a minor at a party he hosted. Taurog offered to have top Hollywood attorney Jerry Giesler fly to Indiana to defend him, but Cooper went with a local attorney who had the charges dismissed. In his book Cooper complains that during those "few desperate months when I was facing criminal charges in South Bend…Norman never wrote me. My grandmother never wrote me. None of my aunts ever wrote me." Cooper was still having troubles with his grades and eventually flunked out of the V-12 program and was inducted into the Navy and sent to boot camp for training, eventually joining Special Services as a drummer with Claude Thornhill's Navy band. He was given a two-week pass before sailing for Hawaii, where he would tour the Pacific battle zone with Thornhill's band, and stopped off in Hollywood to marry June Horne, the daughter of director James W. Horne. It's interesting to note that a *Los Angeles Times* article about the wedding, which took place at the Beverly Hills Hotel on December 11, 1944, reported that Norman Taurog was a member of the wedding party.

When *Please Don't Shoot My Dog* was published in 1981, *Variety* printed an uncomplimentary review, calling the book "quite a 'hate and tell' epic dealing with many people he hated or disliked. Including a long list of stars, directors and other professionals, most of them still consistently active. For a 65-year-old who expects to remain in the business many years, this curious book is not likely to do him good. There's bitterness in it." *Variety*'s reviewer went on to discuss Cooper's relationship with Taurog: "Jackie always suspected his uncle, director Norman Taurog, was his real father. Taurog directed Jackie in a number of films, including *Skippy*, which catapulted the kid to fame. Since Jackie's stepfather was a philandering opportunist, Uncle Norman became the main influence in the boy's life. He did the most for Jackie over the longest period of time—handling his affairs, making decisions for him, giving him professional advice, even using political connections to get him a deferment in the World War II draft and arranging other privileges when Jackie finally was inducted. Yet Jackie disliked Uncle Norman and was continually at odds with him. The overall narrative is choppy. It jumps back and forth, and interpolated throughout are dozens of boxed statements solicited from Cooper's friends and fellow-workers. Their views, of course, are favorable—plainly self-serving puffs. About 40 are from his present wife and children alone—a dizzy and dull repetition—but Taurog, whose views would have been most enlightening, refused to give a statement."

And the Winner Is...

Capitalizing on Taurog's acknowledged success as a director of children, Paramount immediately assigned him to another project featuring youngsters. With Mitzi Green and Jackie Searl as rival child actors in films and Edna Mae Oliver and Louise Fazenda as their dueling stage mothers, *Forbidden Adventure* gave the two adult comedians almost as much screen time as the kids, and they took good advantage of it. Sometimes indelicately described as "horse faced," Edna Mae Oliver was one of Hollywood's leading comediennes, having been a success on Broadway and starring in films since 1923. Even Warners cartoons parodied her unique face. Louise Fazenda had been a favorite of movie audiences since her days with Mack Sennett and her "country bumpkin" character in two-reel comedies. She was married to Warners producer Hal Wallis, who would play an important role in Norman Taurog's later career.

Based on a Sinclair Lewis story called *Let's Play King*, the film, with an adaptation by Agnes Brand Leahy and a screenplay by Edward E. Paramore Jr. and Joseph L. Mankiewicz, took the rival mothers and their precocious children on a trip to Europe, where they meet a child king. The children, discovering that the king lives a restricted life, help him to run away. Their adventures, ending with a kidnapping and a rescue, fill out the remainder of the film's running time. Given an added week to the filming schedule and an increased budget of $270,000, Taurog began filming at the Paramount Ranch in Chatsworth on April 2, 1931, and finished at Paramount Studios on May 7, 1931. *Forbidden Adventure* was released on July 2, 1931 and Philip K. Scheuer, the cantankerous reviewer for the *Los Angeles Times*, while not caring for the film in general, still gave Taurog a back-handed compliment:

"The children in this are bright and natural, Norman Taurog, the director, having inspired them with less camera consciousness than they exhibited in his recent version of *Skippy*."

Paramount wasted no time in reassembling their child actors with their best children's director and announcing to the press that Taurog would direct a sequel to their success of the previous year's *Tom Sawyer* based on Mark Twain's *Huckleberry Finn*, with Jackie Coogan playing Tom Sawyer, Junior Durkin, Huckleberry Finn and Mitzi Green, Becky Thatcher. A full-scale reproduction of the town of St. Petersburg, Missouri, which had been previously constructed for *Tom Sawyer* at the Paramount Ranch in Agoura in the San Fernando Valley, was the setting for much of the filming and the wonderful black actor Clarence Muse was signed to play Jim, the escaped slave. Clara Blandick, eight years before she would portray Judy Garland's Auntie Em in *The Wizard of Oz*, would again portray Tom Sawyer's Aunt Polly. The film was quickly completed during the early summer and opened at the Paramount Theatre in New York on August 7, 1931. Mordaunt Hall of *The New York Times* wrote the following day: "Those clever juvenile players who delighted audiences throughout this country and other lands by their fine portrayals in the film *Tom Sawyer* are to be seen at the Paramount in a pictorial version of another Mark Twain classic, *The Adventures of Huckleberry Finn*. It is an offering which will be heartily welcomed, in spite of changes due to the demands of the screen, by all admirers of the great American humorist." *Variety*'s reviewer avowed that "Norman Taurog's direction was balanced and smooth." *Time* magazine was not as impressed with Taurog's direction: "Director Taurog, while he retains many of the happiest Twain inventions, gives them a less sharply human inflection—almost as though he had been afraid that Mark Twain's conception of his own characters might seem, to contemporary audiences, a trifle quaint." Junior Durkin, aka Trent Bernard Durkin, was only nineteen years old when his career ended tragically with his death in an automobile accident. Returning from a hunting trip with Jackie Coogan and his father, he was thrown from the open rumble seat when the car left the road and rolled over several times.

Paramount, still wanting to capitalize on *Skippy*'s success, decided that a sequel was in order and quickly reassembled virtually the entire team from the previous film, including Taurog, producer, Louis D. Lighton and writers Joseph L. Mankiewicz and Sam Mintz, as well as Norman Z. McLeod who contributed additional dialogue to the screenplay. Their work was based on a Percy Crosby story called *Dear Sooky* and on an earlier screenplay adaptation by Grover Jones and William Slavens McNutt, both of whom had written the screenplay for Taurog's *Huckleberry Finn* earlier that year. Most of the cast from *Skippy*, with the exception of Mitzi Green, was brought back and Arthur Todd replaced Karl Struss as cinematographer. The budget was estimated to be $370,000, with a 36-day shooting schedule, and Taurog's salary was allocated at $1,250 a week for six weeks. A young assistant director named Artie Jacobson was assigned to the film and paid $ 80 a week. He would work with Taurog again on *The Big Broadcast of 1936*, and in 1964 Jacobson would rejoin Taurog as his assistant director on the Elvis Presley feature *Tickle Me*.

It was a short shooting schedule, as the studio wanted to get the film into theaters before the public had a chance to forget *Skippy*, and Taurog managed to complete production in time for the film to have its premiere on December 26, 1931. Like most sequels, the film failed to receive the acclaim of its predecessor, but still managed to reap a small profit for the studio. *Time* magazine's review stated it succinctly: "This picture has the defect of most sequels, in that episodes similar to the ones which seemed spontaneous in *Skippy* now appear to be part of a formula. They are still affecting, touched by gently sentimental sympathy for small children and their sly vagaries."

Shortly after the release of *Sooky*, Hal Roach sold Jackie Cooper's contract to MGM where he would go on to star in 11 pictures, including *The Champ* and *Treasure Island* with Wallace Beery, whom he also disliked intensely. In 1941, with Cooper's child actor days well behind him, Paramount brought nineteen-year-old Jackie back to appear as a fictional version of himself in an unusual little "B" film called *Glamour Boy*; set at Paramount Studios, it was cast with many of the studio's ex-child actors such as Jackie Searl, Edith Meiser, Ann Gillis, and Junior Coghlan and directed by Ralph Murphy. Cooper played Tiny Barlow, the star of the earlier *Skippy*, who comes back to the studio to teach child-actor Darryl Hickman how to take over his old role in a remake. A sizable segment of the original *Skippy* is used to fill out the plot. Never given a New York first-run release, *Glamour Boy* slipped quickly into obscurity.

There's one last sad footnote to the *Skippy* saga involving Percy Crosby, the author and illustrator of the original comic strip. According to his daughter, Joan Crosby Tibbetts, "From 1928 to 1937 Crosby produced 3,650 Skippy strips, ten books of fiction, political and philosophical essays, drawings, and cartoons, as well as numerous pamphlets while mounting a dozen exhibitions in New York City, Washington, D.C., London, Paris and Rome of his oils, watercolors, and other paintings and drawings." In addition there were Skippy dolls, toys and comic books, guaranteeing Crosby the amazing Depression Era sum of $2,350 a week. However, according to his daughter, Crosby's Skippy trademark was pirated by "a bankrupt peanut butter company that later merged with a Fortune 500 company, making a fortune in illicit sales under the Skippy brand name." Crosby fought to reclaim his copyright, but after years of court battles, his health declined and he became an alcoholic, eventually suffering a mental collapse. After attempting to commit suicide in December of 1948, he was committed to the mental ward at King's Park Veterans'

Hospital as a paranoid schizophrenic and spent the last 16 years of his life as a patient, desperately trying to secure his release. He suffered a heart attack in 1964, and after spending several months in a coma, died on his 73rd birthday (December 8, 1964). Joan Crosby Tibbetts fought for years, hiring numerous attorneys and spending great sums of money to regain the Skippy name, but eventually lost a court case in 2008. She is still seeking legal recourse.

1931 was a bellwether year for Norman Taurog; In October, the Academy Award nominations were announced, and Taurog was nominated for Best Director, along with *Skippy* for Best Picture, Jackie Cooper for Best Actor and Joseph L. Mankiewicz and Sam Mintz for Best Writing (Adapted). The Academy of Motion Picture Arts and Sciences hosted its gala 4th annual awards dinner in the Sala D' Oro banquet room of the Biltmore Hotel in downtown Los Angeles on the night of November 10, 1931. Actor Lawrence Grant hosted the event and Charles Curtis, the Vice-President of the United States, was a guest speaker. The Don Lee-Columbia radio network broadcast the ceremony for their West Coast listeners. When Norman and Julie Taurog arrived at the formal affair, Julie was still annoyed that Norman had refused to wear the white tie and tails that was *de rigueur* for the male attendees. Norman had argued that he would have looked like a penguin in such a get-up and had elected to wear a black tie and dinner jacket instead. There was an air of anticipation filling the room since the Academy, for the first time, hadn't announced the winners in advance. Other films nominated for Best Picture included *Cimarron* (RKO), *The Front Page* (Howard Hughes), and *Trader Horn* (MGM). Norman Taurog's competitors for the Best Director award were Wesley Ruggles for *Cimarron*, Clarence Brown for *A Free Soul*, Lewis Milestone for *The Front Page* and Joseph von Sternberg for *Morocco*.

The Academy had decided to award Scientific and Technical awards for the first time and Jackie Cooper, who attended with his mother and was seated at the same table with Best Actress nominee Marie Dressler, fell asleep on Dressler's shoulder as the evening wore on and awards were presented to the Paramount Studio Sound Department for Best Sound Recording and to RKO Art Director Max Ree for Best Art Direction on *Cimarron*. When Dressler won as Best Actress, Jackie had to be transferred to his mother's lap so that the actress could approach the dais to receive her award for her role in *Min and Bill*. When D.W. Griffith announced the Best Actor winner, there was no need to awaken young Jackie, as Lionel Barrymore won the statue for his performance in *A Free Soul*. No one was more surprised than Norman Taurog when he heard his name called out as the winner of the Best Director award for *Skippy*, and in the photograph taken to commemorate the event an unsmiling Taurog stands at the end of the table of winners and presenters, looking more like a deer caught in the headlights of an oncoming automobile than a young man who had just won the most prestigious award in Holly-

Academy Awards Ceremony (1931). Identifiable faces include (L-R) George Arliss, Louis B. Mayer, Marie Dressler, Lionel Barrymore and Norman Taurog at end of table.

wood. To this day, Taurog still holds the title of the youngest director to ever win the coveted statuette.

Shortly after Academy Award Night, Taurog began experiencing severe nausea, vomiting and abdominal pain and was rushed to the hospital to have his appendix removed. As it turned out, while he was in the hospital a series of tests revealed that he was also a diabetic and had been for quite some time. Diabetes patients suffer from abnormally high blood sugar levels when the pancreas isn't producing enough insulin to control it. The majority of diabetics are overweight and fail to observe the proper diet and exercise, a description that fit Taurog perfectly. His intake of sweets was restricted and he was put on a regimen of insulin injections to control his blood sugar, and for the rest of his life he would begin each day by giving himself an injection in his thigh. Sometimes in the afternoon his blood sugar level might drop dangerously low and he would develop hypoglycemia and a feeling of light-headedness. He would then ask for a glass of orange juice to increase the blood sugar level. This condition never affected Taurog's ability to work and few people even knew of its existence, but it would eventually have a profound effect, not only on his career, but his very life.

If all this excitement wasn't enough, while Norman was recovering at home from his appendix operation, Julie learned that she was pregnant. Arrangements were quickly made to convert one of the bedrooms at San Ysidro Drive into a nursery and Patricia Ann Taurog was born on July 26, 1932. Norman and Julie celebrated the arrival of their beautiful little girl by sending out formal announcements to all of their friends. Julie, with the help of a nanny and the household staff, saw to Patricia's needs while Norman, fully recovered, was sent off to RKO Pictures, on loan from Paramount, to direct a Wheeler and Woolsey comedy called *Hold 'Em Jail.*

Bert Wheeler and Robert Woolsey first appeared together in the 1927 stage musical *Rio Rita*, and came to Hollywood in 1929 to recreate their roles in the RKO adaptation starring Bebe Daniels and John Boles. RKO then put them under contract and began producing a series of very popular comedies featuring the duo. They would ultimately make 20 films together and by 1932, *Hold 'Em Jail* would be their eleventh film for the studio. David O. Selznick, then RKO's head of production, had run the script through a phalanx of writers, including S.J. Perelman, Walter DeLeon, Mark Sandrich and five more, before coming up with an acceptable screenplay. In spite of all this talent, the plot is simply a series of sight gags, culminating in an extended sequence involving a grudge football game between the inmates of two penitentiaries. Perelman, who began writing humorous essays for *The New Yorker* magazine, had already written two highly successful films at Paramount for the Marx Brothers (*Monkey Business*, 1931 and *Horse Feathers*, 1932) before he came to RKO to work on *Hold 'Em Jail.* He most likely came up with the idea for the football game as a similar gag-filled match had previously appeared at the climax of his screenplay for *Horse Feathers.* Sandrich had been directing shorts at RKO since 1926, and the following year the studio would award Sandrich with his first feature to direct, *Melody Cruise.* Within twelve months after that, he would be directing Wheeler and Woolsey on a regular basis, before starting *The Gay Divorcee* (1934) and the beginning of his successful series of films with Fred Astaire and Ginger Rogers. Years later, Sandrich's son, Jay Sandrich, would become known for his direction of television comedy series such as *The Mary Tyler Moore Show, The Odd Couple* and *The Cosby Show.* Ex-Vaudevillian Walter DeLeon would return to Paramount with Taurog to work on the script of his next film *The Phantom President*, as well as *The Big Broadcast of 1936*, and briefly at MGM on *Broadway Melody of 1940.*

Taurog and associate producer Harry Joe Brown put together a strong supporting cast for the film, with solid comedians like Roscoe Ates, Edgar Kennedy, Robert Armstrong and Paul Hurst, and Edna May Oliver making a return appearance for Taurog after *Forbidden Adventure.* Playing Edgar Kennedy's sister was a young Betty Grable, in one of her first featured roles; Ward Bond, recently graduated from the University of Southern California's football team, and Olympic champion Jim Thorpe, played members of the opposing football team. While Taurog was on the RKO lot preparing to film *Hold 'Em Jail*, Selznick asked him to direct some retakes for Wheeler and Woolsey's previous film, a 1932 version of the George and Ira Gershwin Broadway musical *Girl Crazy*. In 1943, Taurog would direct another version of this musical at MGM to much greater success.

By the time that *Hold 'Em Jail* was released in September of 1932 to moderate reviews and slightly better boxoffice, Taurog was back at Paramount directing his next project. It was a nightmare from start to finish.

Norman Taurog on the set of *The Phantom President* (1932).

The Phantom President was, as Paramount Pictures proudly announced at the beginning of the film's main title, Broadway star George M. Cohan's first "appearance on the talking screen." Cohan, who had written and produced more than 50 plays, starred in vaudeville, musical comedy, drama, radio and silent movies as well as composing hundreds of songs, was an unhappy camper from the very beginning. He disliked his dual characters, hated the fact that Norman Taurog seemed to be focusing his attention more on his co-star Claudette Colbert and particularly comic Jimmy Durante, who was borrowed from MGM and frankly walked away with the picture. And worst of all, Cohan hated having to work with Richard Rogers and Lorenz Hart on the songs for the film. The studio, feeling that Cohan's music was out of fashion, had brought in the team to supply the songs. Cohan sarcastically referred to them as "Gilbert and Sullivan." He would later reflect on his treatment by Hollywood's executives, calling them short-sighted for not recognizing his immense talent. Personal slights also rankled him, as when the guard at Paramount's main gate refused to allow his car to enter the lot because he was "not a star."

The film's press book was filled with crazy promotion ideas, such as one ad, "A Plank from the Phantom President's platform! Two Hamburgers in Every Bun! Short Skirts for the Statue of Liberty! A Job for Every Relative! One-day week and six-day weekend." Cohan, who was then 54 and hardly leading man material, seemed unduly self-conscious as the patent-medicine man Doc Varney and his doppelganger, Theodore K. Blair. The use of spoken lyrics in place of dialogue didn't help the film's cause, and the songs themselves, whether by Cohan or Rogers and Hart, were unexceptional at best. Surprisingly, none of this seemed to affect Mordaunt Hall's review in *The New York Times* on October 1, 1932: "Notwithstanding the acrimony that burst forth intermittently between George M. Cohan and Paramount Studio officials during the filming of *The Phantom President,* "this feature, in which Broadway's little giant makes his talking-picture debut, is a crackerjack show. It is an adaptation of a novel by George F. Worts and was directed by Norman Taurog, who has to his credit among other productions that splendid shadow venture, *Skippy*. The film is an excellent example of technical skill and many of the episodes are highly imaginative. It was not surprising that it kept audiences at its first exhibition yesterday in a constant state of glee."

In spite of reviews such as this, *The Phantom President* was one of Paramount's biggest flops of 1932, and Cohan made only one more film, a mystery called *Gambling* (1934) for the Fox Film Corporation, after which he retired from the screen and returned to Broadway. He died of cancer at age 64 on November 5, 1942, the same year that he was glorified in the Warners biopic *Yankee Doodle Dandy*.

Elvis, Hawaii and Girls

On August 24, 1960, the Hollywood trade papers carried the announcement that Hal Wallis had signed writer-director Hal Kanter to develop a screenplay for Elvis Presley, to be titled *Hawaii Beach Boy*. Kanter, who had written and directed Elvis' first picture for Wallis and Paramount, *Loving You* (1957), had begun as a gag writer for Eddie Cantor's radio program, then moved on to writing special material for Bob Hope and Martin and Lewis on their television variety shows, and then to writing such films as *About Mrs. Leslie* (1954) and *The Rose Tattoo* (1955). He created the landmark series *Julia* (1968-1971) starring Diahann Carroll, the first African-American actress to star in her own TV series. In later years Kanter would be a mainstay on the annual Academy Award shows, writing special material for the star presenters.

The original story for *Hawaii Beach Boy* was by a young writer named Allan Weiss, a friend of Paul Nathan's. Weiss would eventually work on seven screenplays for Wallis, all but one of which would be for Elvis. His one non-Presley film was *The Sons of Katie Elder* (1965), on which he would share credit with William H. Wright and Harry Essex. Weiss' last writing credit was for *Easy Come, Easy Go* in 1967.

In September, Nathan sent Wallis a memo at the Imperial Hotel in Tokyo, in which he revealed that he was very unhappy with Kanter's work and that he had secretly given the script to Norman Taurog to read. In several instances it appeared that Kanter was trying to make the film too serious for Nathan and Taurog's taste. Three days later Nathan wrote Wallis again, saying that Kanter had delivered the final section of the script and that it was "much better than the first two-thirds." He indicated that he would go over the script with Kanter and make changes. On September 27, Nathan sent a revised script to Wallis's partner Joseph H. Hazen in New York. Kanter delivered what was identified as the "first temporary yellow script" of *Hawaii Beach Boy* on October 1and was taken off salary. On October 11, Paul Nathan sent a memo to Hal Wallis in which he described Taurog's reaction to Kanter's revised screenplay. On the whole Taurog liked it, but he had serious reservations about several plot points; in this draft the Presley character was an orphan who had been adopted and Taurog felt that this point was unnecessary and "gets us nowhere." Nathan pointed out that "since Taurog had adopted children, perhaps he is more sensitive on that point." Taurog, along with assistant director Micky Moore and technical director Fred Zendar, flew to Hawaii on November 19 to check out locations on both Oahu and Kauai. Another writer, Dan Beaumont, came on board and delivered three sets of revisions between late December and January 25, 1961. Kanter then returned to do the final revisions. The 121 page *Blue Hawaii* "white final script" is dated March 17, 1961.

On January 9, 1961, the day after Elvis' 26th birthday, Hal Wallis announced to the press that he had signed the singer-actor to a new five-year contract, starting with *Blue Hawaii*. Casting was in full swing by the first of the

Elvis with Angela Lansbury and Roland Winters (who played his parents) in *Blue Hawaii*.

year. There was a brief interest in Deborah Walley to play Elvis' love interest, but Juliet Prowse was announced as Elvis' co-star on Feb.7. A memo from Nathan to Wallis on February 3, discussed the need for Prowse to either dye her hair black or wear a wig. As it turned out, this was the least of the problems. Prowse refused to play opposite Presley unless three demands were met: permission to use her Twentieth Century-Fox makeup man, travel expenses for her secretary to the Hawaii location, and a change in her billing clause in the contract. In a press release on March 13, a week before filming was to begin in Hawaii, Wallis announced that the part was being recast. Five days later, Prowse's home studio, Twentieth Century-Fox, placed her on suspension and Joan Blackman was announced as Elvis' leading lady in *Blue Hawaii*.

One of the big mysteries to me is why actress Angela Lansbury agreed to play Elvis' mother. Her performance as a clueless Southern belle is so over-the-top that it is almost embarrassing. She certainly wasn't in need of work; she had already made three films that year including a well-received role in *The Dark at the Top of the Stairs* (1960), and would soon appear in her Oscar nominated performance in *The Manchurian Candidate* (1962). Other cast members included character actor Roland Winters as Elvis' father and John Archer and Nancy Walters as another set of lovers who served to complicate Joan Blackman's relationship with Elvis' character.

Elvis on location with Norman Taurog and Hal Wallis at Hanauma Bay Beach Park, Oahu.

On March 20, 1961, Elvis reported to Paramount Studios for wardrobe fittings, and the following day began recording the 14 songs for the *Blue Hawaii* soundtrack at Radio Recorders on Santa Monica Boulevard in Hollywood. The session would last three days and Radio Recorders would become Elvis' favorite studio for recording his soundtracks and be used on nearly every one of his films for the next few years.

Taurog filmed pre-production footage on Oahu from March 20th to the 24th and Elvis flew to Hawaii, along with his clan and Hal Wallis, on March 25. The Colonel had arranged for Elvis to appear that evening at a benefit concert to raise money to build a memorial for the victims of the Pearl Harbor attack entombed in the sunken hulk of the USS Arizona. The concert at the Bloch Arena in Honolulu, which included a performance by Grand Ol' Opry star Minnie Pearl, raised over $62,000 for the memorial. It would Be Elvis' last public performance for seven years.

Filming on *Blue Hawaii* began on Monday, March 27, 1961, at the Hanauma Bay Beach Park on Oahu and continued for three weeks at various locations around Oahu. Final sequences were filmed on the island of Kauai, where the big wedding finale was staged amidst the lagoons at the Coco Palms Hotel. The company returned to the Mainland on April 19 and filming resumed at Paramount Studios, continuing until all filming was completed on May 23, 1961.

On June 20, Wallis flew to New York with a print of *Blue Hawaii* to screen for the Paramount sales and merchandising executives, and the film had its official opening in Hollywood on November 22, 1961. John L. Scott's slightly tongue-in-cheek review in the *Los Angeles Times* began with the following observation: "Most film singers sooner or later get around to warbling on a tropical island, so why not Elvis?" Scott went on to point out, "The picture, in color, does a lot for the 'paradise of the Pacific,' showing its foamy waves, palm trees, luaus and a couple of plush hotels, but not very much for Elvis' fans. What age bracket does he appeal to now?" In his final wrap-up, Scott questioned Elvis' choice of roles: "One of these days Elvis will play a straight role with substance and we'll definitely find out whether he can act or not." *Variety* liked the film, but also had a problem with Elvis' performance: "Presley handles himself with his usual adroitness, although he has a tendency to fall out of character." *The Hollywood Reporter* echoed the view held by most exhibitors at that time: "*Blue Hawaii* restores Elvis Presley to his natural screen element—the romantic, non-cerebral filmusicals—one which he has departed for more dramatic doings in his last few films, with appreciably less commercial success. Since it is this sort of vehicle in which the singing star seems to enjoy his greatest popularity, the kind his vast legion of fans seems to prefer him in, the Hal Wallis production for Paramount should enjoy widespread boxoffice success over the short haul."

Norman Taurog directing Joan Blackman and Elvis in *Blue Hawaii.*

Blue Hawaii would reach #2 after four weeks on *Variety*'s boxoffice survey and would become the eighteenth highest grossing film for 1961, ultimately earning $4.7 million. Within six months of the film's release, the *Blue Hawaii* soundtrack album had sold two million copies, more than any other Presley album. It would be nominated for two Grammy Awards as "Best Soundtrack Album" and Hal Kanter would receive a nomination from the Writers Guild of America for "Best Written American Musical." He lost to Betty Comden and Adolph Green, who won for their screen adaptation of their Broadway musical *The Bells Are Ringing* (1960).

if he's a heavy or a leading man (played with winning charm by Jeremy Slate). Stella Stevens, who plays a nightclub singer, is totally wasted and apparently didn't want to appear in the film in the first place. She fought bitterly with the studio and was threatened with suspension if she didn't comply.

The musical score was made up of a polyglot collection of multi-national songs that seemed to be having a problem finding a common theme, and runs the gamut from Chinese, to Mexican, to Calypso, to finally one memorable performance of "Return to Sender." The non-melodic title tune by Jerry Leiber and Mike Stoller, which opened and closed the film, compounded the problem in a finale filled with dancing girls from every location imaginable, which left Laurel Goodwin smiling awkwardly on the side lines. With thirteen songs performed by Elvis (one of them twice), there was a serious discussion after the film was previewed about cutting some of them. Although several minutes were edited out, in the end none of the songs were cut and the Colonel had his soundtrack album.

Micky Moore, who had already worked with Norman Taurog on six Martin and Lewis films before assisting him on *G.I. Blues* and *Blue Hawaii*, was again the first assistant director on *Girls! Girls! Girls!* Moore would go on to direct Elvis in *Paradise - Hawaiian Style* (1966) and would eventually become the preeminent Second Unit director in the business, famous for his staging of the action sequences in *Butch Cassidy and the Sundance Kid* (1969) and in all of the *Indiana Jones* films. Moore spoke fondly of his time with Norman Taurog, "I enjoyed working with him very much. He was a good director. He would listen to you if you made a suggestion. He didn't reject them, he would consider them and he was just a nice guy to work with." Moore's career would ultimately last a phenomenal 84 years; he would retire in 2000 after directing the Second Unit on *102 Dalmatians* (2000), Disney's sequel to their live-action version of *101 Dalmatians* (1996). Michael "Micky" Moore died of congestive heart failure at the age of 98 on March 4, 2013.

Jeremy Slate, whose first speaking role in a film was as Sgt. Turk in *G.I. Blues*, remembered Norman Taurog as "a pleasure to work with, although he was known to steam off." Slate was referring to an incident that took place on *Girls! Girls! Girls!* during the filming of the scene where Ross (Elvis) takes Wesley (Slate) for a test ride on one the boats he's planning to purchase. Ross deliberately stalls the boat, while examining the engine, manages to squirt Wesley in the face with oil. It was an old gag that Taurog had used many times before and would use again in *Spinout* (1966), but Slate tried to explain to Taurog that the engine wouldn't squirt oil that way. "He lit into me something awful," remembered Slate. "'Who cares about whether there's a choke or whatever? It's a gag!' I was giving him technical instructions on the engine of the boat and I don't think he appreciated it. But anyway that just lasted a few seconds, and he really was a nice man and had a good sense of humor."

Jeremy Slate and Elvis on location at the Bumble Bee Tuna processing docks.

Slate remembered an incident on *G .I. Blues* that illustrated how Taurog kidded with his star: "Elvis and I were sitting and talking and Norman walked up to us. He put his hand on my knee and he looked me right in the eye and he said, 'Jeremy, you were great in that scene. You brought everything there was in that little part. You were fantastic.' And with that, he turned to go and he realized that he had completely ignored Elvis. He turned back and he tapped him on the knee and he said, 'Good work,' and walked away. It was his joke and Elvis caught on instantly and he got a big kick out of that."

Although partially filmed in Hawaii, the actual location of the story was never made clear, and the use of Paramount Studios' New York Street, which figured prominently in the film, didn't help to clear up the confusion. Nevertheless, the filming began in Honolulu, Hawaii, on Monday April 9, 1962 at

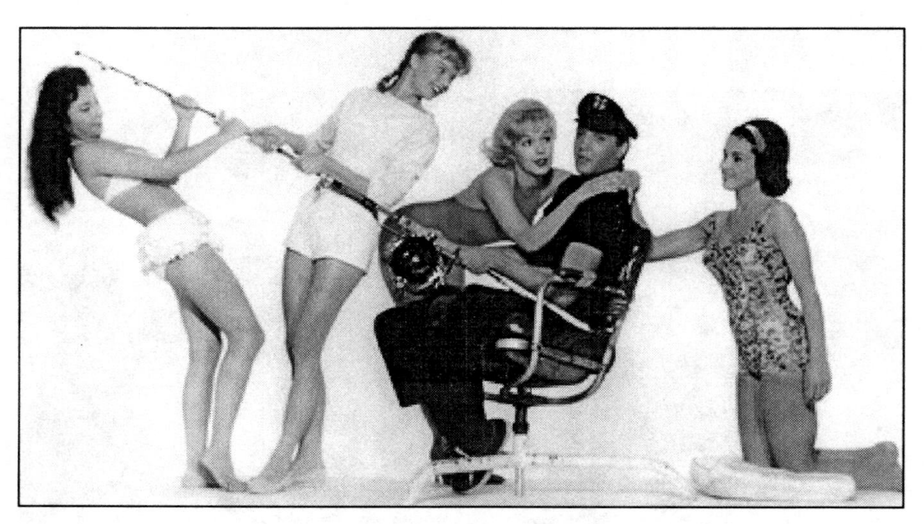

Elvis and some of the *Girls! Girls! Girls!*

various locations, including the Hawaiian Village Hotel, the Marina and the Bumble Bee Tuna processing plant and docks. While filming exteriors on the tuna fishing boat, the reflection from the water gave Norman Taurog a serious sun burn that developed into sun blisters on his lips. He was forced to protect his lips with a white, blocking ointment for several days. On April 26, location filming was completed, except for some second unit photography, and the company returned to Los Angeles. Filming resumed the following Tuesday, May 1on Stage 5 at Paramount Studios and continued for the next nine days. Upon completion of principal photography on May 8, Taurog supervised Elvis' looping session and Elvis then spent a day shooting publicity stills.

Girls! Girls! Girls! had its world premiere in Honolulu on Halloween Eve, 1962, but neither Elvis nor Taurog could attend (they was busy filming *It Happened at the World's Fair* at MGM). The film opened nationwide on November 21 and the reviews were generally positive, if notably influenced by the success of Presley's previous musicals. *The Hollywood Reporter* stated, "A romantic comedy with songs and some production numbers, *Girls! Girls! Girls!* is the new Elvis Presley starrer and will draw most of its attendance from the big following of the popular singer." *Variety* proclaimed, "*Girls! Girls! Girls!* is just that—with Elvis Presley there as the main attraction. Apparently, from the grosses racked up by the performer's earlier pix, he remains generally a salable attraction. This new effort hinges on the popularity of the entertainer, who is given a plethora of songs regardless of whether they fit smoothly into the action." *Film Daily* said it most succinctly: "If you don't like Elvis Presley you're in trouble on this one. Elvis is on screen just about all of the time and has 14 numbers or an average of one every seven minutes or so. Fortunately, watching Presley perform is a pleasant enough chore."

While still well into the profit margin at $2.6 million, *Girls! Girls! Girls!* grossed only half of what *Blue Hawaii* brought in. The single release of "Return to Sender" did better, selling over a million copies, but the soundtrack album with its thirteen songs fell far short of the *Blue Hawaii* album, selling less than 600,000 copies. In 1963, *Girls! Girls! Girls!* was nominated for a Laurel Award by the Motion Picture Exhibitors of America and became the only one of Elvis' features to ever be nominated.

Paramount – 1932

Having survived the unpleasant task of directing George M. Cohan in *The Phantom President*, Norman Taurog moved on to his next assignment at Paramount, a short one: filming the opening and closing segments of an anthology called *If I Had a Million* (1932), a movie that Paramount devised to feature as many of its contract players as possible. From a novel by Robert Hardy Andrews, it consisted of ten sequences (each with a different director), with the screenplays written by a total of 16 writers; a mixture of comedy and pathos, the plot was simple: a dying industrial tycoon can't decide what to do with his fortune. Hating his relatives and despising his employees, he decides to give a million dollars to each of eight people picked randomly from the telephone book. The first name picked is John D. Rockefeller, who is of course quickly rejected and eight more names are selected. In the end, the tycoon decides that he's had so much fun that he isn't going to die and joins his final recipient at her retirement home.

Taurog began filming the prologue, with Richard Bennett playing the tycoon, on Tuesday, October 18, and finished filming the epilogue on Tuesday, October 25, 1932. One of the film's funniest sequences was written and directed by Ernst Lubitsch and contained no dialogue: A clerk, played by Charles Laughton, receives his check in the mail and slowly climbs a series of stairs, moving through various offices, until he comes to the office of the company president. He politely knocks on the door, is admitted and promptly blows a raspberry at his now former boss then turns and leaves. Other stars that appeared in the film included Gary Cooper, George Raft, Charles Ruggles, W.C. Fields, Alison Skipworth and May Robson. Needless to say, the film was a big success and may well have inspired the idea for more star-studded films such as the *Big Broadcast* series. The film's concept was also the basis for a television series called *The Millionaire* (1955-1960), in which each week millionaire John Beresford Tipton (Paul Frees) sends out his representative Michael Anthony (Marvin Miller) to give away one million dollars to a person he has never met.

Maurice Chevalier had been a star at le Casino de Paris, had a successful run at the Palace Theatre in London and appeared in a few silent films in France before he came to Hollywood in 1929 to make his sound film debut in Paramount's first musical, *Innocents of Paris*. Paramount put him under contract and cast him in *The Love Parade*, the first of four films with Ernst Lubitsch and Jeanette MacDonald. By 1933, Chevalier's contract with the studio was running out, Lubitsch and MacDonald had already decamped to MGM, and Chevalier had just two more films left before he would follow them to Culver City. The first of those two films was a remake of a 1927 silent film that had starred Adolphe Menjou called *A Gentleman of Paris* that was based on a novel by Ray Horniman called *Bellamy the Magnificent*. By the time that Waldemar Young, Nunnally Johnson and associate producer Benjamin Glazer had worked it over, the story bore only a slight resemblance to the original, had its title changed to *A Bedtime Story*, and the amusing device of an abandoned baby had been added to the mix. One of the temporary titles for the project was *The Way to Love*, which ended up being the title for Chevalier's final film for Paramount.

Taurog was brought onboard shortly after completing his work on *If I Had a Million* and helped supervise the casting while he prepared for the shoot. The studio had already signed freelance actress Helen Twelvetrees to a two-picture deal and assigned her to play Chevalier's love interest in *A Bedtime Story*. Twelvetrees, whose real name was Helen Marie Jurgens, (she gained the quaint surname when she married first husband, Clark Twelvetrees), came to Hollywood from the New York stage after the advent of sound and had a relatively brief movie career; her final film appearance was in 1939 and she died of an overdose of sedatives in 1958 at the age of 49.

Taurog saw to it that his stars would be properly supported by well-established character actors Edward Everett Horton, George Barbier, Earle Fox and Reginald Mason, plus an infant named Ronald Leroy Overacker, who went under the stage name of Baby Leroy. Baby Leroy, at six months of age, was making his film debut in *A Bedtime Story* and Taurog used him to good advantage, creating a running gag of Baby Leroy gurgling happily as he smashes a series of pocket watches. *The New York Times* review's lead paragraph described his performance this way: "By periodical outbursts of crying, occasional smiles and babbling of some thing that sounds like Da-da or Da-di-da, an infant designated on the program as Baby Leroy gives a performance that rivals in interest that of Maurice Chevalier in the film." Mordaunt

Norman Taurog and Maurice Chevalier audition children for *A Bedtime Story* (Baby Leroy is on left).

Hall, the *Times* reviewer, goes on to praise both the director and the star: "The film was directed by Norman Taurog, who has adroitly refrained from indulging in those obvious jokes. And if one says that Baby Leroy comes close to winning the pantomimic laurels it does not mean that M. Chevalier is any less able than he has been in his other screen works."

Taurog needed Baby Leroy to cry in one scene and he later explained in an interview with an AP correspondent how he managed this. Pointing out Baby Leroy's naturally sunny disposition and the fact that he seldom cried,

Taurog went on to describe his solution to the problem. "We puzzled over it for a week," Taurog said. "The boys wanted to make faces at Leroy, but I knew that wouldn't work. He would have made faces at them. We tried taking his milk-bottle away, and he just looked surprised. Finally, I noticed that he whimpered when a nurse wiped his nose. At first, that was no solution, because, in the picture, you can't show a hand with a handkerchief to your star's nose in order to get a crying scene. We got him in the habit of crying, spontaneously, by picking up a handkerchief near him. In the actual scene, we did that out of camera range. He saw us and began to cry." Later, Baby Leroy would become famous as W.C. Fields' comic foil in three films … whenever he appeared, it was safe to say that the little tyke stole the film right out from under whoever else shared the screen with him. Paramount Pictures put him under contract when he was sixteen months old, making him the youngest actor ever put under contract. They would also take out an endowment policy for his education, to mature when he reached age 15. With the exception of a cameo appearance in the comedy short *Cinema Circus* (1937), his final screen appearance was as a three-year-old in *It's a Great Life* (1935). In 1939, Paramount had planned to costar him with black, child actor Cordell Hickman in *The Biscuit Eater* (1940), but they were forced to replace him on the first day of filming. According to an article in the October 21, 1939, issue of *Variety*, Lonnie Leroy, as he was then called, fell into a creek on the Georgia location and contracted a severe cold. When the doctors informed the studio that he wouldn't be able to work "for at last three weeks," the decision was made to fly child actor Billy Lee to Georgia to replace him; and so ended the film career of Baby Leroy.

Stanley Goldsmith, Taurog's younger cousin, had come out to Hollywood from Chicago, looking to break into the film business. Taurog had arranged for him to work on the swing gang in Paramount's prop department, moving props and set dressings onto various sets as they were being prepared for filming. Taurog later arranged for Stanley to join the *A Bedtime Story* crew as an assistant prop man, and he would continue in this capacity on several more of Taurog's Paramount films, before moving up to a second assistant director post in 1935. Goldsmith would eventually become a highly regarded first assistant director and production manager, supervising such films as, *In Harm's Way* (1965), *The Shoes of the Fisherman* (1968) and *Tora, Tora, Tora* (1970). He would assist his cousin on a number of his films in later years, including, *A Yank at Eton* (1942), *The Beginning or the End* (1947), *The Fuzzy Pink Nightgown* (1957) and *Palm Springs Weekend* (1963).

Shortly after finishing filming on *A Bedtime Story*, Norman and Julie took a well- deserved vacation. He had been working steadily without a break ever since he first started at Paramount in 1930, and Julie could do with a brief respite from the duties of motherhood—so, leaving eight-month-old Patsy Ann with her nanny, they took the train to San Francisco and boarded the S.S.

President Jackson for a leisurely cruise through the Panama Canal, arriving in Manhattan on May 6, 1933. After a week of visiting friends and seeing plays, they returned by train to Los Angeles and Norman reported to the Paramount lot to begin prepping his next film with Maurice Chevalier, *The Way to Love*.

Paramount's foreign department had requested they film a French language version, rather than dubbing the film into French as was usually the case, and Taurog was going to have to do double duty, directing both versions. As it turned out, it would become even more complicated and frustrating than just simply filming the two versions.

Benjamin Glazer, now promoted to producer, and Gene Fowler wrote the screenplay for *The Way to Love*, aided by additional contributors Claude Binyon and Frank Butler. The result of their combined talents was a rather slipshod vehicle for Chevalier that found him as a sandwich-board man, walking the streets of Paris advertising for Professor Bibi (Edward Everett Horton), whose business is making mock postcards for adulterous lovers to send to their spouses from fictitious foreign locales. Instead of Baby Leroy, this time Chevalier has to deal with a scene- stealing dog called Casanova and a carnival performer who is running away from her knife-throwing boyfriend. The cast also included such stalwarts as Minna Gombell, Sidney Toler, Douglass Dumbrille and Mischa Auer.

The Way of Love began filming on June 14, 1933, with Sylvia Sidney in the role of Madeleine, the carnival performer. After filming for just short of a month, Sidney developed a throat ailment that required she have an operation and the production was shut down on July 13 to await her recovery. In the meantime Taurog, with French director Jean Boyer by his side, began filming the French-language version with Chevalier and a French cast.

Sylvia Sidney and B.P. Schulberg were involved in a romantic liaison at the time. Schulberg, who had joined Paramount in 1925, bringing his protégé Clara Bow with him, had recently been "squeezed out" of the company by studio head Adolph Zukor and, perhaps in retribution, Schulberg suggested to Sidney that she take a long rest. Sidney, who was unhappy with her role in the film, took Schulberg's advice, walked out on the picture and flew with him to Europe. Paramount immediately sued Sidney, who eventually settled her contract with the studio, and Paramount. The studio then offered the role to Carole Lombard who turned it down.

Ultimately, Ann Dvorak was borrowed from Warners, and Taurog had to reshoot all of Sylvia Sidney's scenes with Dvorak. Between reshoots and the French version, Taurog virtually filmed *The Way of Love* two and a half times.

The film opened at the Paramount Theatre in New York on October 20, 1933, along with a stage show starring Jack Benny and Mary Livingston. Mordaunt Hall's cursory *New York Times* review gave the cast a few kind words:"M. Chevalier, usually wearing his familiar straw hat, sings delightfully and makes Francois a thoroughly ingratiating vagabond, always good-natured and ever ready to protect an unfortunate girl or even a dog. Ann Dvorak gives a satisfactory portrayal of Madeline. Edward Everett Horton is excellent as Bibi." Norman Taurog's name was not mentioned.

During the filming of *The Way to Love,* Taurog's assistant director was a man named Jack Mintz. It's conceivable that Jack and Sam Mintz were related, possibly even cousins, since both men's families are Russian, but I could find no evidence of a family connection. Jack Mintz was born in Boston, Massachusetts, in 1895, two years before Sam Mintz's birth in Minsk, Russia. Mintz is a fairly common name, even in this country, and it may just be a coincidence that both men found themselves in Hollywood and at different times working for Taurog. Jack Mintz came to Hollywood in the late twenties, finding work in a number of menial positions in the film business. Then, in 1928, he did some writing on a silent comedy for director William Beaudine and the following year worked as his assistant director on a musical comedy called *The Girl from Woolworth's.* The following year he was at MGM as W.S. Van Dyke's assistant on four films, and then moved over to Paramount to assist the two directors that Paramount was pairing on a Cary Grant melodrama, *Gambling Ship* (1933), French director Louis J. Gasnier and writer Max Marcin. Jack Mintz's next film was *The Way to Love* for Taurog and it was the start of a friendship that would last for the rest of their lives. From that point on, Jack Mintz was Taurog's associate on the majority of his films, serving as his idea man, writer and all-around assistant, sometimes with screen credit and sometimes not. He would continue this association until his retirement in 1963 after completing *Palm Springs Weekend*, at which point I would take over these responsibilities for the remainder of Taurog's career.

The End of the Paramount Years

In January of 1934, Norman Taurog began production on his next film for Paramount, a musical version of J.M. Barrie's *The Admirable Crichton* called *We're Not Dressing*. His A-list cast included Bing Crosby, Carole Lombard, George Burns, Gracie Allen, Ethel Merman, Leon Errol and a young British contract player making his second film for the studio, named Raymond Milland. The songs were by Paramount's resident composers, Harry Revel and Mack Gordon, and the screenplay, from an adaptation by producer Benjamin Glazer, was developed by Horace Jackson, Francis Martin and George Marion, Jr. Barrie's basic plot was maintained, with Crosby, a lowly sailor on spoiled heiress Lombard's yacht, assuming a leadership role when the yacht sinks and everyone is stranded on a desert island. In early February, Taurog took the company to Catalina Island, 26 miles as the song says from the mainland, to film extensive beach sequences. He was beset with scheduling problems since both Crosby and Burns and Allen needed to return to Hollywood once each week to rehearse and perform their respective radio programs. On top of that, he had a performing bear that wouldn't perform, and the company was plagued with bad weather. After falling several days behind, Taurog received a call from the head of Paramount's production department asking what the hold-up was. Taurog replied that they were unable to shoot because of heavy fog. The executive replied, "Well, the weather's fine here." So, according to Norman's version told to me years later, he wrapped the company and returned to Hollywood. When the perplexed executive asked why he had done so, Taurog answered, "Your weather was better than mine."

What appeared to be a relaxed atmosphere on the set was deceptive, what with Taurog fighting to get back on schedule and Bing Crosby taking three-

A frustrated Norman Taurog tries to deal with numerous problems on *We 're Not Dressing* (1934).

hour lunch breaks to play golf at the Lakeside Country Club in Toluca Lake. Crosby wasn't yet the super-star he would become, but his popularity on screen and radio was growing since his film debut in *The Big Broadcast* (1932) and, to a certain extent, the studio went along with his demands. Crosby was basically lazy; often too lazy to wear a hairpiece, he would wear hats or caps with little plot justification, accentuating his floppy ears that made him look, as one studio executive complained, "Like a taxi with both doors open." Crosby sang eight songs in *We're Not Dressing*, and Ethel Merman, who had come out to the coast to appear in the film, had several songs that she performed with Leon Errol. It was probably on this picture that Norman Taurog and Roger Edens met for the first time. Edens, who would work with Taurog on several of his films at MGM, was at that time Merman's musical arranger and vocal coach. Merman, who wasn't particularly happy with the pace of the filming, was even unhappier when she attended the New York opening with her family and friends and discovered that her one big solo number, "It's the Animal in Me," had been cut from the film. She and the number would later show up in Taurog's *The Big Broadcast of 1936* and choreographer Leroy Prinz would receive an Academy Award nomination for his staging of the number.

We're Not Dressing opened at the Rivoli Theatre in New York City on April 25, 1934 and the next day's *New York Times* review welcomed the film with the following subdued words of praise: "It has all the plausibility and romantic flavor of the average musical comedy. It is nicely photographed and cleverly directed, the sort of thing that, while it may have too many moaning melodies, is invariably diverting." The *New York World Telegram* called it: "... first rate entertainment for the ear and funny-bone... a gay, melodious bit of musical comedy fluff." And the *New York Mirror* dubbed it a "gay and rowdy musical comedy... lively and nonsensical... catchy songs... [Crosby]fans will delight in 'We're Not Dressing,' which is funny as well as tuneful."

William Claude Dukenfield, known professionally as W.C. Fields, was one of Paramount's major comedy stars in 1934. Having previously been featured for many years in the annual editions of the *Ziegfeld Follies* on Broadway, Fields began starring in silent comedy shorts in 1915 and made his debut in sound films in 1931 in Warners *Her Majesty, Love.* The following year he signed a contract with Paramount and began a seven-year relationship with the studio. Fields, whose famous quote, "Anyone who hates children and animals can't be all bad," was widely repeated, was also famous for his prodigious consumption of alcohol and once said, "I have been asked if I ever get the DTs; I don't know; it's hard to tell where Hollywood ends and the DTs begin." Fields frequently fought with the Paramount executives over the content of his films, preferring to write his own material and direct his own scenes.

Norman Taurog once told me this story: Upon completing his work on *We're Not Dressing,* he was immediately assigned to direct a film version of the Alice Hegan Rice-Anne Crawford Flexner play *Mrs. Wiggs of the Cabbage Patch.* One of his stars was to be W.C. Fields and Taurog was a bit apprehensive: Fields was a noted curmudgeon and difficult to work with. Invited by Fields to meet for breakfast, he presented himself one morning at Fields' home at 24607 Toluca Lake Avenue in the small lakeside community of the same name near Burbank, and was ushered into the study. Fields arrived a moment later and, after a brief exchange of greetings, asked if Taurog would care for some orange juice, which he gratefully accepted. The butler entered bearing a tray with two glasses, an ice bucket, a pitcher of orange juice and a fifth of bourbon. He filled both glasses with ice and a hefty portion of bourbon, and then began to pour orange juice into the nearly full glasses. Fields shouted out in horror, "Hold it! Hold it! Don't ruin the orange juice!" Norman realized it was an act, put on for his benefit, but the glass of "orange juice" was the only breakfast offered to him that morning. Fields lived up to his reputation, developing a strong dislike for his co-star, stage actress Pauline Lord, whom he felt tended to overact.

One day on location at the Shantytown set in Calabasas, Fields arrived and, walking up to a large hog wallowing in some mud, proclaimed: "Good morning, Pauline my dear. You've never looked lovelier." Pauline Lord, who was standing nearby, burst into tears and ran to her dressing room, and it took a great deal of persuasion on Taurog's part to get her to agree to return and film the scene with Fields.

Lord was an immensely successful stage actress who had made a name for herself starring in Eugene O'Neill's *Anna Christie* and *Strange Interlude*. When Lord appeared in the London production of *Anna Christie*, the audience gave her a half-hour ovation. *Mrs. Wiggs of the Cabbage Patch* was Lord's first film and obviously not a pleasant experience for her. After appearing the following year with Basil Rathbone and Louis Hayward in Columbia Pictures, *A Feather in Her Hat*, she gave up films for good and returned to Broadway and her final triumph in *Ethan Frome*. Lord died from injuries sustained in an automobile accident in October of 1950 at the age of 60.

There is an obvious similarity between *Mrs. Wiggs* and Taurog's previous films, *Skippy* and *Sooky*, not the least because of the matching Shantytown settings and the use of children in the stories. In this film Edith Fellows, Virginia Weidler, Jimmy Butler and George Breakston played the Wiggs children and ZaSu Pitts, returning from Taurog's previous comedy *Finn and Hattie*, plays Mrs. Wiggs' fluttery friend, Miss Tabitha Hazy. Fields appears in the final segment of the film as Miss Hazy's mail-order husband-to-be.

Taurog completed filming of *Mrs. Wiggs of the Cabbage Patch* in late July of 1934 and was well into production on his next film when Paramount opened *Mrs. Wiggs* on October 18 at the Paramount Theatre in Manhattan a week later. Andre Sennwald's rather mocking *New York Times* review still managed to praise Taurog's direction: "The cynics who fled down the side streets upon being informed that Hollywood had taken up Mrs. Wiggs may now come back," he wrote. "Norman Taurog and his assistants have wrestled a surprising sum of merriment out of the tearful minor classic which your little sister wagged her pigtails over while you were deep in the perilous histories of Nick Carter." Sennwald went on to itemize several highlights in the film, ending with, "Perhaps the most successful sustained sequence is that which describes the family's visit to the vaudeville show, beginning with Mrs. Wiggs's preparations for the great event. This is Mr. Taurog's brightest style, with a splendid reproduction of the variety entertainment of the early Nineteen Hundreds, the camera playing back and forth between the stage and the row which contains the round-eyed and fantastically delighted Wiggses." *Mrs. Wiggs of the Cabbage Patch* was profitable enough for Paramount to remake it eight years later with Fay Bainter and Hugh Herbert.

In the Jack Mintz papers, held at the Louis B. Mayer Library of the American Film Institute, there is a copy of a stirring speech that the Vice President in Charge of Production at Paramount Studios, Emanuel Cohen, gave to exhibitors in the main ballroom of the Ambassador Hotel on June

19, 1934. Why Mintz kept it is puzzling, but perhaps its encouraging words were a reminder of the hope that kept people pressing on though the daily uncertainty of the Depression era. On that day in June, Cohen admitted to the group of exhibitors that the studio had gone through a "bad period" in 1931 and a large part of 1932, saying, "Our pictures were the second most expensive in the business, and their results at the boxoffice had apparently put them near the bottom of the market's product." He then went on to paint a brighter picture for the coming years, listing the players and directors under contract to Paramount. Coming to the end of the list, Cohen then mentioned the names of the three directors he considered his crown jewels; it's interesting to note that Cohen included Norman Taurog's name in the same sentence with Ernst Lubitsch and Josef von Sternberg. Then, after listing the upcoming productions for 1934, Cohen closed by proudly proclaiming: "I am a conservative by nature and not given to expressions of over-confidence or making statements that are not based on definite facts, and it is with this feeling that I tell you that you will find....that the program for this coming season will be the best that Paramount has had in many a year."

Even in the 1930s Hollywood was always seeking out the youth market, and when somebody came up with the idea of a college musical, Paramount went on a five-year "College" binge with such titles as *College Humor* (1933), *College Rhythm* (1934), *College Scandal* (1935), *College Holiday* (1936) and *College Swing* (1938). It took four writers to come up with the lightweight plot for *College Rhythm*, Paramount's second entry in the "College" series. The previous year, Bing Crosby and Jack Oakie had starred in *College Humor*, and now Taurog would direct Oakie, along with Joe ("Wanna buy a duck?") Penner and newcomer Lanny Ross in the follow-up.

Penner, who had his own half-hour radio program *The Baker's Broadcast* on the Blue Network on Sunday evenings, was making his feature film debut in *College Rhythm*; in 1931 he had starred in a half-dozen Vitagraph shorts... an ex-vaudevillian, he had been introduced to radio audiences on Rudy Vallee's radio show *The Fleischmann Hour* and was voted radio's top comedian in 1934. He specialized in slapstick humor and goofy catchphrases like "Wanna buy a duck?" and "You naaaasss-ty man." and his persona fell somewhere between a nasally adolescent and someone suffering from a speech impediment; by today's standards, a decidedly unpleasant characterization. Penner's career would be cut short by his untimely death from a heart attack at age 37 in 1941.

Jack Oakie, (in later years he would lose his hearing entirely;) learned to read lips after a childhood bout with rheumatic fever affected his hearing. In spite of this handicap, Oakie was an accomplished singer, dancer, musician, comedian and creator of the frequently copied "double-take." He had been making films for Paramount since his feature debut in Clara Bow's

1928 silent comedy *The Fleet's In*. Oakie had become the perennial college boy in films, and his character of Francis J. Finnegan in *College Rhythm* was one more name to add to that list. He would be nominated for an Academy Award in 1941 for his portrayal of Benzino Napaloni, Dictator of Bacteria, in Charles Chaplin's *The Great Dictator* (1940), and would continue in films until 1961, when he would play an amusing Southern Colonel in the Rock Hudson-Doris Day comedy *Lover Come Back*. His final appearance would be in an episode of the television series *Bonanza* in 1966.

Other cast members included Lyda Roberti as Joe Penner's romance-minded co-star, Helen Mack and Mary Brian as Jack Oakie and Lanny Ross' love interests, Dean Jagger in a brief role as the football coach, and George Barbier, one of the screen's best blustering blowhards now playing in his second Taurog film, as John P. Stacy the owner of the department store where much of the action takes place. Several of the film's bit players would become better known as their careers flourished in later years: Kenny Baker, Ann Sheridan, Jane Wyman, Dennis O'Keefe, Dave O'Brian and Joe Sawyer. Ann Sheridan, who also played a small role in *Mrs. Wiggs of the Cabbage Patch*, once listed Norman Taurog as one of her favorite directors, although he never directed her in any of her starring films.

College Rhythm was initially budgeted for $537,000 and Taurog began filming on August 16, 1934. He was under a lot of pressure to shoot the picture, with its numerous production numbers, while at the same time photographing added scenes for *Mrs. Wiggs of the Cabbage Patch*. To add to his problems, Oakie, as was his custom, was fighting with cameraman Ted Tetzlaff over his refusal to wear make-up, and Penner, being relatively new to films, had difficulty singing to a playback and wanted to sing with an orchestra on the set. This sent the Paramount Production Department into a frenzy because a special set would have to be built to film the number and the stage space at the studio was at a minimum. A memo from production executive Sidney Algier to producer Louis D. Lighton, pleading with him to intercede with Penner, was sent on August 18. Judging from an August 23 memo it would appear that Penner won the argument, as it refers to the song being shot on an "interior cover set." A petulant Oakie caused additional delays, according to a September 20 memo sent to production manager R.L. Johnston by the film's assistant director. On several occasions, the assistant director reported, he had to go to Oakie's home and get him out of bed and bring him to the studio and in one case to a location at the Pasadena Rose Bowl. All in all, the assistant director estimated that Oakie cost the company over two days of lost time. In a follow-up memo it was disclosed that Oakie was "unhappy by reason he thinks he isn't getting the 'breaks' and that in the years of his experience with Paramount Oakie feels he is deserving of more consideration." The memo went on to state: "Mr. Taurog has given every consideration to Mr. Oakie so far as this complete production is concerned and has tried in every possible manner to keep all members of the cast in highest spirits and full of enthusiasm for the picture ...Mr. Oakie has not done the mere courtesy to the director of apology for his absence, at any time." Somehow the issues were resolved and Taurog, Oakie and the rest of the cast soldiered on, finishing filming on October 12, 1934.

Paramount produced a ten-minute short called *Hollywood Rhythm,* which they released on November 16, 1934, the week before *College Rhythm* debuted. Made to promote the film and its songs, it purportedly showed the film's composers, Mack Gordon and Harry Revel, hard at work on the songs, with brief cameos by Taurog (looking very stiff and uncomfortable), Lyda Roberti singing and choreographer Leroy Prinz rehearsing his 72 chorus girls for the "Take a Number from One to Ten" number. Mack Gordon, who had been a vaudeville performer before becoming a lyricist, showed a lot of personality while singing and dancing to his own compositions. Jack Oakie and Lyda Roberti appeared in a clip from the film singing a portion of the title tune.

New York Times critic Frank Nugent judged *College Rhythm* to be excellent entertainment, saying, "When the news first was bulletined from the Western front that Joe Penner, radio's duck salesman, was going to make a picture, this corner shuddered slightly and prepared for the worst. The Penner picture, *College Rhythm,* opened yesterday at the Paramount and proves just how wrong one can be in pre-judging a film. It is a question, of course, how much of this credit is due Mr. Penner and how much to the honeyed tenor of Lanny Ross, to the flipness of Jack Oakie, to the accented Lyda Roberti, to the attractive Misses Brian and Mack, to the direction of Norman Taurog, to the words and music of Gordon and Revel. It is a question, but not an especially important one. Let the bows be shared evenly." *Variety* was equally happy with Penner's performance, proclaiming, "Jack Oakie and Mary Brian are well abetted by Joe Penner, who probably meant as much to the picture's drawing potentialities as he does to its amusement quality, meaning plenty in both respects. He is made important to the story and carries most of the comedy burden, yet isn't on long or often enough to wear out the welcome. This favorable beginning should set Penner for pictures."

Taurog was able to take a short break from his busy schedule to celebrate Christmas and New Year with Julie and Patsy Ann at their home in Beverly Hills. The big surprise for two year-old Patsy Ann at Christmas was a special gift that was waiting for her in the backyard and was unique enough to warrant a mention in the "Reel Life" section of the *Boston Globe*: "Out in the garden of the Taurog home, daughter Patsy Ann found a miniature merry-go-round all up and ready to whirl. With six horses, it was complete in every detail right down to the electric piano."

Production reports, those accounts that are sent in each day by the first assistant director (in this case Artie Jacobson), make captivating reading. You can learn about all sorts of fascinating things, such as late scheduling of Ray Noble's shooting call as he worked at the Rainbow Room until 3 AM in the morning. The weather was "dreadfully hot" and production manager Rollie Asher had to change clothes twice a day. He added that if he didn't, his suit would look like a "character suit after it was worn twice." On July 10, the production report noted that filming couldn't begin until 12:30 P.M. "As Miss Dragonette was unable to sing before this time."

After returning to Hollywood, Taurog directed retakes on August 9, with Jack Oakie and Henry Wadsworth on Stage 13, and then shot some additional footage with bit actor Tom Hanlon, playing a radio announcer. *The Big Broadcast of 1936* was screened for the critics during the second week of September, prior to its release, and the reviews were generally mixed. Andre Sennwald in *The New York Times* wrote, "In *The Big Broadcast of 1936* you pays yer money and you takes yer chances. It is a goulash of specialty numbers held together by a hare-brained narrative in which Jack Oakie, Lyda Roberti and Burns and Allen go in for their engaging brand of lunacy…It is as uneven an entertainment as an evening at the radio—except you can't turn it off." The *Motion Picture Herald*, a trade magazine generally prone to hyperbole, was typically more effusive, "*The Big Broadcast* is a big entertainment feature. While it culminates in a super-vaudeville show, it is not an episodic feature. Though it encompasses much, it is motivated by a coherent and well continued comedy premised story. Even without the added feature values, that story could stand on its own feet as novel entertainment. The quality, hokum from start to finish, devotes itself solely to being amusing, with a smart mixture of old and new stuff which the public has demonstrated its appreciation, and doesn't hesitate to ring in a wild and wooly chase together with the U.S. Navy for a flag- waving finale." The Paramount publicity department, with so many big names to sell, got strongly behind the release of the film and inundated newspapers and magazines with colorful ads. In spite of the big push, *The Big Broadcast of 1936*, the most expensive of all of the "Broadcast" films, was the only one to show a loss.

Moving Around Town

By the end of 1935 Norman Taurog's contract with Paramount Pictures was nearing its end; there would be only two more films and one of these would be another loan-out, this time to Samuel Goldwyn Productions. The year before, Goldwyn had bought a *Saturday Evening Post* serial titled *Dreamland* (the name of the amusement park in the story) from Clarence Budington Kelland for $25,000 as the intended basis of Eddie Cantor's annual film for the studio and assigned playwrights Howard Lindsey and Russell Crouse to develop a screen treatment. Not happy with what they turned in, he then put Arthur Sheekman and Sam Perrin on the project. Time passed and they were well into 1935 and nobody, least of all Sam Goldwyn or Eddie Cantor, seemed very happy with the *Dreamland* material. In an act of desperation, Goldwyn's New York story editor, Merritt Hurlburd, made a deal with Owen Davis to write an original story for Cantor, and then met with Damon Runyon for the same purpose; both stories were quickly rejected by Cantor and Goldwyn. Walter DeLeon and Francis Martin were borrowed from Paramount and began work on another draft. Eventually Eddie Cantor's radio writers Harry Einstein and Phil Rapp were brought in to work on Cantor's dialogue.

Cantor, who was to receive $150,000 for the film, had made an arrangement to star in a new Broadway musical that would commence rehearsals on October 15, 1935. He would receive $4,000 per week against 15% percent of the play's gross. Because of the delay in completing a final screenplay, Cantor informed Goldwyn on September 20, of his intention to hold Goldwyn liable for damages if he failed to complete his 1935 film in time. Goldwyn wrote a personal reply addressing Cantor's concerns, but at the same time he had his legal department respond and accelerated preparations to begin filming as soon as possible on what was now called *Shoot the Chutes.*

Ethel Merman would be returning, after *Kid Millions* (1934), to co-star opposite Cantor, this time as torch singer Joyce Lennox, and Norman Taurog would be directing Merman for the third time, after *We're Not Dressing* and *The Big Broadcast of 1936.* The Goldwyn film, which would be the last of seven films that Cantor would make for the producer, had a screenplay that found him playing a meek little man who buys a mail order course called "Man or Mouse - What Are You?" He ends up becoming involved with a gang of crooks who are trying to muscle in on his friend's Dreamland Amusement Park and place rigged slot machines on the grounds. Merman is heavy Brian Donlevy's girlfriend and he uses her to ensnare Cantor into his scheme.

The stunning finale on Dreamland's rollercoaster ride, which Taurog and second unit director Gil Pratt shot mostly at the old Cyclone Racer ride in Long Beach, is filled with awe-inspiring sight gags and stunts that hark back to Taurog's days with Larry Semon. The songs by Harold Arlen and Lew Brown are less than memorable, but the choreography by Broadway dance director Robert Alton, who was making his film debut, was quite striking and innovative—particularly in Merman's "First You've Got Me High, Then You've Got Me Low" number, in which Alton uses a large group of black dancers and singers to back her vocal. Goldwyn, according to A. Scott Berg's insightful biography, kept referring to the song as "First You Got Me Up, Then You Got Me Down." Taurog and Alton would work together again on several films during their joint tenure at MGM.

Sidney Blackmer was originally set to play Vance, the leader of the gang threatening Cantor, but was replaced by Donlevy. Waldo Brian Donlevy was born in Portadown, Ireland, in 1901 and came to this country as a babe in arms. He grew up in Cleveland, and joined the Lafayette Flying Corps in World War I. Donlevy appeared on Broadway in *What Price Glory,* followed by *The Milky Way.* His first featured role in a Hollywood film was Knuckles Jacoby in *Barbary Coast* (1935) for Samuel Goldwyn.

The Goldwyn Girls, the studio's stock company of beautiful dancers, were making their sixth appearance in an Eddie Cantor musical for Goldwyn in *Shoot the Chutes.* They had first appeared in *Whoopee!* in 1930. The girls, including 16 year-old Jinx Falkenburg, were paid $70 per week on a week-to-week contract, and the male dancers were paid $50 a week.

Because of the threatened legal action by Cantor, Taurog didn't have much preparation time on *Shoot the Chutes*; his contract called for him to start with Goldwyn on the day following completion of *The Big Broadcast of 1936.* Taurog's salary was to be $70,000 for 20 weeks work, which broke down to $4,000 per week. A telegram from Taurog's agent Charles K. Feldman to Goldwyn Productions on August 2, 1935, informed the Goldwyn legal department that "Norman Taurog will go off salary Saturday the third day of August, nineteen hundred thirty-five at Paramount and will report to your studio on Monday the fifth day of August for the commencement of his contract with your corporation." Taurog began filming at the Goldwyn Studios on Monday, September 30, 1935, just seven weeks after completing his work on *The Big Broadcast of 1936*. Once again he had to adjust his shooting schedule to allow his star time off every Wednesday afternoon to do his radio program for Texaco on CBS.

Actor Sam Hardy was originally signed to play Copple, one of Donlevy's gang members and Ethel Merman's brother. On October 16, roughly two weeks after filming had begun, Hardy died after an emergency operation and production was shut down. The following telegram was sent to Mrs. Hardy by all of the members of the *Shoot the Chutes* company: "With Saddened Heart and deepest sympathy we extend our condolences in your great loss. It is hard for us to realize that Sam is not with us today and his absence from the set is deeply mourned. It may in some measure lessen your grief to learn that no one in motion pictures was more generally respected and loved than Sam Hardy. Although he had barely started with us on this engagement we all knew him during recent years and everyone from his fellow performers to the most humble members of our staff wants you to know that his memory occupies a tender place in our hearts." The part was recast with William Frawley taking over the role of Copple and Norman Taurog then had to reshoot almost two weeks worth of work involving scenes originally shot with Sam Hardy.

Sam Goldwyn decided he wanted a new title for the film and came across the title of an old musical review that producer Lew Brown had presented on Broadway: *Strike Me Pink*. Goldwyn had his legal representatives contact Brown and negotiate for the use of the title. Brown's asking price was $5,000, but Goldwyn didn't want to pay more than $1,000. After weeks of negotiations, the title was secured for $2,500.

Gilbert Pratt, at Taurog's suggestion, was borrowed from Paramount and paid $400 per week to direct the second unit filming of the climactic rollercoaster chase sequence. Pratt had been an actor and a writer before becoming a director of two-reel comedy shorts. The chase sequence had been budgeted for 32 days of filming from October 7 to November 25 with Taurog supervising and Pratt directing at a cost of $93,920. Two locations were actually used, the Long Beach Roller Coaster and the Seal Beach Roller Coaster.

The second unit continued filming pick up shots throughout production. Also a New York unit filmed establishing shots at Palisades Park and Coney Island of "interesting angles of concessions in foreground and sky scrapers on Manhattan beyond."

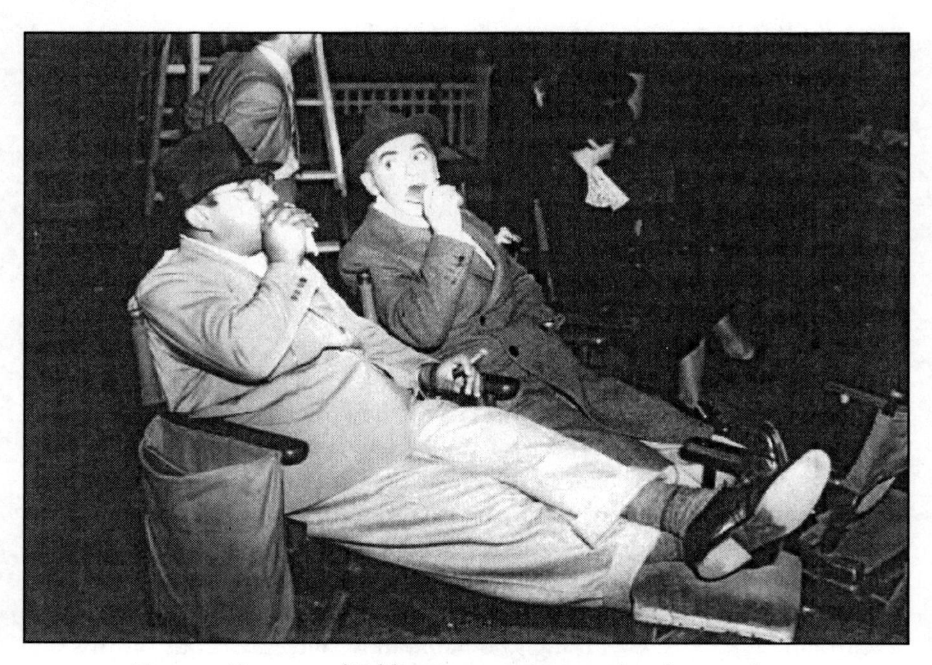

Norman Taurog and Eddie Cantor enjoying a hot dog snack on the set of *Strike Me Pink*.

The majority of the non-chase sequences and the exterior scenes at Dreamland Park were filmed between Friday, October 11, and Thursday, October17.These were interspersed with the musical numbers that were filmed in the *Int. Club Lido* set on various days in October and November. After additional retakes, Taurog completed filming on Monday, December 10, and the film opened in New York on January 16, 1936. Every review singled out the chase sequence finale, heaping it with praise but, with one exception, failing to mention either Norman Taurog or Gil Pratt. The *New York Herald Tribune*: "*Strike Me Pink* is at its best when it reaches its climax and goes in heroically and unashamedly for a splendid finale in the best tradition of the immortal Keystone comedies." The *New York World-Telegram*: "The houseful of guffaws is produced by one of the oldest, simplest and most successful of all cinema devices—the chase… Here it serves to give animation and provide hilarity for an otherwise ambling, unimportant but luxuriously produced and sometimes funny musical comedy." The *New Yorker*: "The classic Sennett chase is here developed, one would think, to its final heights. It's on the grand scale, if anything ever was." It was the *New York Sun* that finally gave Taurog his proper recognition: "Directed by Norman Taurog as slapstick, [it] is for the most part, a mad and merry comedy. It takes a good while getting under way, but once it's really started, however, *Strike Me Pink* goes into a whirlwind finish, a wild, gigantically funny, crazy exciting chase sequence, with the diminutive Eddie pursued by crooks, dressed as policemen and acting like Keystone cops."

On September 19, 1935 a wire was sent from the Paramount Studios in Hollywood to their New York office: "Please register titles *Rhythm on the Range* and *Rhythm of the Range,* original story idea we are developing for Bing Crosby." As it turned out, the former title was already owned by a Mervyn J. Hauser, and on September 20, Paramount and Hauser signed an agreement whereby the studio paid him $7,000 for the rights to his original story and title. Paramount then optioned the rights to three songs from Jacques Wolf and J.K. Brennan for the sum of $2,000 for the songs and their titles: "The Rhythm of the River," "Song of the River" and "Guitars of Love." None of these songs would appear in the final version of the film.

Henry Hathaway was originally penciled in to direct the film, with a tentative start date of December 16. A letter of agreement was sent by Paramount on November 6 to Bing Crosby Productions, in which Crosby approved Hathaway as his director and Frances Langford as his leading lady. On February 24, 1936, production #1087 was assigned to the film with Norman Taurog now set as the director and Frances Farmer as Crosby's leading lady. Taurog would be assisted on the picture by his writer and idea man Jack Mintz and his cousin Stanley Goldsmith, who would move up from the prop department to become a second assistant director for the first time.

Frances Farmer was making her third appearance in a Paramount film since signing a seven-year contract with the studio on her 22nd birthday the year before. Farmer's life has been meticulously and sensationally described in magazine articles, books and films, and in spite of questions as to the veracity of many of these stories, there can be no denying that her life was a tragic one. When she appeared on an episode of *This Is Your Life* in 1958 she adamantly denied that she was an alcoholic, nor that had she been mentally ill. However, Farmer unarguably had a reputation of being temperamental and difficult to work with, and was on a number of occasions arrested for drunkenness. Declared legally insane by her mother, Farmer was committed, against her will, to a mental hospital where she would spend almost five years being treated for schizophrenia. *Son of Fury: The Story of Benjamin Blake* (1942) was Farmer's final screen appearance and she never returned to films after her release from the hospital in 1950, but she did appear on television in several anthology series and had her own local television show hosting afternoon movies in Indianapolis, Indiana, for two years. In 1964 her mental condition started to deteriorate and she began drinking again, forcing the TV station to cancel her contract. After several failed attempts in non-show business ventures, Frances Farmer died of esophageal cancer on August 1, 1970, at the age of 57.

Rhythm on the Range was also the debut for several other actors, the first of whom, radio comedian Bob Burns, was known as "The Arkansas Traveler." Burns was a musician and comedian whose trademark was a musical instrument that he created out of a whiskey funnel and two pieces of plumber's pipe, called a "bazooka." After bouncing around Hollywood, playing bit roles in films, including a couple at Fox with Spencer Tracy and a small bit in *If I Had a Million* at Paramount, Burns went to New York and began appearing with Paul Whiteman on the original *Kraft Music Hall*, and later was a regular on Rudy Vallee's radio program. He came back to Hollywood in 1936 with an offer to appear on Bing Cosby's new version of the *Kraft Music Hall* and later that year, with Crosby's help, he was signed by Paramount to appear in *Rhythm on the Range*; this would be the first of twelve Paramount films he would star in over the next four years. After leaving Paramount he returned to his radio career, starring in his own show on NBC. Burns' final film was a ten-day quickie costing less than $200,000 called *The Windjammer* in which Burns played a character named Bob Burns, an Arkansas farmer who comes to Hollywood to make a film about talking animals. He would die of kidney cancer on February 2, 1956, at the age of 65 at his ranch in Encino, California. There are two stars that bear his name on the Hollywood Walk of Fame near the corner of Hollywood and Vine.

The other newcomer was Martha Raye who, thanks to having been discovered by Norman Taurog, was making the first of fifteen Paramount films that she would star or co-star in over the next four years. Known for her brash personality and large mouth, Raye was literally born into show business. Her parents were vaudeville performers who sang and danced under the name "Reed and Hooper." Raye, who started performing with her parents at the age of three, would entertain audiences in films, on radio and television, and would travel extensively to entertain the troops overseas during World War II, Korea and Vietnam, eventually being awarded the Jean Hersholt Humanitarian Award by the Motion Picture Academy and the Presidential Medal of Freedom in honor of her wartime activities. Raye had been a featured performer on Broadway in several of Earl Carroll's *Sketchbook revues* and also the 1934-35 musical *Calling All Stars*. In 1936 she came out to Hollywood to appear as a featured performer on Al Jolson's radio show, where she would remain for three years.

There was a tradition at this time that every Sunday night at the Trocadero nightclub on the Sunset Strip, stars would get together and entertain each other. One night in 1936 Raye got Jimmy Durante and Joe E. Lewis to act as straight men while she did a comedy drunk routine that she had performed in *Calling All Stars* on Broadway. As it happened, Norman and Julie Taurog were in the audience that night and Taurog immediately made arrangements for Raye to repeat the routine as a cameo in *Rhythm on the Range*. Paramount had to eventually pay composer Lew Brown $500 for the rights to the routine. Everybody liked her performance so much that they added a jive song that Sam Coslow had written for her called "Mr. Paganini," which would become her trademark song. She also joined Bing Crosby and Bob Burns in the "I'm an Old Cowhand (from the Rio Grande)" number. Soon after, Paramount signed Raye to a contract and she stayed at the studio until 1940, before going on to star in a number of films at Universal and appearing with Charles Chaplin in his *Monsieur Verdoux* (1947). From then on it was primarily television and her own show from 1951 to 1956, followed by numerous guest appearances with stars such as Judy Garland and Carol Burnett and as the spokesperson for the Polident denture adhesive commercials. In later years Raye's health deteriorated and she suffered a stroke and a circulatory condition that eventually required the amputation of both of her legs. She died in 1994 at the age of 78.

The "I'm an Old Cowhand" number also featured the singing of several other performers, including the Sons of the Pioneers (along with a young man named Leonard Slye who would soon change his name to Roy Rogers), Louis Prima and his trumpet, and Leonid Kinskey, the wonderful Russian born-comic actor who would always be remembered for his portrayal of Sascha, the crazy bartender who enthusiastically kisses Humphrey Bogart in *Casablanca* (1942).

After location filming in New York's Madison Square Garden for the rodeo sequences where Crosby sang the ballad "Empty Saddles," Taurog com-

The "I'm an Old Cowhand" number featuring (L-R) Roy Rogers (Leonard Slye), Leonid Kinskey, Bing Crosby and Frances Farmer.

pleted principal photography on June 1, 1936. He filmed retakes during the week of June 17 and then he and Julie hosted a wrap party for the entire cast and crew at Victor Hugo's restaurant in Beverly Hills.

July 27, 1936, was designated as "Bob Burns Day" in Little Rock, Arkansas and began with a full-scale parade down Capital Avenue, in front of the Pulaski Theatre, where later that evening Burns would appear with his trusty "bazooka" to entertain the audience before the premiere screening of *Rhythm on the Range*. The film would then begin its country-wide release in New York City four days later at the Paramount Theatre, and Frank S. Nugent's review in *The New York Times* was full of praise for Martha Raye and Bob Burns, but little for Bing Crosby or the film's plot. "Miss Raye is a stridently funny comedienne with a Mammoth Cave, or early Joe E. Brown, mouth," Mr. Nugent crowed, "a dental supply vaguely reminiscent of those frightening uppers and lowers they used to hang over the portals of painless extraction emporia, and a chest which, in moments of burlesque aggressiveness, appears to expand fully ten inches. It's entirely possible that she had several clever lines of dialogue in the picture; we wouldn't know, because every time she opened her mouth the audience started laughing." Nugent then turned his admiration in Bob Burns' direction, "Assisting her in the genial task of stealing the picture from the laryngeal Mr. Crosby and the decorative Frances Farmer is Bob Burns, radio's monologist and bazooka player from Van Buren, Ark. Mr. Burns is tall, dry and drawling. A loquacious and philosophic humorist trained to the vocal requirements of radio, virtually his only concession to Hollywood is that he shifts from foot to foot as he talks instead of remaining rooted to a spot before a microphone. His foot-shifting is intricate, however; and his somnolent phrasing amusing, so we may bid him welcome too." *Newsweek* echoed Nugent's comments, saying, "Martha Raye and Bob Burns lift a mawkish cowboy musical from doldrums to delight."

Paramount and Bing Crosby revisited the "Rhythm" title once again in 1940 in *Rhythm on the River*, a more sophisticated scenario about plagiarized songwriters with Mary Martin, Basil Rathbone and Oscar Levant.

Rhythm on the Range would be Norman Taurog's final Paramount film, until his return in 1952.Taurog would revisit this material once again in 1956 when he would direct Dean Martin and Jerry Lewis in *Pardners* for Hal Wallis—although one might be hard put to recognize any similarity between the two films.

Zanuck Times Three

1935 was one of the worst years of the Depression; the economic slump that had overwhelmed the country was now six years old and there were no signs of recovery. It was in August of that year that Darryl F. Zanuck, the 33-year-old wonder boy who had guided Warners to great success before forming his Twentieth Century Productions with Joseph Schenck, became the head of the newly formed Twentieth Century-Fox Pictures. Shortly thereafter he began the task of turning out films at the rate of one a month. His first, *Metropolitan* starring Lawrence Tibbett, was a critical success, but a boxoffice failure. The second, *Thanks a Million* with Dick Powel did better, but not before a great deal of tinkering on Zanuck's part. Zanuck's next film was chosen to take full advantage of the torrent of publicity that had enveloped the film's subjects the year before. It would be called *The Country Doctor* and it would star the Dionne quintuplets.

The first quintuplets ever to survive infancy were born to Oliva and Elzire Dionne in Ontario, Canada, on May 28, 1934 and thus began the media frenzy known as the "Dionne Quintuplets." Taken from their parents and raised as wards of the Canadian Government, the quints were housed in a specially constructed nursery known as "Quintland" in Northern Ontario, where the public could come and watch the infants through a one-way mirror. Shortly after the quints were born, Dr. A.R. Dafoe, who had delivered all five babies in the middle of the night with the help of two midwives, sent out an urgent plea for an incubator to take the place of the heated bricks he was using to keep the two-month premature babies alive. A reporter with the *Chicago-American* newspaper, Charles E. Blake, flew an incubator to Dr. Dafoe in Callander, Ontario, and managed to gain the doctor's and the family's confidence. Shortly thereafter he wrote a story about the quints that found its way to Zanuck, who bought it and brought Blake to Hollywood to develop the story into a screen treatment. Zanuck assigned writer Sonya Levien to work with Blake on the screenplay. The story was primarily about the Dafoe character, renamed Dr. John Luke, and his fight to obtain a proper hospital for the small town in which he works. The quints make their appearance toward the end of the film.

In 1935, a contract was signed with Twentieth Century-Fox Studios for the quints to appear in a film about their birth and their doctor, A. R. Dafoe. It would appear that Zanuck had Taurog in mind all along to film the quint's biography, as evidenced by an AP story datelined November 12, 1935, that was obviously put out by Twentieth Century-Fox's publicity department and supposedly quoted Taurog as saying he was convinced that the 18-month-old quints had the "ability to play themselves." Taurog supposedly went on to say, "All you need when you have children in pictures is a little ingenuity. These Dionne babies seem to have more than enough intelligence to do the rest." As it turned out it was Henry King who directed the first Dionne film with Jean Hersholt as Dr. John Luke, the fictitious counterpart to the real Dr. Dafoe.

Hersholt took over the role when Will Rogers, who had been set to do the film, was killed in an Alaskan plane crash. Taurog, who had been unavailable to direct the first film due to his Paramount commitments, was signed by Twentieth Century-Fox to a multiple picture contract, with his first film to be *Reunion,* intended as a sequel to *The Country Doctor*.

The screenplay for *Reunion*, which Zanuck intended to personally produce, was based on a story by Bruce Gold. Sonya Levien, who had written the *Country Doctor* script, was given the new assignment and delivered her first draft screenplay dated February 6, 1936. The main portion of the plot focused on the people of Moosetown honoring Dr. John Luke on his retirement with a reunion of all of the babies their celebrated doctor has delivered over the years, including the famous quintuplets. The movie is primarily a love story: Tony Luke, Dr, Luke's nephew, has returned from Toronto to take over his uncle's practice and ends up involved in a love triangle with his true love Mary, Luke's nurse, and Gloria, a woman he has known in Toronto. Sonya Levien delivered a second draft several months later and on July 1, 1936, a meeting was held in Zanuck's office with Norman Taurog and line producer Bogart Rogers. Zanuck was unhappy with the script, declaring that "the general continuity was okay, but the dialogue was very bad throughout the script. The characterizations were poorly drawn. The people talked like characters out of a book." Zanuck then went through the entire script, page by page with specific notes. New writers were assigned to the script and on August 3, Sam Hellman and Gladys Lehman turned in a revised draft, temporarily titled *They Always Come Back*. By the August 4 draft, the title had reverted to *Reunion*, but Zanuck was still not happy. At another meeting, he complained, "The story lacks emotional conflict. There is no excitement or suspense." This was followed by more specific notes from Zanuck, and then Hellman and Lehman went off to create another draft on August 22, followed by a Final Draft on August 25.

Many of the cast members from the original film were brought back, including Jean Hersholt, Slim Summerville, John Qualen, Dorothy Peterson and Montague Love. However, Robert Kent replaced Michael Whalen as Tony Luke and Rochelle Hudson replaced June Lang as Nurse Mary MacKenzie. Helen Vinson joined the cast as Gloria Sheridan.

Director Henry King had taken a production crew to Callander, Ontario, to film the infants in their "Quintland" surroundings for *The Country Doctor*, but had been allowed by law to only film for a maximum of 45 minutes a day. Since the babies were now 27 months old, Taurog was allowed to have them in front of the cameras for one hour a day; still a frustratingly short amount of time, having travelled 3,000 miles to film them. Twentieth Century-Fox had reached an agreement with Canadian Unions on the prior film that they would hire one Canadian union man for each American crew member brought into the country and Taurog's crew of eighty people was matched with an equal number of Canadians. They began filming on August 17 and returned to Hollywood in late September …filming was completed by late October.

Taurog made clear in a syndicated newspaper article what it was like filming the Dionne Quintuplets. "We have a daily 6:45 call for cast and crew," he explained. "With the players made up and everyone breakfasted, we await a call from Dr. Dafoe. He's at the nursery early every morning to check the health of his famous little clients. Having satisfied himself that all's well, he returns to his home, calls us, and we start out." Taurog went on to describe the special blue filter for the lights that been developed for the first film and used to photograph the quints. He then detailed the actual shooting procedure: "The few of us who work near the children wear sterilized surgeons' aprons and masks. Even the electric cables connecting the lights are wrapped in sterilized cloth. I have yet to touch one of the quints. Only the players actually working in scenes with the babies ever place a hand on them. Before going into such a scene, Jean Hersholt and Dorothy Peterson scrub up like surgeons preparing for an operation."

Zanuck rushed through the post-production on *Reunion*, anxious to cash in on the tremendous response to the previous Dionne Quintuplets film. It came in ten minutes shorter than its predecessor and was released on November 20, 1936, eight months after *The Country Doctor*, to lesser (but still acceptable) boxoffice returns. The week after *Reunion* opened in New York, the *New York Times* review damned it with faint praise: "Those charming wards of Edward VIII and Darryl Zanuck, the Dionne quintuplets, are running their limited but endlessly fascinating dramatic repertoire at the Roxy this week, with admirable unaffectedness for such completely bewitching little darlings. They bring with them, perhaps too numerous a supporting cast of grown-ups, for the truth is that *Reunion* is pretty regrettable, as much for the superfluous adult presence on the screen as for the too frequent and too long absences of the Callander glamour girls."

Zanuck and Twentieth Century-Fox tried to exploit the Dionne Quintuplets one more time in 1938 with failed results. The reviews for *Five of A Kind* were less than kind. "It may be ironic justice that the quints have become, in their latest film, the victims of mass production. *Five of a Kind* is an obviously factory-made product, with a synthetically superimposed plot about rival newspaper reporters (Claire Trevor and Cesar Romero) and not a trace of the humor which relieved the two earlier Dionne films. The test of a Dionne picture should not be whether the children are cute to watch (any quintet of 4-year-olds is bound to be), but whether it has any value apart from their presence. This one has none."

Life in Hollywood was good for Norman and Julie Taurog. In spite of the financial crisis that gripped the country, Norman, with his new Twentieth Century-Fox contract, was working steadily and drawing a hefty salary that went to support Julie, Patsy Ann and the rest of their large household at San Ysidro Drive, including Norman's mother, Anita. With unemployment in the country at just under 17% in 1936, the film industry was a bastion of security for its workers, and most particularly for its stars and executives. Newspapers in early January of 1936 carried articles with headlines such as: "Congress Obtains Data in Regard To Large Salaries" and "Pay Checks Show Actors Get Most." One accompanying story reported, that "Congress took a peek into the pay envelopes of the nation's leading money-makers today and discovered that annual salaries of $100,000 are not rarities." Another article stated, "The house ways and means committee figures as submitted by the treasury, showed that Mae West got almost four times as much as Edsel Ford—on the salary roles. And Bing Crosby drew as much as the Mayo brothers together." Figures quoted for annual salaries included, Charles Chaplin, $143,000, Bing Crosby, $104,449, plus $ 88,449 for Bing Crosby Productions, Mae West, $339,166, and Constance Bennett, $176,188. At the bottom of both articles was the following: "Proving that directing movies is profitable too, were the paychecks of Norman Taurog, $118,750, and Wesley Ruggles, $121,415. The producing of the movies paid Cecil B. DeMille $125,000 and B.P. Schulberg $145,563."

In honor of his new Fox contract, Taurog had taken up pipe smoking, or more precisely he began using a pipe as a prop which he only occasionally lit and smoked, but it looked good in the publicity photographs. Julie Taurog enjoyed her status as a famous director's wife, often having her lunches at

Norman Taurog strikes a pose with his new pipe.

fashionable restaurants as reported in the fan magazines. One such article told of a pair of sisters who were visiting Hollywood to see their favorite movie stars. "Lee Heidorn and her sister, Doris, have been in Hollywood only a day or two and they have rubbed shoulders with some of their favorite movie stars: Billie Dove, Lina Basquette, and Arthur Lake." The story was then picked up by one of the sisters and told in the first person: "Our

Jackie Cooper with young Patricia Taurog at Vendome's restaurant.

next adventure was with Jackie Cooper and his charming mother, Mrs. Bigelow. They called for us in the car and had the first wife of Jackie's manager with them. We went to the exclusive Vendome, where we were joined by Mrs. Norman Taurog, who is Mrs. Bigelow's sister and the wife of the famous director. The place was jammed with celebrities. In the various booths, we could see Toby Wing (very heavily made up), H.B. Warner, Frank Fay, Harry Richman, and Bert Wheeler. George Jessel, B.P. Schulberg, Louella Parsons, Laura Hope Crews, Margaret Sullavan (who looked very lovely), and Alice Joyce. Later, Patricia, three-year old daughter of Mrs. Taurog, was brought in by her nurse. After she had some ice cream, we went outside and took some pictures of her and Jackie and then they drove us home."

Julie's brother, Jack Leonard, had tried his hand at acting in early silent films, co-starring with Eugene Pallette and Miriam Cooper in *A Diamond in the Rough* (1914), and appearing in *The Honor of an Outlaw* (1917) with Harry Carey. He later became a writer, co-authoring the original story for Richard Fleischer's film noir classic *The Narrow Margin* (1952). He also co-wrote the screenplay for the Robert Mitchum-Jane Russell film *His Kind of Woman* (1951). He was briefly under contract to MGM where he was credited with three films, all in the "B" Unit. *My Man and I* (1952), *Cry of the Hunted* (1953) and *The Marauders* (1955). There's a mystifying story that Jackie Cooper tells in his autobiography *Please Don't Shoot My Dog* that involves Jack Leonard. When Cooper's mother was dying, he was afraid that his stepfather Charles Bigelow, a man he despised, would try to adopt him after his mother's death. He went to see his Uncle Norman, who advised him to speak with an attorney. Shortly Cooper met with Jack O'Melveny of the law firm of O'Melveny, Tuller and Meyers, who assured Cooper that Bigelow couldn't force an adoption, Taurog called Cooper to his home. As Cooper described it in his book, Taurog told him that he would become Cooper's legal guardian. He added that there were two things Cooper must do: The first was to never mention their conversation to Charles Bigelow, and the second was "to pick up that telephone and call your Uncle Jack and say thanks." Cooper asked why, but Taurog refused to explain, adding as he picked up the phone, "Dial the number. And say to Big Jack, 'Norman said to tell you that even though I don't know what it's for, thanks.' " According to Cooper, Jack Leonard's response to his thanks was, "Oh, I see. Okay Jackie. You don't have to mention it to me again." Cooper leaves the reader with a lot of unanswered questions, saying he never again spoke of the phone call to either Leonard or Taurog and asking the reader, "What had my uncle, Jack Leonard, done for me that required that mysterious phone call?" Cooper never supplied the answer.

Sophisticated comedies, or "screwball comedies" as they were more frequently called, had sprung from the dark days of the Depression. Movie audiences, looking for escape from the hopeless conditions of the 1930s, embraced comedy films like *The Front Page* (1931), *Twentieth Century* (1934),

The Thin Man (1934), and *My Man Godfrey* (1936). Darryl Zanuck's effort to duplicate this formula hadn't met with much success, yet he kept on trying and Norman Taurog's next film was one more attempt; as it turned out, it would be a critical failure and a boxoffice triumph.

Twentieth Century-Fox had purchased a rather melodramatic novel by Frederick Nebel called *Fifty Roads to Town* that Zanuck in his genius decided could be the basis of a comedy and assigned the project to William Conselman to develop. Conselman delivered a "First Story Line" on April 15, 1936, which was followed by a "First Temporary Script" on May 1. Zanuck gave his notes in a memo on May 5 and on June 16, Conselman delivered a first draft screenplay. Willis Cooper did a draft marked "Additional Dialogue." Zanuck then began working with George Marion Jr. and final rewrites came in a script dated September 12, 1936.

The project had been assigned to Raymond Griffith to produce and on October 14, 1936, Otto Preminger was announced as the director. Preminger had just finished directing his first American film for Twentieth Century-Fox: *Under Your Spell* (1936); a "B" picture that Zanuck was using to burn off the studio's contract with Metropolitan opera star Lawrence Tibbett (Tibbett's first film for the studio, *Metropolitan* [1935] had been a flop). For some reason Preminger was then removed as the director of *Fifty Roads to Town* and Norman Taurog replaced him.

The plot of *Fifty Roads to Town*, which bore only a slight resemblance to Frederick Nebel's novel, contained one of the proven comedic ingredients of screwball comedy, mistaken identity. At an upstate New York mountain lodge, Peter Nostrand (Don Ameche), who's running away from a warrant to testify in a divorce trial, meets heiress Millicent Kendall (Ann Sothern), who's running away from an unwanted marriage. Each thinks that the other has been sent to bring them back and tries to foil the other's efforts. When word of an escaped gangster reaches them, Millicent mistakenly believes that Peter must be the gangster and contacts the police. Through all of these plot machinations and more, Peter and Millicent manage to fall in and out of love and then back in love again, all in time for the final fadeout. There's even a time-out for a ballad by Mack Gordon and Harry Revel, sung by the two stars, called "Never in a Million Years."

Taurog's shooting schedule was a quick 32 days starting on January 7, 1937, and ending in early February. This abbreviated schedule placed few demands on him since the film was shot primarily on interior sets at the studio. In fact the atmosphere was so relaxed that Taurog indulged in a few gags on the set. In a scene where Ann Sothern had to fire a revolver at the ceiling to prove it was unloaded, Taurog arranged for one of the electricians overhead to drop a stuffed rabbit at her feet. The startled actress looked at the rabbit in horror, as Taurog, Ameche and the crew howled with laughter.

Fifty Roads to Town was released on April 16, 1937, and the newspaper reviews were "mixed" at best. The *New York World-Telegram*: "The film is superficial, cheerful, lightly amusing, warm weather screen farce." The *Christian Science Monitor*: "Director Norman Taurog and his cast mount their farcical steed and ride off furiously in all directions." But Frank Nugent of the *New York Times* expressed displeasure over the liberties taken with the original story: *Fifty Roads to Town* emerged with its original melodramatic content washed out and an inlay of gibbering farce in its place." The Hollywood trade papers were more enthusiastic, with *Variety* declaring, *Fifty Roads to Town* is diverting situation comedy which distills its entertainment from farcial kidding of the crook mellers, with an ample side order of sexy innuendo. . . Norman Taurog's direction plays creditably for the bantering mood, the laughs, the tricky romance, pointing up the gags and salting down the breezy lines, often with slapstick emphasis." And *The Hollywood Reporter* asserted, "A light farce-comedy, *Fifty Roads to Town* will provide pleasing entertainment on any bill. It belongs to the slightly mad school of nonsense so popular these days. Direction by Norman Taurog is deft in pointing comedy for all the material is worth."

In 1953 Earl Hamner, Jr. the creator of the classic television series *The Waltons*, published his first novel, also titled *Fifty Roads to Town*. Ten years later, Hamner's first screenplay *Palm Springs Weekend* would be produced by Warner Bros. and directed by Norman Taurog.

For Taurog's third and final film for Twentieth Century-Fox, Zanuck picked a musical comedy called *You Can't Have Everything*. Russian-born Gregory Ratoff, a favorite of Zanuck's, had signed a multiple talent contract with the studio in 1936 as an actor, writer, producer and director. In 1936 Ratoff came up with an original story idea that he called *Last Year's Kisses*, which Zanuck bought and assigned to Karl Tunberg to develop. Between 1936 and 1938, Ratoff would also write the original story for *Café Metropole* (1937), co-star in a dozen films and direct two films, all for Twentieth Century-Fox. By 1939 he would concentrate his activities on producing and directing such films as *Rose of Washington Square* (1939), *Intermezzo* (1939), *The Corsican Brothers* (1941) and *The Men in Her Life* (1941). As talented as he was as a director, Gregory Ratoff is probably best remembered by audiences for his performance as Max Fabian, the anxious producer who suffers from acute indigestion in Joseph Mankiewicz's *All About Eve* (1950).

Tunberg delivered a screen treatment for *Last Year's Kisses* on December 9, 1937. A copy of the treatment with Daryl Zanuck's handwritten notes declared that the "last act needs work—surprise too straight line—no twist or climax—needs topper." A new treatment was delivered on January 9, 1937, and Zanuck's copy contained the comment, "Swell Treatment!" It also was filled with his ideas for casting, such as "Warner Baxter or Ameche for

George—Carole Lombard, Pauline Moore or Jean Arthur for Judy—Gypsy Rose Lee or Claire Trevor for Lulu—Fred Allen or Jack Oakie for Dave, etc." At a conference held in Zanuck's office on January 20, he declared that he "considered the treatment a tremendous improvement over the previous one and the script is ready to go into first draft." On March 24, Tunberg delivered a first draft and the title was changed to *You Can't Have Everything*. Norman Taurog was assigned as director and the next set of notes on April 12 contained his suggestions. Over the next few weeks additional rewrites were turned in by Harry Tugend and Jack Yellen.

A typical Twentieth Century-Fox "backstage" musical comedy, *You Can't Have Everything* told the story of Judith Poe Wells (Alice Faye), the great-granddaughter of Edgar Allan Poe; she has come to New York to find a producer for her "serious" play. She meets famous playwright George Macrae (Don Ameche) in an Italian restaurant when she can't pay for her meal and he offers to help. Instead Judy sings for her supper and George is impressed with her vocal ability. He arranges with his partner Sam Gordon (Charles Winninger) to take an option on Judy's play out of pity for her plight. One thing leads to another and Judy and George fall in love, only to have George's ex-girlfriend Lulu (Gypsy Rose Lee making her film debut under her real name, Louise Hovick) create a problem that splits them up. Back in her home town, Judy learns that George has produced her "serious" play as a musical and angrily returns to New York, only to find that her play is a hit. All ends well when she joins George on stage and they embrace.

Zanuck had originally planned to use Jimmy Ritz of the Ritz Brothers as George's friend, but the brothers, who were under contract to Twentieth Century-Fox, rebelled and Zanuck eventually relented, putting all three siblings in the film. Another contract player, Tony Martin, who was just starting with the studio, played singer Bobby Walker and introduced Harry Revel and Mack Gordon's "The Loveliness of You" as well as appearing with the Ritz Brothers and Phyllis Brooks in the "North Pole Sketch."

Taurog began filming on April 22, 1937, and finished in mid-June. *You Can't Have Everything* opened in New York on August 3, 1937 to mixed reviews. The one who seemed to take the heaviest hits was Gypsy Rose Lee with reviewers reacting negatively, such as the *New York Sun*: "Gypsy Rose Lee, erstwhile queen of the strip tease, makes an inauspicious screen debut. If this picture gives an adequate display of her talents, she would do well to abandon her histrionic ambitions forthwith." Or this from *Newsweek*: "Judged solely on her present screen appearance, Gypsy Rose Lee [Louise Hovick] by any other name has a long row to hoe." The coup de grace was delivered by Frank Nugent in the *New York Times:* "*You Can't Have Everything*, besides being a run-of-the-mill musical show. . .will go down in history—and we are careful not to say how far down—as the first time a strip-tease artist has appeared before her public without revealing anything, not even her ability." Some other reviewer, such as Howard Barnes of the *New York Herald Tribune,* actually liked the film, saying, "*You Can't Have Everything* is a vastly entertaining mixture of songs, antics and romance. It has the right ingredients and they have been put together with an expert touch." Or this mention in *Variety*: "[It] is an expert piecing together of story, melody, blackouts, nightclub specialties and production numbers. The fact that it looks as if it were easy to make is the best evidence that it is well done."

On September 4, 1937, shortly after production was completed on *You Can't Have Everything*, Alice Faye married her co-star Tony Martin, the marriage lasted only four years and they divorced in 1941.

Selznick vs. Pasternak

NORMAN Taurog's next film would take a long time finding its way to his doorstep and onto the screen. On December 12, 1936, the following brief blurb appeared in *The Hollywood Reporter*: "H.C. Potter to be borrowed from Samuel Goldwyn to direct David O. Selznick's *Tom Sawyer*. William Wellman was originally scheduled to direct, on a one picture deal, but has been given assignment on *A Star is Born* when *Sawyer* was postponed."

Selznick, famous for his prodigious use of memos, was the son of onetime movie mogul Lewis J. Selznick and had literally grown up in the film business. After working for his father until the elder Selznick's company went bankrupt in 1925, David worked as a story editor at several studios before becoming head of production at RKO in 1931. In 1933 he went to work for his father-in-law Louis B. Mayer at MGM as an executive producer, turning out such hits as *Dinner at Eight* (1933), *David Copperfield* (1935) and *A Tale of Two Cities* (1935). Toward the end of 1935, he left MGM to form Selznick International Pictures, leasing the old Thomas Ince studios in Culver City, and by 1936 had produced two films. The first, *Little Lord Fauntleroy* was a boxoffice success, but the second, *The Garden of Allah*, was both a financial and a critical failure. Selznick and his partner, John Jay "Jock" Whitney, who held a sizable interest in the new Technicolor process, announced in November of 1936 that the company would produce twelve pictures in the coming year, four of them in Technicolor. As it turned out, there were only three films produced by Selznick International Pictures over the next twelve months or so. Two would be in Technicolor, and all would be immensely successful; they were *A Star Is Born*, *The Prisoner of Zenda*, and *Nothing Sacred*. For his next film Selznick returned once again to his favorite source, the classics. As he explained in a speech given to a Film Study Class at Colombia University in November of 1937, "I have had, in any case, some success with resurrecting some of the old books and in bringing them to the screen." Indeed he had, with such films as *David Copperfield, Anna Karenina* and *A Tale of Two Cities* just in 1935 alone.

This time Selznick chose an American classic, Mark Twain's rollicking account of a young boy's escapades in nineteenth century Hannibal, Missouri, *The Adventures of Tom Sawyer*. Selznick had been interested in making the story long before he had first formed Selznick International Pictures, but had been thwarted in his plans by Paramount's filming a version in 1930. Paramount had also registered the title with the Motion Picture Association, which put a hold on it until 1938. In the meantime, in 1936, Selznick purchased from Samuel Clemens' estate for $50,000 the rights to use the Mark Twain name in conjunction with the book's title. Upon learning that Paramount intended to film a sequel called *Tom Sawyer, Detective*, Selznick was forced to purchase the screenplay for the 1930 film in order to stop them. He paid Paramount $10,000 for all material written for the earlier film and handed the project to former silent film director Marshal Neilan to develop a screen story. John V. A. Weaver, a poet and former newspaper book editor, was then assigned to write the screenplay.

Selznick put his research department to work consulting hundreds of sources to insure that the film would have authentic settings, and sought the advice of several experts, including H.L. Mencken and Albert Bigelow Paine. William Wyler was the first director connected to the film and he and Selznick spent several days in the Sacramento River delta looking for locations that would match the Mississippi. Wyler soon left the project to return to his home studio, Samuel Goldwyn Productions, to direct *Dead End* (1937), and William Wellman took over. Since Weaver was taking longer than expected to come up with a script that fulfilled Selznick's expectations, Wellman was reassigned to *A Star Is Born* and H.C. "Hank" Potter was borrowed from Goldwyn. Weaver, who was diagnosed with tuberculosis, had to leave the picture and retire with his wife, actress Peggy Wood, to Colorado for his health. He would die of the disease on June 15, 1938, in Colorado Springs.

A country-wide search for young actors to play the roles of Tom Sawyer, Becky Thatcher and Huck Finn was initiated, and Selznick's publicity director Russell Birdwell, sensing a publicity coup, built it up in all the papers. In a cable to Katherine Brown, the head of his New York office, Selznick, with his usual hyperbole, expressed his support of Birdwell's idea. "I feel that the greatest publicity story and Horatio Alger story in the history of the picture business would be our finding Tom Sawyer or Huck Finn in an orphan asylum, and that this would receive such tremendous attention and arouse such a warm feeling that it would add enormously to the gross of the picture." Supposedly the search for young actors took casting directors to orphanages, reformatories, and public schools, but the final choice, young Tommy Kelly, was actually attending a parochial school in the Bronx when he was discovered and tested for the part of Tom. Ann Gillis (Becky Thatcher) and Ted Limes (Huck Finn) were both established child actors in Hollywood.

After Ben Hecht did a final polish on the script, Selznick was finally satisfied and Potter began filming on March 27, 1937. The delay in starting production had caused Selznick to lose his Technicolor commitment and the film's first sequences were photographed in black and white by cameraman James Wong Howe on the Paramount Ranch location in Agoura Hills, California. After a couple of weeks of filming, Technicolor had a cancellation and Selznick threw out the black and white footage and had them start over, utilizing the giant Technicolor camera and the three-strip process. Technicolor's contract called for their own cameraman and color consultant to be involved in the filming and Howe and Technicolor cameraman Wilfred Cline argued incessantly over the choices of color in the sets and costumes. Cline was supported by Natalie Kalmus, the wife of Technicolor founder Herbert T. Kalmus, who for this film was credited as "Color Supervisor," but as a general rule was "Technicolor Director." Generally considered a nuisance, Kalmus and Cline were overruled by Selznick, who trusted his cameraman's expertise and his own taste over theirs. In Howe's biography, he reports that Technicolor then banned him from shooting any other pictures in color because of his conflicts with them. Howe did film the Leopold Stokowski sequences in Walt Disney's *Fantasia* in 1940, but received no credit. He wouldn't photograph another Technicolor film until *The Eagle and the Hawk* in 1949. In the meantime he did manage to receive four Academy Award nominations for his work on the black and white films *Algiers* (1938), *Abe Lincoln in Illinois* (1940), *Kings Row* (1942), and *The North Star* (1943). Howe would ultimately receive a total of nine nominations and would win two Academy Awards, the first for *The Rose Tattoo* in 1955 and the second for *Hud* in 1963.

After stewing about it for several weeks, Selznick realized that he was unhappy with the results of Potter's work and again shut down production. He offered the assignment to George Cukor, who was under contract to him and penciled in to direct the upcoming *Gone with the Wind*, but much to Selznick's frustration, Cukor turned him down. An early morning phone call then informed Norman Taurog that he was to take over the direction of *The Adventures of Tom Sawyer* and he hastily reported to Selznick International Studios. During Taurog's preparation, some more tinkering was done with the script and some recasting as well. Ted Limes, who was playing Huck Finn, was replaced by Jackie Moran, and the role of Aunt Polly went through several stages of recasting, with Beulah Bondi taking over from Elizabeth Patterson, only to be replaced by May Robson. A couple of future young stars, Lon McCallister and Jean Porter, were cast as Tom Sawyer's classmates.

Taurog put the company back to work on Monday, July 19, 1937, and for the next twelve weeks filming proceeded at various nearby locations and at the studio. Directors never had an easy time on a Selznick picture; some accounts say that Hank Potter wasn't fired, but chose to leave the picture rather than endure any more of Selznick's interference. And for Taurog it was no exception; Selznick was constantly on the set whispering in his ear, or sending him voluminous memos after viewing the rushes. But in spite of all of this intrusion, *The Adventures of Tom Sawyer* still bears the Taurog imprint in the comedy of May Robson as Aunt Polly, and the poignancy of Walter Brennan's Muff Potter, the prissy whining of young David Holt as Tom's cousin Sid, of Tom and Huck Finn's adventures on the river and in the churchyard and the staging of the famous white-washing the fence sequence. Tommy Kelly, a young actor with no prior experience, seems to grow more confident as the film progresses, losing some of the overly cute expressions he resorts to in the earlier portions of the film.

The climax to Samuel Clemens's story takes place with Tom and Becky, who are at a Sunday picnic, deciding to explore McDougal's cave and, after coming upon a large area filled with bats, losing their way. Stumbling upon Injun Joe's (Victor Jory) hideout, the children are pursued by him deeper into the caverns, finally escaping to safety. The cave is then sealed with Injun Joe trapped inside and he eventually starves to death. Everyone agreed that the film needed a bigger, more visual finish, so it was decided that Injun Joe, having chased and trapped Tom on a ledge, should fall to his death when Tom strikes him with his treasured door knocker. The cave sequences are the highlight of the film, due to the combined talents of director Taurog, cameraman Howe and the designs of William Cameron Menzies, who had been hired to assist art director Lyle Wheeler in the creation of the cave set.

On Tuesday, October 5, 1937, a blurb that appeared in *The Hollywood Reporter* under the headline "TOM SAWYER FINISHES," announced "The long shooting schedule comes to an end tonight. Filming started March 27, but twice the footage was junked and a new beginning made. Work on the third try occupied 63 days." Norman Taurog immediately decamped to Universal Studios in the San Fernando Valley to begin preparing Deanna Durbin's next picture for producer Joe Pasternak, *Mad About Music*. He was well into production when *The Hollywood Reporter* announced on December 11, 1937: "David O. Selznick is putting *The Adventures of Tom Sawyer* back into work tomorrow for three days of added scenes. Norman Taurog, now directing Universal's *Mad about Music*, will handle one day's takes, with William Wellman due to take over for the remaining two days." Three days later, the following appeared: "George Cukor will direct three days of added scenes and retakes on Selznick International's *The Adventures of Tom Sawyer.*"

When the film finally went to preview, audiences reacted negatively to Becky's hysterics in the cave sequence and Selznick decided to recut it to eliminate one of Becky's close-ups. He informed Taurog in another of his infamous memos on January 8, 1938, that, "The only criticism we had in the preview cards—and this appeared in a number of them—was that the cave sequence was somehow too horrible for children. . . I studied this even more carefully and came to the conclusion that the offensive part was, hopefully, only the unusually horrible close-up of Becky in which she is laughing hysterically." Whether this did the trick is questionable, as reviews of the film, such as the *New York Herald Tribune*'s, still commented on the fact that "the film has several passages calculated to scare children out of their wits." *The New York Times* took Taurog to task for his slapstick comedy, saying, "Why should the comedy descend to the cheap and obvious splashing of tomatoes, fresh cake icing, whitewash, etc." The trade papers were far more impressed, with *The Hollywood Reporter*'s review headlined: "TOM SAWYER TOP BELLRINGER - Superb Production in Technicolor - Triumph for David O. Selznick, Director Taurog and Child Players." *Daily Variety* raved over the film, proclaiming, "Mark Twain's deathless brief for American boyhood of his generation is beautifully monumented [sic] in film in this great production by David O. Selznick. It will find warm response in every human heart around the world, stir every imagination, delight every critical appraiser and will be commended by enthusiastic word of mouth." The review went on to praise the director: "Great also is Norman Taurog's share in the achievement. His direction is flawless, consists throughout of much more than mere mechanical shrewdness and skill. There is in every scene, in every turn taken by the familiar Twain narrative, an appealing humanity, a deep comprehension of the heart of childhood and an unerring translation of that understanding to the adult sympathy, compassion and delight which would have been commended by the author, as it will be by every grownup and youngster of the myriads who will view it."

These words must have helped to cheer up Taurog as he struggled to overcome numerous problems facing him in the filming of *Mad About Music*. As the pre-production report so presciently stated, the shooting would be hindered by "restrictions on the working hours of our leading lady, Deanna Durbin, and the other twenty-three children working with her. In addition to this, we are handicapped with the problem of finding work to do without Miss Durbin every Wednesday afternoon for a half day because of her broadcast engagements."

Young Miss Durbin was appearing at that time as a guest performer on the Eddie Cantor radio show on CBS. Born Edna Mae Durbin in Winnipeg,

Deanna Durbin appearing on Eddie Cantor's radio program.

Canada, in 1921, she grew up in Southern California. Durbin was first discovered singing in a neighborhood show and signed to a contract by MGM, but after appearing in a short with Judy Garland in which they both sang (Durbin sang operatic, Garland sang pop) her contract was dropped and she was signed by Universal. Taking the name Deanna Durbin, she ultimately made 21 films for Universal and at one time was one of the highest paid actresses in Hollywood. In 1950, Durbin retired from films and moved with her third husband, director Charles David, to a small village just outside Paris, where she lived out of the public's eye until her death at the age of 91 in April of 2013.

Producer Joe Pasternak first came to the United States from Hungary in 1921 and worked in various menial jobs before breaking into films. He assisted Alan Dwan and Wesley Ruggles before returning to Europe and becoming a successful film producer, working for Universal's foreign department in Germany. Pasternak fled Hitler's regime and returned to California and Universal Studios in 1936. His first film with 15-year-old Durbin, *Three Smart Girls* (1936), was such a huge success that it helped to save the studio from bankruptcy, and his follow-up film *100 Men and a Girl* (1937) made Durbin an international star. Pasternak was given a new contract and *Mad About Music* became the third of ten films he would make with Durbin, before moving over the hill in 1941 to MGM Studios in Culver City where he very briefly formalized his credit to read "Joseph Pasternak," and would then spend the next 25 years as "Joe Pasternak" producing 57 films, mostly musicals, and four of them with Norman Taurog.

The original story for *Mad About Music* was written by Marcella Burke and Fred Kohner, with some revisions by Agnes Christine Johnston. The screenplay was competed by Felix Jackson and Bruce Manning in late October and Taurog began filming on November 15, 1937. His cast included Gail Patrick as Durbin's actress mother, Herbert Marshall as a handsome composer, whom she dragoons into pretending to be her father, and two reliable character actors that Taurog frequently used, Arthur Treacher and William Frawley. He also brought in Jackie Moran, who had just finished portraying Huck Finn for him in the Tom Sawyer film, to play Durbin's teenage love interest.

The preliminary budget for the film was estimated to be $680,000, but was quickly revised to "approximately $702, 000," based on a 53-day shooting schedule. The anticipated problems with Durbin's availability and the limited stage time with the young girls who played her fellow students at the Swiss school, caused the filming to eventually expand by 21 days, and the budget to grow exponentially to $858,000. After filming on location at Grauman's Chi-

Herbert Marshall, Norman Taurog and Deanna Durbin relaxing on the set of *Mad About Music*.

nese Theatre in Hollywood, Taurog finally completed everything but some process shots; filming of this process sequence, showing Durbin and some girls riding bicycles during the opening song, was completed the following Tuesday, February 1, 1938. The post-production was then accelerated, with crews working nights and weekends to finish in time for the film's premiere in New York on February 27th. After scoring, dubbing and a quick preview, a composite print of the film was shipped to New York on February 22.

Not just the star, but everyone connected with the film, drew kudos from almost every reviewer for their contributions, with comments such as Jesse Zunser's in *Cue* magazine: "Deanna Durbin, whose astonishing combination of dramatic and musical talents were so evident in *100 Men and a Girl*, proves in *Mad About Music* that her success is no accident. Under skillful direction, and with the aid of a capable cast of juvenile and adult players, she carries her latest picture along through comedy, minor tragedy, and frequent sing-song, to make it completely satisfying film entertainment." The *Hollywood Spectator* declared: "Heart-warming indeed is the story of *Mad About Music* as Norman Taurog tells it, a deeply human story of powerful emotional appeal which loses none of its force by virtue of being told delightfully and with light and amusing touch." *Daily Variety* continued the praise, announcing: "Rarely does a picture come along which so generously fulfills both artistic and commercial requirements, and which so brilliantly redounds to the credit of all who shared in the making. In performance the star transcends even her fine triumph in *100 Men and a Girl*. Herbert Marshall, Gail Patrick, Arthur Treacher, William Frawley and the rest of the cast, distinguish themselves, every one. Delicately and gracefully stated, but always vital in its humorous and pathetic appeal, is the story, tailored to the very essence of Miss Durbin's charm and skylark personality. Flawless is the direction by Norman Taurog, shrewd and showmanly the production guidance by Joe Pasternak."

The Golden Year(s)

1939 is considered by many to be the "Golden Year" for Hollywood films, but for Norman Taurog, the "Golden Year" began in February of 1938, with *The Adventures of Tom Sawyer* and *Mad About Music*, his two huge hits, opening in the same month and playing simultaneously in theaters all across the country, followed by a third even bigger hit opening in September of that year. Taurog's "Golden Year" reached its climax with the announcement on February 5, 1939 of his second Academy Award nomination, but would end on a tragic note.

MGM in 1938 was the preeminent film studio in Hollywood, producing over 40 motion pictures a year and commanding a roster of stars, producers, directors and writers unequaled anywhere else. One MGM publicist described it as "the Tiffany's of the business." The studio complex in Culver City, California consisted of 44 acres divided into six lots, with the main lot containing 37 sound stages, office buildings, commissary, dressing rooms, editing rooms, film vaults, scoring and dubbing stages, art, wardrobe, make-up, props, and special effects departments. The studio had its own film lab, generator plant, police and fire departments, even its own barber shop. The remaining five lots were filled with exterior sets of castles and moats, jungles, railroad stations, New York's Lower East side, and Midwestern streets, a European street, a lake, a full-sized Mississippi riverboat and a three-masted schooner. The studio also had the charming habit of referring to all of its executives, producers, and directors by their last names. Black Chrysler limousines were parked on standby at each stage with a nameplate card in the right hand corner of the windshield that would say "The Taurog Company," or "The Cukor Company," or whoever else was filming that day. Another sign

MGM Studios circa 1940s

on the stage door would identify the production company within in the same manner. The production reports always referred to "Mr. Taurog, Mr. Freed, Mr. Katz, etc."

MGM also had Louis B. Mayer, the pugnacious and sentimental head of the studio. In 1937, Mayer's personal income was $1,300,000, making him the highest-salaried individual in the United States. MGM was still in the midst of recovering from the tragic and unexpected death of Irving Thalberg from pneumonia in late 1936, and much of Mayer's attention was focused on completing post-production work on Thalberg's final film, *The Good Earth* (1937), and preparing for the upcoming filming of Thalberg's long-intended project for his wife, Norma Shearer, *Marie Antoinette* (1938). It was at this point in time that Norman Taurog signed his first contract with MGM and drew as his first assignment a little project that had been bouncing around the studio for a couple of years called *Boys Town*.

John W. Considine Jr. was the son of a colorful former Seattle political boss who later became head of a chain of film theaters. Considine's brother Bob was a noted newspaper columnist and screenwriter, and John had been a producer at MGM since 1933. His credits included *Evelyn Prentice* (1934) with William Powell and Myrna Loy and *Broadway Melody of 1936* (1935) with Jack Benny and Eleanor Powell. Considine had been assigned *Boys Town* in 1936 when MGM bought the rights to a magazine article and paid Father Edward J. Flanagan $5,000 for the rights to the story of his boys' community. The studio was looking for a follow-up role for Spencer Tracy, after his success playing a priest in *San Francisco* (1936), and felt that this could be the story. The original concept was for Tracy to play Father Flanagan with

Mickey Rooney and Freddie Bartholomew as two of his wards. Several efforts were made to come up with a suitable story, none of which satisfied Considine; he had already thrown out an unfinished screenplay and rejected several other story treatments, before Eleanore Griffin was assigned to the project and went to Omaha, Nebraska, to meet with Father Flanagan and tour the facilities. Considine was still unhappy with the results of Griffin's work and asked Dore Schary, a freelance writer working at the studio for $750 a week, to read the material. Schary pointed out the weakness of having Bartholomew play one of the characters and suggested dropping him and focusing on the Tracy-Rooney characters. Considine agreed with this idea and Schary was sent to Boys Town to meet with Father Flanagan. Schary ultimately came up with a screenplay that everyone approved except Tracy, who wasn't happy about being cast as another priest so soon after *San Francisco.*

Tracy, whose deep-rooted psychological problems and fits of depression often led to bouts of drinking and production delays for his studio, had managed to handle a strenuous filming schedule of three pictures in a row without falling off the wagon. He had also just been nominated for an Academy Award for his performance as Father Mullin in *San Francisco,* and the studio, not wanting to upset the apple cart, agreed to shelve *Boys Town* tem-

Spencer Tracy as Father Flanagan with director Norman Taurog on the set of *Boys Town.*

porarily. As it turned out, Tracy, unhappy with having been teamed with Joan Crawford in a potboiler called *Mannequin* (1938), went on a ten-day binge, delaying the start of the Crawford picture. Tracy would lose the Oscar to Paul Muni in *The Story of Louis Pasteur* (1936), but win the following year for his performance as Manuel, the Portuguese fisherman in *Captains Courageous.*

Tracy was before the cameras filming *Test Pilot* with Clark Gable and Myrna Loy when *Boys Town* was put back on the schedule. J. Walter Ruben, who had directed Tracy and Jean Harlow in *Riffraff* (1936), was assigned to direct; he and Dore Schary returned to Boys Town to scout locations and work on the script. By the end of the year, Schary had turned in his revised screenplay and John Considine invited Father Flanagan to come out to the studio to meet with Tracy and him and discuss the film. Flanagan arrived in Culver City on February 18, 1938, and a lunch and a photo session was held with Considine, Tracy, Father Flanagan, and Mickey Rooney. After approving the basic story line of Dore Schary's script and discussing a sales approach for the film, Father Flanagan returned to Omaha and Considine assigned writer John Meehan to do a final revision. It was only after "Jack" Ruben became ill that Norman Taurog was assigned to replace him as director of *Boys Town* and begin what would be the first of six films he would make with producer John W. Considine Jr. They would become good friends and remain so until Considine's death at age 62 in March of 1962. Taurog's initial contract with Metro-Goldwyn-Mayer was for one year, with yearly options for up to four additional years. His salary would begin at $3,000 a week and progress upward to $3,250 for the second year, continue at $3,250 for the third year and rise to $3,500 for the fourth year.

In the late Spring of 1938, while Taurog, Considine, John Meehan and assistant director Horace Hough were in Omaha on a location scout at Boys Town, Spencer Tracy was vacationing in Hawaii with his wife and recovering from another serious drinking bout that had hospitalized him for several weeks. Tracy had won the Oscar for his performance in *Captains Courageous*, but had been unable to attend the ceremonies and his wife Louise had accepted in his place. Mickey Rooney was finishing work on *Hold That Kiss* (1938) with Maureen O'Sullivan and Dennis O'Keefe and doing wardrobe and makeup tests for his fourth installment in the popular "Andy Hardy" series, *Love Finds Andy Hardy* (1938).

Rooney, about to celebrate his eighteenth birthday that September, had arrived at the studio in 1934, when David O. Selznick had hired him to play the brief role of Clark Gable as a boy in *Manhattan Melodrama*. Having already appeared on the stage with his parents when he was three years old, and made over 60 *Mickey McGuire* shorts from 1926 to 1934, Rooney was already a highly skilled performer and he soon caught the eye of entertainment-hungry audiences. Now, thanks to the success of films like *Captains*

Mickey Rooney and Norman Taurog pose for the camera on the set of *Boy's Town*.

Courageous and *Thoroughbreds Don't Cry* (1937), as well as the *Andy Hardy* films, he was about to be proclaimed the top star of 1938 by the Motion Picture Exhibitors of America in their year-end poll.

Taurog brought Jack Mintz in to work with John Meehan on the script, and they were still delivering pages when filming on *Boys Town* began at the studio on June 8, 1938, with the scene where Father Flanagan first meets the cocky Whitey Marsh (Rooney). Although Tracy and Rooney had appeared in two previous films, *Riffraff* and *Captains Courageous*, they'd had very few scenes together, and this would be their first time "de hombre a hombre." Rooney liked to clown around on the set, telling jokes to the crew and then rushing into the set at the last minute to do his scene. He claimed that it helped to psych him up and sharpen his performance. As described by James Curtis in his excellent biography *Spencer Tracy*, when Tracy and Rooney did their first scene together, Rooney started trying to upstage him by fidgeting with his tie or adjusting his pocket handkerchief. Tracy took this for about a minute, then let him have it, saying, "The moment I catch you trying to louse up a scene I'm in, I'll send you to Purgatory. You'll wish you'd never been born, because I can do it." Rooney never tried it again, but he was still behaving like "Peck's Bad Boy" when the company left for Omaha to begin location work at the real Boys Town.

Taurog, Considine, Tracy, Rooney and the rest of the cast and crew of fifty-eight arrived in Omaha by train on June 25, to be met by Father Flanagan and a huge crowd of well-wishers. Gene Reynolds, who was playing the crippled boy Tony Ponessa, has been quoted as saying that "Spencer Tracy rarely relied on a director for guidance." Reynolds described to me what it was like working with Tracy and Rooney: "Tracy was a very kind man, a very sweet man. The crew liked him and he had a nice sense of humor. Very encouraging to me, he was just a great guy. He was very comfortable as Father Flanagan." Reynolds also gave James Curtis his opinion of Tracy's performance: "He was artless, you never caught him acting." Reynolds' memories of Rooney were somewhat less flattering: "Mickey, he was three years older than me, but his social life was decades ahead. One day after filming, we came back to his room at the hotel, and his mother was with him of course, and the first thing he did—and I guess at that time he was only sixteen or seventeen—he went right to the fridge and pulls out a beer and popped it, just like an adult worker. He was way ahead of me and he used to tease me about it. He used to say, 'We're all making out.' We would shoot a scene we were in and then they would send us to school. We would be there, in between shots, until we had put in our four hours—they clocked it—and then we could fool around. At which time Mickey would just be making jokes and doing strange pantomimes and having fun. He had incredible energy."

Reynolds' opinion of Taurog's directing style was very complimentary. "He was a very nice guy, personally, and as a director he was very sure-footed," Reynolds told me. "He knew what he was doing and he was very deliberate. I remember that he took a shot, when we were in Omaha, of the driveway that led up to all of the buildings at Boys Town. It was a tree-lined street and he picked out what I guess was a very nice angle, and he said, 'Okay, give me about fifteen feet of that. Okay print it and let's go.' And Sid

Wagner the cameraman said, 'You only want take one?' And he said, 'I'm only going to use one.' However on other scenes he wouldn't be reluctant to print as many takes as he needed. As for directing Spencer Tracy, what could he say, except 'beautiful'? I do think he was very good with Mickey; he kept a control on him and wouldn't let him play his scenes over the top."

Reynolds also told me a story that illustrated how Taurog and Jack Mintz worked together. "I had this one scene with Tracy," he recalled, "in which Mickey Rooney, in the scene that led up to this, had tried to help me carry my chair. It was a folding chair, and as a cripple—you know I had the club foot—I had a little trouble, as the character, picking it up. Mickey's character stepped in and said, 'Here, kid, let me take that for you.' And I said, 'No, I can do it myself,' and I pulled it away and I was very upset by his condescension. So then I had this scene with Tracy in which Tracy consoles me because I'm so upset with Mickey's character, Whitey, being so crude with me. I cried and said, 'Why do people have to treat me like this?' And Tracy said to me, 'You know, there's a man once who was a cripple, and he became President of the United States.' And I said something like, 'Here I am worried about just getting along here, and here's a guy who was President…—it was something like that. So, Jack Mintz steps forward—I'd played the scene and I thought it was right—and Jack says that I should be much more reassured and gratified and encouraged by Father Flanagan's words. And that's the way I played it, and that's the way Taurog liked it. So that's a case where Jack Mintz earned his money, that's why he was there."

Filming at Boys Town was hard on everybody: 100 ° in the shade, of which there was very little, and then it rained for three straight days, putting the company behind schedule and forcing it to shift to night shooting to pick up the time. After three weeks, the company finally left Omaha and returned to Culver City, to spend the next four weeks completing the film on MGM's soundstages. Rooney, up to his old tricks, had a piano brought in and stashed at the back of the stage. In between takes he would go back there and work on a song he was writing with his old school friend Sidney Miller. Miller was playing Mo Kahn, the Boys Town barber, and his and Rooney's song was called "Love's Got Nothing on Me."

In the first of several autobiographies that Rooney wrote over the years, *Life Is Too Short*, he brags about his ability to turn himself on and off "like a faucet." He would be crying in a scene with Spencer Tracy one minute and as soon as Taurog said "Print," he'd be back at the piano with Miller, working on the song. Although a photograph establishes the existence of a piano, I suspect the story is somewhat apocryphal, as I can't imagine either Taurog or Tracy putting up with those kinds of shenanigans for very long. In the end, everyone managed to survive the heat of Omaha and Rooney's behavior, and Taurog finally wrapped production on August 8, 1938.

Mickey Rooney entertains fellow cast members at the piano.
(Gene Reynolds is seated to the right of Rooney)

The crowds of onlookers that showed up every day to watch the filming at Boys Town caused severe damage to the grounds and Father Flanagan was forced to use most of the $5,000 he had received from MGM for repairs. A few days after filming was completed, an item appeared in Paul Harrison's syndicated *Hollywood* column datelined August 11, reporting that the cast and crew, collectively and individually, had voluntarily sent money to pay the tuition of one or more of the residents of Boys Town. The article ended with the following: "It's nice to know that these gents are not always going around with their tongues in cheeks and cynicism in their souls."

MGM went full out to publicize *Boys Town*; Frank Whitbeck, the studio's publicity director with the rich, baritone voice that frequently set the scene in many of MGM's trailers, even sent director Harry Loud and producer John Nesbitt, along with a camera crew, to Omaha to film a short documentary called *The City of Little Men* that featured the real Father Flanagan. The studio, considering Tracy's performance worthy of another Oscar nomination, was anxious to get the film into release quickly. Editor Elmo Veron was ordered to work around the clock to have the film ready to preview just one week after Taurog had wrapped production. It previewed at the Inglewood Theatre near the studio and received an excellent reaction, with the audience giving it extended applause after the lights came up. A few changes were made after the preview, Mayer gave his okay, the negative was cut, prints were made and *Boys Town* opened at the Capitol Theatre in New York City on September 9, 1938. The newspaper reviews picked on the sentimentality of the script, while the trade papers, recognizing its boxoffice potential, gave it a thumbs up. Frank Nugent in the *New York Times* pointed out that the picture "Gets off to a grand start and keeps its evenly interesting stride so long as Mickey remains the fresh little mug with his guard up against Spencer Tracy's Father Flanagan and the other refining influences of the home. It loses ground and never entirely regains it when the script writers discover they have made Mickey too tough a nut to crack except by resorting to artificial plot leverage." Howard Barnes of the *New York Herald Tribune* agreed, but still found time to accord praise for the direction: "If the picture leaves something to be desired it is because it is heavily underlined with sentiment, and has a highly melodramatic ending. Thanks to Norman Taurog's skillful direction and the generally straightforward performances, though, it still is a provocative and sometimes moving offering." *Variety* also singled out the director for praise: "In his directing of the piece, Norman Taurog once again proves that he is without an equal when it comes to getting a performance out of young players. He keeps the story bubbling and alive, yet pulls no punches when making his sharp, clean-cut points." And *Film Daily* summed it up this way: "Here is a picture containing entertainment value that will appeal to every type of audience. *Boys Town* has entertainment value plus, with a brilliant cast and splendid direction to put it on the screen." *Boys Town* would e go on to gross $4,000, 000 in its world-wide release and garner five nominations and two Academy Awards. It is listed at #81 in the American Film Institute's list of the 100 most inspiring movies of all time.

There were several news items around this time connecting Norman Taurog with *The Wizard of Oz*. On July 16, 1938, Edwin Schallert's column in the *Los Angeles Times* headlined: "NORMAN TAUROG WILL DIRECT

WIZARD OF OZ," with the subsequent article devoting its lead paragraph to the story. "Taurog has moved very much into the ace class of film makers since *Adventures of Tom Sawyer* and *Mad About Music*, Also I hear from John Considine, the producer, that *Boys Town* is to be quite something." Notwithstanding publicity such as this, when Aljean Harmetz interviewed Norman Taurog in 1976 for her book *The Making of The Wizard of Oz,* he claimed he had never been approached to direct the film and had never heard anything about it at the studio.

In fact, Taurog had already been assigned his next film; to be produced by Harry Rapf and starring Franciska Gaal, a Hungarian cabaret singer who looked a little like a chubby Jean Arthur. (Joe Pasternak had discovered her some years before in Europe). *The Girl Downstairs* was a remake of a German-made film called *Catherine the Last* that Pasternak had produced and Henry Koster directed with Gaal in the lead just two years earlier. At Paramount, Franciska Gaal had just finished co-starring with Fredric March in Cecil B. DeMille's *The Buccaneer* (1938), and in a Bing Crosby musical called *Paris Honeymoon* (1939), and Louis B. Mayer was considering putting her under contract. MGM bought the remake rights to the German film, and it was originally to be called *The Awakening of Katrina*, and later *Katherine the Last*, but in the end it was released as *The Girl Downstairs.*

An attempt at a Lubitsch-style comedy, *The Girl Downstairs* hung its hook on a popular plot gimmick of the time, mistaken identity. Harold Goldman wrote the English adaptation of the *Catherine the Last* screenplay by Alexander Hunyady, Felix Jackson and Karoly Noti, and Gerald Savoy did some work on a revised script. In the film, Franchot Tone portrayed a wealthy playboy who thinks he is in love with an heiress whose father doesn't approve of his lifestyle. In order to gain access to the home, he poses as a chauffeur and pretends to woo the downstairs maid. Of course the maid falls in love with him and, thinking he has been fired from his job, uses her savings to buy Tone a dilapidated old taxi. The taxi is so slow that people walk past it and a boy on a bicycle helps to push it. In the final pay-off to the gag, the taxi falls apart piece by piece. All ends well, with Tone and Gaal declaring their love in time for the final fadeout. *The Girl Downstairs* is a film that even Ernst Lubitsch couldn't have made work; in fact, it is almost impossible to watch. Gaal's portrayal of Katarina is like that of a sleepwalker and so simple-minded that you find yourself hoping that Franchot Tone will end up with the down-to-earth heiress played by Rita Johnson. Then there is the moment when Gaal uses the telephone for the first time, screeching "Hello" into the receiver at the top of her lungs so many times that you just want to hang up. As usual, Taurog peopled his cast with wonderful character actors, including Reginald Gardiner, Walter Connolly, Reginald Owen, Franklin Pangborn, Robert Coote and a subdued Billy Gilbert (no sneezing), but it was all for naught as almost every reviewer hated the film. Bosley Crowther in his *New York Times* review called it "An outrageously silly picture, no more plausible than a Dr. Seuss cartoon, made halfway enjoyable by some quaintly amusing touches and the performances of Mr. Tone, Walter Connolly and Reginald Owen." Robert W. Dana in the *New York Herald Tribune* was even harsher: "It is about time that Hollywood realized that Hungarian comedies are no better boxoffice proof than many of the loose jointed, bewildering tales concocted by Coast scenarists in recent seasons, which is a roundabout way of reporting that *Girl Downstairs* is as exciting as a Hungarian derivative of early 1938, *The Baroness and the Butler*." Even the Hollywood trades were dismissive of the film, with *Variety* reporting, "General audiences will find it only mildly entertaining. Picture, aimed to swell the prestige of Franchot Tone, will partially accomplish its purpose. It will not serve similarly, however, for his romantic team-mate, Franciska Gaal, for, appearing at her best, she is handicapped by the scripters' efforts to develop a screenplay around a short story that met with defeat."

Tone soon left Hollywood to return to the Broadway stage, and Gaal went home to Hungary, never to return. And, as if it would make up in some way for the drubbing he received on his last picture, MGM handed Taurog another piece of fluff called *Lucky Night* and rewarded him with star power (Robert Taylor and Myrna Loy), and a reunion with an old friend and associate from his days at Paramount, producer Louis D. Lighton.

Taurog had just begun working on the script of *Lucky Night* with writer Ben Hecht when tragedy struck on November 28, 1938. It had been a day of losses; the *Los Angeles Times* reported that morning that a huge brush fire was threatening several celebrities' homes in Encino, including the home of Alice Faye and her husband Tony Martin. Also on the front page were a photograph and a story about the death the day before of Walt Disney's mother from carbon monoxide poisoning. Norman Taurog wasn't reading the paper that morning; he was returning home from the hospital where his 66-year-old mother had succumbed to a heart attack. Anita had suffered from a heart ailment for many years and her health had been deteriorating for some time. She suffered a heart attack on November 25 and was rushed to the hospital, but died two days later. Anita Taurog was buried the following Tuesday, November 29. It was a grim time for Norman Taurog, but more tragedy, or near tragedy, was still to come.

Ever since the Lindbergh baby's kidnapping in 1932, Hollywood celebrities had been plagued with threats of child abduction. Norman's notoriety had drawn the attention of criminal elements in Los Angeles, and a telephone threat was made to kidnap six-year-old Patsy Ann. Newspapers reported on February 14, 1939, that Beverly Hills Chief of Police Charles C. Blair had assigned two investigators to watch the hillside mansion at 1137

San Ysidro Drive after the child's nurse had received a warning. The FBI was also brought in, and Julie Taurog was reported to be "on the verge of a collapse." Norman, who was busy filming *Lucky Night*, tried to downplay the incident and refused to speak with reporters. In the end, nothing came of the threat, but for Norman, Julie and little Patsy Ann, it was a warning of what might happen, and the fear stayed with them for years after.

Taurog began filming *Lucky Night* on January 16, 1939, from a screenplay by Vincent Lawrence and Grover Jones that was based on a short story by Oliver Claxton. As was the case with all Taurog productions, the atmosphere on the set was relaxed, with time for joking and story sharing between set-ups. In fact, his two stars nicknamed him "Chiefie" and presented him with their caricatures and the cast and crew's signatures on a special parchment at the end of production. Apparently, Taurog liked to keep a record of the people who worked on his films, and as far back as *The Adventures of Tom Sawyer* he'd had a certificate printed up for cast members and crew to sign. Copies of this form were still being handed around for signatures right up to his last film, *Live A Little, Love a Little,* 30 years later. Taurog's cameraman on *Lucky Night* was Ray June, one of MGM's premium cinematographers who had already been nominated twice for Oscars for his work on *Arrowsmith* (1932) and *Barbary Coast* (1935), and like most cinematographers, he worked quietly and quickly. Myrna Loy, who was riding the crest of popularity due to her appearances in *The Thin Man* (1934), its sequel *After the Thin Man* (1936) and *Test Pilot* (1938), had recently married Paramount producer Arthur Hornblow, Jr. and, according to Loy's autobiography, *Myrna Loy: Being and Becoming*, she didn't care too much for the film or for Robert Taylor, who was a bit of a prig in her estimation. She claimed that they got along all right on the set, but in later years, during the Un-American Activities Hearings, she would grow to dislike him intensely for naming names when he appeared as a friendly witness before the committee. A dedicated Liberal, Loy later joined the First Amendment Committee, an organization founded to counter the House Un-American Activities Committee. Taylor, who would marry Barbara Stanwyck shortly after completing *Lucky Night*, would remain at MGM longer than any other of its contract players (1934-1958).

The reviews for *Lucky Night* were even worse than those of *The Girl Downstairs*, with most of the complaints aimed at the writing. *New York Herald Tribune*: "The narrative itself is paper-thin and preposterous." *New York Times*: ". . . one of the most embarrassingly bad scripts ever to be taken seriously by a producer, a director and a cast." *Boxoffice*: "As a romantic comedy, this backfires with a dull thud." *Variety*: "It will excite no boxoffice furore [sic]. . ." *Hollywood Reporter*:

"*Lucky Night* pallid opus hung on anemic script."

Myrna Loy and Robert Taylor present Norman Taurog with a memento from *Lucky Night*.

The Academy Awards nominations were announced on February 5, 1939, and *Boys Town* garnered five nominations, for Best Picture, Spencer Tracy for Best Actor, Norman Taurog for Best Director, John Meehan and Dore Schary for Best Screenplay and Eleanore Griffin and Dore Schary for Best Original Story. When the awards ceremony was held at the Biltmore Bowl in the Biltmore Hotel in downtown Los Angeles on the night of February 23, this time Spencer Tracy and his wife, Louise attended. As did Norman and Julie Taurog, who, with the kidnapping scare only nine days before, were apprehensive about leaving Patsy Ann. The evening ran late, with the presentations not beginning until after eleven o'clock. MGM was thrilled when Tracy won his second consecutive Best Actor Oscar and Griffin and Schary won for Best Original Story, but Taurog lost to Frank Capra, who won his third Oscar in four years for his direction of *You Can't Take It with You*, and the Best Screenplay Oscar went to George Bernard Shaw for his *Pygmalion*. Mickey Rooney and Deanna Durbin were awarded a special Juvenile Award "for their significant contribution in bringing to the screen the spirit and personification of youth, and as juvenile players setting a high standard of ability and achievement."

A few days after the award ceremony, Spencer Tracy sent his Oscar to Father Flanagan at Boys Town, with a special inscription that read: "To Father Flanagan whose great human qualities, kindly simplicity and inspiring courage were strong enough to shine through my humble efforts. Spencer Tracy."

A Brighter Melody

AFTER the kidnapping scare, the Taurogs decided to relocate to a new home at 242 Delfern Avenue in Holmby Hills and try to move on with their lives. It certainly helped that on the same day that Taurog learned that he had been nominated for his direction of *Boys Town*, MGM announced that they had awarded him a new five-year contract. His first assignment under the new arrangement gave a major boost to his reputation, and was the first of the eight musicals he would direct for the Culver City lot.

MGM was famous for its opulent musicals, and for Norman Taurog, directing *Broadway Melody of 1940* with Fred Astaire, Eleanor Powell and George Murphy, and a musical score by Cole Porter, would be both a great opportunity and a challenge. He had directed a number of musicals at Paramount, but with the possible exception of *The Big Broadcast of 1936*, which had been more of a musical revue than a book musical, none matched the scale of *Broadway Melody of 1940*, with its expanded budget, extended shooting schedule, and lavish production numbers.

Broadway Melody of 1940 was the fourth and final film in the series, and the third to star dancer Eleanor Powell. Jack Cummings, who had produced Powell's previous films *Born to Dance* (1936), *Broadway Melody of 1938* (1937) and *Honolulu* (1939), was Louis B. Mayer's nephew. He had started at the studio in the early 1920s as an office boy, later becoming a script supervisor and assistant director. In 1932 he was placed in charge of the studio's shorts department, where he supervised and directed over a dozen short films. His first feature was a "B" movie called *The Winning Ticket* (1935), and after spending time on the troubled *Tarzan Escapes* (1936) along with three other producers and five directors, he finally was given *Born to Dance* to produce on his own. With its success, he settled in to produce over 35 films for MGM before retiring in 1964.

Eleanor Powell had appeared on Broadway in several musical reviews for George White, and her first film appearance was performing a specialty number in *George White's 1935 Scandals* (1935) for Fox Films. She was signed by MGM shortly thereafter and her first film for the studio was *Broadway Melody of 1936* (1935), in which she co-starred with Jack Benny and Robert Taylor. Popular with audiences, she was quickly rushed into *Born to Dance*, followed by *Broadway Melody of 1938* (1937) and Cole Porter's *Rosalie* (1937) with Nelson Eddy. *Broadway Melody of 1940* is still considered to be the best of the series and Powell's performance was enhanced by her dance numbers with Fred Astaire. She married actor Glenn Ford in October of 1943 and they remained married for sixteen years, producing a son, Peter, who also became an actor. By 1943, her popularity had waned and MGM dropped her contract. Powell's final film was an independent production for producer-director Andrew L. Stone, *Sensations of 1945* (1944). In 1981, Powell appeared at the AFI Tribute to Fred Astaire and, after receiving a standing ovation, spoke about their working together on *Broadway Melody of 1940*. "It was always 'Mr. Astaire and Miss Powell,'" she recalled. "You would think we were two scientists in a laboratory, we were so serious. It was Fred's first picture after Ginger, and people expected so much from us." Powell disclosed how they finally broke the ice, with her telling him, "Look, we can't go on like this. I'm Ellie, you're Fred. We're just two hoofers." She spoke of their professionalism and how they would always ask to do it one more time? "We would still be there now," she added, "If somebody hadn't been there to say, 'Look, it's just fine. Print it.'" It's too bad Ms Powell didn't identify that "somebody" as Norman Taurog.

Eleanor Powell's final public appearance was later that same year at the National Film Society Convention in New York City, at their annual Artistry in Cinema Awards dinner, where she was honored with the first "Ellie" Award for her contribution to filmed musicals.

Fred Astaire was returning to MGM after the conclusion of his seven year contract with RKO and his successful run of films with Ginger Rogers. *Broadway Melody of 1940* was his first film there since David O. Selznick borrowed him from RKO, immediately after he'd signed with the studio, to dance with Joan Crawford in *Dancing Lady* (1933); his debut in films, and the only musical Selznick ever produced. Astaire had spent the major portion of his career, up to this point, working with dancing partners: first with his sister Adele on the stage, and then with Ginger Rogers in the nine films they made at RKO. After *The Story of Vernon and Irene Castle* (1939), his last RKO film with Rogers, he had left the studio planning to explore new avenues, and had mixed feelings about being paired with another partner, even one as talented as Eleanor Powell. He would soon change his mind, because, as he wrote in his autobiography *Steps in Time*, "On my list I counted it as thoroughly worthwhile if only for the opportunity of working with Eleanor who certainly rates, as one of the all-time great dancing girls. Her tap work was individual. She 'put 'em down' like a man, no ricky-ticky-sissy stuff with Ellie. She really knocked out a tap dance in a class by herself." Astaire was beginning to think of retiring, and in fact would announce his retirement in 1946, only to be brought back to MGM two years later to replace Gene Kelly in *Easter Parade* when Kelly broke his ankle playing volleyball at his home. He would continue in films until his retirement in 1981, with his final musical being the disappointing *Finian's Rainbow* in 1968.

George Murphy began as a dancer with his future wife Julie Johnson on Broadway in a musical revue called *Shoot the Works* in 1931. His first film was *Kid Millions* (1934), for Samuel Goldwyn, in which he co-starred with Eddie Cantor, Ann Sothern and Ethel Merman. After that he didn't make another musical for three years. He signed a short term contract with Columbia Pictures and proceeded to make four non-musical films, three with Nancy Carroll. He then made a short film which served as his screen test for MGM: *Violets in the Spring*, in which he finally had a chance to sing and dance with Virginia Grey, who was also being considered for a contract. While he was waiting for MGM to decide, Murphy went over to Universal Pictures to star in another musical called *Top of the Town* (1937), which was Universal's overblown answer to the big musical revues that were popular with other studios at the time. In it, Murphy has a terrific tap number called "Jamboree" that also features a young Peggy Ryan. When MGM finally signed Murphy to a term contract, the first film he starred in was a romantic mystery called *London by Night* (1937), but shortly thereafter he was dancing with Eleanor Powell in *Broadway Melody of 1938.* Murphy would stay at MGM for the next 15 years, alternating between musicals and dramas; his final musical appearance was in a loan-out film, *Step Lively* (1944), along with newcomers Frank Sinatra and Gloria DeHaven. Murphy, who had been a Republican for years, entered politics in 1953 after he retired from films, as chairman of the California Republican State Central Committee and was elected to the U.S. Senate in 1965 for one term. He suffered from throat cancer and had to have part of his larynx removed, causing him to speak in a whisper for the rest of his life.

There is a long list of contributing writers on *Broadway Melody of 1940*, including Sid Silvers, who not only appeared in, but co-wrote the screenplay for *Broadway Melody of 1936* (1935), and wrote the original story for *Broadway Melody of 1938* (1937). It is probably Silvers who incorporated the gag of producer Frank Morgan and the mink coat. According to a story Bob Hope once told, his agent Louis "Doc" Shurr used to keep an expensive white mink coat that he'd give to any girl who would go out with him. "He always took the coat back," Hope recalled, "but by that time, it didn't matter." The final screenplay was written by Leon Gordon, who was soon to become a producer at the studio, and George Oppenheimer, who had recently written such diversified screenplays for the studio as *Libeled Lady* (1936) and *A Day at the Races* (1937). Preston Sturges is also listed as an uncredited contributor to the screenplay, but it's hard to determine what his participation could have been. He must have done his work while he was briefly at MGM in 1937, doing revisions on a screenplay he had previously written, based on Marcel Pagnol's *Marseilles Trilogy,* which MGM had purchased from Universal. That film, *Port of Seven Seas* (1938) starring Wallace Beery, Frank Morgan and Maureen O'Sullivan, caused a bit of a stir with the censors due to O'Sullivan's character being unmarried and pregnant.

After several weeks of dance rehearsals with choreographer Bobby Connolly, in which Eleanor Powell later admitted Astaire was a taskmaster, demanding routines be repeated over and over, sometimes just to perfect the hand movements, Norman Taurog began filming in early September of 1938. The filming continued for 66 days, with the book sequences interspersed with various production numbers. Taurog managed to insert a little slapstick humor into the proceedings with a gag involving Astaire constantly knocking

(L-R) Eleanor Powell, Norman Taurog, Ian Hunter and Fred Astaire.

over a prop statuette, but always catching it in the nick of time. The payoff shows that the statuette is made of rubber, bouncing harmlessly on the stage floor. A few weeks into filming, cinematographer Oliver Marsh was replaced by Joseph Ruttenberg. Marsh, who began as a cameraman for Mack Sennett in the Keystone Comedies, had come to MGM in 1925 to photograph Erich von Stroheim's *The Merry Widow* and remained at the studio for the rest of his career. The announcement in the October 21, 1939, issue of *Variety* said that Marsh was being temporarily replaced "because of illness," but like Spencer Tracy, his "illness" was in reality alcoholism. Marsh would return to the studio to film retakes for *New Moon* with Jeanette MacDonald and Nelson Eddy, but would die within eighteen months as a result of his alcoholism. Joseph Ruttenberg had already won his first Oscar for photographing *The Great Waltz* in 1938 and would ultimately win three more for *Mrs. Miniver* (1942), *Somebody Up There Likes Me* (1956) and *Gigi* (1958). He would make three more films with Taurog, the final being the Elvis Presley starrer *Speedway* (1968).

The plot of *Broadway Melody of 1940* is straightforward backstage conflict, with a little mistaken identity thrown in for good measure. However, it still functions well as a device to introduce the eight musical numbers, which, with Astaire and Powell dancing up a storm, are what makes the film so special. George Murphy is surprisingly good as the ambitious King Shaw and holds his own with Astaire in the "Please Don't Monkey with Broadway" number, as well as his singing and dancing "Between You and Me" with Powell. Others in the cast included Frank Morgan, doing his usual absent-minded, fuddy-duddy routines as the producer who discovers Astaire and ends up hiring Murphy by mistake, Ian Hunter as his frustrated partner, Barbara Jo Allen (the future Vera Vague) as their receptionist, and even Mickey Rooney's father, Joe Yule, seated next to Astaire in the producers' waiting room. MGM had this annoying habit of including specialty acts in their musicals, and there were two in *Broadway Melody of 1940*, neither of which did anything but interrupt the action.

Cole Porter contributed six songs to *Broadway Melody of 1940*; the one song that wasn't written exclusively for the film was "Begin the Beguine." Porter had written this in 1935, during a four-and-a-half month Pacific cruise between Indonesia and Fiji with Moss Hart and their families. It was introduced in their hit Broadway musical *Jubilee* at the Imperial Theatre in October of 1935. MGM had put up some of the financing for the play, which featured Mary Boland and Melville Cooper as the king and queen of a fictitious European country, with a young Montgomery Clift and future MGM choreographer and director Charles Walters playing two of their sons. Artie Shaw recorded an extended version of the song for RCA Records that became a best selling record in 1938, rising all the way to #3 on the *Billboard* list of top hits. Because of MGM's previous involvement with the Broadway musical, Porter included the rights to the number, along with the other songs he wrote for *Broadway Melody of 1940*. MGM had originally planned to film *Broadway Melody of 1940* in Technicolor, but opted to go for black & white to reduce costs. It was a decision that paid off handsomely in the look of production numbers such as the "Beguine" number, which wouldn't have looked half as effective in Technicolor with its glittering mirrored floors and deep shadows.

Although Cedric Gibbons and his associate John S. Detlie designed the film's sets, art director Merrill Pye designed the art deco set for the "Begin the Beguine" number; at the time, it was the largest set constructed for a dance number, at MGM or any other studio. It took eight weeks to construct, with thirty-foot mirrors designed to reflect Astaire and Powell as they danced, plus 6,500 square feet of mirrored floor. You can imagine the problems these

Fred Astaire and Eleanor Powell dance the "Begin the Beguine" number on Merrill Pye's multi-mirrored set.

Fred Astaire and Eleanor Powell.

mirrors and the cyclorama behind it, wired with 10,000 light bulbs, created for cameraman Joseph Ruttenberg and his gaffer.

The "Begin the Beguine" number runs nine minutes and thirty-one seconds and consists of two sequences, broken up by a short swing interpolation sung by a girls' vocal group called "The Music Maids." The first sequence, in a tropical setting, introduces the lyrics as sung by Lois Hodnott in a Latin tempo, with Powell and the girl dancers, followed by Astaire, appearing in the giant mirrors and joining Powell in the dance on the mirrored floor. They dance in a flowing, interpretive style for just under three minutes, and then exit as the audience applauds. The four "Music Maids" then liven up the tempo with a new set of jive lyrics, including a reference to "the Merry land of Oz," with a full orchestra reflected in the mirrors behind them. As they exit, the film cuts to an elaborate tracking shot of Powell and Astaire, lasting for over two minutes, with the two of them tapping, at first to an Artie Shaw like arrangement of the tune, and then with no accompaniment. The final moments are Powell and Astaire twirling rapidly for 25 seconds into their final bow. The sequence took days to film, with long breaks needed as the mirrored floor would be polished by grips with dry mops, wearing cloth booties over their shoes. Norman Taurog told me years later that both Powell and Astaire's feet were bleeding from broken blisters by the time they concluded filming the number. As Frank Sinatra reflected when he presented a portion of the number in the 1974 documentary *That's Entertainment*, "You can wait around and hope, but you'll never see the likes of this again."

A blurb in the Wednesday, November 29, 1938, edition of *Variety* announced: "Fred Astaire and Eleanor Powell go before the cameras Friday for their Peirrot and Pierrette number for Metro's *Broadway Melody of 1940* Sequence will require about three days, after which Miss Powell does specialty dance that completes filming." By the end of November, filming was completed and post production work had begun. Alfred Newman conducted the MGM orchestra in the lush orchestral backgrounds for the production numbers, replacing the temp piano tracks that had Bobby Connolly counting out the beats. The final cost for the film was $1.1 million, and the trailer for the film, showing nothing but the musical numbers and none of the dialogue scenes, referred to Astaire and Powell in a title as "The King of Rhythm and The Queen of Taps, Born to Dance Together."

Broadway Melody of 1940 opened to sell-out crowds at the Capitol Theater in New York on February 9, 1940, with Bob Hope on stage, and earned $8,000 on its first day. The reviews were all the same, "not much of a story, but the dance numbers are superb." Frank Nugent in the *New York Times*, after complaining about "the customary hypocritical plot, comfortably designed with large gaps into which carefully prefabricated 'production numbers' may duly be fitted," managed to praise the film at the same time. "It may be just another *Broadway Melody*," he wrote, "but with the Messrs. Astaire and Porter to give it wit and point, it seems much more convincingly Broadway, and much more than usually melodious." The film was released nationwide simultaneously with its New York opening and the reviewer for the *Philadelphia Inquirer* was far more complimentary, if not down-right ecstatic. "Not since the heyday of Rogers and Hart musicals," wrote Mildred Martin, "has there been so lilting or likable a song and dance film as *Broadway Melody of 1940*. In a word, the picture which arrived with the snow yesterday morning at the Stanley has everything—a serviceable, surprisingly fresh story of Broadway dancers, an ear-tickling score by Cole Porter, top-notch and tip-toe direction by Norman Taurog, and not one, but three fleet-footed, completely engaging stars."

Thomas Edison and Arthur Freed

In April of 1940, MGM tore up Norman Taurog's old contract and offered him a new two-year contract, with his salary remaining at the original $3,000. Taurog elected to accept what would amount to a $250- a-week salary cut in exchange for the security of the new two- year contract.

John W. Considine Jr. had a pet project that he had been trying to interest the studio in for several years, the life of Thomas Alva Edison; he'd even hired historian H. Alan Dunn to research and assemble extensive background material on Edison and his inventions. After the success of *Boys Town*, Considine was able to get the studio to give him the go-ahead to develop a screenplay and he handed the assignment to Dore Schary, his good luck charm from the previous film. Within eleven years, Schary would move on from writing to become head of production at RKO, then head of production at MGM, and ultimately replace Louis B. Mayer as studio head. I had the good fortune to work for Schary on the film version of his hit Broadway play *Sunrise at Campobello* in 1960, while I was an assistant film editor at Warners, and I found him to be a warm human being with a keen sense of humor, who enjoyed playing cribbage.

Hugo Butler was assigned to collaborate with Schary on the screenplay and the two men began the monumental task of breaking down the great inventor's life from his birth in 1847, to his death in 1931. Hugo Butler, who had worked with Schary previously on another Spencer Tracy film, *Big City* (1937), as well as having written the screenplays for the 1938 version of *A Christmas Carol* and the Mickey Rooney version of *The Adventures of Huckleberry Finn* (1939), would become a victim in 1951 of the witch-hunt for Communists by the House Un-American Activities Committee and the subsequent blacklist. He and his writer/ actress wife Jean Rouverol and their children would be forced to spend years exiled in Mexico, along with Dalton Trumbo and his family.

Schary and Butler soon realized that there was just too much story to tell for just one film and recommended to Considine that it be broken into two parts, Edison the boy and Edison the man. Their idea was accepted, and MGM was soon announcing that *Edison the Man* would star two-time Academy Award winner Spencer Tracy and that *Young Tom Edison* would feature their number one boxoffice attraction for 1939, Mickey Rooney.

The Rooney film was scheduled to film first and Considine had only one director in mind, his friend and the man who had directed Tracy and Rooney so successfully in *Boys Town*, Norman Taurog. It might have even crossed his mind that Taurog could do both films, but the magnitude of these productions and the fact that the studio wanted to release them back to back would have made that technically impossible; Clarence Brown was assigned to do the Tracy film. After Bradbury Foote, an MGM contract writer who had been at the studio for several years, did a final revision on the screenplay, Jack Mintz incorporated Taurog's notes into the script.

War rumors, which had been flowing rampantly across Europe for months, finally became a deadly reality on the morning of September 1, 1939, when Adolf Hitler's "Blitzkrieg" exploded across the Polish border and swept into Warsaw. What followed were six months of negotiations and counter negotiations known as the "Phony War." Hollywood could see the possibility of their European markets disappearing and began to cut back, but at MGM it was business as usual, or almost as usual. Louis B. Mayer was renegotiating his contract, even as the studio was experiencing its share of problems; the stockholders of Loew's Inc., the parent company, had filed a minority stockholders' suit in the New York Supreme Court charging mismanagement. On top of that, studio workers, including actors and writers, were campaigning for union recognition, eventually throwing up picket lines in front of all of the major studios. These matters would take several years to be resolved, with MGM winning the stockholders' suit, but eventually acquiescing, along with the rest of the studios, to the demands of the workers; with the result that unions and guilds handled future contract negotiations. Mayer's new, five-year contract was formalized with his weekly salary being increased to $3,000 a week, plus an additional bonus of 6.77 percent of Loew's net profits.

Norman Taurog, Jack Mintz and assistant director William Ryan, took the train north to Sonora, California to check out locations for the film. Sonora, which would be the location for Thomas Edison's boyhood hometown of Port Huron, Michigan, as well as for the extensive railroad sequences in the latter part of the film, is located just south of Sacramento. Taurog would return to Sonora to begin filming in late November, just as the chill was beginning to set in. The company completed its work as quickly as possible and returned to the studio to film more exteriors on Lot 3's Western Street and then moved onto the stage for the interiors of the Edison home.

Young Tom Edison wrapped production shortly after the first of the year and a world premiere was held in Port Huron on February 10, 1940, but Taurog was unfortunately unable to attend; having suffered a respiratory illness, he was recuperating in Arizona. Studio files show that the accounting department questioned whether he should be taken off salary, but studio executive Sam Katz responded that Taurog was on leave of absence and on call at all times and he continued to be paid his weekly salary. *The Hollywood Reporter* wrote about crowds so great "that the four major theaters of Port Huron, Michigan, were required to handle the overflow." Henry Ford hosted a dinner party in the executive suite of Ford's River Rouge plant, and gifted Mickey Rooney with one of the original 1939 Lincoln Continental convertibles. *Young Tom Edison* ends with a short promo for the upcoming *Edison the Man*, with Frank Whitbeck's dynamic voice extolling the accomplishments of the great inventor as the camera pulls back from a portrait of the mature Edison to reveal Spencer Tracy admiring the painting. *Edison the Man* was released exactly three months later, to the day.

Mickey Rooney's performance in *Young Tom Edison* is remarkably restrained and his scenes with Virginia Weidler as his sister are quite touching. In point of fact, Taurog guided all of his actors with moderation, with the noticeable exception of Eugene Pallette's overblown performance as the train conductor. The supporting cast, filled with tried-and-true character actors such as Fay Bainter, George Bancroft, J.M. Kerrigan, Victor Kilian, Lloyd Corrigan, Clem Bevans and Harry Shannon, helped to make the somewhat melodramatic story believable at least until it came to the over-the-top climax, with Rooney aboard a rushing locomotive frantically sending a Morse code message with the engine's whistle. The high speed shots of the two trains speeding toward the washed-out bridge reminded one of a sequence from a silent two-reeler. And why not? Norman Taurog had filmed such sequences many times in the past.

In his autobiography, *Life is Too Short* Rooney discussed his approach to the role. "I *became* young Tom," he wrote. "I imagined what and how this young genius would do things and I did them that way. When I wanted to show Tom deep in thought, I pulled furiously on my left eyebrow. That piece of business seemed to work. He loved his mom? Well, I loved my mom, too. I looked at Fay Bainter as if she was my real mom. It worked." Sounds simple, doesn't it? Rooney mistakenly remembered that he was nominated for his performance as Young Tom, but in truth, neither he nor the film received any nominations or awards. His nomination was for another film he had completed just before starting *Young Tom Edison*: his first big musical with his favorite co-star, Judy Garland, *Babes in Arms* (1939).

Rooney would be nominated a total of four times for a Best Actor Oscar, in addition to his two Honorary Oscars. His second "honorary" award was given to him in 1983 and read: "In recognition of his 50 years of versatility in a variety of memorable film performances." He and Taurog would make four more films together, and ultimately he would appear in over 325 films and television productions. Having recently celebrated his 92nd birthday, he is still active in films and television and has at least five titles currently in release or in production.

Frank Nugent's *New York Times* review seemed more focused on Rooney and his performance than on the film and the rest of its cast. "Putting the carte blanche before the horse," Nugent punned, "*Young Tom Edison* seems to be one of those freer biographies whose resemblance to the Horatio Alger School of personal history is no more coincidental than Thomas Edison's resemblance to a Horatio Alger hero... Mickey Rooney's young Tom is an inventive Edison to conjure with, to be regarded with awe and a little terror, to emerge withal as so fascinating a by-product of the Kinetoscope as to make one exclaim, with Mr. Morse, 'What hath God wrought!'" *Variety* was much kinder: "Picture is rich in youthful adventure, and human, homey qualities. Mickey Rooney plays the young inventor with sympathetic restraint. There are no obvious stunts or gags; no overplaying of the dreamy, though deeply serious boy who is laying the foundation for his later achievements." *The Hollywood Reporter* singled out the director for praise, saying, "Norman Taurog, who has plenty of top directorial jobs to his credit, never did a finer one than this. His masterly touch is evident in every scene."

When a studio is turning out over 40 films a year, as was the case with MGM, there are certain demands that are placed upon its contractees. For actors, it was to appear in more than one film at the same time, or to work at a continuous pace without a break. For directors, it was to be able to go from one film to the next with a limited amount of preparation time, and to be available to step in at a moment's notice and temporarily take over another director's film if he becomes incapacitated. Such was the case for Taurog in April of 1940 when director Edwin L. Marin fell ill while directing one of the studio's 'B' movies, *Gold Rush Maisie* with Ann Sothern, and Taurog had to take over the company for a couple of days while Marin recuperated. It was the first time Taurog had seen Ann Sothern since they had worked together at Twentieth Century-Fox on *Fifty Roads to Town* three years earlier. Sothern, now under contract to MGM, was making the third of what would eventually be eleven films in the very popular *Maisie* series.

Considered by many to be the *sine qua non* of his profession, Arthur Freed was arguably the most successful producer of film musicals in the history of Hollywood. He was born in Charleston, South Carolina, in 1894 and grew up in Seattle, Washington. He began as a song-plugger and pianist in

Chicago, and in 1920 he wrote some of the lyrics for a semi-successful Broadway musical revue called *Silks and Satins* that a lesser-known writer, director and performer named William Rock produced at George M. Cohan's Theatre. In 1921 he joined forces for the first time with the man who would become his most frequent collaborator, Nacio Herb Brown, when he wrote the lyrics to "When Buddha Smiles," which was recorded by the Paul Whiteman Orchestra. Freed's next big song success was "I Cried for You," which he wrote with Gus Arnheim and Abe Lyman in 1923. He joined MGM in 1928 as a songwriter and was soon working again with Nacio Herb Brown. Born in Deming, New Mexico, in 1896, Brown had tried his hand at several professions before becoming a songwriter. After attending Manual Arts High School and UCLA, he eventually became a very successful real estate broker in Beverly Hills, but soon changed to his real love, music, and had his first hit "Coral Sea" in 1920. Brown joined Freed at MGM in 1928, and their first assignment was to write the songs for *The Broadway Melody* (1929), followed quickly by *The Hollywood Revue of 1929*. For the latter film they wrote the memorable "Singin' in the Rain" and "You Were Meant for Me." For the next ten years Freed, and frequently Brown, wrote songs for scores of films, including *The Pagan* (1929), *Going Hollywood* (1933), *Broadway Melody of 1936* and *Broadway Melody of 1938*.

Freed had ambitions to become a producer and in 1938 he finally persuaded Louis B. Mayer to give him a chance and was assigned as associate producer on *The Wizard of Oz*. Even though the studio was insisting on a star to play Dorothy, and had first planned to use Shirley Temple and then Deanna Durbin, Freed kept pushing for young Judy Garland and finally won over both Mayer and producer Mervyn LeRoy. It was Freed who fought to keep the song "Over the Rainbow" in the picture, and was proven right when "Rainbow" won the Academy Award for Best Original Song. Freed was given his full producer stripes and his first film was the Rooney-Garland hit, *Babes in Arms* (1939), followed again by Rooney and Garland in *Strike Up the Band* (1940). The success of these films earned Freed a new contract and a raise in salary, and he was given the 1929 Broadway college musical *Good News* as the next vehicle for Rooney and Garland. Realizing that his protégée was maturing, Freed began searching for a vehicle to star Garland as a grown woman; the idea didn't sit well with Louis B. Mayer. Freed bought an old George M. Cohan play called *Little Nellie Kelly* for $35,000 and assigned it to a former Broadway performer and playwright, Jack McGowan, to adapt for Garland. The story called for Garland to play the dual roles of mother and daughter. Cohan's play had opened at the Liberty Theatre on Broadway on November 13, 1922, and had run for 248 performances; almost nothing of the play was retained in the film beyond the title, Garland's dual characters, and two of Cohan's songs, "Nellie Kelly I Love You" and a brief version of "Nellie Is a Darling," sung a cappella by Charles Winninger.

Freed admired Taurog's work on *Broadway Melody of 1940* and *Young Tom Edison* and decided that he was the one to direct Garland's first adult romance. Taurog's salary at this time was $3,000 a week and was charged to the budget for 11 weeks, for a total of $33,000. George Murphy and Douglas McPhail were assigned the roles of the mother and daughter's love interests, and Charles Winninger was to play her father, who refuses to speak to his son-in-law Murphy because they married against his wishes. Taurog brought in Jack Mintz on May 20 to work on the final screenplay with Jack McGowan and they completed their work on July 26. When Taurog began filming on July 28, 1940, Garland was still involved in filming production numbers for *Strike Up the Band* with director-choreographer Busby Berkeley, and Taurog found his star fighting exhaustion from the long hours that Berkeley demanded of his cast and crew.

Taurog developed a rapport with Garland that continued throughout the three additional films that they would make together. Taurog helped Garland with the difficult task of playing the dual role of mother and daughter, as well as the only death scene she played in her entire career. Garland also participated in her first adult love scene (with co-star George Murphy), and afterwards acted out an even better scene for a Hollywood journalist. "I'm so nervous," she confided to the star-struck correspondent. "Isn't it silly? And the silliest thing of all, I just can't look George in the eye. That's never happened to me before. Do you think I'll get over it?" It was a great performance, but the ever-so-embarrassed Garland was already in the midst of a love affair with composer David Rose who, though still married to Martha Raye, would soon become her first husband.

Judy was also beginning to assert her independence. On August 2, 1940, unit manager Sergei Petschnikoff sent the following memo to Arthur Freed: "Judy Garland's mother informed Mr. Taurog today that henceforth Judy's working time would be limited to eight hours per day. Unless we hear differently from you, we will, of course, have to lay out our work accordingly." Although there is no indication of how this was resolved, casting director Fred Datig also sent a memo to Freed's office that same day saying roughly the same thing, but adding: "If she is called in to makeup at 7:30, allowing 1½ hours for makeup and one hour for lunch, she does not intend to work after 6 p.m. In other words, she does not intend to work more than 8 hours in any one day."

Taurog finished filming, after eight weeks and $665,000, on September 19, 1940, there was a day of retakes on September 27. After some preview cards complained that Charles Winninger's portrayal of Nellie's irascible father and grandfather was too heavy-handed, some editing was accomplished to soften his character.

The film opened to mixed reviews, with the *Chicago Tribune* saying, "If you like the simple things of life, you'll like *Little Nellie Kelly*. Judy gives her all and sings pleasingly when the script demands." *Variety* praised it highly, proclaiming, "'Nellie's' power to captivate is not based entirely on the histrionic abilities of the cast, nor on the superb rendition of its tunes by Miss Garland and McPhail, but on that ideal interspersing of comedy and pathos, as provided by Jack McGowan's screenplay, to which Director Norman Taurog has given such deft and meaningful handling. Taurog's piloting stands out on par with the best of his previous piloting attainments." But when the film opened at the Loewe's Criterion on Christmas Eve, Bosley Crowther of *The New York Times* was much harsher: "Loewe's Criterion must have been after forgetting that yesterday was Christmas Eve, for here it was celebrating St. Patrick's Day as big as ever you please with a bit of Irish chauvinism called *Little Nellie Kelly*. The only good reason we can see for this obvious confusion of holidays is that Metro, which made the picture, figured there would be a lot of mellow and tolerant people—especially Irishmen—at this season of the year… *Little Nellie Kelly* is hardly the sort of picture to send folks dancing with Christmas cheer in the street."

In spite of Crowther's opinion, *Little Nellie Kelly* went on to earn over $2 million and remained one of George Murphy's favorite films. Taurog, who was already preparing for his next film, the *Boys Town* sequel, arranged for a print of *Little Nellie Kelly* to be sent to Father Flanagan at Boys Town, and received a note from Father Flanagan in which he congratulated Taurog: "As Director you certainly did the Irish proud and they all owe you a great debt of gratitude. We want you to know, Norman, how much we appreciate the fine spiritual note that you carried throughout the picture. And we feel it is a picture that should have a very successful run because it has everything. Congratulations to yourself and the fine cast headed by Judy Garland."

Back To Omaha and Paramount

On Friday, February 9, 1940, *The Hollywood Reporter* featured an article on its front page, headlined: 100 G's TO HOME FOR BOYS TOWN SEQUEL. The article went on to report: "Outside of production costs, the sequel to *Boys Town* which MGM will make will cost that company $100,000, which goes to Monsignor Flanagan, head of the Nebraska institution, to pay off the debt incurred for the new home which will accommodate 300 more youths."

On Wednesday, April 2, 1940 Louis B. Mayer hosted a luncheon at the studio to kick off the production of *Men of Boys Town* with a radio broadcast over the NBC radio network. Father Flanagan returned to the studio to attend the lunch, and ranking dignitaries of the Catholic and Protestant clergy were invited to attend.

John Considine had writer James Kevin McGuinness, an old MGM hand, developing an original story and screenplay as a sequel to *Boys Town* for several months and now he was ready to go into production. He reassembled his troops from the first film, starting with Norman Taurog, Spencer Tracy, Mickey Rooney and returning cast members Bobs Watson, Sidney Miller, Addison Richards and Robert Emmett Keane. Teenager Larry Dunn was hired to play the paralyzed boy Ted Marley, the fulcrum of McGuinness' new story. Darryl Hickman was signed to play another troubled youth and Lee J. Cobb took over the role of Dave Morris from Henry Hull, who had played the pawnbroker who helped to fund the home in the first film.

McGuinness's convoluted plot was comprised of three distinct storylines for Tracy, Rooney and Dunn, and included individual crying scenes for Rooney, Dunn and little Bobs Watson, who wasn't so little any more.

Larry Dunn as Ted.

As it plays out, *Men of Boys Town* is a combination of the original *Boys Town*, *Angels with Dirty Faces*, and even a touch of *Babes on Broadway* when Rooney and the boys put on a show to cheer up Dunn's character that includes Rooney conducting the band and a slow-motion wrestling routine between Rooney and Sidney Miller that played more like one of their personal appearance routines, which it most likely was.

Filming on *Men of Boys Town* was scheduled to begin on Monday, November 4, 1940, the day before Election Day. In 1940, the fundamental difference between Republican "conservatives" and "liberal" Democrats was President Franklin Delano Roosevelt's "New Deal," the series of economic programs that the president had signed into law during his first two terms in office. Wendell Willkie was running to oppose Roosevelt's third term for president in the 1940 election on a platform of repealing the financial reforms of the "New Deal." Louis B. Mayer, an avid Republican, had made it clear to his employees that he was actively supporting the Republican candidate. On Monday, November 4, the first of two diverse full-page ads ran in *The Hollywood Reporter*. The first ad, paid for by Democratic supporters of President

A taller Bobs Watson tries on his football uniform for director Norman Taurog.

Roosevelt, contained the names of roughly two dozen MGM workers, including Katharine Hepburn, directors George Cukor and W.S. Van Dyke and producer John Considine. It was answered the following day by the Republicans for Willkie, with more than three dozen MGM names, including Lionel Barrymore, Fred Astaire, Wallace Beery, Robert Montgomery and directors Sam Wood and Richard Thorpe. Preferring to keep his political affiliations to himself, Taurog's name was absent from both ads; this preference for political anonymity would only last for a few more years.

After a brief trip to the Boys Town site in Nebraska, where he filmed establishing shots and backgrounds for later use on the process stage, Taurog returned to California and began filming on local locations and at a detailed replica of the Boys Town main building that was constructed on one of the MGM sound stages. He filmed three nights of exteriors on MGM's Lot 2 with his two stars, neither of whom had been required to go to Nebraska. Nobody could generate much excitement for the film; they all realized that all they were doing was making a quick sequel to capitalize on the success of the earlier film. Tracy and Rooney were as professional as ever, with Tracy giving his usual flawless performance as Father Flanagan. George Cukor once described Tracy's style this way: "He was one of those naturally original actors who did it, but never let you see him do it." Bobs Watson, who in later years became a Methodist minister, went to visit Tracy on the set of his last film, *Guess Who's Coming to Dinner?* (1967). Calling him "Uncle Spence," Watson told Tracy that his performance as Father Flanagan was "a major influence" in his decision to become a minister.

After six and a half weeks of shooting, Taurog wrapped production on December 18, 1940. *Men of Boys Town* premiered at the Capitol Theatre in New York on April 10, 1941, and the reviews were pretty much as expected, with the *Times'* Bosley Crowther hating the picture: "The lesson of *Men of Boys Town* is to stay away from sequels. Father Flanagan's Nebraska colony was shown once and shown honestly. This time it is merely used as a point of departure for a catchpenny tale." The Hollywood trade papers, always loath to bite the hand that feeds them, were far less critical, while still acknowledging the problems: "No picture in recent years has more openly bid for sentimental reactions or demanded more cooperation from an audience's tear ducts than *Men of Boys Town*. It is unlikely that film critics will herald the story with much enthusiasm, and they will probably choose 'hokum' as a favorite word to describe it. But wise exhibitors will translate hokum to boxoffice of the most potent sort." *The Hollywood Reporter* even gave Taurog a full paragraph of praise: "He has no equal in the industry when it comes to obtaining the utmost from young actors. He captures on the screen not only the spirit of youths, but their hearts as well. To his record he now adds superlative performances from 11-year-old Larry Nunn and seven-year-old

Darryl Hickman. The restraint of Mickey Rooney and the handling of that diminutive veteran, Bobs Watson, are also to be noted."

On December 13, 1940, Frank Borzage began filming exterior scenes for *Billy the Kid* (1941) with Robert Taylor in Tucson and Flagstaff. When he brought the company back to MGM, the studio decided to reassign Borzage to a Joan Crawford vehicle, *Bombay Nights*, and assign David Miller in his place. *Bombay Nights* never materialized and Borzage was instead given the musical-drama *Smilin' Through* (1941) with Jeanette MacDonald, Brian Aherne and MacDonald's real-life husband, Gene Raymond. Miller had been at MGM since 1935 directing dozens of *Pete Smith* and *Passing Parade* shorts, and *Billy the Kid* would be his first feature assignment. Because of this, the studio asked Norman Taurog to unofficially watch over him for a few weeks and make sure that he got off on the right foot. Taurog did as the studio requested, but quickly determined that Miller was quite capable of doing the job and left shortly after Miller took the company to Death Valley for several weeks of location filming in late January.

On March 11, 1941, *The Hollywood Reporter* carried an article stating that *Billy the Kid* had ten more days of filming on the Metro lot to complete its schedule, adding that the film "has had the longest shooting schedule of any film on the lot since *Gone With the Wind*, following take-over by David Miller of the meg [sic] from Frank Borzage." Then, on April 15, the *Reporter* noted that Brian Donlevy had been recalled from Paramount for retakes and added scenes on *Billy the Kid*. When the final film was reviewed by *The Hollywood Reporter* on May 23, 1941, it appeared that the lengthy filming schedule and retakes hadn't made the film any more attractive for the anonymous reviewer. "It just doesn't seem to matter what you do to a Western," he wrote, "it still comes out as a Western, and whether you spend $50,000 or $500,000 or even more to make one, they all seem to wind up about the same story that has the same entertainment values."

David Miller would have a checkered career, but would always be remembered for having directed a modern Western that many considered to be a classic, *Lonely Are the Brave* (1962) with Kirk Douglas.

For some time Taurog had been experiencing problems with his vision; blurring and a series of dark blobs began to obscure the sight in his left eye. When he returned from Death Valley he went to see an eye specialist, who informed him that he was suffering from nonproliferative retinopathy, a condition brought about by his diabetes. It was caused by changes in the blood vessels of the retina, the light-sensitive tissue at the back of the eye; the vessels would swell and leak fluid, or in some cases abnormal vessels would grow on the surface of the retina. Years later medical science would develop laser treatments, if begun early enough, that would destroy the new blood vessels and seal off leaking ones, thereby halting the progress of the disease;

but for Norman Taurog in 1941 the prognosis wasn't encouraging, the condition was too far advanced for doctors to treat, and in all likelihood he would lose the sight of his left eye. When that eventually happened, Taurog took a deep breath, adjusted to using just his right eye to observe, and kept right on making films. And in all of the years that I knew him, until his condition worsened, I never noticed any compromise in the way he dealt with people or directed his actors.

Back at MGM, Taurog's name was announced for another Mickey Rooney project, *A Yank at Eton*. *Los Angeles Times* movie columnist Edwin Schallert wrote that Taurog would be sailing to Europe to direct the film in London with Rooney and child actress Virginia Weidler. In fact, although Taurog had been assigned to *A Yank at Eton* from May 7, 1939, to July 17,1939, he would have several other assignments, including a loan-out to Paramount, before he would finally get around to directing that particular film, not in London, but on MGM's soundstages in Culver City. In the meantime he once again filled in for a few days for a sick director, this time Edward Buzzell, on a Robert Young comedy, *Married Bachelor* (1941), while preparing for his own next assignment for John Considine, *Design for Scandal* (1941) with Rosalind Russell.

Rosalind Russell had been under contract to MGM since making her film debut in a supporting role in *Evelyn Prentice* in 1934. She signed a seven-year contract and continued in supporting roles until she graduated to stardom in *Night Must Fall* (1936), and several other films with co-star Robert Montgomery, plus *The Citadel* (1938) and *The Women* (1939) and on loanout to Columbia Pictures in *Craig's Wife* (1936) and *His Girl Friday* (1940). Russell always considered herself the second-string replacement for Myrna Loy and found she was frequently farmed out to other studios. Realizing that her studio couldn't always find suitable roles for her, Russell was ready to leave MGM when her contract expired at the end of 1941. Having just co-starred with Clark Gable for the third time in *They Met in Bombay* (1941) and then being rushed through a three-week quickie called *The Feminine Touch* (1941), she had one last commitment to fulfill with a picture called *Miss Achilles' Heel* that she was looking forward to making with Clark Gable, who was replaced at the last minute by Walter Pidgeon when Gable began filming *Honky Tonk* (1941) with Lana Turner.

Miss Achilles' Heel, later called *Achilles and Her Honor*, and finally *Design for Scandal*, was an original screenplay by Lionel Hauser, who had spent the early part of his career writing potboilers for Poverty Row studios and had joined MGM the year before with another original called *Third Finger, Left Hand* (1940), an amusing comedy that starred Melvyn Douglas and Myrna Loy. Hauser liked his plot gimmick of Loy pretending to be married and then having to come up with a husband so much that he used it again to good results some years later in Warners' *Christmas in Connecticut* (1944).

The selection of Walter Pidgeon was an unexpected casting decision in light of the many dramatic roles he had recently portrayed. Pidgeon had just returned from a loan-out to Twentieth Century-Fox, where he had played Mr. Gruffydd, the village minister and Maureen O'Hara's love interest in John Ford's *How Green Was My Valley* (1941). His portrayal of the lovable rascal who woos Judge Rosalind Russell in order to create a scandal and invalidate her ruling in his boss's divorce case was surprisingly charming and effective, and the chemistry between Russell and Pidgeon was quite palpable; it's a shame they never made another film together.

The rest of the cast, all of whom helped to move the fun along, included Edward Arnold as Pidgeon's boss, Lee Bowman as Russell's stuffy boyfriend, Barbara Jo Allen as Russell's friend and confidante, and Guy Kibbee as the presiding judge at the ultimate trial, who practically steals the picture. Taurog began filming on August 18, 1941, on location at Jack Oakie's VeniJay Ranch in the Santa Monica Mountains, which Oakie had named after himself and his first wife, Venita Varden.

Returning to the studio, Taurog completed filming in late September, finishing with process photography of Russell and Pidgeon on their bicycle-built-for -two.

Design for Scandal went into general release in December of 1941 and the Hollywood trade papers loved it. *Variety* declared: "*Design For Scandal* is easy moving, hard hitting comedy, sure to find audience favor… Norman Taurog's direction is another major credit, accounting for the speedy pace, the comedy punch and the undertone of heart that lends substance to many of the top sequences." *The Hollywood Reporter* echoed similar sentiments: "A bright, fast-moving and thoroughly amusing farce comedy, *Design For Scandal* is the kind of light entertainment that will have little trouble in stirring up considerable boxoffice favor… Norman Taurog's skillful direction moves the proceedings along briskly and the clever dialog and bright quips to be found in the script are amusingly embellished with clever, imaginative touches of business." Even the *New York Times* managed to find a few kinds words for the film: "This sort of double-cross occurs every other week on Broadway, so probably no one is going to faint with surprise. But Norman Taurog has directed it with an alert tongue in cheek and the two principals carry off the duel with easy finesse. Credit Edward Arnold for his performance as the badgered tycoon and Guy Kibbee as a choleric old judge. In this case the design is obvious, but the execution neat."

Things had not been going well for some time in the Taurog household, and in October of 1941 they announced that they were separating and Norman moved out of the house in Holmby Hills and into an apartment. They would eventually try reconciliation for the sake of nine-year-old Patricia, and in February of the following year Norman would return to Delfern Avenue. But it was obvious to both Norman and Julie that their marriage was failing.

Around the same time that he separated from Julie, Taurog found himself being loaned out to his old studio Paramount to direct a comedy for producer Fred Kohlmar starring Ray Milland and Betty Field, *Mr. and Mrs. Cugat.* It was based on a novel by Isabel Scott Rorick and a first draft screenplay by Tess Slesinger and Frank Davis. Taurog, unhappy with the material, worked through the month of October with the writers until a revised draft was completed on November 10. With additional work done by Harry Tugend and Jack Mintz, the final draft was at last approved on November 17, 1941. A budget meeting was held that same day and the budget was approved at $552,000 with a 36 day shooting schedule. Four days later, Taurog began filming.

Aware that their script was weak, Taurog and Kohlmar filled their cast with a virtual stock company of comedic character actors, including Eugene Pallette, Charles Dingle, Cecil Kellaway, Charles Lane, Mikhail Rasumny, George Chandler and Jimmy Conlon. Reginald Gardiner, one of Taurog's favorites, was originally signed for the role of Ray Milland's chum, but was replaced before filming began by the equally amusing Richard Haydn. The distaff side was represented by Patricia Morison, Elisabeth Risdon, Kathleen Lockhart and Anne Revere, who had recently appeared in two MGM films for Taurog.

It was a screwball comedy of questionable comedy content: The main character of the film was a scatterbrained wife played by Betty Field, Broadway actress and then wife of playwright Elmer Rice, who had recently made a name for herself in several seriously dramatic roles, such as *Of Mice and Men* (1939) and *The Shepherd of the Hills* (1941). This casting choice was even more confounding when you realize that *Mr. and Mrs. Cugat* later became the basis for a very popular radio series with Lucille Ball and Richard Denning called *My Favorite Husband,* which in turn inspired the enormously successful television series *I Love Lucy*. The success of those shows rested heavily on the comedic talents of Lucile Ball, something Betty Field couldn't possibly match. When a version of the film was broadcast on the *Lux Radio Theatre* a year later, the husband and wife were played by George Burns and Gracie Allen, who probably should have starred in the film version as well.

Taurog once gave an interview in which he discussed the basis of comedy. "While it's all serious," he said, "it's something that you either have or haven't. Good comedians aren't made. They're born with the gift. Seeing the humorous side of life is a twist of mind as native in the comedian as is a scientific bent or a talent for medicine or the ability to be an outstanding portrait painter." Without saying it, Taurog was referring to his directorial abilities as well, and as hard as he tried to pump life into a moribund script, this time he wasn't successful. A few weeks after filming was completed on January 9, 1942, the film's title was changed to *Are Husbands Necessary?*

Paramount finally released *Are Husbands Necessary?* in the early summer of 1942 and the reviews reflected the change in taste brought about by the arrival of the war. The opening paragraph of the *Hollywood Reporter* review said it all: "*Are Husbands Necessary?* is not a comedy of today, but of a yesterday that has been swiftly passed in the march of fast-changing world events. The time is as recent as the 1940s when the era was amused by frivolous and flighty wives whom husbands could afford to keep as pets." Bosley Crowther cared even less for it, "An almost pitiful endeavor to squeeze a few more laughs with frivolous marital farce is made in *Are Husbands Necessary*,"

On December 7, 1941 the United States was suddenly thrust into a war, and for Hollywood and the movies it was a boom time. As the country's industries geared up for heavy war production, unemployment declined and people found that they had more money to spend on leisure activities. In 1940 there were eight million unemployed Americans, but by 1943 and the middle of the war years there were less than a million people still out of work. MGM was facing a major transition; stars like Robert Taylor, James Stewart, and Clark Gable were enlisting in military service. Others, as well as many studio craftsmen, were being drafted. The contracts for some of the studio's biggest female stars (Norma Shearer, Greta Garbo, Joan Crawford and Jeanette MacDonald) were ending and they were being replaced by younger performers like Greer Garson, Jane Powell, June Allyson, Esther Williams and Donna Reed. Louis B. Mayer ordered more scripts written for each of the studio's successful series, *Andy Hardy, Maisie* and *Dr. Kildare*, and Arthur Freed, Jack Cummings and Joe Pasternak were given the go-ahead to start producing musicals. Between 1941 and 1945 MGM would produce 28 highly successful musicals, including such super-hits as *Babes on Broadway* (1941), *Girl Crazy* (1943), *Meet Me in St. Louis* (1944) and *Anchors Aweigh* (1945).

By the time *Are Husbands Necessary?* opened in theaters in June of 1942, Norman Taurog had already reconciled with Julie and was back with his family at his home in Holmby Hills and firmly re-ensconced at MGM with his old friend John Considine Jr, having just completed filming on the Mickey Rooney- Freddie Bartholomew starrer *A Yank at Eton*. In fact, the week after the reviews came out for *Are Husbands Necessary?* Taurog was spending two days filming added scenes for *A Yank at Eton*.

George Oppenheimer had adapted his original story and Lionel Hauser and Thomas Phipps contributed to the screenplay of *A Yank at Eton*; in which Mickey Rooney's widowed mother (Marta Linden) marries Englishman (Ian Hunter) and an unhappy Rooney and his little sister (Juanita Quigley) are uprooted and sent to England to join her. Rooney ends up at Eaton along with Hunter's son Bartholomew, who tries to guide his resentful stepbrother through the hallowed halls and traditions of the old school. All is resolved after some melodrama and much slapstick humor, particularly a scene where Rooney spreads a tube of "stick jaw" into the center of a birthday cake intended for the school bully, only to find that the house master and his wife have been invited to share in the cake. This is climaxed by a "rollicking" moment where all of the principals at the table try to speak while their mouths are clamped shut by the "stick jaw." It was a sight gag right out of Taurog's two-reel comedy days, and his reliance on that type of humor would continue to be a problem for the rest of his career.

Taurog once discussed his ideas of comedy in an extensive interview with syndicated columnist Harold Heffernan. In the interview he predicted that another era of slapstick, comparable to the custard-tossing days of Mack Sennett, would soon be returning. "Everything in the world is really funny," Taurog explained. "The funniest thing perhaps is the case of the puny, weak man, who, in his heart, imagines himself the Napoleon of today. That situation has brought out many of our best comedians, and it's still being used with good results. It will never die. By portraying the realization of a weak little man's hopes of being an overpowering brute, you have a situation that is incongruous but mirthful." Taurog would continue to use sight gags and slapstick whenever he felt the situation called for it. By the fifties and sixties humor would change, but Taurog would continue to fall back on his silent comedy training, some might say far too frequently.

The plot of *A Yank at Eton* strongly resembled an earlier Rooney-Bartholomew picture, *Lord Jeff* (1938), with the roles reversed; coincidentally, Peter Lawford was featured in both films. In the former film it was Bartholomew who played the tough kid who couldn't adapt to the demands of the home for orphaned boys, and Rooney who tried to show him the way. There is a key scene in both films where Rooney refuses to inform on Bartholomew, thereby solidifying their relationships.

Lawford, who was nineteen at the time, but looked younger, was cast as the upperclassman bully Ronnie Kenvil, who makes Rooney's life miserable when he arrives at Eaton. After *Lord Jeff* Lawford was off the screen for four years before returning to MGM to play a bit in *Mrs. Miniver* (1942), followed by his turn as Ronnie in *A Yank at Eton*. Over the next two years Lawford worked all over town, appearing in uncredited roles in films at Columbia, Republic, Universal and Warners. In 1944, MGM signed him to a seven-year contract and featured him as Irene Dunne's son in *The White Cliffs of Dover* (1944). A childhood injury to his right arm kept him out of military service and he rapidly became one of the studio's top romantic leading men.

The rest of the cast was filled with wonderful character actors such as Edmund Gwenn, Alan Mowbray, Alan Napier, Billy Bevan (without his usual moustache) and Aubrey Mather, again playing the family butler, as he had in *Men of Boys Town*. Raymond Severn, a young South African boy of eleven, whose seven siblings all worked as child actors in films, played "Inky," who befriends Rooney when he first arrives at Eaton. Juanita Quigley, who played Rooney's pushy sister Jane, looked remarkably like a young Elizabeth Taylor in certain camera angles, and in fact would play one of Taylor's sisters in *National Velvet* two years later. Both Quigley and Tina Thayer, who played a socially ambitious young lady who Rooney meets on the boat going over and who later shows up at Eaton, were handicapped by poorly written roles that treated their characters more as stereotypes than as flesh-and-blood youngsters—a condition that was exacerbated by Taurog's over-the-top direction.

On March 20, 1942, Taurog signed a new one-year contract with MGM, and three days later began filming the opening sequences for *A Yank at Eton* at El Segundo high school, with scenes of Mickey Rooney playing football at his American high school. From there the company returned to MGM's Lot 2, where art director Cedric Gibbons and his associate Daniel B. Cathcart had constructed an exact duplicate of Eton's Main Hall and Square. The company traveled to Orange County to film the climactic steeplechase sequence at Irvine Park. Filming was completed on Stage 21, where the set for the Willow Club, a roadhouse pub that is the setting for a wild brawl between Rooney, a group of his schoolmates and the proprietor and his men.

Taurog completed filming on May 20, with the added scenes shot on the 18 and 19 of June, and *A Yank at Eton* went into general release in the late summer of 1942. The reviews were not particularly complimentary, with the *Daily Variety* writing: "*A Yank at Eton* suffers as adult entertainment to the extent that it undertakes, with obvious good intent and schoolmasterly emphasis, to propagandize better understanding between American and English folk through a tale about their school-age youngsters… Its approach is too smug, too much like a school lecture, for many of its intended audiences. Rooney plays with his characteristic vigor, giving the role the accentuated American cockiness which he has established as his screen personality." When the film reached New York City in October, Bosley Crowther had his knife out as well; his *New York Times* review began: "Draw a deep breath ladies and gentlemen, and check your sensibilities at the door when (and if) you go to see *A Yank at Eton*, which barged into the Capitol yesterday. The best and by far the safest way to take this international gaucherie is in a state of mental relaxation, masking no demands on reason or on fact… And then you may manage sooner to dismiss it from your mind." Crowther had some negativity left over for the cast as well: "Naturally Mr. Rooney has a field-day all over the place, clowning like Eddie Cantor and jutting his jaw like Jack Holt. Andy Hardy at Eaton is a fearful thing to see. Ian Hunter is just about as smug as an Englishman could possibly be. Freddie Bartholomew is uncomfortably rigid as the misunderstood step-brother and a little lady named Tina Thayer is incredible as a juvenile flirt."

Judy and Mickey

When MGM first purchased the screen rights to Pulitzer Prize winner Booth Tarkington's 1933 novel *Presenting Lily Mars*, they had envisioned it as a dramatic vehicle for Lana Turner. But Turner had recently married her second husband, actor Stephen Crane, and was expecting a child, so the project was turned over to producer Joe Pasternak to develop as a possible musical for Kathryn Grayson. Pasternak, who had already made a film at MGM with Grayson, *Seven Sweethearts* (1942), saw *Presenting Lily Mars* as the perfect medium for a Judy Garland musical, much like the films he had made at Universal with Deanna Durbin, and hired Richard Connell, and later Gladys Lehman, to write the screenplay. Pasternak even had several semi-operatic numbers included in the scenario and cast Marta Eggerth, who had recently signed a contract with the studio and had already appeared with Garland, George Murphy and Gene Kelly in *For Me and My Gal* (1942), to play the temperamental star of the Broadway musical in the film. Eggerth, a beautiful Hungarian-born coloratura soprano, had appeared in dozens of films in Europe and with her husband, the Polish tenor, Jan Kiepura, in concerts in Europe and on the Broadway stage in *The Merry Widow*. Eggerth would make only these two films in Hollywood before returning to Europe to make more films with her husband. She would revive her career after Kiepura's death in 1966 and recently celebrated her 100th birthday, while still making the occasional personal appearance and singing for appreciative audiences.

Pasternak wanted Norman Taurog to direct *Presenting Lily Mars* for several reasons, first because Taurog had already directed Garland in *Little Nellie Kelly* and had developed a rapport with her, and second and perhaps more importantly, because Pasternak believed that Taurog would help to create a film similar in style to *Mad About Music,* Durbin's Universal film. This concept ultimately put Pasternak in an embarrassing position with Louis B. Mayer.

Once again casting was done with the utmost care, and the supporting roles were filled with wonderful character actors, all of whom turned in stellar performances. George Murphy was originally cast as Judy Garland's love interest, but was replaced by Van Heflin, who then became Garland's first romantic, non-singing and dancing leading man; Heflin, who had just won the Best Supporting Oscar for his performance in *Johnny Eager* (1941) played the Broadway producer who at first dismisses Garland's efforts to become an actress, but eventually falls in love with her. In addition to Marta Eggerth, there was Richard Carlson, Fay Bainter, Spring Byington, Ray McDonald, Gus Schilling, Leonid Kinskey, Connie Gilchrist (delivering a powerful cameo performance as an old cleaning lady who was once a Broadway star) Joe Yule, who was still working on his six-month contract that Mickey Rooney had arranged for with Louis B. Mayer and a young lady of twelve named Annabelle Logan who was playing one of Judy Garland's sisters. Logan, the niece of Broadway actress Ella Logan, would years later change her name to Annie Ross and become part of the legendary vocal jazz group, Lambert, Hendricks and Ross. Bob Crosby and his Orchestra, the first of five name bands signed by MGM that year, was given a featured spot in the film, singing with the Wilde Twins, two statuesque blondes that Mayer had put under contract.

Little Patricia Barker played Poppy, the youngest of Lily's sisters, and was absolutely charming, unlike Juanita Quigley, who played Mickey Rooney's pushy sister Jane in *A Yank at Eton.*

Jack Mintz arrived at the studio a few weeks before began filming began to again work with Taurog on final revisions of the screenplay and to be with him on the set. Filming officially began on August 2, 1942, and shut down on October 12 for several weeks of rehearsal with choreographer Ernst Matray on the final production number, "Paging Mr. Greenback," written by E.Y. Harburg, Sammy Fain and Lew Brown. The song was a plea to buy War Bonds and featured Garland and a chorus singing in front of a patriotic background. On October 19, *The Hollywood Reporter* printed MGM's announcement that the number would utilize a chorus of 200 men and women, and then three days later the studio pumped up the number to 400 men and women dancers. In spite of the gallant efforts of the MGM publicity department and the hard work of Ernst Matray and however many dancers and singers, "Paging Mr. Greenback" never appeared in the final version of *Presenting Lily Mars.* There are two versions of what happened, the first being the publicly announced reason that when the film went to preview, audience reactions were muted and Mayer decided to order a new finale to punch up the ending. The second and more likely reason was given by a bitter Pasternak in his interview for John Fricke's book *Judy: A Legendary Career*. Pasternak claimed that the film had been designed to have an intimate feeling, like the Durbin films, but that several of Garland's friends from the Freed unit managed to sneak a look at the film while it was still in the cutting room and reported back to her that it was weak and needed a bigger finish. Pasternak was called up to Mayer's office and given a lecture on the differences between budgets at Universal and MGM. Mayer suggested to Pasternak that he consider filming a production number that really featured all of Judy Garland's talents for the end of the film, and before Pasternak knew what was happening, Arthur Freed and his people were given the job of producing the new finale. It would take several months to prepare; Roger Edens, by now Freed's musical supervisor, would put together an arrangement that included an original song of his, "Where There's Music," interpolated with the old chestnut "Three O'Clock in the Morning," and his boss and Nacio Herb Brown's big hit "Broadway Rhythm." In the meantime, everyone would go off to work on their next project. Pasternak would begin preparing his first big MGM musical, *Thousands Cheer* (1943), in which he would spend lots of the studio's money just as Mayer wanted him to, and use as many guest stars as he possibly could; Garland and Rooney would begin exhaustive rehearsals with Busby Berkeley for the big "I Got Rhythm" production number in Arthur Freed's *Girl Crazy* (1943), and Norman and Julie Taurog would finally admit that their marriage was over and would begin meeting with attorneys.

Charles Walters, a young dancer, recently arrived from Broadway, choreographed *Presenting Lily Mars'* new finale. He worked with Garland for several weeks until she felt comfortable doing the intricate dance steps he had created for her. The number certainly turned out to be as big as Mayer and the others wanted, including twenty-four girl dancers surrounding Garland and wearing costumes similar to the one that Garland would wear in the "Get Happy" finale, which was another last-minute addition to her final MGM film, *Summer Stock* (1950). Also Tommy Dorsey and his orchestra playing on a giant platform that rises above Garland as she and Walters, who became her dance partner, circle and swirl around the giant set created by art director Merrill Pye. Garland appears to be a far more accomplished dancer than she actually was, thanks to Walters' stylish moves that are designed to take the brunt of the complicated dance steps himself and leave Garland to move with her usual impeccable grace.

Presenting Lily Mars went back before the cameras to film the new finale with Roy Del Ruth directing on March 8, 1943, and it opened in New York City the following April. *The Hollywood Reporter*'s review appeared on April 28 and tried to soften its critique by pointing out that, "*Presenting Lily Mars* tells the off-told story of a stage-struck girl. With the girl played by Judy Garland, this MGM picture that owes its origin to a novel by Booth Tarkington

The new finale for *Presenting Lily Mars*, with Tommy Dorsey's Orchestra above and Judy Garland and Charles Walters below.

is a boxoffice attraction of handsome proportions. The entertainment is at its best in the musical interludes- Judy sings four songs and Miss Eggerth three—and in the sequences dealing with the Mars' home life, the accomplished hand of Norman Taurog here being in practiced evidence in his direction of youthful comedy." However, Ted Strauss in *The New York Times* was more to the point: "After having agreed so long on Judy Garland's blithe talents, there is no point in disagreeing now. Miss Garland is fresh and pretty, she has a perky friendliness… No doubt about it, Miss Garland is a gifted young lady. If only MGM did not insist upon having them so obviously exposed. For the film has the unfortunate air of a children's recital in which mama, or in this case MGM, is pushing her precocious child out front and telling her to knock them dead… *Presenting Lily Mars* is uninviting fare; it is glorified monotony. Perhaps MGM should let Miss Garland grow up and stay that way." Alton Cook of the *Herald Tribune* found the story, "All too familiar. The story is one that has been told with slight variation so often in Hollywood musicals maybe the writers couldn't keep their minds on it." Judy Garland, looking glamorous as a young woman dressed in figure-flattering gowns by Irene Shoup, proved that the critics were wrong and *Presenting Lily Mars* took its place in MGM's profit column for the year. Although never considered one of Garland's great films, it still holds a warm spot in audiences' hearts.

While Norman Taurog was awaiting his next assignment, he and Julie were meeting frequently with their individual attorneys. The divorce was not a pleasant experience for either of them, and it took months of negotiations and finally the intercession of a mediator before their attorneys could arrive at a financial settlement agreeable to both parties. The settlement called for the couple's community property to be divided "as near equally as reasonably possible, each taking one-half as separate property." Taurog was ordered to pay Julie $20,000 a year support and Julie would retain custody of Patricia Ann Taurog, whom she would "support, educate and maintain." Taurog was given visitation and temporary custody rights and was strongly advised by his attorney, Lloyd Wright, to accept the agreement and avoid going into court, where California's Community Property law would give Julie half of everything anyway. Taurog's agreeing to this settlement would cause problems for him a few years later with the IRS. Once the agreement was signed, Julie left for Reno, Nevada, to begin her six-week residency and receive her divorce decree. The whole experience must have drained Taurog emotionally and he undoubtedly was delighted to be distracted from this low point in his life by an unexpected phone call from Arthur Freed, summoning him back into service on *Girl Crazy*.

The George and Ira Gershwin musical *Girl Crazy* began life on the Broadway stage at the Alvin Theatre on West 52nd Street on October 14, 1930. It was an immediate hit and played for 272 performances before closing on June 6, 1931. It made instant stars of both Ginger Rogers and Ethel Merman, and much has been written about the members of the theatre's Red Nichols Orchestra, personally conducted by George Gershwin on opening night that included Jimmy Dorsey, Benny Goodman, Gene Krupa, Glenn Miller and a future member of the Arthur Freed unit, Roger Edens. Edens was called up onstage to replace Ethel Merman's pianist, who had suffered a heart attack, and became her accompanist and arranger for her nightclub act. In 1932, RKO produced a highly altered version of *Girl Crazy* with comics Wheeler and Woolsey; Taurog directed some retakes for the film while he was at RKO making another Wheeler and Woolsey film, *Hold' Em Jail*. Now he was being called in to replace Busby Berkeley as the director on Arthur Freed's MGM production of the venerable musical starring Mickey Rooney and Judy Garland.

MGM purchased the rights to *Girl Crazy* from RKO in 1939 and the Freed unit took over its development in 1941. It's interesting to note that Freed didn't ask Jack McGowan, who had co-authored the book with Guy Bolton for the original Broadway version of *Girl Crazy*, to write the screen adaptation, even though McGowan had been at MGM since 1935, specializing in musical screenplays, and had already written four films for Freed. Instead, he hired Fred Finklehoffe, who was also working on Freed's *Best Foot Forward* (1943), to do the screen adaptation. In January of 1942 Finklehoffe's sister was involved in an automobile accident and he had to fly back East to be with her. He was taken off salary as of January 15 with the arrangement (between the studio and his agent Leland Hayward) that if he returned with "some usable work" they would restore the lost pay to him. Finklehoffe did return with "usable work" and continued on the *Girl Crazy* screenplay throughout the spring and summer of 1942, until he received his draft notice and returned to New York to report for duty. Freed then pulled Dorothy Kingsley away from her chores on *Best Foot Forward* and assigned another MGM contract writer, William Ludwig, to work with her on revisions for the *Girl Crazy* script.

Freed's assistant and music supervisor Roger Edens was principally responsible for Judy Garland's participation in *Girl Crazy*. Garland, who was nearing her 21st birthday and whose marriage to David Rose was on shaky ground (they would divorce in 1944), wanted to continue her progression into adult roles, but Edens correctly argued that *Girl Crazy* was another perfect opportunity to continue her highly successful teaming with Mickey Rooney. Rooney, who was twenty-three and having his own marital problems with Ava Gardner (they married in January of 1942 and were now in the midst of a divorce), was resigned to playing Andy Hardy-type roles; as he wrote in his autobiography, "If the people at Metro had had their way, I'd have remained a teenager for forty years."

Edens, whom many considered to be a musical genius, first arrived at MGM in 1935 and joined with Arthur Freed during the making of *The Wizard of Oz* in 1939. Freed soon made him his official music supervisor, and Edens would be responsible for composing and arranging numerous musical highlights, including Judy Garland's paean to Clark Gable "You Made Me Love You," the music for "Our Love Affair," the Oscar nominated song from *Strike Up the Band* (1940), and the "doodle ooh doo" signature opening to Gene Kelly's rendition of "Singin' in the Rain." Edens, as associate producer, would remain with Freed until the producer finally left the studio after his final musical *The Bells are Ringing* (1960). Edens would continue as associate producer on several more MGM musicals, including *Billy Rose's Jumbo* (1962) and *The Unsinkable Molly Brown* (1964).

Casting for the supporting roles in *Girl Crazy* was drawn partially from the list of studio contract players, such as "Rags" Ragland, Frances Rafferty, Henry O'Neill and Guy Kibbee, and partially from a group of players who had appeared in the Broadway production of *Best Foot Forward* and had been brought west by Freed to appear in his film version. June Allyson and Nancy Walker headed that list, but it also included a young actor named Gil Stratton, who was supposed to recreate his role of Bud Hooper in *Best Foot Forward*, but was replaced by another cast member, Tommy Dix, and was moved over to play Mickey Rooney's roommate in *Girl Crazy*. Stratton, who had received his draft notice in late 1942, had been given a temporary deferment to finish his commitment with the *Best Foot Forward* road company. When MGM offered him a contract he was concerned that he wouldn't be able to finish filming before being called up, and wrote to the studio from Chicago, where he was appearing with the road company. Freed had Marvin Schenk of the New York office arrange for Stratton's deferment to continue until he finished appearing in *Girl Crazy*. After the war, Stratton would continue as an actor for a few years before becoming a very popular sports commentator on Los Angeles television.

Budgeted at $1,087,915 for 46 days of filming with 15 rehearsal days and six days of second unit filming, *Girl Crazy* commenced filming on January 4, 1943, with Busby Berkeley as the director. Berkeley was up to his old tricks and had virtually exhausted Judy Garland and Mickey Rooney with his extensive rehearsal schedule before filming even began. He then spent 12 days on Stage 26 filming the "I've Got Rhythm" number with Mickey, Judy, fifty boy and girl dancers and the Tommy Dorsey orchestra. Roger Edens, who had written Judy's vocal arrangement for the song, was furious with Berkeley's over-produced staging, complete with "fringe skirts and people cracking whips and firing guns." Garland, who was already unhappy with Berkeley's dictatorial treatment, was on the verge of collapse when the company moved to Stage 24, where Berkeley rehearsed the "Treat me Rough" number. At this point, Rooney called in sick and the company went on hiatus for four days. Berkeley was called up to Freed's office and informed that

Mickey Rooney, Judy Garland and Tommy Dorsey in the "I've Got Rhythm number.

he was being taken off the picture, officially leaving the film on January 31, 1943. The "I've Got Rhythm" number ultimately cost $203,099—and was $62,128 over budget.

On Monday, February 1, 1943, *The Hollywood Reporter* announced, that "Busby Berkeley, who retired from directing MGM's *Girl Crazy* because of illness, remains off pic permanently. Norman Taurog will shoot remaining sequences on the Mickey Rooney -Judy Garland starrer." The company remained shut down for a month while Taurog familiarized himself with the script, and Garland was confined to her bed to build up her strength for the arduous shooting schedule that lay ahead. After meeting with Freed, Taurog and Jack Mintz presented notes for changes and cuts in the script. There was considerable concern regarding Rooney's routine of impersonations—particularly his use of real names. Trying to get releases became expensive and it took several months to finally secure all releases and pay fees. An interesting side note: A memo from Robert W. Vogel of MGM's Foreign Dept. asked the production team to remember, that in regard to the Rodeo number, "that bucking horses are not allowed to buck in England and that, if any of them do so, we'll louse up a big number." At the same time, a letter to Mayer from censor Joseph I. Breen pointed out that the words "jerk" and "jerky" are on the association's list of prohibited words, and were not acceptable. There was a need for a sense of humor in these matters, as exhibited by Al Block's memo: "Careful research on the part of the local Department, the New York Office and Columbia University, has uncovered the fact that a dildo is a schwanz and consequently must be eliminated from the dialogue in GIRL CRAZY." His reference was actually to the word "Diljo."

Dean Armour: "Could you tell me something?"
Danny: "Yes, sir."
Dean Armour: "Just what is the meaning of the word 'snerpy'?"
Danny: "Well, a snerp is a loogan with a belt in the back; sometimes referred to as a diljo. A diljo is a..."
Dean Armour: "Never mind! I have a rough idea."

By the first of March, production was back in full swing with Taurog and cinematographer William Daniels filming interiors on Stage 24 and Chuck Walters, who had taken over the choreographing chores, rehearsing Garland for the "Embraceable You" number. Walters would again become Garland's dance partner when the number was filmed. One morning Garland ran out of gas on her way to the studio for a 9:30 AM recording session. Garland called the transportation department and requested that a studio car pick her up, but was told that they couldn't do it. Garland then contacted the production department, who in turn called Freed's office. A car was immediately

Judy Garland and Norman Taurog between takes on *Girl Crazy*.

sent to pick her up and deliver her to the scoring stage and the recording session went off as planned. On March 17, Garland was taken ill on the set and sent home, where she remained for the next three days, with the studio examining the cost of holding production for her. Taurog was able to shoot around her and the production stayed on schedule.

Toward the end of the month, with Judy feeling stronger, the company travelled to Palm Springs, some 106 miles away, to film several sequences, including the opening of the film, where Rooney's character Danny Churchill Jr. meets Garland's Ginger Grey under her stalled Model T in the middle of the desert. A great deal of time was spent filming the "Can You Use Me" number with Mickey and Judy in the model T. To make the Palm Springs desert look more like Arizona, the MGM prop department spotted fake saguaro cactus along both sides of the dirt road. For the next two weeks the company worked under a broiling sun and temperatures that frequently exceeded 109 ° in the shade. Because of the heat, the company would halt filming between noon and 2:30 in the afternoon and then resume until 5:30. The actors used tents for dressing rooms on the location, fifteen miles from their home base at the Desert Inn on Palm Canyon Drive, and several times the tents were blown over by sandstorms and filming had to be suspended. In spite of the hardships and delays, all of the location scenes were eventually completed, and Rooney and

Garland's performance in "Can You Use Me" was a rollicking number filled with Rooney's acrobatic shenanigans and Garland's amusing responses.

Girl Crazy spent several days filming on MGM's Lot 3, where the Monterey Street standing set had been reconfigured into the Cody College campus. The company finished filming process photography on Friday, April 9, 1943, and Taurog was back on the stages on May 19 to film additional scenes with Rooney and Garland, with cameraman Robert Planck filling in for William Daniels. Six days later, Taurog and MGM signed an agreement for a new five-year contract, with his salary remaining at $3,000 a week. A few days after that, Taurog wrote a note to Arthur Freed, in which he said, "I can't remember a more pleasant assignment and want to thank you for your ever-present understanding and cooperation." He closed by adding, "The more we do together, the better --- 'them's my sentiments!" Freed's answer the following day was, "Needless to say, you know I feel the same pleasure in working with you and so does all my gang. I am looking forward to many such associations." Apart from directing a sequence or two in *Ziegfeld Follies* (1945), Taurog would direct only one more film for Freed, but it would be a big one.

After several successful previews, *Girl Crazy* opened at the Capitol Theatre in New York City on November 30, 1943. The reviewers were ecstatic, with *The New York Times* leading the parade with the following praise: "Hold your hats, folks! Mickey Rooney and Judy Garland are back in town. And if at this late date there are still a few die-hards who deny that they are the most incorrigibly talented pair of youngsters in movies, then *Girl Crazy* ...should serve as final rebuttal." *The New York Herald Tribune* had this to say: "As pleasant a screen musical as it was on the stage. *Girl Crazy* should make for happy holiday entertainment at the Capitol. Chalk up another musical triumph for the Rooney-Garland Team." *The Hollywood Reporter* gave praise to the staging of "I've Got Rhythm," saying the finale "had a spectacular punch that is among the best effects Busby Berkeley ever staged," and added kind words for Taurog and his male star as well: "Rooney troupes all over the place, just as his enthusiastic following wants him to do in a musical. You can trust the understanding comedy guidance of Norman Taurog's direction for that. The Mick's exuberance is deftly dealt with, but, at the same time, given full play—a neat trick if done as Taurog does it." *The Hollywood Citizen* review on November 26, 1943: "The direction by Norman Taurog shines brilliantly through the surface of this frothy film in which dull moments are as rare as restaurant butter." The British reviews were represented by this one from the *News of the World*: "This is one of the best escapist pictures Metro-Goldwyn-Mayer have [sic] made in a long time. "

Girl Crazy grossed $3,771,000 and Norman Taurog and Arthur Freed were named boxoffice Champions by *Motion Picture Herald* in December of 1944.

The Missing Years 1943–1946

Fresh off a smash hit film, with a new five-year contract in his pocket and drawing $3,000 a week, Norman Taurog should have become one of the busiest directors on the Metro lot, but such was not the case. From October of 1943, when he completed post-production work on *Girl Crazy*, until June of 1945, when he began filming *The Hoodlum Saint*, which was then not released until June of 1946, there is a curious gap in his résumé. For those twenty months, Norman Taurog never officially occupied the director's chair on any MGM picture.

Part of the answer could have been the enormous backlog of films that MGM had ready for release. In 1943, MGM released 32 films, in 1944 the number was 30, and in 1945 it was 29. Another possibility could have been his divorce from Julie Taurog that, thanks to her, was being covered in the pages of every newspaper in the country. When Julie first approached her attorney, John O'Melveny about seeking a divorce, she made sure that Louella Parsons wrote about it, and when in October of 1943 she received her divorce decree in Reno, there was a news photographer conveniently waiting outside the courthouse to take her photograph. Even when Taurog sold the house in Holmby Hills to Sonja Henie at a considerable loss, it made the papers. There is a morality clause in all of the MGM contracts, and it's entirely possible that Norman and Julie's very public divorce may have annoyed Louis B. Mayer. Of course, the fact that Taurog was also now dating Susan Broderick, a very attractive 27-year-old divorcée who just happened to be one of Mayer's private secretaries, might also have had something to do with it.

The official line was that they had met at the home of mutual friends, but the truth was they had caught each other's eye on those occasions when Norman would arrive at Louis B. Mayer's office for a meeting with the boss. They had been secretly dating for some time, although Mayer never knew about it until Louella Parsons broke the story in July of 1944. One can only guess what this self-proclaimed paragon of virtue had to say about it. But whatever his feelings, they were undoubtedly calmed when Norman and Sue were married at the home of Edward Kaufman on Saturday, September 16, 1944, and perhaps his only regret then was that he had lost a good secretary. Susan Ream Taurog was born in Douglas, Nebraska, on March 12, 1916, the only daughter of Ralph Everette Ream and the former Virginia A. Smith, and she would die on November 16, 2008, at the age of 92 at the Motion Picture and Television Country House and Hospital in Woodland Hills. Before her marriage to Taurog, Susan Broderick had been one of Mayer's private secretaries under the supervision of his executive secretary Ida Koverman. Nicknamed "Mt. Ida," Koverman was the power behind the throne at MGM. She at one time had been an assistant to President Herbert Hoover and was actively involved in the California Republican Party. It would appear that Koverman, and indirectly the ultra-right-wing Mr. Mayer, must have applied their influence on Sue Broderick's political education, for in later years as Sue Taurog she was very active in charitable organizations and Republican committees. She was heavily involved in political fundraising for several Republican candidates, including Richard Nixon and Ronald Reagan. She was president of the Los Angeles Orphanage Guild and the KCET-Channel 28 Women's Council, as well as a member of the station's board of directors. In 1964, she was a member of the Republican delegation to the convention supporting Governor Nelson Rockefeller for president. Taurog's political affiliation was also with the conservative wing of the Republican Party. In February of 1944, he was one of the founders of the Motion Picture Alliance for the Preservation of American Ideals, dedicated, its organizers claimed, to "combating Communism and Fascism within the industry." Director Sam Wood was elected president, and Walt Disney, Cedric Gibbons and Norman Taurog were elected vice-presidents. Some other members included actors Robert Taylor, Adolphe Menjou, Gary Cooper, Clark Gable, John Wayne and Ward Bond, and directors and writers Victor Fleming, Borden Chase, Bert Kalmar and Morrie Ryskind. Taurog was actively involved with the anti-Communist movement of the early fifties and supported the House Un-American Activities Committee, along with other right wing personalities Robert Taylor, John Wayne, Jimmy Stewart, Clark Gable and Walt Disney. Norman and Sue Taurog would remain married until his death in 1981 and they would adopt two children soon after they exchanged marriage vows: Jonathan who was born on March 27, 1945, and Priscilla, born on September 1, 1945.

A gentleman by the name of William Smith, who just might possibly be silent film actor Franklyn Farnum using his real name, was Taurog's best man at his wedding and MGM contractee Hazel Brooks was Susan Ream's maid of honor. Hazel was at that time the girlfriend of Cedric Gibbons, and Gibbons, as the head of the MGM Art Department from 1924 to1956, would have worked with Taurog on all of the films that he directed at MGM. Gibbons was also the designer of the Academy Award Oscar statue. Hazel Brooks was under contract to MGM from 1943, when she was just 18 years old, until she left to make a name for herself as the sultry girlfriend of boxer John Garfield in *Body and Soul* (1947). She and Cedric Gibbons would marry later in 1944, when she was 19 and he was 49. The Taurogs and the Gibbons would remain friends for many years and would exchange Christmas cards each year. When Cedric died in July of 1960, the Taurogs sent Hazel a telegram with their condolences. "Dearest Hazel: Please accept our deepest sympathy in the passing of your beloved Gibby. There is little we can say at a time like this, but we are sure that the memory of your beautiful devotion and love will help to sustain you."

To say that Norman Taurog was totally inactive from1943 to 1945 is not quite true. Apart from directing some retakes for a Wallace Beery-Marjorie Main comedy called *Rationing* (1944), Taurog also spent seven days in late January and early February of 1945 filming William Powell as Florence Ziegfeld looking down from his sumptuous penthouse apartment in Heaven for the prologue of *Ziegfeld Follies*, as well as a portion of the "Final Tableau" sequence with Kathryn Grayson singing "There's Beauty Everywhere." The staging for Grayson's song required a complicated combination of rear screen projection, plus the use of a turntable and wind machines. Midway through the song, the film segues into a spectacular dance sequence filmed earlier, with Cyd Charisse and a group of showgirls engulfed in huge, billowing soap bubbles. Charisse, in a later interview, described how the bubbles grew too large and completely blocked the view from the camera, as well as making a number of the showgirls ill. The production reports for Taurog's filming of the Kathryn Grayson number showed that he too had some problems photographing the soap bubbles needed for the transition to the dancers.

Starting in late November of 1943, Taurog was also busily developing a project with his old friend John Considine. It began as an unpublished manuscript by William K. Howard, who was represented by the Myron Selznick Agency, and the 1942 book, *The Church of the Good Thief and the padre of the thieves* by Thomas Francis Ryan. It told the story of the Reverend Ambrose Hyland and his efforts to construct a chapel at Clinton Prison in Dannemora, New York. When Father Hyland was first assigned to be the prison chaplain in 1936, he was given a tour of the prison. In an interview he gave shortly after MGM purchased his story, he described that moment: "I saw the cell block, on which millions had been spent for confinement. I saw the hospital, which cost $800,000, for the care of their bodies. The school, where they could learn, and the industrial building, where they were given occupational training. At the end of the tour I said, I'm the chaplain—where is my church? I was told there were no churches in prison. And why not? The prison was on state property." After Father Hyland was finally able to receive assurances from the governor that a church would be permitted, he set out to raise the money and to build the chapel with the help of volunteer prison labor. He obtained contributions from all over the country and eventually the chapel was finished, complete with a $25,000 pipe organ donated by a group of New York Jewish businessmen.

On December 1, 1943, Norman Taurog was officially assigned to work with producer John Considine and writer Robert D. Andrews on developing a screenplay based on the Father Ryan story. Considine had been extremely busy throughout late 1942 and early 1943 producing two films almost simultaneously. *Salute to the Marines* (1943) with Wallace Beery and *Three Hearts for Julia* (1943) starring Ann Sothern and Melvyn Douglas, but now his only assignment was to supervise the progress on *The Church of the Good Thief*. The "Good Thief" referred to in the title of Ryan's book was St. Dismas, the Penitent Thief who was crucified with Christ and who asked to be remembered in paradise. St. Dismas is the only saint consecrated by Christ himself and the only one sanctified while still alive. On December 28, 1943, Taurog and Andrews took the train to New York to meet with Father Hyland and discuss the story. Three days later, Hedda Hopper's syndicated column carried a typically straightforward story about *The Church of the Good Thief* and Taurog's trip to New York, but then she added a mystifying postscript: "But there's more to this story than meets the eye. I'll tell you more about it some day." Was this an oblique reference to the divorce and Taurog's inactivity?

Taurog and Andrews stayed at the Waldorf Towers and spent several days interviewing Father Hyland and visiting the prison at Dannemora. Father Hyland's narrative certainly contained elements that had worked well in the *Boys Town* films, and the studio's first instinct was to cast their old reliable priest, Spencer Tracy, in the role. But realizing that Tracy was too well remembered as Father Flanagan, their next choice was Walter Pidgeon. Taurog remained with the project until June of 1944, at which time he was assigned to another project called *Seattle*. On August 12, Considine's office sent a draft of Andrews' script (dated July 15, 1944) to Joseph I. Breen of the Motion Picture Producers Association. There were several letters and several drafts correcting certain concerns on the part of the MPPA and eventually approval was granted.

The first indication that there was another project, with the title of *The Hoodlum Saint*, being developed on the lot that might conflict with *The Church of the Good Thief*, came when *The Hollywood Reporter* announced in August of 1943 that writer-producer Casey Robinson had been signed to write the screenplay. Robinson, a long-time writer at Warners, had just completed writing and producing *Days of Glory* (1944) for RKO. He apparently spent some time at MGM and may have worked briefly on the *Hoodlum Saint* script, as well as *Adventure* (1945), Clark Gable's first film after returning from military service. However, the real action on *The Hoodlum Saint* front started when writer James Hill was assigned to develop a screenplay based on an original story by Frank Wead. At some point, a "B" level producer by the name of Cliff Reid, who had just finished supporting director John Ford as his associate producer on *They Were Expendable* (1945), was assigned to the film. There is a strong connection between Frank Wead, who became a successful screenwriter after suffering a debilitating accident in 1926 in which he fractured his neck while serving as a Naval Aviator, and Cliff Reid, whose main experience as a producer had been at RKO, where he produced most of the *Mexican Spitfire* series with Lupe Velez. Wead wrote the screenplay for John Ford's *They Were Expendable* and Reid worked closely with Ford as his associate producer on several films beside *They Were Expendable*, including *The Lost Patrol* (1934) and *The Informer* (1935)

The Hoodlum Saint was primarily the story of a bitter World War I veteran who uses people to gain his fortune that he then loses in the stock market crash of 1929. Through an earlier connection with a neighborhood church, he learns of St. Dismas "the hoodlum saint", and ends up preventing the church's St. Dismas fund from being stolen. One good deed deserves another, and the girl he'd jilted earlier returns to his arms. When the studio brass decided to scrap *The Church of the Good Thief* and go with *The Hoodlum Saint*, their decision was undoubtedly influenced by the former story's similarity with the Father Flanagan films, as well as the joint references to St. Dismas. Another story with a similar theme was eventually produced many years later by actor Don Murray: *The Hoodlum Priest* (1961), which told the story of the Reverend Charles Dismas Clark and his fight for the rights of former convicts and against capital punishment.

Whatever the studio's reasons, *The Hoodlum Saint* was given the go-ahead, and Norman Taurog began filming in mid-June of 1945, with William Powell, Esther Williams and Angela Lansbury in the leading roles. Both Williams and Lansbury were just beginning their careers, and although Angela Lansbury had been nominated for an Oscar for her first two films, *Gaslight* (1944), and *The Picture of Dorian Gray* (1945), she'd followed it up with a series of stock supporting roles in *National Velvet* (1944), and *The Harvey Girls* (1945), and while the studio had finally put Esther Williams, after a number of unremarkable dry-land roles, into the water in *Bathing Beauty* (1944) and *Thrill of a Romance* (1945), in *The Hoodlum Saint* neither of these actresses would be given a chance to showcase their talents. Powell, whose career at MGM was winding down after eleven years of popularity, would make only one more film, *Song of the Thin Man* (1947) before leaving the studio and moving to Universal-International, where he would stay for the next six years enjoying success with such films as *The Senator Was Indiscreet* (1947) and *Mr. Peabody and the Mermaid* (1948).

The rest of *The Hoodlum Saint*'s cast was reminiscent of a Frank Capra or Preston Sturges movie, filled with wonderful character actors such as James Gleason, Lewis Stone, "Rags" Ragland, Frank McHugh, Slim Summerville, Chester Conklin, Louis Jean Heydt, Roman Bohnen, Henry O'Neill, Addison Richards, Byron Foulger, and even good old Mrs. Hudson from the *Sherlock Holmes* films at Universal, Mary Gordon. This would be "Rags" Ragland's final film before his untimely death of uremic poisoning at the age of 40 in 1946.

As part of a publicity stunt for the picture, William Powell who lived in Palm Springs when he wasn't at work, was presented with a special portable dressing room on the set that was dressed with several truckloads of sand, Joshua trees and a picket fence. Deck chairs were set out beneath a fancy umbrella and a canvas desert panorama that was hung behind, along with a cardboard sun suspended from wires. A photographer took a still of Powell and Norman Taurog posing stiffly in front of the dressing room, which later appeared in an issue of the studio's promotion magazine *Lion's Roar*.

Although Taurog completed filming in mid-September of 1945, the studio held up the film's release until June of the following year. When the film premiered in New York on June 26, 1946, the *New York Times* reviewer had this to say: "In producing *The Hoodlum Saint* ...Metro obviously set out with a worthy and unusual theme. But a tediously involved plot, unwieldy dialogue, pat situations and flat characterizations add up to a somewhat jumbled and tepid drama. All this is perhaps better phrased by Angela Lansbury, a torch singer, who remarks to William Powell, early in the film, 'Isn't it sort of risky to be fooling around with religion?' Apparently it was, for this story of a cynical newspaper man turned utilities magnate who finds faith through the inspiration of St. Dismas, the Good Thief, is more often uninspired than stimulating." Some of the other reviews were even harsher. Cecelia Ager in *PM* called it "an MGM attempt to invade Bing Crosby's profitable Church with some imitation Damon Runyon characters. But they wind up empty-handed because Runyon did not write them, and because whoever did was unable to simulate the spark of genuine reverence deep down in Crosby's church that inspires his audience and thus makes it profitable." Joe Pihodna of the *New York Herald Tribune* wrote, "MGM has spared neither actors nor director. *The Hoodlum Saint* is a hodge-podge." Eileen Creelman in *The Sun:* ". . . an outstanding example of bad taste, if of nothing else. The little drama tries to be one of those religious pictures that are often so popular, forgetting that great dramas about religion are written out of conviction. 'The Hoodlum Saint' is a synthetic piece, a phony tale from the start."

The Beginning Or The End

On the morning of August 6, 1945, a United States Army Air Force B-29 bomber named *Enola Gay* dropped the first wartime atomic bomb on the Japanese city of Hiroshima. Three days later, another B-29 dropped the second bomb, designated "Fat Man," on the city of Nagasaki. All told, over 218,000 people would die from the blasts, or later from the results of the radioactive fallout. On August 14 the Japanese Emperor Hirohito announced Japan's surrender, followed by the signing of the surrender documents onboard the battleship USS *Missouri* in Tokyo Bay on September 2, 1945. This became known as V.J. Day and marked the official end to World War II.

The development of the Atomic Bomb had been a classified secret for many years and now the public was curious to learn the story of how it came to be. Newspaper and magazine articles would be written, and eventually a film would be produced. Several studios were anxious to be the first to come out with a film about the Atomic Bomb and Metro-Goldwyn-Mayer suddenly found itself in the forefront of that effort. Around the first of November 1945, MGM producer Sam Marx, who had produced *Lassie Come Home* (1943), received a phone call from Tony Owens, Donna Reed's husband, asking for Marx to meet him at the Beverly Wilshire Hotel for breakfast. At the breakfast, Owens showed Marx some letters his wife had received from her former high school teacher, Dr. Edward Tompkins of Oak Ridge, Tennessee. These letters explained to Miss Reed something of the non-classified scientific side of the Atomic Bomb, and the professor wondered if the motion picture industry would want to tell the people of the world some "inherent facts about this bomb which they should know." Marx brought this to the attention of the powers-that-be at MGM and soon he and Owens were on a plane to Oak Ridge. They were met by Dr. Edward Tompkins and Dr. Paul Tompkins (no relation) with the following greeting: "We are very happy that you are here. We hope you can soon tell the world the meaning of this bomb, because we are scared to death!" Upon his return to the studio, Marx set down his experiences at Oak Ridge in a 19-page outline and presented it to L.B. Mayer. It would be more than a year before Mayer would give the production his okay, and even then its final go-ahead was influenced by the interest of other producers in the same subject. Eventually, newsman Bob Considine, brother of MGM producer John Considine was hired to develop a treatment based on Marx's research and soon after writer Frank Wead was assigned to the project.

On December 11, 1945, *The Hollywood Reporter* published MGM's first announcement regarding *The Beginning or the End*: "MGM announced yesterday that Spencer Tracy, Clark Gable, Van Johnson and other top stars were being groomed for roles in *The Beginning or the End*, the story of the atomic bomb, which Bob Considine is readying for shooting." As it turned out, none of the stars mentioned would appear in the film.

Three days later, *The Hollywood Reporter* carried the following story: "Hal Wallis returned to his desk on the Paramount lot yesterday after ten days in New York and Washington, where he went in connection with his plans to produce a feature around the atomic bomb. Wallis, immediately upon reaching Hollywood, signaled the start of filming on his *The Searching Wind*, then started a writer round-up for the development of his bomb story."

A memo from Frank Wead to Sam Marx, dated December 31, 1945, suggested various possible scenes to be included in the screenplay, while making note that: "many scientists worked on the bomb with great misgivings."

On January 2, 1946, *The Hollywood Reporter* headlined; "MGM GUNS ATOMIC PIC TO BEAT OTHERS." According to the article, "Faced with the threat of Hal Wallis' projected picture based on the atomic bomb and Sol Wurtzel's efforts to be first to the screen with a similar story for 20th-Fox release, MGM's top executives yesterday gave that studio's bomb picture top priority over every other production on the huge lot. Louis B. Mayer ordered that Sam Marx, producer of the Culver City studio's *The Beginning or the End* be given a green light on all facilities in order to bring the story to the screen with the utmost speed." On January 4, *The Hollywood Reporter* continued to feed the rivalry by running a boxed blurb on page three headlined "ATOM WIRE BURNING." The story claimed that producer Sam Marx was having writer Bob Considine wire his original story treatment page by page to the studio, "where it's rushed into the hands of scripters."

Soon other writers were at work on *The Beginning or the End*, including Beirne Lay, Jr. who would later write the novel and the screenplay for *Twelve O'Clock High* (1949). On January 22, 1946, Lay turned in a treatment titled "Chain Reaction Among the Scientists." Basically a study of the conflict between secular scientists and those of religious beliefs, the final paragraph read: "The atomic scientists who have mastered the secret of the energy of the sun are close-mouthed with their prophecies. But it is their hope that Americans will not dismiss lightly the scientists' conviction that the miracle wrought in their laboratories has enjoined us to make haste with the fulfillment of the prophecy of Isaiah: 'They shall beat their swords into plowshares and their spears into pruning hooks; nation shall not lift up their sword against nation, neither shall they learn war anymore.'"

Over at Paramount, Wallis was still busily at work on his Atomic Bomb project, now titled *Top Secret.* A document entitled, "Suggested Opening for *Top Secret*" by Robert Smith and dated February 6, 1946, posed the question, ". . . that men of good will all over the world are asking today. Should we have the atom bomb at all?"

On that same day, Norman Krasna and Glenn Tryon submitted a treatment entitled "ATOM BOMB PROLOGUE AND EPILOGUE" to Marx. In it they suggested a quasi-newsreel of the burying of a time capsule, followed by scientist Robert J. Oppenheimer speaking directly to the audience, all of which was eventually used in the final version of film. Their epilogue involved a "Speaker" who explains the contents of the time capsule and voices the comment that was later written out in the film's final title: "To the people of 2446 A.D. This was THE BEGINNING, only you, and those who have lived between us and you, can know THE END."

In the archives of the Margaret Herrick Library of the Academy of Motion Picture Arts and Sciences in Beverly Hills I read a screen treatment by Ayn Rand dated February 24, 1946 and containing a rather self-important (typical Rand style) preface with a cynical father and the birth of his son, who would become John K., the "everyman" in the telling of Rand's version of the story. The progress of various real scientists is intercut with John K.'s education–his having problems, starting to drink, partying, growing to hate the subject of science, etc. Eventually war is declared and John K. goes into battle, is wounded, and becomes a spiritual wreck. At some point he is called in to his commanding officer and ordered to become the bodyguard of Dr. Oppenheimer. Ultimately John K. becomes a believer and speaks the final line in the film: "Man can harness the universe, but nobody can harness man." Huh???

A headline in the March 18, 1946, *Hollywood Reporter* declared that "MGM AND WALLIS MERGE FACILITIES ON ATOM BOMB PIC." The article went on to explain "Metro-Goldwyn-Mayer and Hal Wallis Productions will merge story properties and other production facilities in turning out the story of the atomic bomb, thus eliminating duplication of effort on the nation's screen, it was announced yesterday. The picture will be made on the MGM lot, with Sam Marx producing, Norman Taurog directing and

Sam Marx and Norman Taurog pose for publicity photo announcing the start of production on *The Beginning or the End*. (Photo courtesy Photofest)

Wallis serving in an advisory capacity." "The deal calls for the transfer to Metro," the article continued, "of all story material and research information that has been gathered by the Wallis organization for its contemplated $1,500,000 'Top Secret'. Metro will combine the Wallis material with its own on *The Beginning or the End*."

The choice of Norman Taurog to direct a picture of the size and scope of *The Beginning or the End* might seem at first glance to be an unusual one. However, there were several reasons why it made sense. One might be that Taurog and Marx were old and dear friends, and would remain so for many years to come. Another and more important reason could be that, despite the earlier announcements heralding important casting and priorities, the budget on the picture was not in the realm of a super-production and neither was the shooting schedule. Taurog was certainly a well-proven director of dramatic stories who was also known to be a director who brought his pictures in on schedule.

The casting for the film took some time to accomplish, inasmuch as there were over 180 speaking roles to be filled; many of the lead roles were given to MGM contract players such as Robert Walker, Tom Drake, Audrey Totter and Hurd Hatfield. The two major historical figures involved in the development of the bomb, Dr. Robert Oppenheimer and Major General Leslie R. Groves, were played by Hume Cronyn and Brian Donlevy respectively. Lionel Barrymore was initially cast to play the late President Franklin Delano Roosevelt, but Mrs. Roosevelt objected to Barrymore portraying her husband because of comments he supposedly made during the previous election, in which he supported Thomas Dewey.

Taurog began filming on Monday, April 29, 1946, and the next day *The Hollywood Reporter* announced that Sergei Petschnikoff had been assigned as unit manager, with Stanley Goldsmith and Frank Myers as assistant directors. On May 2, *The Hollywood Reporter* announced "MGM on Monday slipped quietly into the start of *The Beginning or the End*, its film based on the development of the atom bomb, under producer Sam Marx and director Norman Taurog. Agnes Moorehead was the only cast topper called for the early sequences, supported by several minor players." If Ms Moorehead did indeed work in the film, her scenes must have been deleted later, as she does not appear in the final version.

On June 5, production of scenes with Lionel Barrymore as President Franklin D. Roosevelt were put on hold until a letter he had written to Mrs. Roosevelt was answered. The following day the studio announced that Barrymore had withdrawn from the film and British actor Godfrey Tearle would take over the role. Roman Bohnen, who was originally signed to play President Harry Truman, was replaced by Art Baker. As it turned out, both replacements bore a stronger resemblance to the presidents they portrayed than the original actors, even though only the back and side of Baker's head was photographed, in keeping with the tradition that a living president is never impersonated on the screen.

On July 26, *The Hollywood Reporter* ran a blurb announcing that *The Beginning or the End* had finished production ahead of schedule in 48 days. Three days later, Sam Marx took out an ad in the *Reporter* in the form of a Western Union Telegraph, saying "It's true *The Beginning or the End* finished shooting ahead of schedule but the credit for that job certainly goes to Director Norman Taurog, Unit Manager Sergei Petschnikoff, Assistants Stanley Goldsmith and Frank Myers, Cameraman Ray June and the great crew who took such a vital interest in this particular project."

However, production on *The Beginning or the End* was far from over. On August 1, Taurog began filming six pages of retake material, and on September 24, John Lee Mahin delivered a cut-and-paste version of a new ending that Louis B. Mayer had ordered. Using newly released Signal Corps film, it was a vivid depiction of the devastation that engulfed Hiroshima that day, with some voice-over narration by Tom Drake's character. Interestingly, the tone in Mahin's initial writing was more upbeat than in the final version; however, the major portion of his work was used in the final film. Mahin would revise it once more on October 1, making some cuts in his original material and eliminating Drake's narration.

In mid-November, James K. McGuinness, a writer who had worked his way up the ladder to become part of L.B. Mayer's executive committee, accompanied the film to Washington, D.C., where President Truman's aides Charles Ross and Matt Connelly were to view it. Both men were unhappy with a scene that depicted President Truman making the decision to use the bomb. They particularly disliked a line of dialogue where Truman said, "I think more of our American boys than I do of all our enemies." To Ross and Connelly it made the president look as if he made the decision too quickly, without giving it enough thought. McGuinness returned to the studio and quickly wrote a new scene in which Truman spent more time deliberating before deciding, ordering leaflets to be dropped warning the people of Hiroshima of "what is coming" (something which never actually happened), and predicting the bomb will "shorten the war by approximately a year."

On November 22, *The Hollywood Reporter* ran a new datelined story announcing "Several changes in MGM's *The Beginning or the End* were ordered here and in Washington when the print was brought East recently by James Kevin McGuinness for official inspection." The article also reported that "all of the necessary legal clearances have not yet been secured on the picture, tentatively scheduled for February release." Many of the scientists portrayed in the film, including Albert Einstein, did eventually sign the necessary releases, but several of the European scientists refused, including Lisa Meitner of Germany and Sir James Chadwick of England, who declined when the studio refused to incorporate sequences that he had written about himself. Danish Physicist Dr. Niels Bohr, who was portrayed in the film by Belgian actor Victor Francen, at first agreed, but after the film was completed changed his mind, requiring many of his scenes to be cut from the film and his character's name changed to Dr. Marre. Consequently, none of the foreign scientists who contributed to the development of the bomb, with the exception of Drs. Einstein, Fermi and Szilard, appear in the film.

The *Daily Variety* of December 9, 1946, announced "In order to include hitherto undisclosed details of President Truman's historic decision to drop the atom bomb on Japan, Metro-Goldwyn-Mayer's exciting story of the bomb, *The Beginning or the End* has been sent back to the sound stages for an added scene."

The Beginning or the End had a special preview-premiere in Washington, D.C., on February 19, 1947, followed by premieres in London, New York, Sidney and Ottawa the following day. Soon after it went into general release in 138 key cities.

The reviewers seemed almost reluctant to say anything negative about *The Beginning or the End*; they praised the film for its depiction of the scientific scenes and hesitantly panned it for, as the *Daily Variety* reviewer put it, "an inept mixture of atom and hokum." However, the reviewer then quickly qualified his comments by adding, "Unfortunately such world-shaking events as the invention and first use of the atom bomb, spectacular as they

(L-R) Robert Walker, Audrey Totter, Brian Donlevy, Tom Drake and Beverly Tyler in *The Beginning or the End*.

may be, are not necessarily the stuff of which screen drama is made." *The Hollywood Reporter* actually described the film this way: "The Production by Samuel Marx may well be one of the most important ever attempted in Hollywood." This review then added, "Norman Taurog's direction is a major factor in keeping the exposition from dragging." The *New Yorker* reviewer correctly pointed out, "There is a considerable attempt in the picture to justify the bombing of Hiroshima. The actor playing President Truman makes as good a case for the government's side of the matter as anybody could." As usual, Bosley Crowther's review in *The New York Times* didn't bother to mince words: "Metro has made a motion picture which fairly re-enacts the main events in this almost incredible story and which gravely points out the fearfulness thereof. . . But unfortunately, in making this picture, Metro has seemed to confuse the humbleness of its achievement with the magnitude of atomic power. . . For, despite its generally able re-enactments, this film is so laced with sentiment of the silliest and most theatrical nature that much of its impressiveness is marred."

Crowther then managed to put a fine point on the matter by writing a second review the following day. In this review he wrote: "*The Beginning or the End* treats this most grave and urgent subject with mere theatrical solemnity. It is not a new type of motion picture to scan a vast and revolutionizing force in such a way that our poor imaginations may conceive it as the cosmic thing it is. It is not even a scrupulous picture in its limited theatrical frame. It is just a romantic documentation of recent historic events. Let us hope that the screen, our greatest medium for communicating the drama of nature and man's soul, will do a lot better by this subject as we plunge on into this atomic age."

Taurog was ill-served by a pedantic script that spent most of its time either preaching for world peace, or spouting unintelligible scientific jargon. Ayn Rand wasn't the only one guilty of delivering proclamations; in the finale of the film, Robert Walker's character, while arming the bomb on Tinian, prevents a chain reaction explosion by plunging his hands into the bomb's mechanism, thereby exposing himself to a deadly dose of radiation. As he dies he proclaims, "God has not shown us a new way to destroy ourselves. Atomic energy is the hand He has extended to lift us from the ruins of war and lighten the burdens of peace." Taurog's large cast, made up mostly of MGM contractees, performed professionally with the jarring exception of a young starlet named Beverly Tyler, who played Tom Drake's wife and whose unconvincing emotional exhibitions made your teeth ache.

There would be numerous films made by Hollywood about the Atom Bomb, some good and many not so good. MGM tried again with questionable results in 1952 with *Above and Beyond*, the story of Col. Paul Tibbetts who piloted the *Enola Gay*. In 1959, Stanley Kramer produced and directed *On the Beach*, his adaptation of Nevil Shute's apocalyptic vision of the first Atomic War. Many other films were made such as *Fat Man and Little Boy* (1989) and the first of numerous post-apocalyptic films, Arch Oboler's *Five* (1951). Television dealt with the subject in the TV movies *Enola Gay: The Men, the Mission, the Atomic Bomb* (1980) and *Day One* (1989), as well as in many TV documentaries. Whether Bosley Crowther's hopes were ever realized is questionable, but 68 years later mankind is still here and that's something.

Changing Times

With the end of the war, many things began to change in the country. Returning GIs were buying homes and having children; new families required automobiles and washing machines, and people were starting to spend less on entertainment. Inflation was taking hold of the economy and television was making inroads into the nation's homes. Although movie attendance had reached an all-time high in 1946, profits dropped precipitously the following year.

Metro-Goldwyn-Mayer was facing another transition as well: Its profit statements from 1946 to 1947 showed a decline from $18,000,000 to just over $4,000,000, the lowest since 1933. Profits from the foreign market, instead of growing, were shrinking, with Britain, Italy and France's decision to heavily tax large portions of the profits from American releases. The stock market responded and MGM's stock sank to an all-time low, just as the company committed to bond issues totaling $55,000,000. What still lay ahead for the studio was the Supreme Court's anti-trust decision that would force MGM and many other Hollywood studios to sell their theatre chains, and the House Un-American Activities Committee Hearings that would begin in the late summer of 1947 and create havoc within the entire film industry. In addition, Louis B. Mayer's growing obsession with horse racing was a major cause of concern for the Loew's Board of Directors and its chairman, Nicholas Schenck; Mayer was spending too much time at the tracks and not enough at the studio. He was eventually forced to sell his stable of racehorses and in 1948 a new (or rather an old face) was brought on board as vice-president in charge of production.

Dore Schary had moved on from screenwriting to become a producer for David O. Selznick's newly formed independent division, Vanguard Productions. When Selznick folded Vanguard a few years later, Schary moved over to RKO as a producer, but was soon promoted to head of production. Schary and the studio's new owner, Howard Hughes, didn't get along and Schary eventually asked for his release. It was at this point that Schenck and the Loew's Corporation's Board of Directors offered him the job at MGM. 1947 had been a disastrous year for MGM, with one flop after another. Films like *The Sea of Grass, Lady in the Lake, Song of Love* and *Desire Me* failed to even make their costs back at the boxoffice. With Schary's arrival on July 1, 1948, things began to improve, if only temporarily, and not right away.

The two program pictures (the studio's polite synonym for a "B" picture) that Norman Taurog directed during 1947 were no exception; both films were held on the shelf until March of 1948, when they were both tossed into general release within a week of one another, making hardly a ripple in the boxoffice waters. *The Bride Goes Wild*, originally titled *Virtuous*, was an original comedy by Albert Beich that starred June Allyson and Van Johnson, while *Big City* (the third time the studio had used that title) was an adaptation of a story by Miklos Laszlo called *Catherine (Unfinished Symphony)*, and starred the studio's popular but aging child star, Margaret O'Brien. The pseudo sophisticated screwball comedy of *The Bride Goes Wild* seemed more suited to the 1930s than to post-war 1948, but its story was still head and shoulders over the homeless waif being adopted by three diverse bachelors, which was the main plot for *Big City.* Based on a story originally conceived in Europe in the 1930s, its sentimentality was overwhelming. These were the type of films that Louis B. Mayer loved and Dore Schary hated; the tension between the two was already increasing because of another film that Schary had brought with him from RKO, a World War II drama called *Battleground.*

Two of MGM's brightest stars of the war years were beginning to lose some of their radiance by the time they appeared in *The Bride Goes Wild*, but Van Johnson and June Allyson still gave it their all and Albert Beich's screenplay gave them some amusing scenes to play, particularly with a new discovery, child actor "Butch" Jenkins. Hume Cronyn, finishing out his MGM contract, had a chance to exercise his comedy muscles after having played the very solemn Robert Oppenheimer in Taurog's previous film. Una Merkel, playing in her first of what would become five films for Taurog and veteran character actor Lloyd Corrigan added more comedy luster, and red-headed Arlene Dahl added glamour.

Johnson played an alcoholic author of children's books who hates children and literally bumps into Allyson in his publisher's office. She learns of his true feelings about children and threatens to expose him, but Cronyn, Johnson's publisher, tells her that Johnson is actually a widower who drinks because of his grief and his worries over his young son. Cronyn finds an irascible little brat (Jenkins) at a home for boys and stashes him in Johnson's apartment for Allyson to meet. Dahl is Johnson's socialite girlfriend and Richard Derr plays Allyson's stuffy boyfriend. After numerous misunderstandings, childhood pranks and delayed weddings, true love prevails and Allyson ends up in Johnson's arms.

Taurog started filming *The Bride Goes Wild* on June 17, 1947, with veteran Metro cameraman Sid Wagner in charge of the photography. Wagner had been an MGM fixture since arriving in 1938. His first feature was *Boys Town*, and he had worked with Taurog again on *Young Tom Edison*; he'd been nominated twice for Academy Awards for his work on *Northwest Passage* (1940) and *Dragon Seed* (1944). A young man, Wagner was only 46 when he suffered a fatal heart attack in his car on the way to the studio early on Monday morning, July 7, 1947. When word reached the set, Allyson and Johnson were so upset that they went home for the day and filming was suspended. According to Hedda Hopper's reporting of the incident, when someone from the production department asked Taurog to get them back on the set, he supposedly replied, "You ask them, I can't. We all loved the guy." Ray June took over as director of photography. Filming resumed a few days later and was completed in mid-August.

Howard Strickling's MGM publicity department managed to come up with a few inconsequential promotional ideas for the picture, such as having Van Johnson join a long list of stars who had appeared in the forecourt of the Grauman's Chinese Theatre to have their footprints immortalized in cement, and for Arlene Dahl to commentate at a Cole of California swimsuit fashion event at one of the Broadway Department stores.

When *The Bride Goes Wild* finally opened at MGM's Capitol Theatre in New York City on June 3, 1948, Bosley Crowther's *New York Times* review was surprisingly complimentary: "For a movie with as inauspicious a title as *The Bride Goes Wild* ...this patchwork of sentiment is a surprisingly genial little show. And if you'll take it as nonsense entertainment, it will give you a pretty good time. . . In the first place, that title means nothing—absolutely nothing at all. More appropriate to the evident activities would be 'The Picture Goes Wild.'- In the second place—Albert Beich, who is credited with the story... finished his script in a burst of inventive flashes ... which Director Norman Taurog ably got into fast action for the screen." *Variety* was equally complimentary, saying: "*The Bride Goes Wild* is merry fun and nonsense, type of comedy which every class of audience will find hugely diverting and a gem of smart picture making." *The Hollywood Reporter* praised Taurog's "polished directorial job," commenting, "His experienced hand accounts for the artful mixture of broadly slanted comedy situations and gentle heartwarming pathos." Apparently audiences were unimpressed with these glowing reviews and stayed home.

Joe Pasternak had been interested in doing a story with a theme of racial tolerance for some time. He'd purchased Hungarian author Miklos Laszlo's story *Catherine* (*Unfinished Symph*ony) in 1937 while he was still at Universal and had brought the story with him to MGM. In 1942, he had writer Nanette Kutner develop a screen treatment based on an original idea of his and incorporating Laszlo's story, which she called *Brothers of the East Side* and told of an abandoned infant girl who is adopted by a Jewish Cantor, a Protestant minister, and a Catholic policeman. Mary McCarthy, Charles Lawson and Warner Low then wrote additional treatments, with Lawson and Low starting a screenplay, but abandoning it in November of 1945. Another attempt by Anne M. Chapin and Whitfield Cook, now titled *Home Is Where the Heart Is,* was completed on May 9, 1947, and Abel Kandel then did some work on revisions for several weeks. Pasternak then did a cut and paste compilation from all of the scripts and treatments himself, which he continued working on well into the time that *Big City* started filming.

The star of the film, little Margaret O'Brien, was MGM's answer to Shirley Temple and had been making money for the studio ever since she first appeared as a five-year-old war orphan in *Journey for Margaret* (1942). Born Angela Maxine O'Brien on January 15, 1937, she was the only child of circus performer Lawrence O'Brien (who died before she was born) and flamenco dancer Gladys Flores. O'Brien took the first name of her film persona in *Journey for Margaret* as her stage name and quickly became the darling of audiences all over the country. Her most memorable role was "Tootie" in *Meet Me in St. Louis* (1944), in which she sang and danced with Judy Garland. By the time that now ten-year-old Margaret began filming *Big City*, her films were beginning to lose the appeal of such earlier hits as *The Canterville Ghost* (1944), *Our Vines Have Tender Grapes* (1945) and *Three Wise Fools* (1946), a fantasy about three elderly men who befriend a young orphan girl, which bore more than a slight resemblance to the premise of *Big City*. I attempted to contact O'Brien, asking for her memories of working on *Big City*, but she failed to respond, perhaps because, as she had said in her eponymously titled biography, "Although it was pleasant to work on, it wasn't as memorable to me as some of my other films." Taurog, however, did remember little Margaret and told his favorite story about her in an interview he gave to AP correspondent Bob Thomas in 1951. At the beginning of the picture she inquired of Taurog, "When is my big crying scene?" and he replied, "I'll tell you when it comes." When every dramatic scene came up, she'd again ask, "Is this my crying scene?" and Taurog would continue to put her off. When the final scene of the picture was filmed, Taurog turned to Margaret and said, "Okay, now you can have your crying scene." He explained his reasoning to Thomas: "I wanted the audience to cry, not Margaret."

To play O'Brien's three benefactors, MGM signed Robert Preston to play Reverend Phillip Y. Andrews and Danny Thomas as Cantor David Irwin Feldman. George Murphy was called up from the contract ranks to play Officer Patrick O'Donnell. Murphy had already worked with O'Brien in 1946 on *Tenth Avenue Angel*, which was still sitting on the shelf awaiting release and wouldn't reach theaters until February of 1948, one month before *Big City*'s release. The rest of the cast included Butch Jenkins, returning as a neighborhood brat heckling young Margaret, Edward Arnold as the judge who must decide O'Brien's future, Taurog favorite Connie Gilchrist, Karin Booth and German-born actress-singer Lotte Lehmann making one of her rare appearances in a Hollywood film. Also joining the cast was Betty Garrett, fresh from her triumph on Broadway in *Call Me Mister* and making her film debut, receiving "And Introducing to the Screen" billing and having her songs staged by MGM's utility dance director, Stanley Donen, who had also recently arrived at the studio.

When *Big City* was finally released in March of 1948 it received generally negative reviews, with *The New York Times* leading the pack: "At a time when tolerance, an often elusive virtue, is most needed, a film thematically stressing brotherly love should be a shining golden nugget in a world of dross—a veritable needle in a haystack of hate. But *Big City*, which obviously was turned out with much love by the artisans at Metro, displays only the slightest speck of intolerance to justify its story and hardly any reason for the standard and, sometimes maudlin, sentimentality with which it is copiously laced." The Hollywood trade papers were equally unhappy, with *The Hollywood Reporter* saying, "*Big City* has solid boxoffice names and the kind of musical elements which will prove pleasing to great numbers of the motion picture public. That these highly substantial points are not backed up by a more judiciously contrived story is the factor which will militate against the complete success of the production." And *Daily Variety* predicted that, "*Big City* will find it a touch-and-go proposition in the key deluxers." Margaret O'Brien would make only two more films for MGM before leaving the studio in 1949. She would have difficulty in making the transition to adult roles and her career, from that time on, would consist of guest star appearances in television series and the occasional low-budget feature. At one point she would travel to Lima, Peru, where she would live for several years and host (in Spanish) a daily soap opera. While there, she would marry a wealthy businessman and return with him to California. She would ultimately marry and divorce three husbands and have one child, a daughter, by her second husband. In 1972 she would appear in an episode of *Marcus Welby, M.D.* and reunite with Robert Young, with whom she co-starred in *Journey for Margaret*. She still lives in Southern California.

In December of 1949, writer Walter Abbott filed a plagiarism suit against Loew's, Inc. claiming that MGM got the idea for *Big City* from his story "Choir Boy." A February 1953 news article in the *Hollywood Citizen-News* quoted his attorney Edward M. Rose saying that Abbott "received a very good settlement from Loew's, Inc." Considering that the writing credits for the film included the names of five different writers credited for the screenplay, the adaptation and the original story, plus another for additional dialogue, it would appear that Joe Pasternak either cribbed some ideas from Abbott's story, or more likely, the studio paid him off to avoid a nuisance suit.

Words and Music

Shortly after he completed filming retakes for *Big City* on December 30, 1947, Taurog moved over to the Arthur Freed unit to begin work on a project tentatively entitled *The Lives of Rogers and Hart*. Freed, in his constant search for new material, had begun to examine biographical subjects such as Jerome Kern *Till the Clouds Roll By* (1946) and had now decided to give Rogers and Hart's lives the full MGM treatment, complete with as many songs from their songbook as he could secure stars to perform them.

The project began with a letter from attorney Howard E. Reinheimer, dated April 19, 1944, confirming Richard Rogers' interest in the possibilities of a film about his and Lorenz Hart's careers and their music. Dramatist Guy Bolton, who had worked on several previous Freed productions, was hired by MGM on February 14, 1946, and immediately began holding meetings with Rogers. By the end of May, Bolton had completed a story outline and was awaiting Rogers' reaction. In a letter to Freed on May 28, Bolton described his story and discussed his previous conversations with Rogers. It appeared that Rogers had approved the idea of Frank Sinatra portraying Larry Hart, with Gene Kelly as Rogers , but had expressed his concern that Hart's character would overshadow him, because of his being a "bit of a vagabond." At no time in the letter, or in any subsequent discussions, was Hart's homosexuality ever mentioned, although his drinking was always an issue. Bolton officially delivered his treatment to the studio on May 31, 1946, and on September 25, contracts were drawn up between Loew's Incorporated and Richard Rogers and the Lorenz Hart estate. The agreement called for MGM to pay Rogers and the Hart estate the sum of $250,000. MGM also agreed to pay for the music releases; however, if the cost exceeded $60,000, then Rogers and Hart would share equally any excesses up to $40,000.

Beginning toward the end of 1946 and continuing throughout the early months of 1947, writer Jean Holloway began developing a screenplay while holding additional meetings with Richard and Dorothy Rogers, in which she was given access to Rogers' scrapbooks and records. In the early summer of 1947, Loew's executive Sidney Phillips wrote to Arthur Freed suggesting that he might consider hiring Richard Rogers' brother-in-law Ben Feiner Jr. to help. Freed hadn't yet responded to Phillips' letter when he received a note from Richard Rogers in which he made the same request. Feiner, who was Dorothy Rogers' older brother and was portrayed in the film by Richard Quine, was hired to represent Richard Rogers' interests on the project and was given an "Adaptation By" screen credit.

Jean Holloway completed work on her screenplay, dated December 10, 1946, and Isobel Lennart came on board to handle revisions based on Freed's notes. On December 12, Feiner sent some suggested notes to Lennart at her home in Malibu. With his opening paragraph he attempted to soften the blow by writing, "The following suggestions and/or criticisms are entirely Mr. Feiner's and do not necessarily coincide with those of anyone else whosoever living or dead. I might also add that Mr. Feiner quite expects that certain ones (or all) may be tossed out the window." Feiner would deliver additional memos to Freed in which he discussed his impressions of Richard and Dorothy Rogers' personalities as well as that of Larry Hart. Fred Finklehoffe, the co-author of the hit Broadway play *Brother Rat,* who had done such a wonderful job on the screenplay for *Girl Crazy* as well as *Meet Me in St. Louis* (earning an Oscar nomination for Best Screenplay), was hired on December 29 and began work on revising the script. Ben Feiner would continue to sit in on various script conferences with Finklehoffe and Freed. A script conference was held in Freed's office on March 19, 1948, with Norman Taurog joining Finklehoffe, Feiner and Freed, and several other meetings were held over the next few weeks. A copy of the revised script was sent to Mickey Rooney on March 24, 1948.

Rooney hated the script and thought that "the writers had come up with a terrible turkey." Although Rooney matched Hart in stature, there was very little else that they had in common. Lorenz Hart was a closeted homosexual, physically unattractive and an alcoholic, who suffered from deep depression about his inability to find a meaningful relationship with men or women. This darkness would often be expressed in the lyrics of his songs. None of this came close to matching the screen persona of the happy-go-lucky, girl-loving Mickey Rooney. The fact of the matter was that the *Words and Music* screenplay contained very little about either Lorenz Hart or Richard Rogers that was even remotely accurate. Rogers, as written and portrayed by

Tom Drake, was, as critic Bosley Crowther described him, "a solemn and sentimental-soggy thing," more reactive than active; and Rooney's manic-depressive antics as Hart, ending with his melodramatic stumbling through the rain-soaked streets to die in front of the shop where he once bought a pair of elevator shoes, is patently ridiculous, not to mention totally fictitious.

Another script conference was held on April 2, 1948 between Roger Edens, Feiner, Taurog, and Jack Mintz. A series of changes, some minor and some of more consequence, were listed in a covering memo. On April 6 another conference was held to specifically discuss the "Hollywood Sequence" and this time Freed joined the others. There was a great deal of discussion about the ending for the film, with Taurog wanting to shoot a scene in Larry's apartment with Dick and Dorothy going over his things and Dick finding a book of poetry and reading the line, "Out of my great sorrow, I make little songs…" and then dissolving to the tribute and Dick finishing the quote. Freed and Edens voted against this idea, but since the ending was up for grabs, it was decided to shoot the apartment sequence and decide later. A new memo was distributed covering the group's decisions.

Words and Music began rehearsals on March 23, 1948, with Lena Horne reporting to MGM's Rehearsal Hall "B" to work with choreographer Robert Alton on the "Where or When" and "That's Why the Lady Is a Tramp" numbers. Horne's rehearsals would continue for three days, during which time she was also fitted with her wardrobe. On March 26, Taurog shot color wardrobe and makeup tests with Tom Drake, Janet Leigh, and Lena Horne. Horne then continued rehearsals for six more days.

On April 1, Ramon B. Perez and his twin brother Royce, otherwise known as the Blackburn Twins, reported to Rehearsal Hall "C" to begin rehearsing "Where's That Rainbow?" with Ann Sothern and "Thou Swell" with June Allyson. Freed was considering signing the brothers to a term contract, but after performing another specialty dance in *Take Me Out to the Ball Game* (1949), the twins left MGM and continued their careers on television.

Unit manager Dave Friedman published his estimated budget, showing *Words and Music*'s costs to be $2,659,065. Friedman added a note of warning: "Due to musical numbers being created as picture progresses—all estimates pertaining to numbers are approximations."

Mickey Rooney, who had been unhappy with the studio's choice of films since his return from military service the year before, was by his own admission drinking too much and "hanging out with the wrong crowd." He wrote about it in his autobiography: "Drink was poison to me, but I hadn't quite realized it yet. After a few drinks, I'd have a hangover that might last for five days. I started not showing up for work on Mondays." Rooney was scheduled to report to the wardrobe department at 10:30 A.M. on Monday morning

March 29 for fittings and discussions with Taurog and unit manager Friedman. At 9:15 on Monday morning Rooney notified the wardrobe department that he would be in on Tuesday. Taurog had a story conference on that day with Arthur Freed, Roger Edens and Ben Feiner, so the meeting was rescheduled for the following day. A rehearsal was then called for 2:30 P.M. Tuesday April 6 with Rooney, Robert Alton, Tom Drake and Marshall Thompson. On Monday at 6 P.M. Rooney notified the studio that he was in San Francisco. He finally reported for work the following day and rehearsed the "Manhattan" number with Drake and Thompson.

Freed's assistant Lela Simone sent a memo to Freed informing him that the "total pre-recordings for *Words and Music* was one hour and twenty-three minutes." There would be seventeen songs filmed, but not all of them would remain in the final version of the picture.

Two separate units were involved on *Words and Music*; Robert Alton was in charge of filming the musical numbers with Harry Stradling as his cameraman, and Norman Taurog directing the story sequences with Charles Rosher as his cameraman. This arrangement would continue throughout the spring and summer of 1948, with occasional breaks to rehearse each new number before putting it on film. Alton began filming first on April 5, 1948, with both of Lena Horne's numbers in the *Int. Ritz Plaza Roof Garden* set, and Taurog would begin a week later, with sequences in Hart's home.

(L-R) Mickey Rooney, Tom Drake, Betty Garrett and Janet Leigh.

MGM's Scoring Stage (Stage One) was a hectic place on the morning of May 28, 1948. First, Perry Como, who had been borrowed from 20th Century-Fox for the film, was laying down the vocal track for Rogers and Hart's "Blue Room," and following him, Mel Torme, who had made his screen debut a few months earlier in *Good News*, prerecorded "Blue Moon." Ironically, "Blue Moon" was never performed in any of Rogers and Hart's Broadway musicals and was twice cut from MGM films in the 1930s, before having its lyrics rewritten for a third time for Shirley Ross to sing in *Manhattan Melodrama* (1934) as "The Bad in Every Man." At the insistence of Jack Robbins of MGM's publishing company, Hart then wrote new, more romantic lyrics for the song and with its new title "Blue Moon" it became a popular hit.

Later that afternoon, under the supervision of Roger Edens and musical director Lennie Hayton, Mickey and Judy prerecorded "I Wish I Were in Love Again," which would become the pair's last film duet, and at that, it almost didn't happen. Garland's marriage to Vincente Minnelli was in trouble and the emotional turmoil was having its effect on Judy's mental condition. On June 2, she had a 10:00 A.M. makeup call and a 1:00 P.M. shooting call to begin filming the "Hollywood Party" sequence in Larry Hart's Beverly Hills mansion. According to the production manager's report, she was late for makeup, didn't arrive on the set until 3:05 P.M. and was then unable to work. She was sent home and Taurog filmed sections of the party sequence without her. Over the following four days Garland called in ill each morning and Taurog continued filming around her. Garland finally returned to work on June 8 and her portion of the party sequence was completed, including the number with Rooney. In the end, their performance of "I Wish I Were in Love Again" is one of the highlights of the film.

The studio arranged for Richard Rogers and Oscar Hammerstein, along with their wives, to come out on the Super Chief to California for a month in May of 1948 to watch some of the filming and to listen to the prerecorded musical numbers. When he returned to New York, Richard Rogers sent Freed a telegram thanking him and everyone concerned. He was "delighted with the soundtracks—they are all quite brilliant." In November, Rogers apparently viewed some of the filmed musical numbers and wrote to Freed about how happy he was with the orchestrations and with "the performance of these songs by such an extraordinary cast of stars." His enthusiasm wouldn't last.

Words and Music officially wrapped on July 14, 1948, with added scenes and retakes being completed on August 7. Final estimated costs showed that, due to delays in filming and added scenes, it came in $140,000 over budget. The first sneak preview was held on September 12, and the following day a memo with a list of cutting notes was sent to editors Albert Akst and Ferris Webster. The film was too long and several musical numbers were either shortened or eliminated completely. A love scene between Mickey Rooney and Betty Garrett needed to be rewritten, and the preview audience's reaction indicated that Judy Garland's appearance in the "Hollywood Party" sequence was too brief and another song was to be added. A list of seven songs, one of which was "Johnny One-Note," was included in the memo.

On September 9, 1948 Jack Mintz turned in a revised Sc # 82 in which Betty Garrett's character, Peggy, tells Hart why she can't marry him. When production was reopened for retakes, Taurog shot this scene on September 27. Taurog and Robert Alton then filmed the "Johnny One-Note" number with a much healthier Judy Garland on October 1 on the reconstructed Beverly Hills mansion set. In fact Garland had gained so much weight that her gown had to be redesigned in an attempt to hide the extra pounds. Many of the critics would later make note of the differences in her appearance. Garland would go on to make *In the Good Old Summertime* (1949), followed by *Summer Stock* (1950), which, after thirteen years and twenty-seven pictures, would sadly be her final film for MGM.

Taurog's five-year contract had expired on August 9, 1948, and the studio's new offer of a week-to-week arrangement with his salary reduced from $3,000 a week to $2,000 was, to say the least, an unpleasant surprise. Nevertheless, Taurog was no fool; he could see the drastic changes that were taking place all over Hollywood, and knew that he had little choice in the matter. Not wanting to leave his home base of the past ten years and believing in the old proverb, "A bird in the hand is worth two in the bush," he reluctantly accepted an arrangement that would continue for more than fifteen months, before MGM would finally present him with a new one-year contract.

Words and Music opened at the Radio City Music Hall on December 9, 1948, and had the third highest non-holiday MGM opening day for the year with $19,224. By the end of the week it had earned $138,546 and at the end of six weeks it had earned $691,747 in New York alone. In Los Angeles it opened in three theaters and earned a total of $38,034 for the weekend. It ultimately was held over for two weeks. The Motion Picture Herald announced in its year-end report that *Words and Music* had earned $1,642,000.

The Hollywood Reporter's review stated: "Norman Taurog's direction, prescribed as it is by the script, is filled nevertheless with Taurog touches of clever business and overall warmth. He is most successful in blending the action into production sequences." Howard Barnes of the *New York Herald Tribune* felt that the film was "grandiloquent and gaudy…it is both silly and saccharine." Bosley Crowther (*New York Times*) felt it was a "patently juvenile specimen of musical biography, as far from the facts in its reporting as it is standard in its sentimental plot." He went on to single out Mickey Rooney's death scene as "…among the most horribly inadequate and embarrassing things this reviewer has ever watched." However, *Variety* called it a "smash in every sense of the word—a lavish, pretentious, star-studded musical and lasting tribute to Lorenz Hart and Richard Rogers." Taurog was given a nice plug: "Norman Taurog directed the mellow Fred Finklehoffe screenplay with a knowing hand, never allowing the story to take itself too seriously for any length of time."

As for Richard Rogers' reaction to *Words and Music*, he is quoted as saying, "They had a story written that at times impinged on the truth, but not very often." Rogers' believed that MGM's only interest in doing their life story was to get access to the Rogers and Hart music library. Years later, when author Hugh Fordin requested an interview with Rogers for his book *MGM's Greatest Musicals*, he received a rather curt letter in reply from Rogers' secretary, Rita M. Chambers, in which she quoted Rogers as saying, "I knew Arthur Freed but not very well and did not work with him closely. I am afraid there is no interview with me on Arthur Freed."

The Sound of a Gavel and the Voice of a Tenor

Patricia Taurog, Norman and Julie's fifteen-year-old daughter, was not getting along with her mother; it was a situation not uncommon with a teenager beginning to assert her independence. Patricia was smarting at her mother's insistence that she be chaperoned on dates and had moved into her father's home at 606 Stone Canyon Road in Bel-Air, where Norman and Sue were more lenient with her. In late September of 1947, Patricia, accompanied by her father, went to court with a petition to have Norman appointed as her guardian. Julie Taurog made a surprise appearance and informed Superior Judge Newcomb Condee that she had just retained an attorney to contest the proceedings and needed more time to prepare the case. The judge put the hearing off until mid-December and ordered court investigators to look into the matter and report back to him. Judge Condee also allowed Patricia to continue living with Norman and Sue until the new hearing date.

On December 18, 1947, Norman and Patricia returned to Judge Condee's courtroom for the hearing. Julie was there with her attorney, but as it turned out she had decided not to contest Patricia's request. According to a reporter's first-hand account in the *Los Angeles Times*, Julie wept softly at the counsel table while Patricia told Judge Condee that she preferred to live with her father. Judge Condee stated that under California law a child beyond the age of 14 had the right to nominate a guardian, and the court was bound to accept the nomination unless the guardian could be proven unfit. According to the county's probation report, no such finding was found for either parent. The *Time*s article went on to quote the following conversation, with Judge Condee asking Patricia, "You are quite sure that this is the way you want it?" and Patricia responding, after glancing at her mother, who was daubing at her eyes with her handkerchief, "Yes, I am sure." Judge Condee granted the petition after advising Patricia to be more attentive to her mother, even though she was now legally permitted to reside with her father. Patricia continued living with Norman and Sue Taurog until her marriage six years later.

In December of 1948, as an investment, Taurog became a partner in a camera shop on Sepulveda Boulevard in Westchester, not to far from the Los Angeles International Airport. Hedda Hopper dutifully reported, "Van Johnson, Esther Williams, and Claude Jarman were on hand to help Norman Taurog unveil his new camera shop in Westchester." Taurog would remain an owner until the late seventies, when he and Sue would sell the shop and their home in Beverly Hills and move to Palm Desert. That same month, Taurog was back in court contesting an IRS decision that the property settlement in his divorce from Julie was a gift and not, as he claimed, a division of property. The IRS was claiming that taxes were due and delinquent on $118,181.52. Because Taurog had agreed to and signed off on the division of property, as his lawyer had recommended, before the divorce degree was granted, the court ruled that the amount being contested was indeed a gift and Taurog was responsible for the delinquent taxes.

Taurog's legal woes were still not over. In February of 1949, he and Julie were back in court, with Julie contesting the reduction in alimony payments since Patricia had moved in with her father. Julie informed the court that Taurog had agreed, at the time of their divorce, to pay her $20,000 a year for her and Patricia's support, but had decreased payments since he had become Patricia's legal guardian, claiming he now took care of Patricia's expenses and that his salary had been reduced. No resolution was reached that day, and in fact, the alimony battle would drag on for over three years before Norman and Julie reached an out-of-court settlement in July of 1950 in which she agreed to have her alimony cut in half.

Shortly after completing *Words and Music*, Taurog moved from the Freed unit back to the Pasternak unit and began preparing a film that was called at that time, *Music in Their Hearts*. It was to star a new discovery that Louis B. Mayer had heard singing at a Hollywood Bowl concert and had signed to a contract. His name was Alfredo Cocozza, an ex-GI who, after studying and making his debut in *The Merry Wives of Windsor* at the Tanglewood/Berkshire Music Festival, changed his name to Mario Lanza. Born in Philadelphia, on January 31, 1921, Lanza-Cocozza's career was interrupted by World War II, when he joined the Army Air Corps and was assigned to Special Services. He toured in the wartime production of *Winged Victory* and was part of the ensemble in the 1944 film version. Upon his discharge from the Army, Lanza returned to his singing career and appeared in numerous concerts all over the country, eventually being hired to replace tenor Jan Peerce on the CBS radio program *Great Moments in Music*. He was signed by

RCA Victor and made a few test recordings. Somehow one of these recordings came into the possession of Ida Koverman, who played it for her boss. It was shortly after this that Mayer saw Lanza perform at the Hollywood Bowl and, after a successful screen test, signed him to a limited contract, paying him $750 a week. Lanza was allowed to continue his concert appearances and travelled with bass George London and soprano Frances Yeend, appearing in 86 concerts throughout the United States, Canada and Mexico during the remainder of 1947 and early 1948.

In January of 1949, Lanza began his first film for MGM, now titled *That Midnight Kiss*. His co-star was a young coloratura soprano, Kathryn Grayson, who had been under contract to MGM since 1941 and had already starred with Gene Kelly in *Anchors Aweigh* (1945) and Frank Sinatra in *It Happened in Brooklyn* (1947). Grayson, a Southern girl from Winston-Salem, North Carolina, was born Zelma Kathryn Elisabeth Hedrick on February 9, 1922. She studied voice with Frances Marshall of the Chicago Civic Opera and was signed by RCA Red Seal records when she was only fifteen years old. Mayer heard her sing, signed her to a long-term contract and had her study acting with the studio's drama coach Lillian Burns, before placing her in her first film opposite Mickey Rooney, *Andy Hardy's Private Secretary* (1941). Her most recent film was *The Kissing Bandit* (1948) with Frank Sinatra; she later claimed that this was her least favorite film and for good reason. *The Kissing Bandit* was one of MGM's most famous flops.

Kathryn Grayson and Mario Lanza in *That Midnight Kiss*.

The trailer for *That Midnight Kiss* proclaimed, "Two voices that belong together," and it was certainly true. Unfortunately, even though they would make a second film, Mario Lanza's relationship with Kathryn Grayson was strained at best, as she considered him coarse and ill-mannered. She was offended that he mauled her in their love scenes and that his breath often reeked of garlic. Lanza was a crude and arrogant man whom Taurog detested. He once told me that Lanza would go behind the flats to urinate, rather than take the time to leave the stage and go to the men's room. According to Taurog, Lanza often smelled as if he needed a bath, was intractable and undisciplined with a giant ego, constantly complained and possessed a foul temper. Lanza loved to eat, a problem that caused him to gain considerable weight and, like Elvis Presley twenty years later, this forced him to go on crash diets to prepare for each new film assignment. Unlike Presley, who never showed anger on the set, Lanza's dieting would affect his temperament and he would become even more unpleasant to his fellow workers. Johnny Green, who was the head of MGM's music department at the time and worked with Lanza on his opera sequences, was quoted as saying that Lanza felt insecure because he hadn't performed more operatic roles before coming to Hollywood. Lanza, who had barely finished high school, had difficulties handling his finances and was frequently short of funds, and this frustration added to his unpleasant demeanor on the set. He always felt that people were trying to take advantage of him and this situation would only grow worse as Lanza's fame increased.

Taurog began filming *That Midnight Kiss* on January 10, 1949, while still on his week-to-week arrangement with the studio. Joe Pasternak gave the script by Bruce Manning and Tamara Hovey a good solid cast of MGM contract players that included Jose Iturbi and his sister Amparo, Keenan Wynn, J. Carrol Naish, Jules Munshin, Marjorie Reynolds, Arthur Treacher, Thomas Gomez and Ethel Barrymore, who had only recently signed an exclusive contract with the studio and was appearing in her second film after *The Great Sinner* (1949).

That Midnight Kiss was previewed for the press at the Village Theatre in Westwood, California, on August 17, and the reaction was better than hoped for. *The Hollywood Reporter*'s opening paragraph said it all: "A bright, new singing star, Mario Lanza, is introduced in *That Midnight Kiss*, and his presence in the cast, as much as any factor, will account for lively boxoffice interest in the Joe Pasternak, Technicolor musical." When *That Midnight Kiss* had its world premiere in Lanza's home town of Philadelphia on September 2, 1949, it grossed $24,500 in its second week, which better than doubled Pasternak's previous hit of 1948, *Luxury Liner* ($11,000). The New York opening on September 22 brought somewhat mixed reviews, with Kate Cameron of the *Daily News* referring to the film as a "light Cinderella theme, in reverse," that was "amusingly handled by director Norman Taurog." *Motion Picture*

Herald acknowledged, "Producer Joe Pasternak gave the production his customary proficient handling, utilizing big budget to eye-filling advantage, and Norman Taurog's direction is successful in making the characters plausible and frequently amusing." The *New York Times'* Bosley Crowther, who rarely had a kind word to say about anyone or any film, admitted that Mario Lanza's voice had "quality and warmth and he had a very nice personality. We'll have to wait to see how he can act. A slight disposition to be too radiant and follow Mickey Rooney's footwork style betrays his youthful inexperience. No doubt he will improve."

The Hollywood opening in October brought out the hometown cheerleaders, with Sara Hamilton of the *Los Angeles Examiner* borrowing the opening line from bucolic radio news reporter Gabriel Heatter's opening exclamation on his nightly radio show: "Ah yes, there's good news tonight at the Los Angeles, Fox Wilshire and Egyptian Theaters, where *That Midnight Kiss* is packing them in. Mario Lanza, a young man with an out-of-this-world voice, is the 'news,' and maybe you think MGM isn't clapping its patty-cakes over this find." Edwin Schallert in the *Los Angeles Times* echoed these sentiments, with his opening paragraph proclaiming, "Mario Lanza in *That Midnight Kiss* shows every indication of becoming a new screen sensation. In personality and in song he achieves a brilliant first bid for fame... He has spirit and naturalness in his acting. His operatic numbers received unusual applause."

Thrilled with the success of *That Midnight Kiss*, the studio rewarded Lanza with a $10,000 bonus and ordered Pasternak and Taurog to immediately begin preparing a follow-up film for Lanza and Kathryn Grayson. RCA Victor spent $40,000 to promote the release of an album of Lanza singing ballads and operatic arias from the film, and his rendition of "Che Gelida Manina" from *La boheme* was recognized as the Operatic Recording of the Year by the National Record Critics Association of the United States. But the clock was ticking; Mario Lanza had only four years left before he and MGM would part ways.

A new producer had arrived on the MGM lot and his reputation had preceded him. Val Lewton, onetime story executive for David O. Selznick, had made a name for himself producing stylized, low-budget horror films for RKO Studios. Films such as *Cat People* (1942) and *I Walked with a Zombie* (1943), made for practically nothing, had become profit bonanzas at the boxoffice. Now he was at MGM and those expecting him to continue his trend of baroque horror subjects were disappointed when the title of his first production was announced as *Please Believe Me*. As it turned out, the title referred to an original comedy by Nathaniel Curtis that was to star British actress Deborah Kerr and be directed by Norman Taurog. It was Lewton's hope that producing a comedy would prove to the industry that he was capable of producing more diversified subjects than just horror films.

Lobby card for *Please Believe Me*.

The story had Kerr playing Alison Kirbe, a quiet little English lass who learns that a lonely soldier she had befriended during the war had died and left her his Texas ranch. On the ship sailing to America to claim her inheritance, Alison meets three attractive young men, Terry (Robert Walker), a gambler heavily in debt, Jeremy (Peter Lawford), a millionaire playboy, and Matt (Mark Stevens), an attorney trying to keep Jeremy out of trouble. A fourth passenger is Vincent (James Whitmore), a sleazy attorney who draws Matt's suspicion that he and Alison are working a scam. By the time the ship docks, Alison, who is flattered by all of the attention she is getting, decides to remain in New York for a week. Further complications include the discovery that Alison's land is worthless, with Matt convinced that she is out to swindle Jeremy, and Alison unwittingly running up a gambling debt at Lucky Reilly's (J. Carrol Naish) club while trying to help Terry pay off his debt. Everything is eventually sorted out and all three men propose, with Alison enthusiastically accepting Matt's offer.

Kerr's co-stars were lower echelon leading men, but still very personable. Peter Lawford, who had been under contract at MGM since co-starring with June Allyson in *Good News* (1947) and Esther Williams in *On an Island with You* (1948), had played second leads in *Easter Parade* (1948), *Little Women* (1949) and *The Red Danube* (1949). Mark Stevens, who had garnered industry attention the previous year co-starring with Olivia de Havilland in *The Snake Pit* (1948), had just finished out his Twentieth Century-Fox contract playing opposite William Powell and Betsy Drake in *Dancing in the Dark* (1949) before travelling down Motor Avenue to MGM Studios to appear in *Please Believe Me.*

Robert Walker was the one big question mark. He had made only one film since completing *Till the Clouds Roll By* in May of 1946 and that was a loanout to Universal for *One Touch of Venus* in February and March of 1948. The tragedy of Walker's life is well known; shattered by his divorce from Jennifer Jones, he began drinking to excess. He once said, "My personal life has been completely wrecked by David Selznick's obsession for my wife. What can you do to fight such a powerful man?" Walker impulsively married and then quickly separated from Barbara Ford, John Ford's daughter. In December of 1948 he was arrested for drunkenness and shortly thereafter suffered a nervous breakdown. A decision was made by his father and by Dore Schary (who agreed that the studio would cover all expenses) that he be committed to the Menninger Psychiatric Clinic in Topeka, Kansas, for treatment. After a six-month stay Walker was released in May of 1949 and returned to California, anxious to see his two sons and to resume his career. He readily accepted the role of Terry Keith in *Please Believe Me*, and although still fragile, his humorous performance helped to make the role of a con artist, who is after heiress Kerr's presumed fortune, more sympathetic.

Of the other cast members, James Whitmore, after being nominated for a Tony award for his Broadway debut performance in 1947 as Tech Sergeant Harold Evans in *Command Decision*, was making his second MGM film after his Oscar- Golden Globe-nominated performance in *Battleground*. Dore Schary was so impressed with Whitmore's performance as the grizzled master sergeant in *Battleground* that he placed him under contract and even tried starring him in a few films. Whitmore was better suited as a character type where he functioned best supporting the stars, as he did so well in *Please Believe Me*. In later years, Whitmore would travel around the country in a series of one-man shows about Mark Twain, Will Rogers and Harry Truman, and it was in this last production that he received his Best Actor Academy Award nomination when it was filmed in 1975. Another tried-and-true character actor was J. Carrol Naish. Creating his second of three consecutive screen characterizations for Taurog, he would return in *The Toast of New Orleans*. Others offering strong support included Spring Byington, George Cleveland and Ian Wolfe.

Please Believe Me had its press preview at the Egyptian Theatre in Hollywood on March 3, 1950, and opened nationally in May. It received generally good reviews from the trade press, with *The Hollywood Reporter* telling its readers "*Please Believe Me* is a charming comedy mix-up with a collection of stars to give it boxoffice punch, a light, frothy story to entertain, and some very bright gags to provide laugh content." *Weekly Variety* took a swipe at the writing while managing to give the director a compliment: "Norman Taurog's direction manages considerable smoothness in unraveling the erratic story twists." And *Daily Variety* reported that, "Metro's *Please Believe Me* is a pleasing comedy despite a super-abundance of characters and more plot complications than necessary. . . Norman Taurog's direction of the Val Lewton production is smooth as it winds and wends its way to an inevitable conclusion." As usual, it was up to the *New York Times* to come down hard on everyone and everything: "In producing *Please Believe Me* the powers over at Metro must have been firmly convinced that the paying customers were anxious to view Deborah Kerr being pursued by three swains instead of one, the standard for the course. And, while the race is a mite more complex than the normal, the chuckles and amour distilled from this item ...could have been handled, it seems, by fewer and less noted operatives. For this romantic comedy is much ado about a tissue-thin tale, which, at its best, is only mildly diverting."

Please Believe Me turned out to be the only production of Val Lewton's career at MGM and he left shortly after completing it for a new arrangement at Universal, where he produced only one film, *Apache Drums* (1951), before his untimely death of a heart attack on March 14, 1951, at the age of 46.

Robert Walker would deliver two more memorable performances, in Alfred Hitchcock's *Strangers on a Train* (1951) and Leo McCarey's anti-communist screed *My Son John* (1952) before succumbing to what many thought to be a doctor's fatal error on August 28, 1951. Suffering from an emotional relapse, he was being treated by several psychiatrists at his home and was given an injection of sodium amytal. He lapsed into a coma and expired before emergency crews could revive him. It was later discovered that he had been drinking and the alcohol, mixed with the amobarbital, caused his death. Robert Walker would have celebrated his 33 rd birthday on October 13, 1951.

Mario, O'Malley and Malone

With the unexpected success of *That Midnight Kiss*, MGM's sales department was anxious for another Mario Lanza film to be in theaters as quickly as possible to capitalize on his popularity. Joe Pasternak had two writers working on stories with various titles, including *Kiss of Fire*, *The Weekend is Yours* and *Serenade to Suzette.* By the time Taurog returned to the Pasternak unit, the final draft by Sy Gomberg and George Wells had been retitled *The Toast of New Orleans*.

The distinguished Broadway choreographer Eugene Loring, who had been under contract to MGM for a brief period in the early '40s as a choreographer and actor, and had staged the impressive Fred Astaire-Lucille Bremer production numbers in both *Ziegfeld Follies* (1945) and *Yolanda and the Thief* (1945), returned to the studio to stage the dances in *The Toast of New Orleans*. Georgie Stoll and Johnny Green supervised the music. Nicholas Brodszky, who had been working in England for several years, returned and with Sammy Cahn wrote the songs, one of which, "Be My Love," was nominated for an Academy Award as Best Original Song and would become the first of Lanza's million-selling singles. Brodszky and Cahn would repeat their success two years later with their title tune for Lanza's fourth film, *Because You're Mine* (1952). The huge New Orleans set by Cedric Gibbons and Daniel B. Cathcart, which took up three connecting sound stages, was photographed by three-time Academy Award nominee William Snyder, who would still be photographing musical numbers on MGM sound stages in 1980 for the hit television series *Fame*.

David Niven was signed to play the opera director and Kathryn Grayson's mentor, Jacques Riboudeaux, and J. Carrol Naish returned as Lanza's uncle Nicky, an inflated performance that grew tiresome very quickly. Others in the cast included an eighteen-year-old Rita Moreno, making her first of several MGM musicals; James Mitchell, another new arrival from Broadway, where he had won the Walter Donaldson Award for his performance in the original production of *Brigadoon*; Sig Arno as the apoplectic mayor of Bayou Minou; Romo Vincent, reprising Thomas Gomez's rotund tenor from the previous film; and the ubiquitous MGM contract player Clinton Sundberg as Niven's assistant.

The happy-go-lucky character that Lanza portrayed in *The Toast of New Orleans* belied the truth. Success had gone to Lanza's head and he was even more intractable and unpleasant during the filming than he had been on *That Midnight Kiss*. In addition to his over-eating, he had now added alcohol to his addictions and the combination caused his 5'7" frame to blow up like a balloon. By the time he reported to the set he had managed to lose some of the extra weight and was able to stuff himself into his costumes, but on screen he still looked considerably heavier than he had in his initial film.

Taurog began filming *The Toast of New Orleans* in late December of 1949, shortly after MGM had handed him a new one-year contract with a slight raise in his weekly salary to $2,500. Taurog managed to keep his leading lady from killing her co-star and to keep his own temper under control and completed filming the dialogue scenes, as well as the operatic sequences, by early March of 1950. Lanza went off immediately to begin preparing for his role as Enrico Caruso in *The Great Caruso* (1951) and Taurog began preparing his next film, *Mrs. O'Malley and Mr. Malone* (1950). Grayson's next film would be one of her most successful, the 1951 remake of Edna Ferber's *Show Boat,* with a musical score by Jerome Kern and Oscar Hammerstein, II.

RCA Victor expressed interest in producing an album with both Lanza and Grayson singing duets from the film's soundtrack. Emanuel "Manie" Sacks of RCA Victor wrote a letter to Pasternak, suggesting that such an album would be a great promotion for *The Toast of New Orleans*. The problem was that Grayson was now under contract to MGM Records and not contractually available, and RCA wouldn't reciprocate by allowing Lanza to record an album with Grayson on MGM records. Several letters passed back and forth between Sacks and Pasternak, but neither MGM nor RCA would compromise and the album never materialized.

The final post-production work was completed in early August and *The Toast of New Orleans* was presented to the industry press with a special preview held at MGM Studios on the night of August 17, 1950. Specially printed programs containing the names of the cast and crew members were handed out to the press representatives and then everyone settled back with anticipation as the houselights were dimmed. The studio's high expectations were realized, as the various reviews indicated. Edwin Schallert of the *Los Angeles Times* wrote, "*The Toast of New Orleans* will afford the expected enjoy-

David Niven, Kathryn Grayson and Mario Lanza in *The Toast of New Orleans.*

ment to devotees of MGM musicals and particularly of those supervised by Joe Pasternak… Norman Taurog directed with more finesse than usual using a routine screenplay by Sy Gomberg and George Wells." *Variety* showed more enthusiasm, saying, "*The Toast of New Orleans* looms as a likely loot-gatherer for Leo, thanks to lighthearted plot, smartly projected new tunes and geared-to-the-popular-taste operatic arias, and the pleasing presence of Kathryn Grayson and Mario Lanza, neither of whom has ever shown to such advantage." *The Hollywood Reporter* was equally enthusiastic: "[T]he production of Joe Pasternak thrills the ear even as it delights the eye with exquisite New Orleans backgrounds. The story is slight, but it holds attention largely because of the interesting romantic characterizations of a crude fisherman with a God-given voice and an elegant, polished operatic diva. Most of the complications are played for fun—thus giving *New Orleans* pep and tempo. Norman Taurog puts the players charmingly through their paces and sees to it that the action is kept fluid and lively." When the film opened in New York on September 29 even Thomas M. Pryor of the *New York Times* managed to spread a few kind words in amongst his criticism: "[This] is a case where the soundtrack is triumphant, for the comedy-romance follows a formula that is devoid of novelty or sparkle. But it is amazing how bright a picture can be spun from tarnished words and situations when the physical qualities of the production, the photography and sets, really enhance the atmosphere of the story. Producer Joe Pasternak, an old hand at creating an illusion of gaiety, has turned the trick again... with the assistance of Norman Taurog's direction, by breathing life into an inanimate script." The *New York Mirror* also liked the film with Frank Quinn praising it as "a refreshing package of melody and merriment... *The Toast of New Orleans* is pleasing and melodic. We liked it."

The Toast of New Orleans was a smashing success, exceeding by far the grosses of *That Midnight Kiss*. Lanza's next film *The Great Caruso* was an even greater success with the public, but his popularity brought criticism from some music critics who began faulting his performances. A *Time* Magazine cover article, published on August 6, 1951, criticized Lanza's singing style and mocked his weight problem, even attacking his intellect and personal habits. "Lanza, who once weighed close to 300 lbs peeled down to a svelte 169 for his first movie, 1949's *That Midnight Kiss*; that time Director Norman Taurog kept a scale on the set and weighed him in like a jockey every morning. . . Lanza's idea of dieting, based on his own theory that proteins can add no weight, is to pile chicken legs, half-pound chunks of rare steak and a mound of barbecued kidneys on his plate, devour them and then heap on a second helping. For breakfast, he holds down to a steak and four to six eggs."

In his next film, a minor entry called *Because You're Mine* in which he played an opera singer who is drafted into the army, Lanza so mistreated his co-star, Broadway performer Doretta Morrow, that she walked off the set on several occasions and left Hollywood as soon as the picture was completed, never to return. Lanza's weight fluctuated throughout the filming to such a degree that in some of his scenes he could barely fit into his uniform. Rumors of his boorish behavior were beginning to be reported by the press, with Hollywood columnist Sheilah Graham noting in one of her columns, "Now it's Norman Taurog who isn't talking to Mario Lanza. Norman directed Mario's first two pictures." *Because You're Mine* was a moderate success, but the public was growing tired of the formulaic scripts and the studio decided it was time to make a change.

Lanza's next film was to be a remake of *The Student Prince* with his co-star from *The Great Caruso*, Ann Blyth, and Lanza was told that it was imperative that he lose weight for the film. Lanza went on a crash diet and was in fighting shape when he reported to the studio to begin recording the soundtrack. His director was Curtis Bernhardt, and according to Hollywood legend, there was friction between them from the start. Bernhardt was supposedly present on the scoring stage when Lanza was recording one of Sigmund Romberg's songs and complained to Lanza that his performance displayed "too much passion." Lanza was furious and supposedly went to Dore

Schary, demanding that Bernhardt be taken off the picture. Another version, validated by articles in *The Hollywood Reporter* and other trade publications, reported that Lanza failed to show up for the first day of filming on August 20, 1952, and MGM suspended him, threatened legal action and prevented him from appearing on his weekly NBC radio program. Lanza reported for wardrobe tests on August 22 and the suspension was lifted; however he failed again to report to the set when filming was scheduled to resume on August 25 and was immediately suspended again. By the beginning of September it was clear that Lanza, who had failed to report for work a third time, wasn't returning and the studio abandoned the film. MGM-Loew's Incorporated sued Lanza for more than $5,000,000 for breach of contract. The suit was finally settled when Lanza gave permission for his vocal recordings to be used in a revived version of *The Student Prince* starring Edmund Purdom and Ann Blyth, with Purdom lip-syncing to Lanza's voice. Ironically, this new film would not be directed by Curtis Bernhardt but by Richard Thorpe, who had directed Lanza in *The Great Caruso.*

I've often wondered whether there might not be a self-destructive chromosome in the DNA of some creative personalities. Perhaps that would explain why so many destroy themselves while they are still young, with their careers not fully realized. Just as in the case of Robert Walker, Judy Garland and Elvis Presley, Mario Lanza, severely depressed and beset by the cost of his lavish lifestyle and a series of bad investments, continued drinking to excess, which, along with his overeating binges, began to seriously affect his health. He would make a few more films, several in Europe, but would never again reach the heights that he achieved with his first few MGM films. Lanza suffered a mild heart attack in Rome in August of 1959 and upon his recovery began a controversial sleep treatment diet program in preparation for a new concert tour. He would die from a pulmonary embolism while undergoing this treatment on October 7, 1959, at the young age of 38, a mere twelve years from the time he had first arrived at MGM.

The first film that Dore Schary chose to star James Whitmore in, after his outstanding supporting performance in John Huston's *The Asphalt Jungle* (1950), was something of an anomaly. In *The Next Voice You Hear...* (1950), God spoke on the radio to everybody in the world—not exactly your everyday film fare. Whitmore and the future First Lady, Nancy Davis, did a credible job of portraying Mr. and Mrs. Average American, but the message-laden plot overwhelmed them and the film garnered little attention or much in the way of boxoffice returns. For Whitmore's next starring vehicle, Schary chose the writings of well-known mystery authors Craig Rice and Stuart Palmer and their short story "Once Upon a Mystery (The Loco Motive)" that appeared in the October 1950 issue of *Ellery Queen Mystery Magazine.* Rice was the nom de plume for Georgiana Ann Randolph Craig, author of comedy-mystery stories featuring John Joseph Malone, a hard-drinking small-time lawyer. Palmer had been successful for many years with mystery stories featuring Hildegarde Withers, a spinster schoolteacher and amateur detective. Both writers had previously written for Hollywood, with Rice's Malone character appearing in an adaptation of her mystery *Having Wonderful Crime* (1945) for RKO as well as an unsold pilot for ABC Television in 1950. Rice had also written the screenplays for two of the RKO *Falcon* series. Stuart Palmer's Hildegarde Withers was portrayed for RKO by character actress Edna May Oliver in three adaptations of his books, and then by actresses Helen Broderick and ZaSu Pitts in three more films. Palmer himself wrote screenplays for three of the *Bulldog Drummond* series for Paramount, as well as collaborating with Rice on the screenplay for *The Falcon's Brother* (1942). Rice and Palmer collaborated again on the *Ellery Queen* magazine story, in which they involved Malone and Withers in a murder that took place on a train. However, due to problems securing the film rights to the Withers character, screenwriter William Bowers was forced to change her name to Hattie O'Malley and make her a cantankerous widow from Montana who had won a radio quiz contest and was travelling with her young niece to New York City to collect her prize.

William Bowers was as big a character as any of his screen creations. A good-natured two-time Oscar nominee who enjoyed a good joke and shar-

James Whitmore and Marjorie Main in *Mrs. O'Malley and Mr. Malone.*

ing a cocktail or two with his friends, Bowers had an irreverent sense of humor that frequently showed up in the hard-hitting dramas that he wrote. After working as a newspaper reporter in Long Beach, California, his first screen credit was the Bob Hope comedy *My Favorite Spy* (1942), but his greatest claim to fame came seven years later for his screenplay of the classic Gregory Peck western, *The Gunfighter* (1950) and another western, *The Sheepman* (1958), which were his two Academy Award nominations. Bowers wrote several film noir thrillers, *Cry Danger* (1951), *Split Second* (1953) and *5 Against the House* (1955), and in later years, the successful comedies, *Imitation General* (1958), *Advance to the Rear* (1964) and *Support Your Local Sheriff* (1969), for which he was also the producer.

James Whitmore's co-star in *Mrs. O'Malley and Mr. Malone* was the venerable character actress Marjorie Main, who was known to be a trifle unusual. Although her husband had died in 1935 after fourteen years of marriage, Main was known to go off in a corner of a film set and speak with her dead husband, asking his blessing of the scene they were about to shoot. She would then return to the set and announce to the director and the other cast members that her husband approved of the scene. Margaret O'Brien wrote in her autobiography of seeing Main set a place for her husband at the location lunch table. Despite her eccentricities, she was a born scene-stealer and a perfect choice to play the boisterous Hattie Malone.

Main had made her Broadway debut in January of 1928 in a religious-themed play starring Pauline Lord, *Salvation* that ran for only 31 performances. Her first big success was in a Jerome Kern-Oscar Hammerstein, II musical called *Music in the Air* that opened at the Alvin Theatre on November 8, 1932, and ran for 342 performances before the Depression forced it to close in September of 1933. Hollywood called and Marjorie came out to the Coast to recreate her role in Fox Films' version of *Music in the Air* (1934) starring Gloria Swanson and John Boles. She then returned to Broadway to appear as "Babyface" Martin's mother, as part of the large ensemble cast in Sidney Kingsley's drama *Dead End*. Main enjoyed a 14- month run that was interrupted only by her leaving the play to appear with another ensemble cast in Clare Boothe's comedy *The Women* in December of 1936. She was again called away in April of 1937 to recreate her original role in Samuel Goldwyn and William Wyler's film version of *Dead End*. While she was waiting to begin filming *Dead End*, Goldwyn had Marjorie play the small role of Barbara Stanwyck's mother in *Stella Dallas* (1937). Main decided to remain in Hollywood and ended up appearing in four more films that year and twelve films the following year. She worked off and on at MGM beginning in 1938 and was placed under contract to the studio in 1940, when she was hired as a possible replacement for the late Marie Dressler. She co-starred in five films with Wallace Beery, played opposite Judy Garland in *Meet Me in St. Louis* (1944) and *The Harvey Girls* (1946), and had been nominated for a Supporting Actress Oscar in 1947 when MGM loaned her to Universal to play Phoebe "Ma" Kettle in *The Egg and I.* MGM ended up sharing her contract with Universal, who immediately exploited her popularity in two films with bucolic themes, *The Wistful Widow of Wagon Gap* (1947) with Abbott and Costello and *Feudin', Fussin, and A-Fightin'* (1948) with Donald O'Connor and her *Egg and I* co-star Percy Kilbride. Universal ultimately starred Main and Kilbride in seven *Ma and Pa Kettle* films between 1949 and 1955, and after Kilbride became ill during the filming of *Ma and Pa Kettle at Waikiki* (1955), made two more, *The Kettles in the Ozarks* (1956), with Arthur Hunnicutt playing Pa Kettle's brother Sedge, and *The Kettles on Old MacDonald's Farm* (1957), with Parker Fennelly in the Pa Kettle role. After this film, Marjorie Main retired from films at the age of 67 and lived another eighteen years, before succumbing to lung cancer on April 10, 1975.

Most of William Bowers' screenplay takes place on a train speeding eastward from Chicago to New York, which gives the film a certain film noir quality that Norman Taurog used to good effect, what with several murders and mysterious characters lurking in the dimly lit train's passageways. Taurog began filming on May 29, 1950, with a marvelous cast of supporting actors that included, Ann Dvorak, Phyllis Kirk, Fred Clark, Dorothy Malone, Don Porter, Douglas Fowley—and of course, who else but Clinton Sundberg? Main and Whitmore worked well together delivering Bowers' caustic dialogue, with Main even singing a fast ditty with the mind-boggling title of "Possum up a Gun Stump." The filming progressed smoothly on to its completion in late June.

Mrs. O'Malley and Mr. Malone had its press preview at the Egyptian Theatre on November 1, 1950, and all of the revues praised the film, with *The Hollywood Reporter* proclaiming, "There is some of the most cheerfully macabre humor and one of the liveliest corpses ever seen on the screen in *Mrs. O'Malley and Mr. Malone* and the combination results in 70 minutes of solid hilarity." *Daily Variety* followed with, "William Bowers' slick screenplay hits a high laugh-per-minute pace during the proceedings, the chuckles frequently tripping over themselves. Norman Taurog's deft direction puts the cast effectively through its paces without a letdown." *Weekly Variety* seemed to agree with everything but the running time of the film: "Metro has an effective piece of screen entertainment in *Mrs. O'Malley and Mr. Malone.* It's a broadly treated situation comedy with a mystery basis, played strictly for laughs... Marjorie Main and James Whitmore, in the title roles, sparkplug the fun to be found along the racy 69 minutes. Most of the plot is mild, but the comedy dressing keeps it laughable and likely. It has good scripting by William Bowers, enlivened by snappy dialogue, and smart, fast direction by Norman Taurog." On its New York opening at the Palace Theatre on Febru-

James Whitmore, Norman Taurog and Phyllis Kirk on the set of *Mrs. O'Malley And Mr. Malone.*

ary 22, 1951, Howard Thompson of the *New York Times* joined in the praise: "The stars' teamwork is graceful and Norman Taurog's direction is so nimble that the shoestring budget is barely noticeable… William Bowers' script is consistently amusing, the pace is bouncy and the cast scald each other—and two corpses—with withering sarcasm from beginning to end."

With such solid approval from the critics, it was to be expected that there would be sequels, but such was not to be the case. Even if MGM had wanted to pursue a second film, Georgiana Craig (Craig Rice) spiked that plan by selling the rights to the John J. Malone character to ABC for a television series. *The Amazing Mr. Malone* starring Lee Tracy ran for one season from 1951to 1952.

Rich, Young and Pretty and Goodbye

Norman Taurog's MGM contract was due to expire by the end of November 1950, and it was becoming apparent that the studio and his agents at MCA Artists couldn't agree on terms for a new one. However, while Arthur Park, his representative at MCA, began talking to other studios, Taurog still had one last film commitment to fulfill at MGM with his old friend Joe Pasternak. Pasternak had been preparing a screenplay with writer Dorothy Cooper called *Welcome to Paris* since early in 1950. In July, Sidney Sheldon was assigned to work on the screenplay; the title was changed to *This Must Be Love* because the studio felt that the original title was too close to their currently filming production *An American in Paris* (1951). The title *This Must Be Love* was eventually scrapped as well, since everyone felt it was too ordinary, and when Sheldon turned in his final revised screenplay it bore the title *Rich, Young and Pretty.*

It was always intended as a starring vehicle for Jane Powell; Ricardo Montalban was initially penciled in as one of her co-stars, but was soon replaced by a new arrival to MGM, Argentine actor-singer Fernando Lamas, who was joined by French actress Danielle Darrieux to play Powell's mother and Lamas' love interest. Another early announcement had Marjorie Main playing Jane Powell's travelling companion, but she was later replaced by Norman Taurog favorite Una Merkel and then went off to Universal to make another of her *Ma and Pa Kettle* films. Wendell Corey, still a good, solid character actor at this point in his career, left his home base at Paramount and began a three-picture run with MGM by playing Powell's father, and Vic Damone, who had just begun his long-term contract with the studio by performing briefly in the Mickey Rooney starrer *The Strip* (1951), assumed his first full role as Powell's love interest. The rest of the supporting cast included Richard Anderson as Powell's Texas boyfriend, Marcel Dalio as a portrait artist involved in Darrieux's surreptitious attempts to meet the daughter she gave up as a child, and Hans Conried as a self-important maître d'.

Danielle Darrieux was returning to Hollywood films for the first time since appearing in her first and only previous American film *The Rage of Paris* (1938). Born in Bordeaux, France, in 1917, Darrieux had been starring in French films since 1931 and American audiences knew her from her role as Charles Boyer's doomed lover in *Mayerling* (1936) and as Emma Breitkopf in Max Ophuls' *La Ronde* (1950). She would make one other American film, *Five Fingers* (1952), before returning to France, where she continued her amazing 80-year career by appearing in over 100 films, including *The Earrings of Madame de...* (1953), Lady *Chatterley's Lover* (1955) and *Alexander the Great* (1956). In 2007, she supplied the voice for one of the characters in the French animated film *Persepolis*.

Fernando Lamas had first made a name for himself as an award-winning sportsman in horsemanship, fencing and boxing, as well as winning the South American freestyle swimming championship in 1937. By the time he was 27, he had already starred in a number of Argentinean films, and in 1950 he came to the United States to pursue a career in Hollywood. After appearing in a small role in *The Avengers* (1950), a Republic Picture starring John Carroll and Adele Mara that filmed in Buenos Aires, MGM signed him to a long-term contract in 1951 and his first film for the studio was *Rich, Young and Pretty*. He would have a chance to once again display his excellent baritone, singing opposite Lana Turner in *The Merry Widow* (1952), and his future wife Esther Williams in *Dangerous When Wet* (1953), but he would spend the majority of his time on loan-out to Paramount making a series of "B" pictures for Pine-Thomas Productions. In later years he would turn his talents to directing, mainly in television, and would eventually direct his son, Lorenzo Lamas, in his television series *Falcon Crest*.

Despite a pleasing screen personality, Vic Damone was totally miscast as Andre Milan, a French government clerk, whose lack of a French accent is unconvincingly explained away with a couple of lines of dialogue. Damone had been discovered by Milton Berle after he had won the top prize on the *Arthur Godfrey Talent Scouts* program. Berle arranged for him to appear at the New York nightclub, La Martinique, which brought him his own radio show on WHN and soon after, a recording contract with Mercury Records. His contract with MGM led to his also appearing in *Athena* (1954), again with Powell, and a cameo appearance in *Deep in My Heart* (1954), singing two of Sigmund Romberg's composition, before his career was interrupted by his being drafted into the Army. Upon his return, he resumed his contract with MGM and appeared again with Jane Powell in *Hit the Deck* (1955) and with Ann Blyth in *Kismet* (1955), before leaving the studio and pursuing a career as a nightclub performer and recording artist. Damone officially retired in 2001, after performing before a packed house at the Kravis Center in West Palm Beach, Florida.

In most musicals the plot is usually there merely to hang the songs on, and in the case of *Rich, Young and Pretty*, this was certainly the case. Texas rancher Jim Rogers (Wendell Corey) his daughter Elizabeth (Jane Powell) and their housekeeper Glynnie (Una Merkel) are on their way to Paris, where Jim is to make a speech before a United Nations committee. Marie Devarone, (Danielle Darrieux), Elizabeth's mother, who left Jim when Elizabeth was two, is living in Paris and wants to see her daughter. Then there is the son of Jim's colleague, Andre Milan (Vic Damone), who becomes romantically interested in Elizabeth, much to her father's dismay. The songs by Sammy Cahn and Nicholas Brodszky, the same team that had written the two Oscar-nominated songs for the Mario Lanza films, wrote a very tuneful score, with their ballad "Wonder Why" again winning the pair an Oscar nomination. A new vocal group on the scene, the soon to be very popular Four Freshmen joins with Damone and Powell on the cleverly staged and catchy tune, "How D'Ya Like Your Eggs in the Morning."

When Taurog began filming on November 14, 1950, he already knew that his future employment worries had been resolved. His agent Arthur Park had set him up with a two-picture contract at Warner Bros. and a commitment from Paramount and Hal Wallis to direct an upcoming Martin and Lewis comedy. Taurog also discovered that his female star was suffering from morning sickness. Jane Powell, who had married figure skater Geary Steffen, Jr., the year before, was pregnant with her first child and not having an easy time of it. Some articles have stated that Taurog and his cameraman, Robert Planck, were forced to shoot Powell from the waist up and hide her behind pieces of furniture, but the facts were that Powell wouldn't give birth to her son, Geary Steffen III, until six months after filming on *Rich, Young and Pretty* was completed, and despite her bouts of nausea she delivers an engaging performance.

This was probably the first Norman Taurog film that I can remember seeing, and as a callow teenager of sixteen I thought it was terrific. I loved the songs, thought Jane Powell was lovely, and found the story breezy and fun to watch. I became an immediate fan of the Four Freshmen and can still sing the lyrics to "How D'Ya Like Your Eggs in the Morning." When I viewed the film recently, I still found myself smiling and humming along with the songs; shows you how sophisticated I've become. The reviewers were not so enthusiastic. *Time* magazine called it "a light cinemusical subject with the butterscotch-caramel sentimentality of the bobby-soxers it is designed to please." I presume they were referring to me. *The New York Times* described it as "pretty as a picture postcard and just about as exciting." The *Los Angeles Times* was a little kinder, but not much: "The title, *Rich, Young and Pretty* would seem to indicate romance, and that's just what it does. A sprightly, somewhat sugary film story *Rich, Young and Pretty* is for the most part beguiling—a pleasant hour and a half." Only *The Hollywood Reporter* gave it anything like a good review, saying: "Joe Pasternak's production in Technicolor is studded with rich physical values as it wanders engagingly from a Texas ranch to the bright boulevards of Paris." Even Taurog managed to get a nice mention: "Director Norman Taurog, a wise old hand in dealing with youthful foibles, fills the piece with disarming touches that, like the music, contribute sizably toward overcoming that old film musical obstacle, story." *Rich, Young and Pretty* didn't create much excitement at the boxoffice, but still managed to turn a small profit for the studio.

When Metro-Goldwyn-Mayer celebrated its 25th anniversary in February of 1949, Louis B. Mayer ordered Howard Strickling to have his publicity department recreate *Life* magazine's famous "More Stars Than There Are in the Heavens" photograph that had appeared in a 1944 issue of the magazine commemorating the studio's 20th Anniversary. Strickling went even further and added a command performance luncheon on one of their sound stages, invited the Hollywood press and filmed it for the newsreels. Every MGM star was there, even the supporting actors, seated in alphabetical order on four tiers of tables with Louis B. Mayer right in his element, seated in the center. However, seated right next to him was his new VP of production, Dore Schary, and even then the atmosphere was frigid.

By 1951, Dore Schary had been at MGM for several years, and had won his battle with Louis B. Mayer over the making of *Battleground* (1949), which Mayer had dubbed "Schary's Folly" claiming that audiences were tired of war films. But *Battleground* had been a rousing success at the boxoffice, also winning four Academy Award nominations (Best Picture of 1949, Best Director, Best Supporting Actor, Best Film Editing) and winning Oscars for Best Screenplay and Best Cinematography. 1949 also saw the release of two more highly successful war films from other studios, Republic's *Sands of Iwo Jima* and Twentieth Century-Fox's *Twelve O'Clock High*, both of which were also nominated for Academy Awards; it was embarrassingly clear that other studios (and audiences) failed to share Mayer's concern about the popularity of war stories. Schary had followed up on his success by green-lighting several more quality films that succeeded at the boxoffice including 1950's *The Asphalt Jungle, Father of the Bride,* and *King Solomon's Mines*. Mayer was feeling isolated; he had fought with Schary again over *The Red Badge of Courage* (1951), a film that to him was doomed from the start, but Schary had appealed to Nicholas Schenck and gained approval for the film to be made. As Mayer had predicted, the film was a financial failure, but Mayer was furious with Schary for going over his head and after several other incidents where Schenck backed Schary over him he brought the matter to a head by calling Schenck and demanding, "It's either me or Schary. Which?" Schenck, who felt that the studio's product had considerably improved since Schary's arrival, told Mayer that he would continue to back Schary. On April 16, 1951 *The Hollywood Reporter*'s gossip column, the *Rambling Reporter*, featured the following item: "The Schenck-Mayer differences have the MGM lot in an uproar." On May 15, *The Hollywood Reporter* announced, "Dore Schary and his assistant Walter Reilly due in New York for conferences with Nick Schenck." Mayer announced his resignation to the press on June 22, 1951, to take effect on August 31, however he left the studio before that. There is a story, quite possibly apocryphal, that as Mayer was driving off the lot, his car was stopped at the main gate because it was a studio car. He was made to wait until one of his personal cars could be brought from his home and he could continue his humiliating exit from the studio that he had helped to create. It was truly the end of an era. Mayer was paid $2,750,000 for his residual rights to all films produced by MGM up to the time of his departure. Several weeks later, Schary met with Schenck and the Loew's Board of Directors in Chicago and was officially promoted to become head of production and immediately set about shortening production schedules and cutting overhead.

Rich, Young and Pretty's theatrical trailer was a lackluster affair featuring the film's musical director David Rose seated at a piano and speaking directly to the audience. Rose promised that they wouldn't use adjectives or exaggerations in this trailer, but would merely show the audience who's in the film and let them judge for themselves. The trailer has virtually no dialogue, just short clips from a couple of the songs and is in fact an extremely unimaginative promotion for a film that had a lot of entertainment to offer. About a month after the film opened, Joe Pasternak wrote a memo to Dore Schary complaining about the lack of exploitation on the picture. In fact he wrote two versions of the memo on the same day and it's not clear which of them was sent, or if he in fact changed his mind and sent neither. In either event, nothing is recorded of Schary's opinion of the film, or its lack of proper promotion. Whatever the outcome, *Rich, Young and Pretty* played out its dates and disappeared into the MGM vaults and Norman Taurog left the studio, not to return for twelve years.

Martin and Lewis, and Then Cary Grant?

Hedda Hopper announced Norman Taurog's departure from MGM in her column on February 14, 1951, but with a slightly different slant on things. Headlined "CHANGE OF PACE," the story went on, "Norman Taurog, who hasn't been getting good stories at MGM, resigned from the studio and moved across town to Paramount, where he'll direct Dean Martin, Jerry Lewis and Polly Bergen in *The Stooge*. Naturally he's delighted and so is Hal Wallis, who's producing the picture. It was Norman who made his nephew, Jackie Cooper famous."

The comedy team of Martin and Lewis was a phenomenon that began in July of 1946, when the team first appeared at Atlantic City's 500 Club. After a rough first show, they threw out their script and ad-libbed the second show, with what basically became their routine for the rest of their careers together: Dean would sing and Jerry would interrupt him with his childishly squeaky voice and slapstick gags. Their success rapidly built and they were soon appearing at nightclubs such as the Copacabana and on their own NBC radio program. From there it was only a short hop to appearing on the Ed Sullivan television show *Toast of the Town* and then to star in the opening episode of NBC's early TV variety show *Welcome Aboard*. In 1949, Hal Wallis signed them for his film based on the popular radio series *My Friend Irma* starring the original radio Irma, Marie Wilson. By 1951, they had already made five films for Wallis and their popularity was still growing.

Hal B. Wallis was one of the industry's most influential producers. He had begun his career in Hollywood with a job as an assistant publicist in the Warner Brothers publicity department in 1923. By 1927 he was studio manager and took on the job of production manager on the studio's first sound film, *The Jazz Singer.* Within a few more years he was producing films for Warners starting with *Little Caesar* (1931), on which he shared responsibility with another up-and-coming producer on the lot, Darryl F. Zanuck, although neither received screen credit. Over the next twelve years he continued to supervise practically every film made at the studio, sometimes receiving screen credit and sometimes not. He left Warners in 1943 over an incident involving his boss, Jack L. Warner: When *Casablanca* (1942) was announced as the Best Picture winner at the 1943 Academy Awards, Warner was the first out of his seat, beating Wallis (who had produced the film) to the stage and accepting the award. Wallis was so infuriated that he broke his contract and left the studio and a year later formed an independent production company with former Warners attorney Joseph H. Hazen, who had left the studio along with Wallis. Wallis and Hazen then signed a new contract with Paramount Pictures and began a twenty-four year association with the studio.

Wallis had seen Martin and Lewis at the Copacabana nightclub in New York in 1948 and hadn't been terribly impressed with their act, but a year later, when the team headlined at the newly reopened Slapsie Maxie's on Wilshire Boulevard in Los Angeles. Wallis was there along with practically every other studio head. The boys had picked up a new manager, fast-talking agent Abner J. Greshler, and when the audience went crazy that night, Abby Greshler quickly made the rounds of the tables, listening to the many offers forthcoming. Wallis beat out the competition by offering Martin and Lewis $50,000 a picture for seven pictures over five years. Greshler negotiated a sweetener in the contract that allowed the team to appear in one "outside" picture a year, and the boys and Greshler formed their own production company and named it York Productions. After they completed *My Friend Irma Goes West* for Wallis in March of 1950, Greshler arranged for independent financing for their first film in which they would receive star billing and Greshler would executive produce. *At War with the Army* (1950) was filmed from July to August of 1950 at Motion Picture Center Studios from a screenplay by Fred F. Finklehoffe, who also produced. The film was helmed by Hal Walker, one of Paramount's better contract directors, who had directed the boys in *My Friend Irma Goes West* and would guide them through two more films within the year; Paramount Pictures released the film and it returned a handsome profit for everyone and made Martin and Lewis boxoffice stars. By the time they began filming *The Stooge*, their fourth film for Wallis and Paramount, their salary had been revised upward to $75,000 a picture.

According to author Arthur Marx, when Wallis introduced Jerry Lewis to Norman Taurog, Lewis got down on his knees and in his squeaky voice, pleaded, "Please Mr. Director, say you'll do a picture with us. Say you'll do it!" Undoubtedly Taurog was amused, if somewhat nonplussed by Lewis' behavior, but since he had already signed his contract with Wallis-Hazen Inc., he probably smiled guardedly in agreement. Jerry Lewis was a cruder, louder version of the comics of an earlier era, comedians such as Charlie Chaplin, Harold Lloyd and Buster Keaton, who used sight gags to portray their comedy, and Taurog was the ideal director to help Lewis perfect his type of humor. Taurog would later say that at first Lewis was "a doll," doing everything that he instructed him to do, when he wasn't breaking up the crew with his antics both on and off the set. After a while, though, Lewis began to get into everyone's hair, asking for changes and making suggestions; albeit he often knew what he was talking about. Taurog managed to last through six pictures with Martin and Lewis and two more with Lewis alone, but many years later he expressed to me his intense dislike for Jerry Lewis, an opinion echoed by many others who worked with Lewis over the years.

The Stooge was based on an original story idea by Fred Finklehoffe and Sid Silvers. In the 1920s Silvers had appeared in vaudeville as a stooge for comedian-accordion player Phil Baker, heckling him from the audience, and *The Stooge* was based to some extent on his experiences. Finklehoffe, who had worked with Taurog on several MGM films, had written the screenplay for *At War with the Army* and would also work on the screenplay for *The Stooge*, along with Martin Rackin and Elwood Ullman. The story was set in the 1930s with Martin playing Bill Miller, a popular vaudeville entertainer who marries singer Mary Turner (Polly Bergen) and announces he is leaving his partner (Richard Erdman) and going on the road as a solo act. Miller bombs and his agent (Eddie Mayehoff) talks him into taking on a stooge to add humor to the act. Ted Rogers, the stooge (Lewis), becomes more and more popular and Bill's ego gets the better of him and he fires Ted, much to Mary's dismay. Everything ends happily, with Bill finally admitting that he can't do the act without Ted and reconciling with both Mary and Ted.

The irony of *The Stooge's* story is that in real life, in Martin and Lewis' performances on television and in nightclubs like the Copacabana, the situation was reversed. It was Dean who was Jerry's stooge, as he stood there with egg on his face while Jerry romped around the stage doing his knockabout comedy routines with Dean playing his straight man.

The cast of *The Stooge* included Polly Bergen, who had played her first featured role in *At War with the Army*, and Eddie Mayehoff, who had come from the New York stage and television and had just played the memorably pushy father in *That's My Boy* (1951), who wants his awkward son, (Lewis) to follow in his footsteps on his college's football team. Other cast members were Marion Marshall, as Frecklehead Tait, the girl who pursues Lewis and gives him his first kiss. Marshall was married to director Stanley Donen at the time and had recently completed a long-term contract with Twentieth Century-Fox. She had also appeared in *That's My Boy* and would return in Martin and Lewis' *Sailor Beware* (1952). Playing Lewis' mother was Frances Bavier, a

Broadway actress who would become a regular on numerous television series in the '50s and '60s, but would be best remembered as lovable Aunt Bee on the *Andy Griffith Show* and *Mayberry RFD* television series.

Filming began on February 19, 1951, and moved as smoothly as possible what with Jerry and Dean's penchant for playing practical jokes on everyone; it was completed on March 24. The jokes were generally Jerry's idea, but Dean would often go along with them. One of their favorite gags was to cut off the ties of visiting dignitaries, which would embarrass Hal Wallis who had brought them to the set as a courtesy. The order went out, "no more tie -cutting," but the practical jokes continued, with people's laughter encouraging Lewis to go further. One time he climbed into the rigging and tied and gagged one of the electricians. If Dean and Jerry were good and played their scenes without interruptions, Taurog would give them gag lollipops as a prize.

For some reason, after *The Stooge* was completed it was put on the shelf for almost two years. The published explanation was that the studio was afraid the film had too many dramatic scenes and not enough comedy, but the more likely reason was probably that Wallis and Paramount were concerned that Dean Martin's egotistical character was too unlikable for audiences that were just getting to know him. Whatever the reason, by the time the film opened in February of 1953, Norman Taurog had already completed two more films with Martin and Lewis, as well as another musical for Paramount and a film with Cary Grant at Warners.

After viewing the film at the Paramount Theatre in New York, Bosley Crowther, never a Jerry Lewis fan, seemed to agree with the studio's concerns, stating in his *New York Times* review, "Here is some information that is likely to shatter your faith in man: Dean Martin and Jerry Lewis have gone dramatic in their current film. *The Stooge* which put in an appearance at the Paramount yesterday after languishing for almost two years in Hal Wallis' studio vaults, has the two rambunctious comedians playing characters in a sentimental plot and actually pawing at the heart-strings before it comes to an end. Students of the exotic and the brazenly bizarre are likely to find the display more intriguing than will the addicts of straight belly-laughs. . . Now we don't want to take the position that Mr. Martin and Mr. Lewis could not play a straight dramatic show, if they wanted—even *Hamlet* to mention the extreme. But the mixture of slapstick and sentiment that is tossed off in *The Stooge* is a little bewildering for them, not to mention their customers. The going gets rather sticky and unfunny toward the end. This is not only oddly depressing; it is perilous to one's simple faith in man." In spite of Mr. Crowther's rather one-sided concern, the film still brought money into the Paramount coffers.

Taurog's contract with Warner Bros. to direct *Room for One More*, which he signed in November of 1950 just as he was about to start filming *Rich, Young and Pretty* at MGM, called for him to be paid $75,000 at the rate of $3,750 a week. A rider to the agreement optioned his services for a second film for an aggregate sum of $130,000.00 for both films. When Taurog returned to Warners in 1957 to direct *Onionhead*, the contract was revised, paying him $75,000 for the second film as well. Having already been approached by Hal Wallis and Paramount about a new arrangement to direct more Martin and Lewis films, Taurog was unquestionably enjoying one of the most successful periods of his career.

Warners had purchased the rights to the novel *Jimmy John* for $9,000 from Anna Perrott Rose Wright and assigned it to veteran producer Henry Blanke, who had been with the studio since 1928. Blanke, a dapper little man, born in Germany, began as an assistant to Ernst Lubitsch and accompanied him to Hollywood in the early '20s. He was soon at Warners supervising production and over the years produced nearly forty films, generally receiving the title of associate producer which was the practice at many of the studios at that time. In 1942 he was granted full producer status and went on to produce such films as *The Treasure of the Sierra Madre* (1948) and *The Fountainhead* (1949). Blanke would leave the studio in 1961 and would make one more film at Paramount, *Hell Is for Heroes* (1962), before retiring.

The writing team of Jack Rose and Melville Shavelson wrote a charming screenplay based on Wright's autobiographical story and Jack L. Warner was so pleased with the results that he decided to give the production more firepower by casting an established star in the lead. Warner was able to entice Cary Grant to return to the studio by offering the co-starring role of his wife to Grant's real-life wife Betsy Drake. Grant's deal of $300,000 plus a profit participation of 10% of the gross was no doubt another enticement.

Room for One More told the story of a happily married couple, George and Anna (Grant and Drake), with three children, whose household keeps growing because Anna can't resist bringing home abandoned pets. She also offers to become a foster parent and ends up with an emotionally disturbed girl with a history of suicide attempts. Anna eventually succeeds in helping the girl, Jane (Iris Mann), to feel accepted by the other children and to gain confidence in herself. As the family is about to go off on a holiday, George adamantly objects when Anna proposes they take in a young, handicapped boy named Jimmy-John (Clifford Tatum, Jr.). George finally gives in and the enlarged family heads off for their beach cottage, where mean-spirited Jimmy-John destroys one of the girl's bicycles in the midst of a tantrum and then is caught peeking in one of the girl's windows. George, who the children affectionately call Poppy, gives Jimmy-John a crash course in the facts of life, but when the boy, frustrated by his handicap, throws another tantrum, Poppy decides he must be returned to the welfare agency. However, when the children vote for Jimmy-John to stay and Jimmy-John is accepted into the local Boy Scout troop, things begin to improve. The finale involves Jimmy-John

George "Foghorn" Winslow and Cary Grant in *Room for One More.*

earning a merit badge by taking a difficult ten-mile hike and being awarded the rank of Eagle Scout at the Boy Scout Court of Honor.

With a cast that included one of the most popular actors in Hollywood, five children and a dog, Norman Taurog had his work cut out for him. He tested a number of children and finally settled on Gay Gordon and Malcolm Cassell as Trot and Tim Rose, and a wonderful little five-year-old named George (Wentzlaff) Winslow, whose deep voice belied his age and would later earn him the nickname "Foghorn."

Winslow had been discovered by Grant on Art Linkletter's television show *People Are Funny* and had recommended him to Taurog. Winslow, with his deadpan delivery as Teenie, the youngest of the Rose clan, was a comedy delight. Iris Mann, a twelve-year-old actress who had earned recognition as one of the "possessed" children in the Broadway production of *The Innocents* the previous year, was signed to play the role of Jane. Clifford Tatum Jr, another Broadway child actor, had appeared in *Annie Get Your Gun* with Ethel Merman.

Wanting to spend some time working with the children and the dog, as well as with the rest of the cast, Taurog got the studio to agree to a ten-day pre-filming rehearsal period that began on August 8, 1951. Filming officially began on Monday, August 20, and was completed on Friday, October 12, 1951. The final budget for the film was $1,079,000. As was generally the case with all of Taurog's films, the atmosphere on the set was relaxed and playful; one of several publicity shots taken on the set shows Taurog, Cary Grant and Betsy Drake handing out packages of candy to the children. Taurog was once asked by columnist Bob Thomas how he managed to get along so well with children, and he answered, "I guess it's because I just like kids, but you can't handle them with kid gloves all the time. Before the picture starts, I warn the mothers that I might have to speak sharply to their children during the filming of the picture. Discipline is important; otherwise the kids will take advantage of you. After the first day, I've never had any trouble with any of them, not even Mickey Rooney." Taurog also explained that it was important to keep the children natural, "and to prevent them from becoming 'actors.' That's the mother's responsibility. When I see a kid starting to get self-conscious, I have the mother removed from the set."

Room for One More is a highly sentimental film that seems to work on all levels. Taurog's experience with animals and kids came in handy and he delivered a nice comedy-drama that even brought a lump to my throat on several occasions. The kids are all believable and not too cute—even little George Winslow. The two "problem kids" make the transition from nasty to nice for plausible reasons as they are accepted by the other family members. Grant and Drake are credible as a married couple (not surprising since they

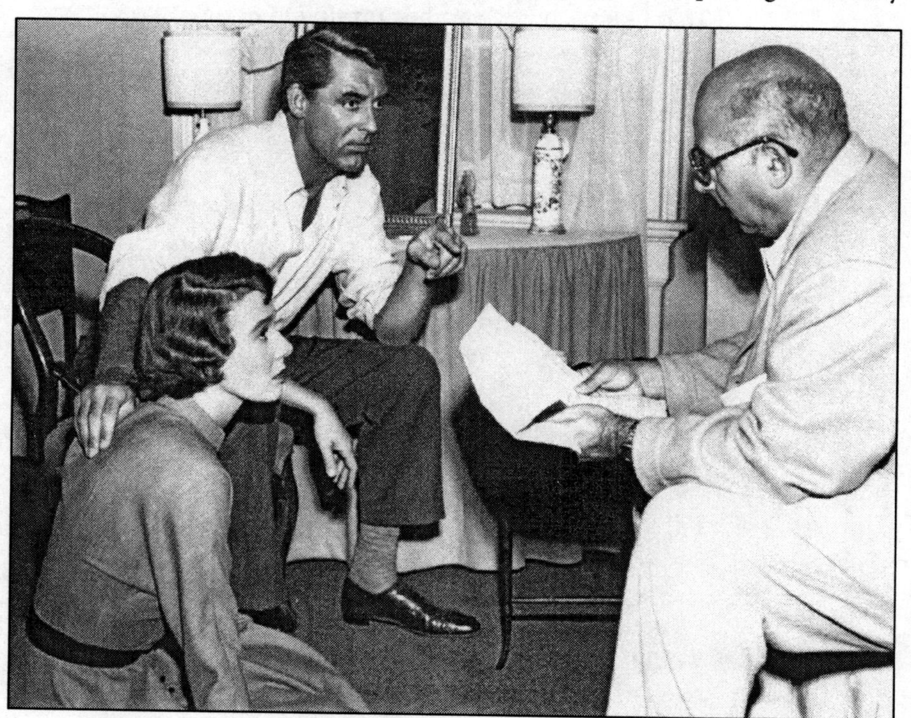

Director Norman Taurog with actors Betsy Drake and Cary Grant.

were married at the time) and the humor comes out of situations and is not forced. The Eagle Scout ceremony in the finale, although reminiscent of the finale in *Boys Town*, was just as effective.

The film opened in New York on January 14, 1952, and went into general release on January 26. Three days after the New York premiere, Jack L. Warner received a letter from Albert S. Howson of Warners New York office informing him that Father Patrick Masterson, executive director of the National Legion of Decency, was objecting to two situations in the film. Howson enumerated the Legion's objections, saying, "The Legion feels that the sequence in which Cary Grant tells the little boy about how babies are born is objectionable in a picture designed for entertainment purposes." The sequence in question was a charmingly played, sensitive moment between Grant's character and young Jimmy-John. Just for fun, here are some of the "objectionable" lines of dialogue as they appeared in the film:

POPPY
(drawing in the sand)
Now, this is a woman --

JIMMY-JOHN
That I know, but what I been trying to find out
is how babies get born.

POPPY
(clearing his throat)
I see this is an *advanced class.*
(he scratches his head)
Well, look—you know how chickens and birds
lay eggs?
(Jimmy-John shakes his head)
They lay them in a nest, and keep them warm with
their feathers until the babies peck open the
eggshell and hop out.

JIMMY-JOHN
I didn't hop out of no eggshell.

POPPY
Of course not. It wouldn't work with people. What
would happen if they sat down on their eggs and
tried to keep them warm enough to hatch?

JIMMY-JOHN
They'd bust. And anyhow, who's got feathers?

POPPY
No one in our set. So instead, women keep a nest inside them where the eggs are warm and safe. When the baby is old enough, it's born ready-made.
(he draws in the sand)
Like this.

JIMMY-JOHN
(watching closely)
Pretty good system.

POPPY
I'm glad you approve. Now we won't have to change it.

Needless to say, J.L refused to make any changes in this scene or in scenes where "the husband's physical desire for his wife is over-done." Not just as a matter of principle, but because the film was already in release and hundreds of prints had been sent out to the exchanges. The Legion gave *Room for One More* a "C" rating, which didn't hurt its boxoffice one bit.

Betsy Drake and Cary Grant with the children of *Room for One More*. (L-R) Iris Mann, George Winslow, Clifford Tatum Jr., Malcolm Cassell and Gay Gordon.

The reviews were almost unanimous in their praise, with *The Hollywood Reporter* leading off with, "*Room for One More* is a delightful domestic comedy, stunningly produced by Henry Blanke, warmly directed by Norman Taurog and played to the hilt by Cary Grant, Betsy Drake and as beguiling an aggregation of moppets as you'll ever encounter." *Variety* praised, "A nifty scripting chore by Jack Rose and Melville Shavelson wins chuckles for situations and dialogue that combine friendly humor with humanness and develop an honest marital feel between the parents. Also, script has a frankness not often used on the screen. In this respect, Grant's remarkably straightforward explanation of procreation to a curious young boy is not a bad model for parents." TAKE THAT, LEGION OF DECENCY! *The Los Angeles Examiner* and the *Hollywood Citizen News* both had nice things to say about the film, with the *Examiner* singling out Taurog's contribution thusly: "[One of its blessings] is the warm, so very human direction of Norman Taurog, who has no peer when it comes to handling children on the screen. And he's just as great handling those 'big kids'—the adult actors." The *Citizen News* added, "There's a lot of good clean fun all the way through this film. The dialogue is clever and amusing. So are the dramatic situations. The dog steals most of the scenes, but some of the youngsters don't do half bad either."

Of course there was still the dyspeptic Bosley Crowther in the *New York Times* to complain rather primly about scenes where the children interrupt with "the cuddling of Ma and Pa." Crowther actually delved into psychological depths in his complaint, saying with a straight face, "An intricate Freudian situation is suggested in the handling of this gag, and that's not a very fortunate suggestion in an essentially uncomplicated film, having to do with children and the joyful recompenses thereof." Once again Crowther's comments were lost to the crowds lining up to see the film and *Room for One More* was a joyful success.

A decade later, Warners produced a television series based on the film. Starring Andy Duggan and Peggy McCay, it ran on the ABC network for one rather unsuccessful season in 1962.

Jerry, Jerry, Jerry!

On November 19, 1951, just over a month after finishing work on *Room for One More*, Norman Taurog was back at Paramount and about to begin his second film with Martin and Lewis. The film, *Jumping Jacks,* was based on an unproduced screenplay called *Ready, Willing and 4F* written in 1944 by Robert Lees, Fred Rinaldo and Brian Marlowe and intended as a vehicle for Bing Crosby and Bob Hope. Hal Wallis purchased the completed screenplay from Paramount and assigned Herbert Baker to adapt it for Martin and Lewis. James Allardice and Richard Weil did some additional work on the script and Wallis quickly put it into production.

After only five films, the team of Martin and Lewis was the hottest thing in Hollywood and the boys were beginning to get a little too full of themselves. A sign went up on the stage door, "This is a closed set." Taurog, whose patience was being sorely tested, tried to accept Dean Martin's lackadaisical attitude. "He knew his words when he came on the set," Taurog once told Arthur Marx, "but he did it *a la* Crosby." According to Taurog, Martin was lousy in rehearsals, just mumbling his way through the scene, but when the cameras rolled, he'd come alive and play the scene the way he was supposed to. "He wanted to get through the scene as quickly as possible," explained Taurog, "so he could get onto the golf course." When Lewis would come and ask for the day off, Taurog would try to accommodate him by rearranging the schedule whenever he could, but if he couldn't shoot around him he would have to say no. "The next day," recalled Taurog, "he'd suddenly wind up with a terrible stomach ache and we'd have to send for the doctor, and I would end up giving him the day off."

Dean Martin and Jerry Lewis in *Jumping Jacks* (1952).

Principal photography on *Jumping Jacks* began on December 3, 1951, on location at the Airborne Department of the Infantry School at Ft. Benning, Georgia, with Mona Freeman as Dean's love interest, Don DeFore as his company commander and Robert Strauss as his sergeant. Don DeFore, a freelance actor who had begun his career on Broadway and transferred to Hollywood in 1936 where he made a career playing the good-natured buddy in a number of films, had recently appeared in *My Friend Irma* (1949) and *Dark City* (1950) at Paramount. DeFore would go on to co-star in a number of television series, such as *The Adventures of Ozzie and Harriet* (1952-1957) and *Hazel* (1961-1965). Robert Strauss had appeared on Broadway in *Detective Story* and *Stalag 17*, and had made a couple of films in New York before coming to the West Coast earlier in 1951 to appear with Martin and Lewis in *Sailor Beware*. Strauss would recreate his character of "Animal" in Billy Wilder's film version of *Stalag 17* (1953). Also in the cast as fellow soldiers were Richard Erdman, credited as "Dick, Erdman" and Danny Arnold. Erdman, the perennial bushy-haired juvenile in a number of wartime films at Warner Bros. had recently impressed Hollywood with his performances as a cynical paraplegic in *The Men* (1950) and a smart-talking alcoholic in Dick Powell's film noir, *Cry Danger* (1951). Danny Arnold, who acted in three Martin and Lewis films, would soon move into writing where he would remain for the rest of his career. Arnold would work with Taurog and me in on *Palm Springs Weekend* in 1963, before his great success with the Emmy winning series *Barney Miller* (1975-1982). The last time I saw Danny Arnold, years later, he was sitting in a booth in the front section at Chasen's in Beverly Hills, smoking a huge cigar, surrounded by his cronies and enjoying his success. He waved at me.

The company finished location filming on December 14, 1951, and left Ft. Benning to return to Hollywood. After a month's hiatus over the holidays, during which Martin and Lewis fulfilled a nightclub engagement, the company resumed filming at Paramount Studios on January 10, 1952, and finished on January 23. The next day Taurog filmed a few retakes and a special trailer with Martin and Lewis. Although *Jumping Jacks* still showed a final cost of $1,187,420, Taurog had managed to complete the picture in just 28 days.

On February 15, 1952, the following item appeared in Mike Connolly's *Rambling Reporter* column in *The Hollywood Reporter*: "Four of the six scripting credits on Hal Wallis' *Jumping Jacks* belong to writers named in Un-American Activities Committee hearings as Reds. They are Robert Lees, Richard Weil, Fred Rinaldo and Brian Marlowe, latter being a dead Red…" By 1952 the "Cold War" and the "Red Craze" had reached its zenith and the Blacklist, although never acknowledged as existing, was obliterating the careers of actors, writers and directors. Billy Wilkerson, the 62-year-old founder of *The Hollywood Reporter,* was an avid anti-Communist and had previously written numerous articles in his daily "Tradeviews" column, naming supposed Reds and Red sympathizers and supporting the Un-American Activities Committee. His reasons were partially an inflated patriotism, but more precisely a desire to exact revenge on the Hollywood studio heads who had denied him entrance into their private club when he had tried to build his own studio in the late '20s. By destroying their talent pool, he felt he was achieving his goal.

Hal Wallis was not about to sit idly by and watch his multi-million dollar investment in Martin and Lewis go down the tubes, and on February 21, his attorney Loyd Wright sent a letter to *The Hollywood Reporter* demanding that it be published in the paper. In his letter Wright elucidated the history of the screenplay's previous development and then goes on to say, "The Wallis version was written by Herbert Baker, James Allardice and Richard Weil, of whom the latter was mentioned, along with 150 others, as having been seen at one time at a meeting attended by communists. Weil has not been questioned by the Un-American Activities Committee. Neither Lee, Rinaldo, nor the estate of Brian Marlowe benefit financially from the sale to Hal Wallis Productions of *Jumping Jacks*. They receive credit as determined by an arbitration committee in accordance with our standard contract in force with the Screen Writers Guild." By early June, a month before the film's release, Wallis had secured an official endorsement from the Department of the Army, and an injunction against an anti-communist group called the Wage Earners Committee, prohibiting them from picketing theaters where the film was playing. In November of 2012, Billy Wilkerson's son, W.R. Wilkerson III, published a formal apology in *The Hollywood Reporter* for his father's role in the notorious Blacklist.

Jumping Jacks opened simultaneously in New York and Los Angeles on July 23 and the reviewers once again raved about Jerry Lewis' comedy. Even good old Bosley Crowther had to grudgingly admit that there was something in Lewis' humor: "There is grotesqueness yes, in the gawking that Mr. Lewis does," he wrote. "The fumbling of hands, the looking cross-eyed, the childish pouting, the walking pigeon-toed and the frequent horrendous hiation [sic] of an incredibly mammoth mouth. There is also a trace of genuine burlesque in the silly way he lifts and cracks his voice, and sometimes his clumsy gestures are most adroitly and amusingly timed." *The Hollywood Reporter* looked at the film from the opposite end of the prism, saying, "There is no restraining influence in *Jumping Jacks*. It's just sheer Martin and Lewis and their outrageous antics which bring audiences close to hysteria in what shapes up as the top laugh-getter for the team to date." *Variety* once again singled out Taurog for praise: "Thanks to Norman Taurog's very able direction and a situation comedy plot perfectly tailored to show off Lewis' uninhibited miming and Martin's pleasant way of handling straight-man chores and singing, this is the comics' funniest film venture since *At War With the Army*. Just as nonsensical, but with smoother production and situation framing, Taurog's handling makes it a constant attack on the funny bone with a succession of laugh highlights, some of which will literally roll an audience in the aisles."

Over the next four years Taurog would direct four more films with Martin and Lewis, technically for their production company York Pictures, but also for Hal Wallis, who still owned a one-third interest in the boys' contract, along with Paramount. All of the films would be released by Paramount and be produced by Taurog's old friend Paul Jones. Taurog and Jones had known each other during the 30s, when Taurog had first arrived at Paramount and Jones had been an assistant director. Jones had later become a producer and had remained at Paramount for all these years, producing films such as *The Lady Eve* (1941), *Road to Utopia* (1946) and *My Favorite Spy* (1951). Each of the Martin and Lewis films, starting with *The Caddy* (1953) and followed by *Living it Up* (1954), *You're Never Too Young* (1955) and *Pardners* (1956), became increasingly an ordeal for both Taurog and Jones. Now that Jerry Lewis was in effect a producer of his films, he became more unmanageable; his demands grew more frequent and more unreasonable. Taurog speaks of the numerous times that they would be about to film a scene and Jerry would suddenly hold up his hand and shout, "Wait a minute! I've got a funnier way of doing it." This would then necessitate reblocking the scene and relighting it. The delays would exasperate Dean, who just wanted to get the scene shot and go home. One time when Martin was having trouble with a line of dialogue, he looked heavenward and exclaimed, "Don't just look down on me, God. I told you to help me, not destroy me." Taurog apparently liked that as he adapted a version for himself; any time something went wrong on the set interrupting a take, he would look up and mutter, "Don't just look down… help me!" It would generally break up the crew and the actors and release some of the pressure.

A syndicated columnist visited the *Caddy* set when the company was filming on location at the Riviera Country Club and described some of Lewis' antics: "He always arrives on the set loaded with trick devices from novelty stores. During the shooting of one of the big scenes in the picture, he managed to slip seven or eight ice cubes into Dean Martin's trousers pockets and the scene had to be shot all over again when Martin discovered he had suddenly become a refrigerator.

When director Norman Taurog chided him for this, he gave Taurog a five-minute lecture on how he didn't have any sense of humor and should be shooting sea epics. He continually halted the cameras to demand a comb for those idiotic locks of his. The fact that all this tom-foolery was costing a ton of money, and some of it his money because he and Martin own a third of the picture, didn't bother him a bit."

But it bothered Dean Martin. Taurog even had the prop man make up a large card that said, "It's your money," which he'd hold up when Jerry was pulling one of his time-consuming practical jokes, and Dean would say, "Let's get going!" As time passed, Taurog could see that the team was beginning to have problems: Arguments would take place on the set between the two men, and once Jerry decided that he could sing, conflicts would constantly arise over who would get which song to sing. Jerry would go to Taurog and say, "I should get that song, Dean has enough songs to sing in the picture." Starting with *The Caddy*, Jerry would meet with the writers every day to go over the script and make suggestions to build up his part and cut down Dean's. Arthur Marx describes a situation where Taurog suggested doing what was called a "high and dizzy," a physical gag from Taurog's old days in two-reel comedies. It would involve the boys being on a high ledge of a building, hanging on for dear life and trying to escape from the heavies. Dean liked the idea, but Jerry told Taurog he couldn't do it. When Taurog tried to explain that there would be no danger as they would film it against a process screen, Jerry still refused, saying, "It's not Jerry Lewis being funny—it's the gag."

The entourage that followed Jerry around kept growing until there was at least eight or nine members who laughed at his jokes and ran errands for him. Dick Stabile was the orchestra leader for their nightclub dates and for their segments of *The Colgate Comedy Hour* on NBC; he and his brother Joe would remain with Lewis for many years, long after the team broke up. Another member was Mack Gray, a bit actor who had once worked for George Raft and would remain with Dean Martin after the split. Danny Arnold had started as a minor borscht-circuit comic and played in a number of the Martin and Lewis films before coming up with an original idea called *So Where's the Money?* Arnold's original story had no role for Dean Martin and Paramount initially turned it down. Sensing he had the power, Jerry Lewis demanded they make it their next film or he would refuse to appear in any more pictures for Paramount. He emphasized his point by walking off the lot and refusing to return. Paramount gave in and hired Hal Kanter and Edmund L. Hartmann to create a vehicle for Martin and Lewis, and Arnold was later brought in to work on the screenplay, which became known as *The Caddy*.

By the time filming began on *The Caddy* in late November of 1952, Jerry Lewis' hyperkinetic style had begun to take its toll on his health and mid way through, production had to be halted when Lewis became ill. Taurog was able to shoot around him for a couple of days, but on January 8, 1953, production was suspended for 23 days when Lewis entered Cedars of Lebanon Hospital with a 102 ° fever. The studio paid the hospital for his care and

Marin and Lewis and Norman Taurog on the set of *The Caddy* (1953).

a special budget report showed that the delay cost Paramount $61,423. The final cost of the film was $1,864,112, the most expensive Martin and Lewis film to date.

Wallis and the studio realized that they were running out of concepts for Jerry Lewis and had the story department start digging through their files for more ideas. Consequently, the next few Martin and Lewis films were remakes of previous productions; *Living it Up* was based on the 1953 Broadway musical *Hazel Flagg*, which in turn was based on the 1937 David O. Selznick film *Nothing Sacred. You're Never Too Young* was a remake of the 1942 Brackett-Wilder film *The Major and the Minor. Pardners* was a remake of the Bing Crosby film *Rhythm on the Range*, which Taurog had directed for Paramount in 1936. One other film, *Artists and Models* (1955), which Frank Tashlin directed, bore no connection to the previous Paramount film of 1937, but merely shared its title and its setting of the annual Artists and Models ball. Whatever the source of their films, Martin and Lewis were voted the number one draw at the boxoffice for 1951 and 1952 by the Motion Picture Exhibitors, and for the next two years after that they held the number two position. By 1955 they had dropped to number seven in the list.

By the time that Taurog began preparing his sixth and final film with Martin and Lewis in 1956, things had changed dramatically with his two stars. The film's title, *Pardners*, was deeply ironic as the Martin and Lewis partnership was on the verge of breaking apart. Dean had already legally notified Jerry that he intended to fulfill his contractual obligations, but that he no longer wanted to continue as a team beyond that point, nor to maintain any form of personal contact except on the set. Martin felt that the scripts no longer featured him beyond that of a colorless romantic lead who sang a few songs, and he was fed up with Lewis' ego and his constant meddling in every aspect of the production, which caused the films' budgets to grow. As an example, Mala Powers had originally been signed to play Jerry Lewis' love interest in the film, but after filming tests with him she informed the studio that she didn't wish to appear in the film and Jackie Loughery replaced her. Powers never revealed what had turned her against appearing with Lewis, but whatever it was, it must have happened while they were filming the tests.

Lewis' hi jinks continued, but now they were bigger and cruder gags that frequently had a tendency to be cruel. He would often take a pair of scissors to a subordinate's shirt or his tie and cut it to pieces, or unexpectedly pour cold water over someone's head. One of his most ambitious gags caused a tremendous brouhaha at Paramount when he had an oil painting that belonged to Cecil B. DeMille altered. When DeMille's Biblical epic *Samson and Delilah* (1949) was released he'd had an artist paint a reproduction of Victor Mature as Samson tearing down the Temple columns and hung the painting in the studio commissary just above his personal table. Lewis had another artist remove Mature and insert his image into the painting in the same pose and had it re-hung in the commissary. When DeMille saw it he was furious, although most everyone else thought it very funny. Undoubtedly DeMille ordered the offending painting taken down; however in 1964, when I was on the Paramount lot making *Tickle Me* (1965) with Taurog and Presley, I saw the painting hanging in the studio commissary in its original spot. By that time of course, DeMille was dead and Jerry Lewis' current film, *The Disorderly Orderly* (1964) was making a lot of money for Paramount Pictures.

As production was about to begin on *Pardners*, Taurog was appraised by the head of the studio Don Hartmann of the need to keep the amount of exposed negative to a minimum. On January 20, 1956, Taurog wrote Hartmann a memo informing him that the length of the first assembly by the cutter was 10,480 feet (1hour and 58 minutes) against the original estimate by the production department of 11, 089 feet. Taurog's original estimate was 10,028 feet. He ended by saying, "So there was not much difference one way or the other. Thanks very much for your help. Sincerely, Norman Taurog." One has to wonder what "help" Taurog was referring to.

You could cut the atmosphere on the *Pardners*' set with a knife, it was so tense; Dean wasn't speaking to Jerry and his unhappiness showed in his acting, and Jerry seemed to be trying to compensate by acting up with greater frequency. To make matters worse, when the company arrived in Phoenix, Arizona, on December 8. 1955, to begin location filming, it began to rain. After sitting idle for four days, the company returned to the studio. Filming officially ended on Saturday, January 28, 1956.

The final breakup was filled with incidents, including one very public explosion over the premiere for *You're Never Too Young* at a Catskills resort where Jerry had first started. Dean was angry that Jerry had arranged the event without first checking with him, and when the day of the premiere came Dean was in Hawaii with his wife. On June 18, 1956, UP columnist Aline Mosby broke the story under the headline: "DEAN MARTIN, JERRY LEWIS BREAKING UP." Datelined Hollywood, Mosby announced, "Dean Martin and Jerry Lewis, one of the most famous teams in show business, confirmed today they are breaking up after a farewell nightclub tour in the East. The final 'divorce' of the team came to light when Martin played golf instead of attending a party yesterday to celebrate their last movie together, ironically titled *Pardners.* Lewis said the pair had huddled with Paramount executives Friday and agreed to go their separate ways."

While Paramount was willing to let the team split, Hal Wallis wasn't so sanguine; he still had a contract calling for four more films from the team and the only way he would settle would be to divide the contract into four films from each man. It would take years, but Wallis would see his contracts fulfilled.

The team of Martin and Lewis gave their final performance at the Copacabana nightclub in New York on July 25, 1956, the tenth anniversary of their first teaming, and it was a memorable night. The boys did every part of their old routine and then some, and when they finally left the stage, to a standing ovation, Jackie Gleason leapt on the stage and led the cheering.

It would take awhile for Dean Martin to find his niche as a solo performer. His first film *Ten Thousand Bedrooms* (1957) at MGM was a flop, but his performance in his next film, *The Young Lions* (1958), brought him wide acclaim and he was soon in Howard Hawks' *Rio Bravo* (1959) with John Wayne. From that point on, his career blossomed with more films, his own television series and nightclub dates. His films with Frank Sinatra and their joint Vegas shows would become popular events and he would eventually make over 30 films, including his Matt Helm series. Martin would retire from films after appearing in *Cannonball Run II* in 1984 and began to withdraw from public appearances after his son, Dean Paul, was killed in a 1987 jet crash while flying with the California Air National Guard. He completely retired when he was diagnosed with lung cancer in 1993 and succumbed to the disease on Christmas morning, 1995.

Jerry Lewis remained at Paramount making films for Hal Wallis, as well as for his own very successful production company; for several years he was Paramount's biggest boxoffice attraction. In 1966, after his films began to lose money, he left Paramount and moved his company to Columbia Pictures where he made five more films, none very successful, followed by one more at Warners, *Which Way to the Front?* (1970). After the unreleased *The Day the Clown Cried* (1972) it was the occasional guest star role on television and films; Lewis made a cameo appearance in Billy Crystal's *Mr. Saturday Night* (1992) and co-starred with Robert De Niro in *The King of Comedy* (1983), he played a Jewish gangster in six episodes of the 1988-1989 television series *Wiseguy* and is currently playing the title role of an aging widower in the independent film *Max Rose*.

After fifty-plus years of hosting the annual Labor Day Muscular Dystrophy telethon, MDA announced on August 3, 2011, that Jerry Lewis would no longer be hosting the event and that he had completed his tenure as the National Chairman of the Muscular Dystrophy Association. The announcement was somewhat ambiguous as to whether he was fired or had resigned and Lewis remained silent on the matter. His health still being somewhat of an issue, Lewis returned to doing one-man shows all over the world. Then in June of 2012, he collapsed from hyperglycemia at a New York Friar's Club event and had to cancel a personal appearance in Sydney, Australia.

Lewis had been working on a musical adaptation of his 1963 film *The Nutty Professor* for the past six years. With book and lyrics by Rupert Holmes and score by Marvin Hamlisch and directed by Lewis, the musical had its pre-Broadway world premiere at the Tennessee Performing Arts Center in Nashville in July of 2012. The local reviews (there were no out-of-town reviewers in attendance) gushed their praise, although all made note of the play's heavily 60s retro ambiance. On August 17, 2012, Marvin Hamlisch died suddenly of lung failure just before he was due to travel to Nashville to view a performance and help with any needed revisions. Although several Broadway theatre owners viewed performances during the play's four-week engagement in Tennessee, as of this writing nothing further has been announced about a Broadway opening.

A Lot of Stars Are Singing

As a welcome break from the mad world of Martin and Lewis, Norman Taurog also directed two other films for Paramount during this period, the first of which was *The Stars Are Singing* (1953). Based on an original story called "The Goddess" by Paul Hervey Fox, the project had been in development for several years, with writers Valentine Davies and Jo Swerling running it through their typewriters. By 1952, Liam O'Brien, brother of actor Edmond O'Brien, had completed a screenplay called *Reach for the Stars* that the studio planned to use as a follow-up vehicle for Italian soprano Anna Maria Alberghetti, who had first appeared in Gian Carlo Menotti's film version of his opera *The Medium* (1951) and had made her American film debut the previous year with Bing Crosby in *Here Comes the Groom* (1951). Paramount also planned to use the film to introduce Rosemary Clooney, whose recording career had exploded the previous year with the release of "Come On-A My House," a song she despised, but would have to reprise in *The Stars Are Singing*.

Norman Taurog was just finishing up the post-production on *Jumping Jacks* in late February of 1952, when producer Irving Asher approached him about directing his upcoming production *The Stars Are Singing*. A deal was quickly made with Paramount, by Taurog's agent Arthur Park, for Taurog to receive $75,000 on a fourteen-week guarantee. Taurog and Asher had known each other at MGM, when Taurog had briefly overseen tyro director David Miller on Asher's production *Billy the Kid* (1941).

Casting began immediately with Lauritz Melchior, whom Taurog had missed directing while they were both at MGM, signed to play Jan Poldi, a once great, now alcoholic opera star who helps to shelter illegal immigrant Alberghetti when she jumps ship. Rosemary Clooney plays a struggling singer and one of Poldi's neighbors who tries to help Alberghetti. Tom Morton, a young dancer who gained recognition as one of the talented cast of the Broadway revue *Lend an Ear*, was given the role of Buddy Fraser, another neighbor in the apartment building who tries to help. Taurog's old standby Fred Clark played McDougal, the immigration officer searching for Alberghetti, and John Archer played Clooney's boyfriend.

Pre-production preparations continued throughout April and May, with choreographer Jack Baker beginning rehearsals for several weeks with his dancers. The day before Asher directed makeup and costume tests with Alberghetti and Morton, a second unit under Arthur Rosson's direction flew to New York to shoot backgrounds on May 9, 1952. The company filmed for seven days at various Manhattan locations, including the Washington Produce Market and Greenwich Village. Victor Young was assigned as the musical director and on May 3, began recording the classical numbers with Alberghetti; at some of these sessions Anna Maria's mother accompanied her on the piano. Taurog shot makeup tests on the afternoon of May 14 with Clooney, and on Tuesday, May 20 with Alberghetti. Filming officially began on Monday, June 2, 1952 and the last vocal recording was on June 28, when Clooney recorded "Haven't Got a Worry to My Name." All of the popular songs in the score were written by Jay Livingston and Ray Evans, with the exception of "Come On-A-My House," which was written by Ross Bagdasarian and his cousin, author-playwright William Saroyan. The company completed filming on July 15, but reopened production for one day on September 23 to film an added scene with character actor Lloyd Corrigan. The estimated budget for the film was $1,268,000, but the final costs were $1,264,337, as Taurog brought the picture in slightly under budget.

Toward the end of the film, Alberghetti's character is about to be deported, but President Eisenhower intercedes on her behalf and calls her on the phone. When told who's calling, Alberghetti asks, "Ike, Ike who?" After filming and post-production was completed, Anna Maria returned to her home in Rome, and sometime around October of 1952, Paramount requested that she record one line of dialogue in Rome for the picture. The line was "Adlai, Adlai who?" For this she was paid $416.66 (one fifth of her weekly salary) plus $50 expenses. The line was a protection in case Adlai Stevenson beat Dwight Eisenhower in the upcoming election and the studio would have to replace the original line. Needless to say it wasn't needed.

The Stars Are Singing was press previewed at Paramount Studios on January 13, 1953, and all the reviews sang the praise of Rosemary Clooney, with *The Hollywood Reporter* announcing, "A good story, fine warbling, amusing comedy and pleasant performances combine to make this Irving Asher production a genuine treat that should send Rosemary Clooney soaring toward stardom." *Variety* heaped on more praise: "Miss Clooney's disc-selling ability should lure some customers to the ticket windows and word-of-mouth will do the rest. Under Norman Taurog's good direction, her personality comes over on the screen and she has a naturalness that will be liked." Kay Proctor in the *Los Angeles Examiner* said it quite succinctly: "There's a special excitement in *The Stars Are Singing*, and her name is Rosemary Clooney." Bosley Crowther, in *The New York Times* a few weeks later, had this to say about Ms. Clooney in his usual acerbic manner: "The chatter around the Hollywood show-shops is that Rosemary Clooney is being groomed to take over the top roles at Paramount that Betty Hutton recently resigned. . . She's a pleasant enough young lady, a little forced and self-conscious with the charm and, for those who like modern balladeering, done with vigor and bounce, she's right there. . . But it's questionable whether she's ready to fill Miss Hutton's Paramount shoes, and it is certainly questionable whether the studio has presented her as to do her the most good."

The Stars Are Singing was a moderate success for Paramount, but Rosemary Clooney's film career was short-lived, with only three more films for Paramount and a guest appearance in then-husband Jose Ferrer's MGM film *Deep in My Heart* (1954). She would continue her career with a number of hit recordings for various labels during the '50s and early '60s and would appear frequently on television, including her own musical-variety show on NBC. She even made a guest appearance on her nephew George Clooney's television series *ER*. Rosemary Clooney, who died of lung cancer, is still considered one of the greatest interpreters of American song, and was awarded the Lifetime Grammy Achievement Award in March of 2002, just four months before her death on June 29, 2002. Unable to attend the event because of her health, her eldest son actor Miguel Ferrer accepted the award on her behalf.

The 1950s saw considerable changes, not only in the film industry, but in the country as a whole; the post war optimism was being eroded by McCarthyism, the Korean War, and Jack Kerouac's Beat Generation. The major studios were eliminating their contract lists, and actors, directors and writers were finding assignments on a free lance, picture-by-picture basis. Norman Taurog was still directing the Martin and Lewis films, but at the rate of only one picture a year. Between *The Caddy* (1953), *Living It Up* (1954) and *You're Never Too Young* (1955) there were long periods of inactivity. He was now 57 years old and there were younger directors starting to fill the ranks, many from the so-called "Golden Age of Television." On Sue's advice Taurog hired a press agent, and in May of 1954 announced the formation of Tau-Ream Productions and their first project called *Three Days of Grace*. Over the next year or so, several more items appeared in newspapers, with the company's name now changed to Taurean Productions and the participation of a writer named Allan J. Kenward, who had in 1942 written and directed a wartime drama on the Broadway stage called *Proof Through the Night* that MGM had purchased and produced as *Cry 'Havoc'* (1943). The press releases first stated that Kenward was writing a screenplay that Taurog hoped to make "with the cooperation of a major company." He wouldn't reveal the title of the property just that it was "a story about grown-ups as seen through the eyes of this kid." A later press release revealed that the screenplay Kenward was preparing was based on Ralph Moody's autobiography of growing up in Colorado during the early1900s called *Little Britches.* The first of a series of books about his family, Moody's *Little Britches* had been published in 1950. Taurog's instincts were sound: a story with a young boy as its protagonist was right up his alley. Unfortunately, nothing came of the venture. A 1981 film starring Burt Lancaster, called *Cattle Annie and Little Britches,* was based on a novel by Robert Ward and not on the Moody books.

In 1954, Taurog made his first "contractual" foray into television. David O. Selznick, for whom the word "spectacular" seemed almost synonymous, came up with the idea of saluting the 75th anniversary of Thomas Edison's invention of the electric bulb by producing a two-hour, star-filled television tribute entitled *Light's Diamond Jubilee* that would air simultaneously on all four networks (NBC, CBS, ABC, and Dumont). Selznick enlisted his long-time writer Ben Hecht to adapt the works of Irwin Shaw, John Steinbeck and Mark Twain, and that's where Taurog came in. Selznick decided to include the fence-painting sequence from his 1938 film *Tom Sawyer,* and made a financial arrangement with Taurog for his participation. This generated the following comment by the *Variety* reviewer: "The mosaic of events fabricated designs of diverse elements and some may have wondered why Tom Sawyer and his fence whitewashers were given such prominence... It was all a part of the pattern of humanity." Taurog would also direct an unsold TV pilot called *Skinny and Me* for Jerry Fairbanks Productions in April of 1959, but that would be his sole television venture and after that he returned permanently to feature films.

1954 also saw the marriage of Norman Taurog's eldest daughter Patricia to a young Air Force Reserve officer, Sheldon Schrager, the son of an auto parts manufacturer. The marriage took place on July 18 at the Beverly Hills Hotel, and was a star-studded event with more than 150 guests, including Louis B. Mayer, Doris Day and her husband Marty Melcher, and a woman who would become Sue Taurog's best friend and partner in many of the charities she would be involved with over the years, Sybil Brand. After Schrager was discharged from the Air Force, he would, with Taurog's help, become an assistant director and work his way up through the ranks, eventually becoming a producer and an executive with Columbia Pictures. According to Jackie Cooper, Schrager made a number of attempts to affect a truce between Cooper and Norman Taurog, but their get-togethers were always uncomfortable and Cooper eventually elected to permanently end the relationship. Cooper also wrote that Patricia Schrager was estranged from her father and never saw him, but on several occasions during the '60s I would see Patricia and Sheldon Schrager at events to which my first wife and I were invited by the Taurogs, and she always seemed to exhibit an affectionate attitude toward both Norman and Sue. Patricia and Sheldon Schrager's marriage lasted for 20 years and they had one son, Michael. A year after their 1974 divorce, Patricia married Leo Devery, and Sheldon married actress and former Miss Israel, Aliza Gur in 1978. Patricia is now widowed and living in North Carolina, and Sheldon, who was divorced from Aliza Gur, passed away in 2011. Patricia declined to be interviewed for this book.

By early 1954, Norman and Sue Taurog had moved into their final Beverly Hills home, 527 North Hillcrest Drive, and the event was immortalized with a three- page photo spread featuring Sue, Patricia, Priscilla and Jonathan in the Sunday *Los Angeles Times* Rotogravure section. In June, Taurog agreed to stage the show the following September at the Makeup Artists and Hair Stylists Ball at the Hollywood Palladium with Bette Davis as mistress of ceremonies, and in December he and Sue became grandparents for the first time, when Patricia and Sheldon, who was now on duty with the Air Force in Japan, announced the birth of their son Michael in Tokyo.

On August 17, 1955, Taurog had signed a contract with Paramount Pictures for a two-picture deal that would have him directing another new television star, George Gobel, in a remake of Preston Sturges' *The Lady Eve*. The second film was to be for Martin and Lewis' York Pictures Corporation, and was tentatively entitled *Where Men Are Men,* but would eventually become known as *Pardners* (1956). Over the 40 weeks that this contract was in effect, Taurog's aggregate salary would be $200,000.

A stand-up comedian with a laconic style of delivery who referred to himself as "Lonesome George," George Gobel was one of the hottest TV personalities in 1955; his weekly NBC comedy-variety series, which had debuted the previous year, was at the top of the ratings and had won an Emmy Award. His appearance on Selznick's *Light's Diamond Jubilee* in 1954 had been considered the highlight of the two-hour event, and his dry comment, "If it weren't for electricity we'd all be watching television by candlelight," is still considered a classic. Paramount, with high hopes that Gobel could recreate his television success in films, signed him to an exclusive contract in 1955 and cast him in the Henry Fonda role in their musical remake of *The Lady Eve*, now called *The Birds and the Bees.* His co-stars would be the vivacious Mitzi Gaynor, who had just completed a long-term contract with Twentieth Century-Fox and was beginning a multi-picture pact with Paramount, and popular British actor David Niven, who would follow this performance with his starring role in Mike Todd's wide-screen extravaganza *Around the World in 80 Days* (1956). Once again Taurog filled his supporting cast with reliable character actors, many of whom he had worked with before: Reginald Gardiner, Hans Conried, Harry Bellaver, Margery Maude, Clinton Sundberg, Milton Frome, Mary Treen, King Donovan, Rex Evans, Charles Lane, Bartlett Robinson and Fred Clark, who would be making his fifth of what would ultimately be ten films for the director.

Sidney Sheldon had twice won a Writers Guild Award for Best Written American Musical (*Easter Parade* in 1949 and *Annie Get Your Gun* in 1951) and an Oscar in 1948 for his original screenplay *The Bachelor and the Bobby-Soxer* (1947) and he had worked with Taurog on *Rich, Young and Pretty* and *You're Never Too Young.* Sheldon had been developing a screenplay based on the 1941 Sturges comedy under the generic title of *The Gobel Story.* In June of 1955, Sheldon delivered his rather lengthy first draft to producer Paul Jones, who had also produced the original Sturges production. Sheldon spent a week or so going through the script with Norman Taurog and Jack Mintz, and presented his still lengthy 125-page final draft screenplay on July 5, 1955.

After filming various wardrobe and makeup tests, Taurog shot some background footage at Hollywood Park racetrack on July 9, 1955, and officially opened production on July 11 with George Gobel, David Niven and Peggy Moffitt in the *Int. Ship's Dining Salon* set on Paramount's Stage 9. The following day Mitzi Gaynor reported sick and production was shut down for two days, resuming on July 15. On Saturday, August 6, Gaynor and Gobel reported to the Paramount Scoring Stage to pre-record the numbers "The Birds and the Bees' and "La Parisienne," by Harry Warren & Mack David, with musical conductor Walter Scharf. The company finished filming on September 3, and then reopened production on November 10 to film a retake with Harry Bellaver in the flooded process tank on Paramount's back lot.

An establishing shot of an ocean liner was needed to open the film and that became a major hassle for the studio. First there was the problem of using a Coast Guard Sikorsky S-55 helicopter as a filming platform. Someone forgot to contact the admiral in charge, so even though the Coast Guard offices in Washington D.C. gave their approval the admiral, whose nose was out of joint, refused to grant permission until a formal letter of request was sent to his office. Finally, on July 22, a second unit crew flew to New York to film various shots of the liner over several days.

Paramount rolled out *The Birds and the Bees* with a series of invitational premieres starting on March 20, 1956, and initial reviews were mostly positive, but with a note of concern. *The Hollywood Reporter* advised, "This gay slapstick comedy with music should be sold as a laugh-getting movie that happens to have a TV comic for its leading man, rather than a mere feature-length expansion of the usual George Gobel Show." *Variety* followed with, "George Gobel segues from video's small tube to VistaVision's big screen in easy style and if his fans follow him into the nation's theaters then *The*

Birds and the Bees, a remake of *The Lady Eve*, will shape to good boxoffice." However, when the film opened at Paramount's New York flagship theatre on April 22, the *New York Times* pointed out the basic problem with the film: "Mr. Gobel and his well-known halting delivery have a comic charm all their own. There is, however, not enough original material to sustain him and it all tends to become repetitious." *Newsweek*'s reviewer stated it more succinctly: "30 minutes of distilled drolleries on TV is one thing. The lengthy demands of a two-hour movie make labor of Gobel's gagging."

George Gobel's film career was short-lived; Although *The Birds and the Bees* made it to *Variety*'s list of early 1957 top money making movies, Paramount ended their deal with him. His next and final film, *I Married a Woman,* made later that year for RKO Pictures, was not released until May of 1958 when RKO went out of business and sold a package of unreleased films to Universal. Gobel then returned to television, where he guest-starred in numerous series and specials over the years and in the late '80s became a regular on the original version of the hit comedy game show *The Hollywood Squares*. He would die on February 25, 1991, as the result of a series of strokes, brought on by bypass surgery.

Rising Stars and Falling Stars

Even before MGM star Debbie Reynolds married popular singer Eddie Fisher in September of 1955, they had already become the new version of "America's Sweethearts," with their photographs on the covers and stories about them in all of the fan magazines. RKO had been playing around for some time with the idea of remaking their earlier comedy hit *Bachelor Mother* (1939); George Jessel had announced plans to film it with Betty Hutton starring in 1954, but nothing came of it. When two years later RKO decided to go ahead with the project as a musical, producer Edmund Grainger and the studio brass thought they had come up with a natural winner by casting Reynolds and Fisher in the leads. The studio borrowed Reynolds from MGM in May of 1956, unaware that she was already four months pregnant with her first child, future actress Carrie Fisher. Although costume designer Howard Shoup was given the job of hiding Reynolds' condition from the camera, the publicity department made a point of featuring it in the film's press releases. What they didn't mention was the fact that the Reynolds- Fisher marriage was already on the rocks and the couple were frequently not speaking to one another.

Writers Robert Carson and Arthur Sheekman were given the job of adapting Norman Krasna's 1939 screenplay (based on an original story by Felix Jackson), and composers Mack Gordon and Josef Myrow came up with the five songs for Debbie and Eddie to sing in the film. Norman Taurog, who had known Reynolds since she first arrived at MGM in 1950, was hired to supervise the film, now called *Bundle of Joy,* and found himself once again directing a baby (actually twins) playing the foundling that Debbie discovers on a doorstep and who complicates her life. Filming began at RKO Studios

Eddie Fisher suggests a change to his wife Debbie Reynolds and a skeptical Norman Taurog on the set of *Bundle of Joy*. (Photo courtesy Photofest)

on June 8, 1956, and finished in early August. The cast, as usual, was filled with accomplished character actors, lead by dapper Adolphe Menjou as Fisher's father and the owner of the department store where Reynolds works, and Una Merkel as Reynolds' landlady, who helps to care for the baby. Other cast members included Tommy Noonan, Melville Cooper, Bill Goodwin, Howard McNear, Robert H. Harris, Mary Treen, Edward Brophy and Gil Stratton.

RKO held an invitational Hollywood premiere on December 21, at the Egyptian Theatre on Hollywood Blvd, with Eddie Cantor as master of ceremonies. The reviews the following day were filled with compliments for Fisher's acting and for Taurog's direction, with Harrison Carroll in the *Los Angeles Herald & Express* informing his readers, "It's no news that Debbie Reynolds is an expert comedian but, considering that this is his first film, Fisher displays a surprisingly light touch. And he puts over the catchy tunes of the score with all the persuasiveness that might be expected." *The Hollywood Reporter* continued the praise: "Fisher is not yet an accomplished actor, but this lack of technique does not show and what does come though is the picture of a very warm and charming young man. His intrinsic sincerity is projected with considerable tenderness and strength. He comes off very well. No doubt he has been aided by Norman Taurog's good direction, which is sure throughout." *Variety* wrote, "Through the skillful comedy knowledge of Norman Taurog, whose direction never misses a bet, the Edmund Grainger production emerges as a clever piece of showmanship with Fisher warbling five numbers and dueting with his wife in another." Edwin Schallert in the *Los Angeles Times* summed it up by saying, "*Bundle of Joy* has a freshness, gaiety and wholesomeness that will make it especially appealing to the family audience." Trust Bosley Crowther to come up with the one sour note, as he did in his *New York Times* review on December 20: "It is fortunate for Eddie Fisher and Debbie Reynolds that they have a large following of fans who would probably applaud this nice young couple in anything they chose to do. It is also fortunate for the Capitol Theatre, where *Bundle of Joy* was presented last night. For this new Technicolored musical picture, which has the Fishers (they are married you know) as stars, is a sadly deficient entertainment when looked at objectively."

When Carrie Fisher was born on October 21, 1956, RKO took out an ad in the trades the next day promoting *Bundle of Joy* as "The most prosperous holiday gift you ever had." Unfortunately Debbie and Eddie did not draw the crowds as expected and the film did not do well at the boxoffice. Fisher, once he had left Reynolds for Elizabeth Taylor, appeared in only one more film, *BUtterfield 8* (1960) before his career took a nosedive. Reynolds returned to MGM, where her performance in *The Unsinkable Molly Brown* (1964) earned

Jane Russell and Norman Taurog on the set of *The Fuzzy Pink Nightgown*.

her an Academy Award nomination. In 1958, when the Debbie-Eddie-Liz Taylor- Richard Burton scandal broke, there were rumors that Universal (who had inherited the studio's library when RKO ceased to exist) planned to reissue the film. Louella Parsons wrote in her syndicated column on September 22, 1958: "*Bundle of Joy* will not be reissued according to one of the top executives of Universal-International. 'We feel it would be the height of bad taste to capitalize on this tragic story in that way.'"

Taurog's next assignment was an independent film for Jane Russell's production company, Russ-Field Productions, *The Fuzzy Pink Nightgown* (1957). Jane Russell, who had exploded onto the motion picture screen with her lusty performance in Howard Hughes' *The Outlaw* (1943), and then spent the next ten years under contract to Hughes and RKO playing "sexy broads," found that her career had peaked with *Gentlemen Prefer Blondes* (1953). Since then she and her husband, pro quarterback Bob Waterfield, had been starring her in films that they produced themselves. *The Fuzzy Pink Nightgown* would be their fourth and final production, and Russell's last feature film of any stature. It was based on a novel by Sylvia Pate, bearing the slightly dissimilar title of *That Fluffy Pink Nightgown*, and a screenplay by Richard Alan Simmons. Simmons had been a contract writer for Universal-International and would later gain fame and a few Emmy nominations in television for his writing and producing of the *Columbo* series with Peter Falk and its spin-off *Mrs. Columbo* starring Kate Mulgrew.

The Fuzzy Pink Nightgown told the story of a Hollywood star who is kidnapped by a couple of bumblers on her way to the premiere of her newest film, *The Kidnapped Bride*. The confusion over whether it is a real kidnapping or a publicity stunt fills out the rest of the story, with Russell's character eventually falling in love with one of her abductors.

Taurog apparently tried to interest Dean Martin in playing the romantic lead opposite Russell but Martin, who was in the process of splitting up his partnership with Jerry Lewis, opted instead to make the first and only big flop of his career, *Ten Thousand Bedrooms* (1957). Ray Danton, a television actor who had appeared in a few films including *I'll Cry Tomorrow* (1955), was signed for the role, but after a few days of filming was replaced by Ralph Meeker, an established star since he played Mike Hammer in *Kiss Me Deadly* (1955). The official reason for Danton's departure was a case of laryngitis, but unofficially it was rumored that Danton (ten years younger than Jane Russell) was let go because he looked too young on the screen to play opposite Russell. Once again Taurog filled the supporting roles with solid character actors, including some from his last film (Adolphe Menjou, Una Merkel and Robert H. Harris). Other members of Taurog's rapidly expanding stock company included old reliable Fred Clark and his real-life wife Benay Venuta in one of their rare appearances together, Keenan Wynn and Milton Frome.

Filming began on location at Paradise Cove, near Zuma Beach, in late December of 1956, but almost immediately production was halted by the outbreak of what became known as the Newton-Hume-Sherwood brushfires in the Santa Monica Mountains and along the Malibu shore; it ultimately destroyed over 35,000 acres and 250 structures. Filming resumed on January 2, 1957, near the Paradise Cove Pier and on the bluff above at the home of Wright Merrifield, which had somehow miraculously escaped being damaged by the fire. Interiors were completed at the Samuel Goldwyn Studios by January 25, 1957.

The Fuzzy Pink Nightgown had its world premiere in London at the Leicester Square Theatre on May 9, 1957, and opened in Los Angeles in selected theaters on August 21. Audience reaction at the sneak previews had cooled United Artists' enthusiasm for the film and it was paired as a double bill with a "B" western called *Outlaw's Son* (1957). The reviews weren't very encouraging, with the *Los Angeles Times* describing the film as "diverting, mild entertainment," and *The Hollywood Reporter* complaining, "There does not seem to be much connection between the title and the screenplay of this Russ-Field production for United Artists, but when it provides the opportunity for advertisements and marquees that can read Jane Russell in *The Fuzzy Pink Nightgown*, why quibble?" *Variety* noted: "Basic idea had a good

Hollywood columnist Hedda Hopper (C) visits with Ralph Meeker, Jane Russell and Adolphe Menjou on the set of *The Fuzzy Pink Nightgown*.

deal of comedy potential... This kind of situation, to be gotten across with top comedy effect, required a clever satirical treatment or sharp delivery of snappy dialogue. But neither is the case. The amusement comes but intermittently; for the most part the writing is unimaginative and Norman Taurog's direction is routine." *The New York Times*, never one to be outdone, slipped the knife in this way: "An ordinary piece of feminine night clothing is a pretty flimsy excuse for putting together a long, long movie."

If *The Fuzzy Pink Nightgown* were to be remembered at all, it would be due to an incident involving another Hollywood sexpot known as "The Body." On the night of January 3, 1957, Marie McDonald, wife of Harry Karl (who would later marry Debbie Reynolds), claimed she was abducted from her home by two men who demanded her money, her rings and supposedly raped her. After learning that she had made three phone calls during the time she was missing, none to the police department, and a medical exam produced no evidence of rape, the police found MacDonald's claims to be highly unlikely. When told that a copy of the novel *That Fluffy Pink Nightgown* was found in McDonald's home, a grand jury ruled that there was no evidence of a crime and the case was dismissed. Marie McDonald would die of a drug overdose on October 21, 1965, at the age of 42.

Norman Taurog returned to Warner Bros. Studios in 1958 to fulfill the second half of his 1952 contract and make a film with another rising star, Andy Griffith. Having created the role of Will Stockdale in the hit Broadway production *No Time for Sergeants* in 1955, Griffith starred in Elia Kazan's *A Face in the Crowd* in 1956 and then came out to California in early 1958 to recreate his role in the film version of *No Time for Sergeants* for Warners. The film was such a success that he was now returning to play the lead in another service comedy, *Onionhead.*

Jack Warner purchased the rights to Weldon Hill's novel *Onionhead* in 1956 for $75,000 after having been given an advanced copy of the galley proofs. Hill, whose real name was William R. Scott, based his novel on his own experiences in the U.S. Coast Guard during World War II. Nelson Gidding, who began his writing career with a novel based on his experiences as a prisoner of war during the Second World War and then branched into television, wrote for a number of the early series including *Sgt. Preston of the Yukon* (1955), on which he also served as story editor. Gidding had just finished writing his first feature screenplay for Warner Bros., at first called *The Jazz Age* but later *The Helen Morgan Story* (1957). He would go on to write the screenplay for *I Want to Live!* (1958), the story of Barbara Graham, whose controversial murder trial and execution made newspaper headlines in 1955. Gidding and his co-writer Don Mankiewicz would receive an Academy Award nomination for that screenplay, and this film would mark the beginning of Gidding's 17-year association with director Robert Wise, for whom he would write four more highly successful screenplays, including The *Haunting* (1963) and *The Andromeda Strain* (1971).

Producer Jules Schermer sent a revised first draft of Gidding's *Onionhead* script to Jack Warner on May 17, 1957, with a note explaining that changes had been made "to get a better flow and also for economic reasons." On June 5, 1957, Schermer sent a memo to Steve Trilling, Warner's executive assistant, suggesting that Stanley Donen would be available as soon as he finished co-directing The *Pajama Game* (1957) with Broadway director George Abbott and "would be an excellent choice for *Onionhead*." Jack Warner's initial choice for a director was Gordon Douglas, a lackluster director of "B"-level films who was under contract to the studio. It was obvious that Warner didn't want to spend the money for Donen and eventually the studio went for Taurog, who owed them a picture on his old *Room for One More* deal. Taurog signed his revised contract on July 1, 1957, reported to the studio shortly thereafter and proceeded to go over the script with Jack Mintz. A second revised script was sent to Andy Griffith on August 5. A production meeting was held at the studio on Thursday, August 15, 1957, and an estimating budget was prepared shortly thereafter for $960,000, which allowed for 43 shooting days including 2 days of filming at the Coast Guard Station in Alameda, California and 7 days filming at Terminal Island in San Pedro, California.

Andy Griffith and Felicia Farr in *Onionhead*.

On Tuesday, August 20, Taurog shot talent tests with Murray Hamilton, Joanna Barnes, Erin O'Brien, and Dorothy Provine. Steve Trilling had initially rejected Felicia Farr (future wife of Jack Lemmon) for the role of Stella, but eventually changed his mind after seeing her performance as the seductive barmaid in *3:10 to Yuma* (1957). Schermer sent him a thank you memo, in which he wrote: "I can probably say this better in writing than tell you face to face, but I did want you to know that I feel it takes a big man to do an about face on your decision regarding Felicia Farr. You know I believed in her for the part and I am grateful for your decision." Farr was borrowed from Columbia Pictures for eight weeks at the rate of $1,250 a week with a $10,000 guarantee.

Erin O'Brien was cast as Griffith's college sweetheart whose rejection leads him to enlist in the Coast Guard and become a cook. Joey Bishop, a stand-up comedian who was just finishing appearing in another Warner film, *The Deep Six* (1958), and had previously portrayed one of the platoon members in *The Naked and the Dead* (1958), was cast as Gutsell, one of Griffith's fellow mess cooks. Other cast members included Joe Mantell, James Gregory, Claude Akins, Tige Andrews, and Ray Danton as the disagreeable ensign in charge of the ship's mess. The big surprise was the casting of Walter Matthau as the crusty head cook, "Red" Wildoe, complete with bleached blonde hair and an over-the-top but enjoyable performance. He was paid $5,000 a week with a five-week guarantee.

The official start date for the picture was September 16, 1957, and Andy Griffith was to report to the studio on September 9 for pre-production meetings and wardrobe fittings. However, Griffith and his wife Barbara flew to California on September 2 and reported to the studio on the 3rd. They stayed at the Hollywood Roosevelt Hotel until they could move into the house at 3375 Coldwater Canyon that they had rented when Griffith had made *No Time for Sergeants* earlier that year. Since Griffith reported one week early, the studio agreed to pay for his and his wife's roundtrip airfare and to pick up his hotel bill. Norman Taurog shot wardrobe tests with the principals on September 17 and 19 and filming officially began on September 23, 1957.

The schedule called for the company to shoot at Terminal Island on Oct. 14 and 15 and then travel to Alameda on October 16 by plane and begin filming upon their arrival. When the studio limousine arrived at Norman Taurog's home at 527 Hillcrest Road to take him to the location, it had already stopped just up the block to pick up cameraman Hal Rossen, who lived at 613 Hillcrest Road. On October 22 the company returned to Terminal Island for more filming; they stayed at the Hacienda Motel in San Pedro and filmed aboard the Buoy Tender USCGC Heather for six days, requiring the use of a tug as a camera boat. The studio reimbursed the Coast Guard the sum of $19,875 for repainting the Heather in wartime gray and installing two 20mm anti-aircraft guns and depth charge racks, Y guns and empty depth charge cans. On November 9, the company returned for a second location shoot (six days) at Terminal Island.

Things did not always go smoothly; toward the end of filming, Andy Griffith reported for work complaining he was ill. A doctor confirmed that he had the flu and production was stopped for several days while he recuperated—only to then have both Felicia Farr and Erin O'Brien come down with the flu. Then Joey Bishop pulled a muscle in his groin and was unable to complete the sequence he was filming. He was able, later that afternoon, to appear in a less strenuous scene involving process photography.

Filming was eventually completed on November 29, 1957 and Taurog supervised post-syncing with his cast on December 4 and then proceeded to work with editor William Ziegler on his director's cut until late December. The film was previewed on February 18, 1958, at the Westwood Village Theatre and audience reaction was somewhat mixed, as were the reviews. Both *The Hollywood Reporter* and *Variety* predicted commercial success based on the popularity of Griffith and the success of his previous film *No Time for Sergeants*. However, both trades as well as the reviewers for the *Los Angeles Examiner* and the *New York Times* pointed out the film's lack of definition with a plot that moved between comedy and serious drama.

Onionhead was an attempt to capitalize on Griffith's success in *No Time for Sergeants* and was promoted as a comedy follow-up. However, the storyline is far more serious and Griffith's character more sophisticated than his character in *Sergeants* and at times almost unlikable as he pushes himself on several women. The script also has a problem delineating character traits in Felicia Farr and Erin O'Brien, with both women exhibiting contradictory personalities—first turning Griffith down, then swooning over him. Farr's character is even harder to fathom as she seems to be demure at first (even bringing a girlfriend as chaperone to dates), then becoming a raging nymphomaniac, unable to resist any man. The shipboard scenes remind one of *Mister Roberts*, but without the raw humor of that play and film. What plot there is, apart from Griffith's love life, involves his learning to be a cook and his problems with his immediate boss Walter Matthau (looking fat and strange with bleached hair) and his executive officer (played with the proper nastiness by Ray Danton) who is stealing from the ship's supply fund.

Joey Bishop plays a lecherous seaman, and the running gag with him pinching various buxom ladies' bottoms has the film's one good laugh in its payoff. The film was a financial failure, as audiences expected the big laughs from *No Time for Sergeants*, which just weren't there. Taurog directed in a straightforward manner with few sight gags beyond a sequence with yeast-filled dough exploding from the oven. The title comes from the gag of Griffith's pal (Joe Mantell) encouraging him to shave his head and rub it with an onion solution to encourage hair growth, which doesn't seem to go anywhere beyond the initial shock of seeing Griffith's bald pate.

Onionhead was such a major disappointment for Andy Griffith that, according to an interview he gave many years later, after one more film, *The Second Time Around* (1961), he gave up acting in feature films for many years and concentrated on his two successful television series *The Andy Griffith Show* (1960-1968) and *Matlock* (1986-1995) and their spin-offs, as well as guest starring in a number of mini-series and TV movies.

For Norman Taurog, whatever disappointment he had would be short-lived, for he would soon be embarking on an entirely new adventure: a series of films with arguably the most popular singer in the world at that time, Elvis Presley. These films would ultimately carry him to the end of his lengthy career.

Out With the Old – In With the New

Norman Taurog filmed *Pardners,* his final film with the team of Martin and Lewis, between late November of 1955 and late January of 1956. After that he would still have two more films to make with Jerry Lewis, *Don't Give Up the Ship* (1959) and *Visit to a Small Planet* (1960), and then he would be free of a man who, although he admired Taurog and once described him as "an expert," was becoming more and more involved in the directing and producing of his own films, and would sometimes forget that he wasn't the guy in charge on the Taurog set. Norman Taurog gritted his teeth and soldiered on, but never forgave Lewis for his frequent bouts of ego-inspired interference and unreasonable demands. One time Lewis, having asked and been denied permission, still left the set of *Visit to a Small Planet* early on a Friday to take a weekend flight to New York to act as toastmaster at the Founders Dinner of the Eleanor Roosevelt Institute for Cancer Research. Taurog once expressed his theory on how not to let someone like Lewis give him ulcers. "I found out very early in Hollywood," he said, "that the way to last in this business was not to take your studio problems home with you. When the day's shooting is done, I go home, take a shower, have dinner, rest a while and then go to my study for an hour. I don't go there to wrestle with myself over the imperfections of that day's work. I go there to lay out the next day's work in the cool, cool of the evening. I emerge feeling fine, and the rest of the evening is mine to share with my family. I go to bed relaxed, sleep well, and get up early a refreshed and well-rested man. I am at the studio by eight and work alone until nine, when the office staff comes in. I give them their day's work, and after that I'm on top of my problems for the rest of the day. What wears men out is trailing when they should be leading."

Between *G.I. Blues* and *Blue Hawaii*, Taurog was asked back to Twentieth Century-Fox to help guide the embryonic film career of yet another record idol of the nation's teenagers. His name was Pat Boone and according to *Billboard Magazine* he was the second highest selling artist of the late 1950s, after Elvis Presley. Famous for his trademark white buck shoes, Boone had 38 Top 40 hits, sold over 45 million albums and had already appeared in four films with varying success, He and Norman Taurog met to prepare a film that was called at that time *Warm Bodies*.

In 1958 screenwriter Jay Sommers secured the rights to a recently published novel called *Warm Bodies*, written by Donald R. Morris and based on his experiences in the U.S. Navy. Sommers then proceeded to develop a "spec" screenplay and upon its completion had his agent submit it to various studios. Twentieth Century-Fox liked the script as a vehicle for their new star Pat Boone and made an arrangement with Sommers to buy his screenplay and hire him to continue his writing duties on the project. Oscar Brodney, himself a successful screenwriter, was assigned as the producer and worked with Sommers on further developing the screenplay. By the summer of 1960 a revised screenplay was submitted to both the Shurlock Office and the Office of the Navy. The script received a few notes, mostly technical corrections from the Navy, and the film was okayed for production.

Taurog was a natural choice to become the director, having just helmed three service comedies practically in a row. Ever since the success of the 1955 version of the Thomas Heggen-Joshua Logan play *Mister Roberts*, service comedies had become very popular with the studios; besides Taurog's *Onionhead, Don't Give Up the Ship* and *G.I. Blues*, there had been the film adaptation of John Patrick's *The Tea House of the August Moon* (1956), *Don't Go Near the Water* (1957), *Operation Mad Ball* (1957), *No Time for Sergeants* (1958), *Operation Petticoat* (1959) and *The Wackiest Ship in the Army* (1960). So *Warm Bodies,* renamed *All Hands on Deck*, seemed like a natural fit for both Pat Boone and Twentieth Century-Fox, and Taurog was just what the doctor ordered to direct this comedy.

The problem was that the script lacked originality. Once again Taurog was given a plot that stretched credibility to the max, with an eccentric Chickasaw Indian sailor (played by comic Buddy Hackett) who happens to be very rich, keeps a pet turkey aboard his ship and hates movies where the Indians lose to the Cavalry. He is being watched by Washington politicians because his wealth interests them. Boone's character, the executive officer on an LST operating out of Long Beach, California, meets and falls in love with a pretty reporter (Barbara Eden), who smuggles herself on board when the ship is ordered to make a trial run to the Aleutians, where the turkey mates with a pelican who hatches an egg and… I think that's enough, you get the idea.

Fox released *All Hands on Deck* (1961) as the upper half of a double bill with a Hugh Marlowe western called *The Long Rope*, and the reviews were anything but impressive. The *Los Angeles Times* headline declared, "*ALL HANDS ON DECK* STANDARD SERVICE FARCE." *Variety* elucidated the problems by reporting, "The 20th-Fox release should generate some teen response via Pat Boone, but for most grownup wicketeers it will amount to little more than a drab and predictable variation on dozens of service comedies that have preceded it to the screen… Norman Taurog has directed with a light touch, but the material leaves too much to be desired." *The Hollywood Reporter* continued on the same tack, adding: "The fault in *All Hands on Deck* seems to be that the material is overly familiar, and a joke with a predictable conclusion does not usually get a laugh." *The Hollywood Citizen News* finished it off by proclaiming, "The story could have been written in Script Writing I and the dialogue is a masterpiece of the ludicrous."

Pat Boone's career in films tapered off after *All Hands on Deck* and he began to focus on gospel music and appearing as a motivational speaker at conventions. He became more and more outspoken about his support for conservatism and began campaigning for various Republican candidates, including Ronald Reagan and George W. Bush. He declared himself an avid anti-gay activist and likened liberalism to cancer. By 2009 he had become a "birther," declaring that Barack Obama was "not eligible to serve as president."

In January of 1961, Colonel Tom Parker began the process of killing the goose that laid the golden egg. First he negotiated with Hal Wallis to tear up their old contract and write a new one for five pictures, with Elvis getting $175,000 for the first three pictures, and then being raised to $200,000 for the final two. An additional bonus of $90,000 was to be paid upon the completion of the last film, and this was to be split evenly between Elvis and the Colonel. Within weeks of signing this contract, Parker negotiated another contract with MGM for four additional Presley films. This arrangement called for Elvis to be paid $400,000 per picture, with additional sums of $75,000 in general expenses and $25,000 for musical expenses. After the studio recouped $500,000 on each film, Presley would receive 50% of the profits. As sweet as the financial arrangements were, these deals called for Elvis to make nine films in five years. If that wasn't enough, before these contracts expired Parker had entered into a deal with Allied Artists for another film and a two-picture arrangement with United Artists. The end result was that between 1960 and 1966 Elvis Presley made 17 films, and some of these films were released within months of each other. Regardless of the quality of the scripts, and that was certainly questionable, is it any wonder that Presley's box office appeal began to crumble?

Elvis' first film for MGM was assigned to Ted Richmond, who produced the film under his Ted Richmond Productions banner. Richmond had begun work in the early 40s making ultra-low budget films for Poverty Row studio PRC, and then moved only slightly up the ladder to "B" movies at Columbia Pictures. He would remain at Columbia for six years, producing a number of the studio's very successful *Blondie* series with Penny Singleton, then move over in 1950 to Universal International and more program films. In 1953, while still at Universal, Ted Richmond would produce Tyrone Power's *The Mississippi Gambler* (one of the first films to give a star profit participation) and the beginning of a three-picture association between Richmond and the actor. Their final film together would end in tragedy when Power suffered a fatal heart attack on the set of *Solomon and Sheba* (1959). After a two-year gap, Richmond signed a producing deal with MGM and produced the Bob Hope comedy *Bachelor in Paradise* (1961). His next film would be Elvis' *It Happened at the World's Fair*, and with Colonel Parker's recommendation, he signed Norman Taurog to helm the picture—an assignment Taurog later told me was made unpleasant by Richmond's abrasive personality. This depiction of Richmond was also repeated to me by another friend of mine, screenwriter Herb Meadow, who had written one of Richmond's earlier Columbia films, *Count Three and Pray* (1955) and had found him to be quite obnoxious at times.

A few months before Taurog began filming *It Happened at the World's Fair* (1963), his fourth film with Elvis Presley, something happened that would eventually bring the two of us together for the first time. I had been an assistant film editor at Warner Bros. for several years, and in May of 1962 I was working on a film being produced by Richard Zanuck and directed by George Cukor, *The Chapman Report* (1963). The original editor had come over from Twentieth Century-Fox with Zanuck, and after a year on the film had returned to his home studio. I was then moved up to temporary film editor to finish what work was needed and to make eliminations in the film based on a series of censor notes from the Shurlock Office and the Catholic National Legion of Decency. *The Chapman Report* was based on a novel by Irving Wallace that had caused quite a stir when it first came out, due to its depiction of a medical sex survey similar to the actual Kinsey Reports on the "Sexual Behavior in the Human Male and Human Female" published during the late 1940s and early 1950s. The film used face-to-face interviews by highly trained specialists of four disparate suburban housewives to dramatize their personal lives. Both censor boards (particularly the Legion of Decency) found a great many parts of the film to be objectionable and were demanding changes. A screening was held in Jack Warner's private projection room and the Legion's notes were discussed. There were many but, from what I could tell, not that difficult to accomplish. However the big problem was that they had summarily dismissed the film's ending and wanted the studio to shoot a new one. Jack Warner was wringing his hands in dismay; if the Legion gave the picture a "C" (condemned) rating as they had threatened, then members of the Roman Catholic faith would be forbidden from seeing it both in the United States and throughout the world. After listening for what seemed like forever to the arguments going back and forth between Warner, his executive vice president Steve Trilling, and the representative from the Shurlock Office who had brought the notes, I decided to put in my two cents and asked Warner if I could make a suggestion. His answer still rings in my ears all these many years later: "Why not, kid? Everyone else has." My suggestions, including a way to satisfy the Legion's demands about the ending, must have impressed Warner, because the next morning I was called up to Steve Trilling's office and informed that Jack Warner was promoting me to producer.

My first assignment as producer, apart from writing and supervising the filming of the new ending for *The Chapman Report*, was to be a film that Warner wanted to make about the influx of teenagers into Palm Springs during the Easter vacation break. Warner had even selected the title, *Palm Springs Weekend*, which never made sense to me because the Easter break generally lasted for a week or sometimes two. Nevertheless, that was his title and who was I to argue with the man who had just given me the chance of a lifetime. A few days later I was again called into Trilling's office and introduced to a young man named Earl Hamner, Jr. who I was told was to write the screenplay for *Palm Springs Weekend*. The studio had recently purchased Earl's novel *Spencer's Mountain* and was in the process of turning it into a big-budgeted movie starring Henry Fonda and Maureen O'Hara. Earl would later create the beloved and long-running television series *The Waltons* (1971-1981), based on *Spencer's Mountain,* and then the equally long-running and popular *Falcon Crest* (1981- 1990). In its infinite wisdom the studio didn't have Hamner write the screenplay for his novel, but instead sent him off to Palm Springs during Easter Week to soak up the atmosphere for an original screenplay. Hamner clearly remembers that first meeting with Jack Warner, and his impression of the head of the studio not as "a forbidding legend, but rather a short, mustachioed, smiling man who put me at ease right away." After complimenting Hamner on his book, Warner brought up the subject of an assignment for him. "He explained that he had an army of young people under contract," remembered Hamner, "and he liked to keep them busy, actors like Connie Stevens, Troy Donahue, Bob Conrad and others. He said that he had recently seen a movie called *Where the Boys Are* [1960] which was set in Florida during Spring Break, and that he had a hunch there might also be a movie about Spring Break in Palm Springs where young college and high school students went to celebrate. Would I be willing to go over to 'the Springs' at Easter and see if there was a movie in the notion? Of course I would! I came back from my week in Palm Springs, wrote a treatment and wonder of wonders, got the go-ahead to write a major film!" Warner's explanation to Earl Hamner about his reasons for making *Palm Springs Weekend* was similar to the one I was given when I was called into his office the day I received my promotion, with one exception: Warner added two pieces of advice for my life as a Warner producer: "Don't be in a hurry to get yourself an agent, and don't step on my lines." With these words of wisdom firmly implanted in my brain, Hamner and I set out to create a screenplay that would insure that the "Colonel," as he liked to be addressed, wouldn't regret giving two neophytes a chance.

While Hamner was writing the first draft screenplay for *Palm Springs Weekend*, Taurog was on location in Seattle, Washington, filming *It Happened at the World's Fair.* The idea for the film originated with a suggestion from Washington Governor Albert Rosellini that struck a responsive chord with the MGM brass, and on May 30, 1962, *Variety* announced that Ted Richmond had hired "Seaman Jacobs and Sy Rose for their first feature film assignment on *Take Me to the Fair.* Writers have been associated with the *Bachelor Father* TV series." Taurog reported to MGM in late June, soon after completing his post-production chores on *Girls! Girls! Girls!,* to begin preparing for filming. One of his first actions was to fly to Seattle with his production staff to check out locations and to visit the Seattle Century 21 Exposition, the official name for the World's Fair. The park's monorail system

Joan O'Brien and Elvis in the "Happy Ending" finale for *It Happened at the World's Fair.*

Jack Mintz working with Elvis and Vicky Tiu on board the monorail at the Seattle World's Fair.

and the 605-foot high Space Needle with its 360 ° rotating dinning room at the summit were both scheduled to appear in the film, and Taurog had his art director Preston Ames take photographs and measurements so that he could recreate the interior of the restaurant on an MGM sound stage.

When Elvis reported to MGM Studios on August 28, 1962, he was fighting a sore throat that developed into a full scale cold a few nights later when he began recording the songs for the picture at Radio Recorders Studios in Hollywood. He was able to record one song before his throat closed up on him and he canceled the recording session after a few hours. With location filming scheduled to begin within a few days, Elvis' failure to return to Radio Recorders until after the Seattle shoot forced Taurog to film, with one exception, all of Elvis singing against background plates instead of on the actual location as planned. That one exception luckily turned out to be "Happy Ending" by Ben Wiseman and Sid Wayne, a rollicking number staged by choreographer Jack Baker as the finale for the film, complete with a 100-member marching band.

The fact that Elvis would be working within the Fairgrounds with hundreds of spectators milling around was a cause of deep concern for the Colonel and MGM, so a large contingent of Seattle police, augmented by plainclothes detectives from the Pinkerton Detective Agency, were assigned to protect the star. In addition, members of the Memphis Mafia (Elvis' entourage) who were travelling with Elvis were given special jumpsuit-style uniforms to identify them while on the set and functioning as Elvis' personal bodyguards.

Filming began at the Hallweg Monorail Terminal, next to the Seattle Century 21 Exposition, on Wednesday, October 5, 1962. Over the next seven days, filming continued throughout the Fairgrounds and at the base of the Space Needle. An extensive sequence with Elvis and little Sue-Lin (Vicky Tiu) touring the park was used to showcase the Fair's many exhibits, and frankly slowed the pacing of the film down to a crawl. Vicky Tiu, who would grow up to marry the Governor of Hawaii, Benjamin Cayetano in 1997, was the younger sister of Ginny Tiu, who played Mai Ling in *Girls! Girls! Girls!* The Jacobs-Rose script was nothing more than a framework upon which to hang the ten songs that Elvis sang at the drop of a music cue. Elvis was more relaxed and his relationship with little Vicky Tiu seemed genuine and underplayed. The rest of the plot, including a heavy (H.M. Wynant) and an illegal airplane flight, allowed Elvis and his buddy (Gary Lockwood) to have several fights. The love story with Joan O'Brien followed the usual formula of cute meeting—misunderstanding—reconciliation. I don't know whose idea it was for men's clothier Cy Devore to design Elvis' wardrobe for the film, probably producer Richmond's, but although Elvis looked great he appeared overdressed, always wearing different outfits with a jacket and tie.

Filming concluded in Washington on Thursday, September 13, 1962, and the company returned to Los Angeles to resume filming at MGM on the following Monday.

Apart from a second location junket to Camarillo in Ventura County, California, to film the airplane sequences at the Camarillo Airport, and the sequence where Walter (Kam Tong) and Sue-Lin first pick up Elvis and Gary

Garry Lockwood, Elvis, Vicky Tiu and Kam Tong at the Camarillo location for *It Happened at the World's Fair*.

Lockwood in their truck, one of the remaining sequences still to be filmed was the romantic dinner that Elvis and Joan O'Brien have in the rotating restaurant atop the Space Needle. It was on this set, which Preston Ames and his associate George W. Davis had recreated so effectively, that I first laid eyes on Elvis Presley and met Norman Taurog.

We had reached the point where it was time to sign a director for *Palm Springs Weekend* and the studio had recommended Taurog, a director with a huge list of credits in his résumé that went all the way back to silent films. He seemed like the perfect choice, but my biggest concern was how he was going to feel about working with a first-time producer. I went out to MGM Studios to meet with him for lunch and was directed by the guard at the front gate, an affable fellow aptly named Kenny Hollywood, to the stage where Elvis and Joan O'Brien were playing their scene in the replica of the Space Needle restaurant.

The real restaurant rotated 360° every thirty minutes, but on this set it was the painted background, seen through the glassless windows, that rotated for the same effect. I didn't meet Elvis that day, that wouldn't happen for a couple of years, but I watched with amusement as he joked with Taurog and other crew members over a flubbed line of dialogue. When the company broke for lunch, Taurog escorted me to his office where a selection of chicken sandwiches and iced tea was laid out for us. Norman and I hit it off instantly, I think he enjoyed my company and I certainly enjoyed his. He had a wonderful sense of humor and immediately made me feel at ease. We discussed the script, which the studio had previously sent him, and Norman made suggestions on what still needed to be done to improve it, trading ideas back and forth. I liked his way of thinking and left our lunch feeling comfortable that we could work together and that he would listen and respect my point of view. It was, to quote Humphrey Bogart's immortal line to Claude Rains at the fadeout of *Casablanca* (1942), "The beginning of a beautiful friendship."

After a considerable amount of process photography that took more than a week to complete and included the filming of at least four of Elvis' songs, production on *It Happened at the World's Fair* concluded on November 8, 1962. When MGM released *World's Fair* the following March, the reviews were much like those of Elvis' other recent films, with *Variety* warning that viewing the film would "apt to be tedious going for all but the most confirmed of Presley's young admirers." The *New York Herald-Tribune* described it as an "inoffensive bit of escapist fluff, like a marshmallow frappe with a musical topping." And the *New York Times* bemoaned the fact that "Elvis Presley's budding dramatic talents have been neatly snipped in the Seattle story, which emerges as a dismal parody of the Metro-Goldwyn-Mayer musicals of old." Although nobody at the studios seemed to be reading it, the handwriting was definitely on the wall.

Norman Taurog reported to Warners in mid November to begin prepping *Palm Springs Weekend.* One of the very first things we did was for Norman, Earl Hamner and me to travel to Palm Springs for a location survey. Since the picture was now officially in pre-production, several key personnel had been assigned, including a production manager and an art director, both of whom accompanied us. I had heard rumors that the Palm Springs officials were already expressing concerns that our film would show the city in a bad light, so the studio's publicity department arranged for our group to have lunch with Mayor Frank Bogert and members of the City Council to assure them that they had nothing to worry about.

I'd been receiving a number of letters from a local real estate agent who had sent me a dreadful idea for a screenplay called *Mr. Palm Springs* that he desperately wanted the studio to buy. I had tried to politely reject his submission, but he continued to bombard me with letters, and I suspected that he was behind the movement to derail our filming permits. At the luncheon, held in a private dining room at the newly opened Palm Springs Riviera Hotel, Norman, Earl and I did our best to charm the members of the City Council, Mayor Bogert and Chief of Police Gus Kettman. Norman accidentally spilled iced tea on the sleeve of his jacket and managed to turn it into a

Earl Hamner is fourth from left, next to art director LeRoy Deane. I'm standing next to Chief of Police Gus Kettman and Norman Taurog stands between him and Mayor Frank Bogert.

joke that everyone enjoyed. We seemed to successfully allay everyone's fears for the moment, but they reserved judgment until after they'd read our final screenplay, which we promised to send as soon as it was finished. I mentioned the real estate agent to Mayor Bogert, who assured me that the guy was a crackpot and not to worry about him.

One evening just before we were to return home, Norman informed me that we had been invited to dinner at Colonel Parker's home. I'd heard a lot about the famous "Colonel," and was anxious to meet him. The Colonel and his wife Marie owned a typical Palm Springs ranch-style house overlooking the lights of Palm Canyon Drive. We arrived just before sunset and settled down in their attractive den, while Marie, a very pleasant, plump housewife, served drinks. It was plain to see that Norman and the Colonel were good friends from the way they kidded one another, but I couldn't shake the feeling that the Colonel was showing off for me. I already knew his background and how, as an illegal Dutch immigrant and ex-carnival barker, he had assumed the title of Kentucky Colonel and taken a patent medicine with high alcohol content, renamed it "Hadacol" and sold it as a cure-all for arthritis and the common cold; but this evening the Colonel wanted to talk about how he'd "snookered" another producer named Hal Wallis.

The story bears repeating, if for no other reason than to show the unmitigated ego of the man. The Colonel had a habit of buying expensive suits and then having the tailor sew in a label from an inexpensive men's store named "Jim Clinton's." The Colonel loved to play the country hick and the label was the icing on the cake. When he was seated in Wallis' office, he turned back his coat so that the label was showing while he gave Wallis the figure he wanted for Elvis' new movie contract. Wallis balked at the figure, so the Colonel got up and started out of the office, informing Wallis that if he made it to the door the figure would go up by $50,000 and for every minute he was kept waiting in the outer office it would go up an additional $50,000. Wallis was not a man to be bluffed easily, but according to Parker, he gave in when the figure had risen by $100,000 and signed the new five-year contract. I was certain that the story was apocryphal, but it gave me an insight into a man who craved power, and who I would grow to dislike more and more as I worked with Elvis in the years to come. I don't believe that Colonel Parker ever spoke to me again, although we would see each other on various sets over the years. I seem to remember Norman reintroducing me to him on the set of *Tickle Me* and reminding him that I had been a guest at his house in Palm Springs, but Parker just nodded and walked away.

Palm Springs Weekend

After returning from Palm Springs, Earl Hamner began revising the script based on our location selections and further suggestions from Norman Taurog. The next step for Norman and me was to finalize the casting, and since Jack Warner's goal was to use as many of the studio's young television personalities as possible, the process turned out to be fairly straightforward. The studio at one point was considering Tuesday Weld to play the role of Gail, the high school student trying to pass as a Beverly Hills rich kid, but eventually decided on Connie Stevens. Troy Donahue had been in mind from the beginning for the role of Jim Munroe, the basketball hero. I had asked Earl to write a part for Ty Hardin, who had impressed me with his work in *The Chapman Report*, and Earl came up with a wonderful character of an ex-cowboy named Stretch who worked as a stunt man in pictures. Norman and I agreed that Bob Conrad, one of the stars of Warners television series *Hawaiian Eye* (1959-1963) was a perfect choice to play Eric, the spoiled rich kid who leads Connie Stevens' character astray. Unfortunately Steve Trilling had apparently told Edd Byrnes, who was becoming very popular as "Kookie," the hair- combing parking attendant on Warner's *77 Sunset Strip* (1958-1964), that he had the role of Eric. Byrnes hand-wrote a thank you note to Jack Warner, addressing him as Colonel Warner, and the good Colonel informed me that I had the unpleasant task of telling Byrnes that we had decided to go with Conrad, one of his rivals on the lot.

Despite what has been previously written Suzanne Pleshette was never considered for the role of Bunny, Troy Donahue's love interest. I was a big fan of Suzanne's and had even tried, unsuccessfully, to interest the studio in reviving a long dormant screenplay called *Letter from Peking* with her as the star. How-

(L-R) Troy Donahue, Stefanie Powers, Ty Hardin, Connie Stevens and Robert Conrad in *Palm Springs Weekend.*

ever, even though she was in her early twenties and was dating Troy, which would have been a nice publicity gimmick, Suzanne was much too mature to play any of the girls in *Palm Springs Weekend.* We found our Bunny, the chief of police's daughter, in a Blake Edwards thriller for Columbia Pictures called *Experiment in Terror* (1962): Stefanie Powers was actually the youngest of our cast and had only been featured in three films before *Weekend*, but nevertheless she did a terrific job for us. Stefanie was borrowed from Columbia Pictures for "not more than eight weeks," and Columbia was paid $1,875 per week for her services. My guess is that Stefanie saw less than half of what Columbia received.

We cast Dick Van Dyke's younger brother Jerry and a young actress name Zeme North as the two comedy lovers, and eight-year-old Billy Mumy as Boom-Boom, the ten-year-old terror who comes between them. On orders from on high, Warners' casting department had already penciled in three character actors who were also under contract to the studio for featured roles in the film: Andrew Duggan, who had played Dr. Chapman in *The Chapman Report*, and Jack Weston and Carole Cook, who had just finished co-starring with Don Knotts in the still unreleased half animated, half live-action fantasy called *The Incredible Mr. Limpet* (1964). When Norman and I

Suzanne Pleshette and Stefanie Powers watching filming on *Palm Springs Weekend*. (Photo courtesy Photofest)

ran this picture we both fell instantly in love with Carole Cook and I thought that Jack Weston was simply terrible. I even wrote an impassioned memo to Steve Trilling in which I called Jack "Probably the unfunniest man I had ever seen." As it turned out I lived to regret my words, as Jack took what was an over-the-top character as written and directed and turned in a wonderfully droll performance. I became good friends with Jack and we continued to see one another after the completion of filming—even going on a fun-filled trip to San Francisco along with Jerry Van Dyke and all of our wives.

Carole Cook and Jack Weston in *Palm Springs Weekend.*

Earl Hamner finished his revisions and the script was sent to the Production Code Administration, otherwise known as the Shurlock Office after its boss, Geoffrey M. Shurlock. The Shurlock Office approved our script with a few minor word changes; we couldn't show a sign reading, "Stamp Out Virginity," or refer to "rose bushes covered with girl's underclothes." At the same time, as promised, the script was sent to the Palm Springs City Council and their reaction was considerably more detailed and vitriolic. According to an article by reporter Frank Scully that appeared in *Weekly Variety*, one member of the City Council, a man named Harry Paisley whom we had met at the luncheon, said that the script read "like the work of a 13-year-old boy, the most terrible thing I ever read. They have made a fool of our chief of police, our hotels and everything else." Mr. Paisley's opinions were considerably overstated, but it was clear that we weren't going to get official cooperation unless some script revisions were made. One scene where kids poured soap detergent into a fountain in the center of town was based on an actual incident that had occurred a few years before, but the council wanted it removed for fear it would inspire others to do it again. At Norman's suggestion, Earl rewrote it into a marvelous comedy sequence involving Boom-Boom at the La Casa Yates' swimming pool, the motel where our kids were staying; it became one of the highlights in the film. A phone call from Jack Warner to Mayor Bogert, reminding him that Warner owned a home in Palm Springs and that filming there would bring a lot of money to the city, smoothed things over and we got our cooperation.

Although I thought that the script was now in pretty good shape, Norman felt it still needed some more work. So David Schwartz, who had just finished working on the screenplay adaptation of Helen Gurley Brown's best-seller *Sex and the Single Girl,* was hired to do a quick polish on the script. His results didn't satisfy anybody and the studio authorized hiring another writer. Norman suggested Danny Arnold, a writer he had worked with at Paramount on the Martin and Lewis films, and in January of 1963, Arnold was signed on a week-to-week basis at $1,500 a week to do a polish. Danny lived in Palm Springs, so we first met at the Holiday Inn Hotel next to the 405 Freeway in Bel Air, where he was staying temporarily. Then, when we moved down to Palm Springs to start filming, we continued to meet at my suite in the Riviera Hotel. Norman requested that his old associate Jack Mintz be the film's dialogue director and I authorized his hiring at $500 a week. As it turned out, this would be Jack's final film, as he retired from the business shortly after completing *Palm Springs Weekend.*

Even though work was still being done on the script, the studio insisted that the budget be finalized and a production meeting was held in the main meeting room of the production department on Thursday, January 17, 1963. Norman and I, along with the production manager Charles Hanson, were joined by all of the department heads, as well as Norman's cousin Stanley Goldsmith, who would be the film's first assistant director. We went through the incomplete script and Norman attempted to fill in the blanks as best he could, describing certain scenes and locations that were yet to be written, so that our art director LeRoy Deane could get an idea of what he had to design and construct. The final budget for the film came in at $1,565,000 and Steve Trilling, who had never approved of Warner's decision to make me a producer and had since become my nemesis, heatedly objected to the cost. I had tried to delay the start date and the budget meeting until all work on

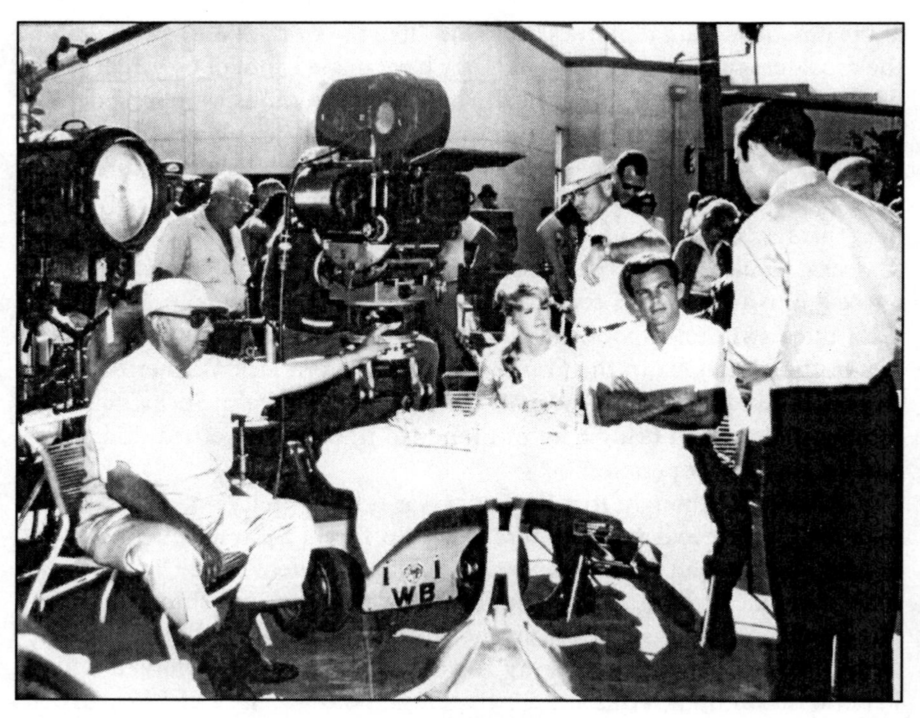

Norman Taurog directing Connie Stevens and Robert Conrad at the Riviera Hotel pool.

the screenplay was finished, but Trilling had insisted, and here we were at a standoff that wouldn't be resolved until we returned from Palm Springs.

On February 10, 1963, a studio car picked up Norman and me at our homes and drove us to Palm Springs where we checked into the Riviera Hotel, which would become our headquarters as well as one of our principal location sites. Filming began in front of its main entrance on February 12, 1963, and Norman immediately introduced one of his infamous sight gags. Two of Troy Donahue's basketball team members (Robert Gothie and Jim Shane) pull up in a Model T and wave to the doorman as they walk away, leaving the poor man to watch in shock as the car slowly disintegrates in front of him. The doorman was played by Mike Henry, former Pittsburgh Steelers and L.A. Rams linebacker and future Tarzan in three films in the late '60s. Gary Kincaid, another member of the basketball team whose real name was Gary Knafelc, was also an ex- pro football player for the Green Bay Packers. Knafelc dropped his screen name when he went back to Green Bay in 1964 to become the team's public address announcer, a position he held for over 40 years until his retirement in 2004.

Filming continued for the next few weeks around the Riviera Hotel, a gas station on Indian Avenue, some streets in Palm Springs, and the exterior of the Congress Inn, just off of Highway 111, which doubled for the exterior of the La Casa Yates motel; LeRoy Deane was building the motel's interior on Stage 7 at Warner Bros. There was also an extensive road race between Eric, Stretch and Jim that required several stunt men, a special effects team to stage a crash and a camera car to film running shots on the road. Unfortunately we began getting hit with severe wind storms which blew sand everywhere, making filming impossible. This caused us to fall a couple of days behind schedule and the decision was made to scrub some location filming and return to Burbank. The biggest loss was not being able to shoot the night exterior of an actual gambling casino in Cabazon, just outside of Palm Springs, which figured heavily in the film's finale. An exterior of the casino and parking lot had to be built at the studio and the end result, with an unconvincing background cyclorama and a very large and very phony-looking rock right in the foreground, was not very satisfactory. On top of that it added $24,000 to our set budget. The estimating department came out with a new schedule and cost estimation that showed that we would run five days and $91,000 over budget. Steve Trilling was immediately on the phone, demanding we cut scenes to catch up, and Norman and I went through the script very carefully, managing to find a few scenes we could lose, but not enough to make an appreciable difference. In the end, Norman managed to pick up a couple of days on the schedule and the studio allowed us to continue filming all of the needed scenes.

Troy Donahue and Jerry Van Dyke manage to survive being engulfed in soap suds in *Palm Springs Weekend*.

There were a few other minor problems, such as the day that Troy Donahue reported to the set with several pimples on his face. Our cameraman, Harold Lipstein agreed that he couldn't be photographed and he was sent to his physician, who informed the studio that Donahue would need at least two days before he could be photographed in close up. Troy was back at work a few days later when Norman began filming the pool sequence with the bubbles on Monday, April 11. It took three days to complete, but Norman filled the sequence with several wonderful sight gags and Troy and Jerry Van Dyke were good sports and didn't complain about being submerged constantly in soap suds.

Toward the end of April we filmed the final scene in the picture, where Connie visits Ty in the hospital and tells him the truth about herself. We still needed several days of process filming with Connie, Bob, Troy and Ty in cars, for several sequences including the chase, and a second unit was sent back to Palm Springs to film the process plates we hadn't been able to get because of the bad weather. Norman returned to the studio to film process shots on Monday, May 13, and the film officially wrapped on the following Thursday, May 16, 1963.

Norman was kind enough to include me in his editing sessions with our editor Folmar Blangsted, and when we had the picture in shape we ran it for Jack Warner, who seemed to like what he saw. Steve Trilling, on the other hand, started his usual nitpicking until I thought I'd go crazy. Warner finally overruled him, declaring that we should first see how the film played in front of an audience before we did any more cutting. *Palm Springs Weekend* was turned over to the music and sound effects departments, and as it turned out our composer was Frank Perkins, whose daughter and I had dated briefly in high school. Frank had written the song "Stars Fell on Alabama" a pop standard in every performer's repertoire, and for our picture he wrote a wonderful jazz-fused score.

When it came time to sneak preview *Palm Springs Weekend*, it turned out that Jack Warner was away from the studio, taking his annual vacation in the South of France, and on the night of the preview, Norman Taurog came down with a bad case of the flu. We previewed at the Warners Theatre in Huntington Park and as the film unspooled I could tell that the audience was thoroughly enjoying it. Afterward, as was the custom, everyone trooped upstairs to the manager's office to hold a post-mortem. On the way upstairs all of the department heads were congratulating me on a successful preview. Normally, when Jack Warner was present at a preview, he would sit behind the manager's desk and, if the picture had problems, he would mention his biggest concerns, tell one of his corny jokes and dismiss the meeting. The following morning a complete set of Warner's notes would arrive at the editor's cutting room and the problems would be addressed. Tonight, it was Steve

Trilling seated behind the manager's desk, and instead of telling a corny joke, he announced to the room that the picture "needed a great deal of work." He then began to enumerate all of the changes he had brought up at the earlier screening with Jack Warner and, as if on cue, the department heads began agreeing with him. Since neither Warner nor Taurog were there to disagree, I realized that there was no one there to stop him but me and I ended up making some damaging remarks—damaging to my career, that is. My public, disrespectful challenge of Trilling's authority cost me my job; I received a written notice that my option was being dropped and I would be leaving the studio in six weeks.

Norman and I had discussed the possibility of continuing to work together, and I had already given him a play that I thought had screen possibilities. The play was called *State of Mind* and had been written by a very successful science fiction author named Nelson Bond. Bond's play told of a harried Long Island business executive, who discovers an old land grant assigned to one of his ancestors by the Continental Congress of the United States for services rendered during the Revolutionary War. The grant deeded most of what was now Long Island to his ancestor, and our hero then decides to secede from the Union. The problems that this causes make up the main plot of the play. It was a very funny political satire, on the order of films such as *Passport to Pimlico* (1949) and *The Mouse That Roared* (1959). Norman also saw its potential and we secured an option on the play and Norman gave it to his agents at Chasin, Park Citron. In short order, they put together a package with Fred MacMurray as the star, Claude Binyon (a writer Taurog had worked with years before at Paramount) to write the screenplay, Norman as the director and me as the producer. MacMurray had just finished filming another comedy for Warner Bros. called *Kisses for My President* (1964) and the studio was looking for a follow-up for him. Arthur Park took the package directly to Jack Warner and got an immediate commitment from him, and we were back in business. I even had the pleasure of running into Steve Trilling in the hall one day and having him begrudgingly greet me with, "Well, it looks as if you're going to be staying around awhile."

Palm Springs Weekend opened nationwide on November 5, 1963, and the reviewers all seemed to like the film, with the *Hollywood Reporter* announcing, "Warners has come up with another good job of picture-making in *Palm Springs Weekend*, peopling it with bright, young, pleasant-looking players and giving it a topical story—and a production sheen in keeping with the rest of the studio's product. Michael A. Hoey produced and Norman Taurog directed the feature, which by virtue of it being cast with many TV stars, may find wide acceptance at the boxoffice." *Variety* liked some of our lesser-known players as well: "Comedy, broad and plentiful, owes much to the strong second team—particularly Zeme North as the perennial plain Jane;

Jerry Van Dyke, as her male counterpart; and Jack Weston and Carole Cook, who have a more glandular approach to romance than do their youthful charges." John L. Scott in the *Los Angeles Times* wrote, "These up-and-coming young people throw themselves into a topical story with vigor. Norman Taurog, the director, has always had a way with youngsters, and mixes action, romance and comedy elements fairly judiciously." Even the *New York Times*, now *sans* Bosley Crowther, had some nice things to say about our efforts: "Say this for the young people in *Palm Springs Weekend*. They're one heck of a lot more palatable than those braying, wiggling adolescents in the recent *Beach Party*. Somehow, the ingredients have merged for a harmless, good-natured little romp, where restless youngsters aren't averse to good manners, a principle or two and, glory be, some blithe practicality about sex. For the most part, director Norman Taurog keeps his high-spirited cast in sensible check. The young people are generally personable, if hardly memorable, and more than matched by a handful of oldsters. Finally, here is one groovy saga that doesn't imply that anybody over 21 is ready for the glue factory."

Palm Springs Weekend didn't make *Variety*'s list of the top grossers of the year, but individual box-office reports throughout '63 and '64 showed that the film returned an ample profit for Warner Bros.

The Year of Desperation

While we were waiting for the contracts to be drawn up for *State of Mind*, Norman Taurog asked me to help with a project he was going to do for the Harvard School for Boys which his son Jonathan was attending. Harvard was an Episcopal day school-boarding school that was also a part-time military academy, located on a twenty-three-acre campus on Coldwater Canyon in the San Fernando Valley. Many of Hollywood's elite sent their sons to the school, including Darryl Zanuck's son Richard, who had graduated in 1952, and Gregory Peck's sons, Stephen and Cary, who were still attending the school at that time. Founded in 1900, the school had moved to the Valley location in 1937 and was now in need of expansion to increase its current enrollment of 350 boys to a maximum of 600 boys. Norman had in mind to produce a short fund-raising film and he asked me to write and produce it with him. We called it *A Step Toward Manhood* and predictably, Norman suggested that we tell the story through the eyes of a five-year old boy who sneaks into the school and ends up getting a guided tour from the headmaster, Father William Chalmers. Through his connections at Paramount Studios, Norman was able to secure the equipment and a film crew, including his old friend Academy Award cinematographer Loyal Griggs. After a few weeks spent writing the screenplay, we were all set to start shooting. Gregory Peck had agreed to speak the narration and we found a cute little guy, the younger brother of one the students, to play Tommy our five-year old.

November 22, 1963, was a Friday, and Norman and I had agreed to meet at the Harvard School with our crew to go over the filming requirements before we began production on the following Monday. I was in my car, driving in from Woodland Hills on the 101 Freeway, when the radio announced that President Kennedy had been shot in Dallas. By the time I'd reached the Harvard campus, the world had learned that John F. Kennedy had died. Norman and I went through the motions with our crew without saying anything to each other about *State of Mind*, but both of us knew that our project had just been cancelled. Sure enough, the call from Arthur Park came later that afternoon: Warners had pulled out of the deal, not wanting to be involved in making a political satire at this tragic time for our country. *State of Mind* never did get made and Warners delayed the release of *Kisses for My President* for almost a year.

We finished making *A Step Toward Manhood,* and it was so successful, raising almost $3 million for the school, that four years later they asked us to come back to update it. This time Dick Zanuck, who was now head of production at Twentieth Century-Fox, gave us a crew and facilities to do the work, and Gregory Peck kindly agreed to come back to record the new narration.

I left Warner Bros. in early December and shortly thereafter Jack Warner fired Steve Trilling. Warner's son-in-law William T. Orr had been appointed vice- president in charge of all television and feature production and there really was no place for Trilling any more. It must have been a great shock to a man who had devoted over thirty years of his life to the studio, for a few months later Steve Trilling suffered a fatal heart attack at the age of 61.

Norman and I announced in the trades that we were forming an independent production company. I had an exciting idea for a television series called *Hunters Three*, about a trio of international agents, an American, a Japanese and an Englishman, who travel the world spying for an unnamed agency like the CIA. A terrific writer by the name of Ron Bishop, who had been working with me while I was still at Warners on a western script I was supposed to produce, joined with me in creating a pilot script, and Bob Conrad, who had also left the studio, agreed to be one of our stars. If Sheldon Leonard hadn't sold *I Spy* to NBC that season, I think we might have had a chance, but unfortunately he did and we were out of luck. If all of this bad news wasn't enough, in late May of 1964, Norman Taurog contracted a severe case of hepatitis and was hospitalized at St. John's Hospital for nine weeks and then spent a long time at home recuperating. It seemed as if a black cloud was hovering overhead and was just not going to go away, but Norman never lost his sense of humor, and when I would visit him at his home, he was always full of good spirits.

Like most of the homes in this section of Beverly Hills just south of Sunset Boulevard, 529 Hillcrest Road was set back from the street behind a large lawn and manicured flowerbeds, which were separated by steps and a brick walkway that led to the ornate glass and wood front door of the two-story, five-bedroom house. As you entered the living room with a baby grand piano on your right and the study on your left, a hallway led through past a winding staircase to a sunroom containing a small glass dining table. Norman's study was warm and comforting. A large window, which looked out onto the front lawn and the tree-lined street beyond, filled the room with bright sunlight, illuminating the large bookcase that held his morocco-bound scripts and his Oscar. A collection of clown figurines and a self-portrait of Red Skelton as a clown, given to Norman by the comedian, occupied another of the shelves. Norman would sit in a large easy chair, his back to the window, and his guests on a comfortable couch opposite him. Since he was already blind in one eye and his eyesight was failing in the other, he preferred to view his guests with the sunlight at his back. The Taurogs had two African-American servants, a cook-housekeeper and a houseman named Leon who also served as Norman's driver. Whenever I would come to the house, Leon would greet me at the front door with a friendly, "Hello, Mr. Holy," No matter how hard I tried I couldn't convince Leon that my last name had no "L" in it, and eventually even Norman began calling me "Mr. Holy" as a joke. That's how he always greeted me after that, for as long as I knew him.

While Norman was recuperating during the long, hot summer of 1965, Sue Taurog was busy with her charity and her political work with the Republican Party. Earlier in 1962, when Richard Nixon had begun his unsuccessful run for governor of California, she had hosted a lunch for Nixon at Romanoff's in Beverly Hills, as well as organizing a telethon and a closed circuit dinner for him the following week. When Nixon lost to Democratic incumbent Pat Brown, he gave his famous "You won't have Nixon to kick around any more" speech to the press. The following year, Sue co-chaired, with her friend Sybil Brand, the annual USC's Town and Gown banquet of the cinema fraternity Delta Kappa Alpha honoring Mary Pickford and Harold Lloyd, and the year after that an all-star, charity fashion show for the premiere of Ross Hunter's film *The Chalk Garden* (1964). This event at Universal Studios was a big success in spite of the fact that it was held in a pouring rain. In June of 1965, Sue was elected president of the Los Angeles Orphanage Guild, about the same time that Norman became increasingly involved with USC's Cinema Department. That summer it was his turn to be honored, along with Rosalind Russell and Robert Wise, at the annual Delta Kappa Alpha fraternity dinner.

The dark clouds finally lifted toward the end of summer, when Norman called to say that he was fully recovered and was starting a new picture with Elvis for Allied Artists in a few weeks. He wondered if I would like to work with him, as his old associate Jack Mintz had decided to retire. I of course accepted immediately, knowing that I would learn a lot about writing and directing from working with him on the set. The money was good, but the only title I could have was what Jack had received, dialogue director; how-

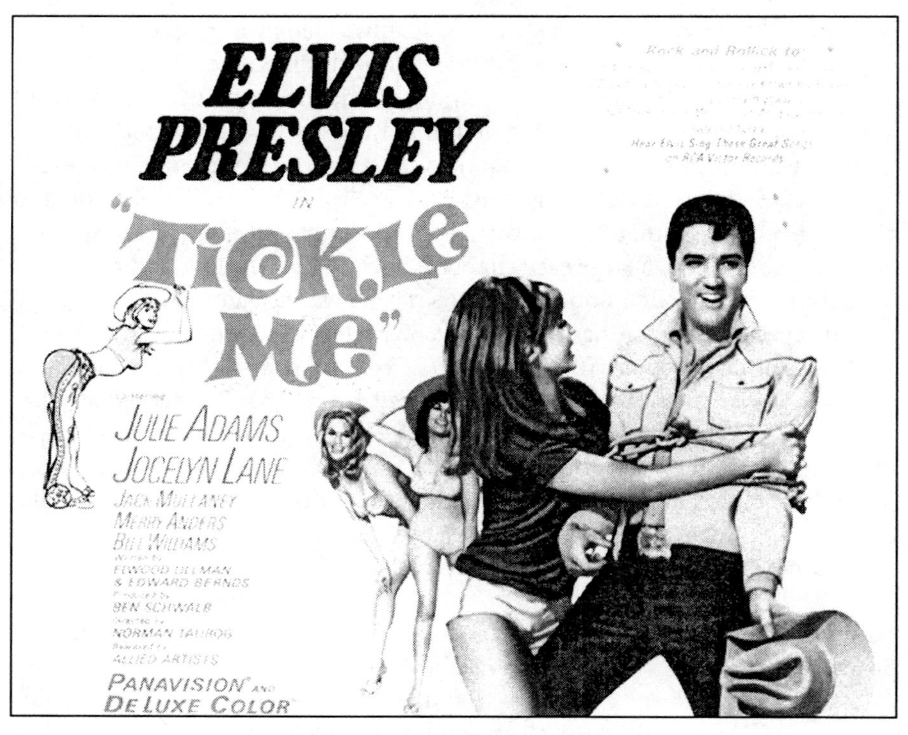

Lobby card for *Tickle Me*.

ever, since the Directors Guild now objected to the use of the word "director" in that title, it became dialogue coach and eventually dialogue supervisor. Whatever my title, I would spend the next four years writing and rewriting scripts and standing beside Norman Taurog on the set, learning firsthand about filmmaking as he directed the last six films of his career.

Colonel Parker's deal with Allied Artists came about because Elvis suddenly found himself short of cash. According to what Norman told me later, the IRS had come down hard on Elvis and he desperately needed money to pay his income tax, so the Colonel cobbled together a quick, one-picture deal with Allied Artists Pictures. Allied Artists was the upscale named offspring of Monogram Pictures the onetime member of Poverty Row that occasionally aspired to make important pictures, provided the budgets weren't too high. The deal that the Colonel brokered would pay Elvis (and the Colonel of course) $600,000 plus $150,000 in expenses and 50% of the profits. To keep the budget at $1,500,000, the Colonel arranged with RCA for enough unreleased music tracks to fill the soundtrack, thereby eliminating the need and the cost of recording any new songs. I'm not sure why it was decided to film the picture at Paramount, but I'd imagine it was a combination of things, including the fact that the Colonel had his office on the lot and didn't feel like moving. I also think that Norman probably correctly pointed out to the film's producer, Ben Schwalb, that Paramount had better facilities and its crews were familiar with working with Elvis. At any rate, Allied Artists entered into a rental agreement with Paramount which included stage rental at $1,200 a day and $1,000 a day for the studio's Western Street. The agreement also included the use of standing sets, camera, sound, electrical, and grip equipment, cutting rooms, dubbing and recording stages, and offices. *Tickle Me* would be the least expensive Elvis Presley film on record. With a below-the-line estimate of $399,750, it eventually went $6,650 over budget and finished at $406,400.

I reported to Paramount some time around the first of October and started going over the script with Norman. He looked pretty rugged having lost over 70 pounds during his illness, but his energy seemed to be there, and his sense of humor was certainly unaffected. The *Tickle Me* screenplay, which was originally called *Isle of Paradise*, was written by a couple of slapstick comedy writers, Edward Bernds and Elwood Ullman, who had begun their writing careers creating shorts for the Three Stooges, before turning their talents to the *Bowery Boys* series at Monogram. The plot of *Tickle Me* began by placing Elvis at a women's dude ranch surrounded by lots of gorgeous women and then progressing into a complicated series of situations involving a lost treasure and an old western ghost town. As it turned out, I did quite a bit of writing on the script, particularly in the last act, which Norman and I virtu-

With Norman Taurog on the set of *Tickle Me*.

Julie Adams and Elvis.

Jocelyn Lane and Elvis.

ally rewrote from scratch, inserting a lot of haunted house gags, filled with creaking doors, stormy nights and characters lurking around in fright masks.

In addition to Elvis, the other leads in the film were Julie Adams, the sexy victim of Universal's Gil Man in *Creature from the Black Lagoon* (1954) who played the seductive owner of the resort. Jocelyn Lane, a young British actress who had made a name for herself as a fashion model and had previously appeared in several sex-and-sand opuses, played Elvis' love interest and the inheritor of the map to a hidden fortune. Jack Mullaney, who had been co-starring in the TV series *My Living Doll* (1964-1965) with Robert Cummings and Julie Newmar, was Elvis' bumbling friend Stanley Potter. Jimmy Hawkins was also up for the part of Stanley, and he remembered that was how he first met Norman Taurog "I was called into his office at Paramount. He was very frank with me, he said, 'There's another guy that we're trying to get and if he's not available I would very much like you. I've seen your work and I'd like you to do it if things don't work out with this other actor.' So I said, 'great, I'd love to work with you, sir.' Of course they got the other person." Hawkins would end up making two films with Elvis, *Girl Happy* (1965) and *Spinout* (1966), the latter for Norman Taurog; in it, both he and Jack Mullaney played members of Elvis' band. In a somewhat similar situation, Edward Faulkner, who played Brad Bentley, Elvis' rival for the attention of the health resort's many young women, had first worked briefly for Norman Taurog on *G.I. Blues*. "I remember I was just getting started," he told me, "and it was in 1960, when they were shooting *G.I. Blues*. I was at Paramount for some reason, and I was walking down this long hallway. I'd been to see somebody in casting, and this small man behind me called out, 'Pardon me, are you an actor?' I recognized that he was Bill Meiklejohn, then head of casting at Paramount, and I said, yes. He asked me if I would like to do a picture with Elvis Presley and I said I would be delighted. So I went on the set and met Mr. Taurog and he okayed me and I didn't have that large a part, I played Red, one of the soldiers in the train station some place in Germany. That was my first experience with Mr. Taurog, and I found him very easy, very congenial, and easy to work with. Some years later my agent called me and said, 'You're to go to Paramount Studios to see Norman Taurog, he's directing an Elvis picture.' So I met with Mr. Taurog again and he started describing the part to me, and I said, 'Mr. Taurog, I don't think I'm physically right for this part. I could handle the fight scenes, that's no problem, but you want a big, muscle-bound kind of a guy and I just don't think physically I would fit into this part.' He asked me if I had any film where I was in a fight and I said he could look at *McLintock!* [1963], where I had a great fight scene with Pat Wayne. And then he said, 'Do you have any pictures where you might be stripped to the waist?' And I said, 'Yes, as a matter of fact, in *How to Murder Your Wife* [1965] with Jack Lemmon, I was one of his entourage and we had some scenes in the gym.' So he said, 'Well, let's take a look at those.'" Faulkner immediately went to a phone and called his agent and they both agreed that he wasn't right for the part. Faulkner drove back to his home in Palos Verde Estates, which was over an hour's drive from Paramount, and almost as soon as he arrived home he received another phone call from his agent's secretary asking him to return to Paramount for another meeting. When he arrived, Taurog told him they had looked at his film and then asked him to remove his shirt. Faulkner remembers removing his shirt and striking several poses, adding with a laugh, "So that's how I became Brad."

Other featured players were Bill Williams from television's *The Adventures of Kit Carson* (1951-1955), who played the friendly deputy sheriff that turns out to be the head crook. Merry Anders was signed for a featured role as one of the girls at the resort who was always hungry, and Norman's old friend, Connie Gilchrest played the resort's Swedish masseuse. Louis Elias and Robert Hoy, both terrific stunt men, were cast as two untrustworthy resort workers and were featured heavily in fights and stunts throughout the picture and particularly in the haunted house sequence.

Taurog's crew was comprised of many familiar faces, including cinematographer Loyal Griggs, who in addition to just having filmed *A Step Toward Manhood* for Norman had previously photographed *G.I. Blues* and *Girls! Girls! Girls*! Robert Goodstein, who had spent many years at Paramount as a prop man on a number of Taurog's earlier films and had moved into production was the unit manager, and Artie Jacobson, who had been the first assistant on several of Taurog's previous films, was again on the set with him. Micky Moore once again headed up a second unit shoot. Editor Archie Marshek had edited a number of films for Norman Taurog, including three Martin and Lewis comedies and *The Fuzzy Pink Nightgown.*

Elvis reported to Paramount on Tuesday, October 6, 1964, for wardrobe fittings. When I first met Elvis Presley in a dressing room of the wardrobe department at Paramount Studios, where he was trying on his *Tickle Me* costumes, my initial impression was that he was standoffish; he barely looked at me as we were introduced. However, I soon came to realize that he was incredibly shy and felt uncomfortable around strangers. He would prefer to spend his leisure time with the group of guys that travelled with him at all times. With them he could laugh, play music and watch television, indulge in some very physical sports, and eat the Southern fried foods that he loved. Elvis' coterie, the so-called "Memphis Mafia," became so famous that there's even a calorie-stuffed deep-fried fritter with banana chunks and cinnamon glaze, topped with chocolate chips that's served at an Oregon restaurant that's called the "Memphis Mafia." Elvis would have loved it.

The gang was an odd assortment of young men, close to his age, who were either related, like his cousin Billy Smith, or had grown up with him

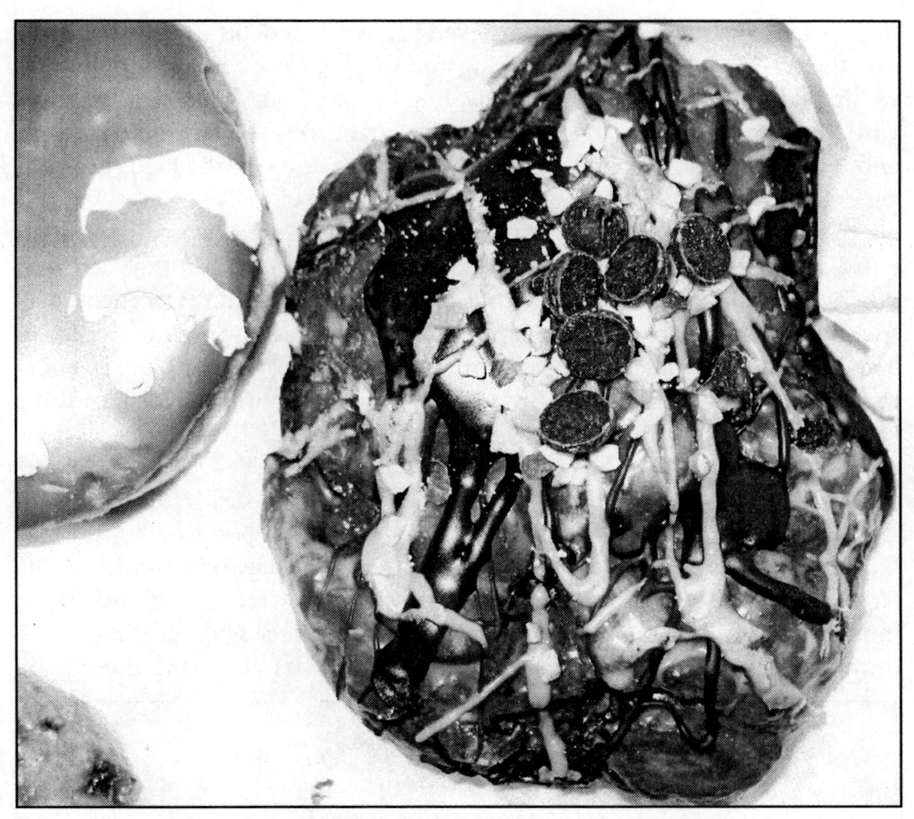

The "Memphis Mafia" deep-fried fritter.

in Memphis, like Red and Sonny West, Marty Lacker, Lamar Fike, and Jerry Schilling, or served with him in the army, like Joe Esposito and Charlie Hodge. There was no question that these "boys" clearly loved him and would do anything for him—and frequently did, including procuring drugs for him. They each had specific jobs to do, some official and some unofficial, and there was a defined hierarchy to the organization. Joe Esposito, who had first met Elvis in Germany when they were in the Army, was the "major-domo," whose job it was to run the organization and see to it that Elvis would report to the set on time. He also successfully trod the narrow path of pleasing both Elvis and Colonel Parker at the same time. He apparently lost favor with Elvis at one point and was briefly replaced by Marty Lacker, before being allowed to return. Others like Red West had gone to high school with Elvis and had been with him since 1955. Red would introduce his cousin, Sonny West, to Elvis at a roller rink in 1958 and Sonny would go to work for Elvis in 1960 when he got out of the Air Force and Elvis had returned from Germany. Elvis relied on "the boys" to do everything. In later years when he began touring, their responsibilities would become even more detailed, but at the time that I met them their jobs included cooking and driving for Elvis and functioning as his bodyguards. Billy Smith, Elvis' first cousin from Kentucky, who was with him as a companion beginning in the early fifties and lasting to the very end, and several others, including Jerry Schilling and Charlie Hodge, would generally hang out on the set with Elvis.

Some members, like Joe Esposito and Charlie Hodge, would present an outwardly friendly attitude to outsiders even if they didn't feel that way, and others like Red West, his cousin Sonny West and Jerry Schilling were genuinely friendly. Still others like Marty Lacker and Alan Fortas saw no importance in being friendly and often appeared hard-faced and aloof. Lamar Fike, an enormously fat man who first met Elvis in 1954 and went to work for him three years later, was not with him on the movie sets that much. I'd see him occasionally, but most of the time he was probably at the house in Bel-Air or at Colonel Parker's offices in one of the converted dance studios on the MGM lot.

Elvis supported the "boys" with salaries, Christmas bonuses, houses, Cadillacs and other gifts. And he rewarded his most loyal associates with a glittering necklace bearing the letters "TCB"—for "Takin' Care of Business," Elvis's motto—above a lightning bolt motif. In later years, after Elvis' death, most of these same men would continue to trade on Elvis' name, giving interviews,

(L-R) Unidentified, Sonny West, Red West, Elvis, Jerry Schilling, Lamar Fike, Joe Esposito, Vernon Presley and Taurog's son Jon, who was briefly with the group.

writing books, making personal appearances, even making videos. Today, most of their stories are benign, humorous anecdotes about water fights, bachelor parties and other celebrities, but there was a time when these same men would write and talk about Elvis' drug addiction, including a video in which many of the original members spoke about Elvis' addiction to speed and how they too had to take the pills, just to keep up with him. At the same time they declared there was nothing they could do to stop Elvis's decline into oblivion. It always rang hollow to me, particularly since those that are still alive have built careers around Elvis' legacy and travel the world giving lectures.

Elvis certainly loved women and they certainly loved him and on *Tickle Me* he was surrounded by women. There were, count 'em, 16 beautiful ladies, all dressed in a variety of skimpy outfits and eagerly hovering around him. For Elvis it was a veritable smorgasbord of pulchritude. As his cousin Billy once described Elvis and his women, "He was so charismatic that they were like moths, flying around a flame." Lamar Fike described it this way: "You've got wealth and looks; they're really going to come and their going to came fast and hard. And what you had to do on a continual basis, was weed 'em out. Because you got to weed the squirrels out from the lambs, and the squirrels cause you more trouble than a lamb ever caused… Because they're crazy." As far as I could tell, there weren't any "squirrels" on *Tickle Me*, and however many of the "lambs" Elvis managed to corral, it didn't affect our shooting schedule.

We started filming *Tickle Me* on October 12, 1964, on Paramount's Stage 5 in the *Silver Queen set.* It was a stylized flashback sequence, a parody of old western movies told in an amusing tongue-in-cheek style. Jocelyn Lane looked incredibly sexy in a tight-fitting gold lamé gown, Elvis had a chance to show off his fast-draw ability in a quick shootout with Ed Faulkner, and of course it was one of many excuses for Elvis to sing. This particular song, "Put the Blame on Me," fit nicely into the western parody setting, but some of the other songs seemed to be dragged in from left field and had so much reverb added to Elvis' vocals that they sounded like what they were, songs for a record album and not as if Elvis was actually singing them in the film. Paramount art director Arthur Lonergan designed two extensive sets on Stages 8 and 9 for the resort's pool area and the exterior and interior of several cottages. The main exterior for the Circle Z dude ranch was a redressed set that had been constructed for some previous Paramount production in the studio's main process tank and permanent sky cyclorama. There were several days scheduled on the studio's western street and we could only be there whenever Paramount's hit television series *Bonanza* (1959-1973) wasn't using it.

Tickle Me filmed for a total of 23 days, one of the shortest schedules for any Elvis movie, plus two days of second unit photography for desert exteriors in the Palmdale area. The second unit footage, of which there was quite a bit, helped to give the film some "air," as we filmed all the rest of the exteriors on studio sets, with a desert background that looked just as phony as the one in *Palm Springs Weekend*. The final day of filming, November 11, was spent shooting process shots on Stage 2 and several pick-up shots in the Palace Hotel corridors on Stage 5. All in all it had been a very easy and quite pleasant shoot. Elvis had been very cooperative, and at the wrap party, held in the Corral Club saloon set, he and Colonel Parker handed out posters and record albums to everyone. I got Elvis to autograph one of the posters, which hung in my daughter Karin's bedroom for many years.

The film was press previewed at the Hollywood Paramount Theatre on May 13, 1965, and received generally good reviews. *The Hollywood Reporter* said, "*Tickle Me* is the latest Elvis Presley, somewhat better than average in this special class, which means it will do Presley business with a plus. The Allied Artists release is a comedy with songs, and Norman Taurog has directed with a light and inventive hand, so the comedy is frequent enough to make it pleasant... Directed well, as he is here by Taurog, Presley has a facility for genteel comedy. He seems to be kidding himself, not taking his romantic charms too seriously, in a manner that is ingratiating. He gets good help from Jack Mullaney, playing one of those all-thumbs, two-left-feet characters. Mullaney is very funny, and Taurog has wisely given him footage to develop." *Variety* even singled out our ghost sequence in its review: "Screenplay ...is wispy thin, but allows singer to rock over nine numbers from past albums to good effect. He gets good comedy backing from a competent cast and a flock of young beauts [sic] cavorting in near-bikini attire, and a wind-up finish, fast and corny, should tickle the palates of his natural audience as well as furnishing a field day for moppets." Only Howard Thompson in the *New York Times* really disliked the film, saying, "Elvis Presley had better watch his step after *Tickle Me* ...This is the silliest, feeblest and dullest vehicle for the Memphis Wonder in a long time. And both Elvis and his sponsors, this time Allied Artists, should know better."

Well, as it turned out, Allied Artists did know better. *Tickle Me* contained nine songs (David Winters did the choreography), five fights and sixteen beautiful women—a perfect formula for success—and that's exactly what Allied Artists got. On Monday, July 26, 1965, *The Hollywood Reporter* carried a story in which Steve Broidy, the president of Allied Artists, announced that *Tickle Me* had already grossed $1,028,000 from 2622 engagements and that the United States rentals alone would be at least $3,000,000 and worldwide billings should bring in between $4,700,000 and $5,000,000. *Tickle Me* became the third highest grossing film for Allied Artists and saved the studio from bankruptcy for a few more years. Allied Artists ceased to exist in 1976, when it merged with consumer producers Kalvex and PSDP, Inc. and became known as Allied Artists Industries manufacturing mobile homes and pharmaceuticals.

Sergeant Deadhead and *Dr. Goldfoot*

Shortly after the holiday break in 1964, Norman Taurog signed a two-picture deal with American International Pictures, the company famous for their *Beach Party* films and for Roger Corman's baroque Edgar Allan Poe horror films. It was a simple move, from the Paramount lot directly across Melrose Avenue to Producers Studios one of the oldest facilities in Hollywood, having begun as Famous Players Fiction Studio in 1915. The studio's decaying edifice was an appropriate setting for the company founded by James H. Nicholson (later joined by Samuel Z. Arkoff) and based on the formula of minuscule budgets and even smaller shooting schedules. I was sorry to see Norman associate himself with such low-grade productions, but I suspected that the twelve months he had been laid up with his illness had made him anxious to get back to work; and now that he had proven with *Tickle Me* that in spite of having just celebrated his 66th birthday he was still in good form, the AIP offer looked appealing, particularly since they were willing to pay close to his usual fee. On March 10, 1965, AIP sent out a press release announcing that Taurog would direct their upcoming production, *Sergeant Deadhead*, to star Tommy Kirk. They followed this up with a flyer, sent to every publication in town, announcing the picture, featuring Taurog's name in bold letters and proudly referring to him as "the celebrated Hollywood director of such films as *G.I. Blues, All Hands on Deck, Visit to a Small Planet* and *Blue Hawaii*."

Sergeant Deadhead (1965) was written by a man named Louis M. Heyward, who used the nickname "Deke." Heyward had been a television writer at several studios before coming to AIP, where he became director of motion picture development. His writing experience had been as a comedy writer

Lobby card for *Sergeant Dead Head.*

for Garry Moore and Ernie Kovacs. "Deke" Heyward would write a number of other scripts for AIP including *Pajama Party* (1964) and *The Ghost in the Invisible Bikini* (1966) that matched the quality of *Sergeant Deadhead*, which I can only describe as a mindless, unfunny comedy.

The plot, if you can call it that, involved a mild-mannered Air Force sergeant, played by Frankie Avalon who replaced Tommy Kirk, who accidentally gets shot into space in a test rocket. The experience changes the sergeant's personality and he becomes a power-mad skirt-chaser that blackmails the Air Force into giving him everything he demands or he'll reveal the truth about the failed rocket experiment. Since for some reason Avalon's character keeps switching back and forth between personalities, poor Deborah Walley, a talented AIP starlet who was cast as his love interest, can't keep up with his shenanigans. *Sergeant Deadhead*, as film historian Tom Weaver pointed out in a *Videoscope* article about the film, goes from one genre to another, from service comedy to sci-fi to bedroom farce. "It's like three or four movies in one," he added. "And none of 'em any good."

The one saving grace was the cast of wonderful character actors that Taurog managed to secure for the film, including Eve Arden, Gale Gordon, Cesar Romero, Reginald Gardiner and Fred Clark, most of whom had worked with Taurog before. Eve Arden, who played a love-starved WAF lieutenant, even performed a Guy Hemric-Jerry Styner song, "You Should Have Seen the One That Got Away," choreographed by Jack Baker. It came out of nowhere and was completely out of character for her to break into song, but she socked it over with the same caustic humor that she had displayed in all of her old Warners films, as well as her big success on television *Our Miss Brooks* (1952-1956). Other cameo roles were portrayed by Pat Buttram, Ed Faulkner, John Ashley, Harvey Lembeck, and Donna Loren.

There was one other notable performer appearing in *Sergeant Deadhead*, the great silent comedian Buster Keaton. He was probably the saddest man I ever met. Once one of the most popular silent comedians in movies and still revered for films like *Sherlock Jr.* (1924), *The General* (1926) and *Steamboat Bill, Jr.* (1928), Keaton had fallen on hard times and was now reduced to appearing in silly cameo roles in *Beach Party* films; this would be his fourth film for AIP. He was married to a younger woman, Eleanor, who was always by his side on the set and watched over him like a mother hen. Keaton was very withdrawn; he would say "Good morning," but that would be about it. In an interview, Claire Bloom remembered Keaton on the set of Charlie Chaplin's *Limelight* (1952), "He didn't really talk to anyone," she recalled. Bloom remembered his showing her a postcard of a Hollywood mansion and saying, "That used to be where I lived." *Sergeant Deadhead* would be Keaton's final film for AIP; after completing a redeeming cameo in *A Funny Thing Happened on the Way to the Forum* (1966), Keaton died at the age of 70 on February 1, 1966.

"Deke" Heyward didn't waste time trying to create gags for Keaton; the script would simply say, "Buster does a bit here," and Keaton would come up with something and show it to Taurog. We shot for several days at a location in the east end of the San Fernando Valley that was supposed to be the parade grounds for the Air Force Missile Center. It was actually a new prison that had just been completed by Los Angeles County and hadn't yet been activated. Keaton came up with a gag involving a hose (the water keeps cutting off and on) that was right out of one of his old movies; in fact, one of

Deborah Walley, Buster Keaton and Frankie Avalon perform one of Keaton's "gags" in *Sergeant Deadhead.*

the film's reviewers wondered about "the progress of screen comedy in some six decades of filmmaking." Nevertheless it was funny and Taurog gave it the screen time that it deserved.

Sergeant Deadhead was press-previewed at the Academy Award Theatre on August 3, 1965, and the reviews were kinder than I had expected. *Variety* called it ". . .an entertaining space-age comedy with some younger thesps [sic] surrounded by vets who carry the load. Good direction and production values plus six tunes enliven a script that touches all bases." *The Hollywood Reporter* headlined: "AIP PRODUCTION A BRIGHT SHOW," and continued: "American International shifts its stock company from the beach to the army in *Sergeant Deadhead*, and it is likely the audience for these farces will shift right with them… For solid base there are usually a batch of experienced actors. For fluff and trimming there are the pretty young people. This is the mixture in *Sergeant Deadhead*, and under Norman Taurog's creative and well-paced direction it achieves the proper creamy style." Harry Gilroy of the *New York Times*, who wasn't a fan of the *Beach Party* genre, did give Buster Keaton and Eve Arden a few small compliments. The film managed to recoup its costs and make a small profit for AIP, and that was all that was expected of it.

While Norman was preparing to film his next project for AIP, *Dr. Goldfoot and the Bikini Machine* (1965), I moved across the lot to direct a low-budget sci-fi film that I had adapted from a novel by Murray Leinster. I called it *The Nightcrawlers*, but the producer (curse him) changed it to the absurd title of *The Navy vs. the Night Monsters* (1966). Because of this producer, making the film was an upsetting experience for me and after six weeks I was happy to return to the AIP offices to join Norman and the crew on an extensive location shoot in San Francisco, where we filmed a highly imaginative comedy car chase sequence all over the Bay Area. We had some of the best stunt men in the business, including Carey Loftin and Bill Hickman, who a few years later would stage the great car chase in *Bullitt* (1968). Others who worked with us were Paul Stader, Troy Melton, Jerry Summers, Ronnie Rondell, Bob Harris, Louis Elias, and two of the greatest stunt men in the business going all the way back to silent days, David Sharpe and Harvey Parry. Our cameraman was Sam Leavitt, who had won an Oscar for *The Defiant Ones* (1958), and our art director was Daniel Haller, the man who had designed all of the sets for Roger Corman's AIP Poe films; Claude Binyon Jr. the son of the writer who would have written the screenplay for *State of Mind*, was our first assistant director, as he had been on *Tickle Me*. You couldn't ask for a team better than that.

The script for *Dr. Goldfoot* had been written by Robert Kaufman, from a story idea that Jim Nicholson (using the name James Hartford) had come up with. The original plan had been to follow the AIP formula and have songs integrated throughout the film, but Norman brought in Elwood Ullman to do

Stunt men Jerry Summers and Ronnie Rondell double for Dwayne Hickman and Frankie Avalon on San Francisco's Golden Gate Bridge.

a rewrite while I was away directing my film, and the final script read like a good-natured spoof on the James Bond films with no songs. This apparently disappointed Vincent Price, who had been looking forward to singing and complained about it to an interviewer. There was no real story, just a silly plot involving Frankie Avalon's character, Secret Agent 00&1/2, searching for Dr. Goldfoot's sexy robot (Susan Hart) who is seducing wealthy Dwayne Hickman out of all of his money. The real fun was in the sight gags in Dr. Goldfoot's dungeon and the chase sequence throughout San Francisco, Sausalito and Tiburon. We actually filmed on the Golden Gate Bridge; the bridge personnel would briefly hold up traffic as we'd get shots of a trick cable car crossing toward Sausalito and then they would let the traffic flow in behind us.

Another funny gag was a special motorcycle and sidecar with stunt doubles for Vincent Price and Jack Mullaney that was rigged to separate at high speed. *Dr. Goldfoot* was the first AIP film to have a budget that exceeded $1,000,000 (actually $1.4 million) and a shooting schedule that went over 30 days. Our cast included AIP's favorite star Vincent Price in the title role, and Frankie Avalon, Dwayne Hickman and Susan Hart as co-stars. Jack Mullaney and Fred Clark supplied the comedy, along with Milton Frome, Hal Riddle and Vince Barnett. Of course the robots produced in the "Bikini Machine" were played by a covey of beautiful, bikini-clad young ladies, including comedian Mort Sahl's wife China Lee and Jim Nicholson's two daughters Luree

Frankie Avalon and Dwayne Hickman react to the sudden appearance of knives between their fingers, as Vincent Price and Jack Mullaney look on in amusement.

Holmes and Laura Nicholson. Some of the group had previously appeared in *Sergeant Deadhead.* Other AIP stars who made brief appearances were Annette Funicello, Deborah Walley, Harvey Lembeck and Aron Kincaid.

Vincent Price was a joy to work with, and seemed to take pleasure in portraying the campy Dr. Goldfoot. He obviously enjoyed working with Jack Mullaney, who played his assistant Igor, and it was evident in the way they bounced their performances off each other. Price also loved being directed by Norman Taurog, who was reaching back to his days as a two-reel comedy director for most of the tried and tested gags. It was a little over the top, but what the hell? In this picture, *everything* was meant to be tongue-in-cheek.

Although it wasn't common knowledge at the time (at least not to us), Susan Hart was married to Jim Nicholson—not that it made any difference, Nicholson made no special requests and Susan never tried to throw her weight around. She worked like a trooper in a very difficult role, coming up with several different dialects and occasionally speaking in foreign languages, even Japanese. She had to do some tough things, sometimes looking pretty stupid, and she pulled it off. She was very pretty and a very smart lady and she enjoyed working with Norman, later telling film historian Tom Weaver, "He was probably one of the sweetest men I've ever met in my entire life. He was so caring. I think of all the directors I've worked with, he was the most helpful; there was, again, a sweetness about him that I never saw in any of my other directors." The admiration was apparently mutual; shortly after filming was completed, Taurog sent a letter to Hart, in which he complimented her performance: "Yours was a difficult and taxing role which called for infinite understanding and professional skill. I have never worked with anyone who was more cooperative and attentive to direction." Hart would appear in only one more film for AIP, *The Ghost in the Invisible Bikini* (1966), and a few television shows before retiring from acting to concentrate on her marriage to Nicholson and to raise her son, also named Jim. Nicholson left AIP in 1971 and became an independent producer at Twentieth Century-Fox where he developed two films, *The Legend of Hell House* (1973) and *Dirty Mary, Crazy Larry* (1974), the latter a big moneymaker. When Nicholson died unexpectedly of a brain tumor in December of 1972, Hart took over as executive producer and saw both films through to completion.

When Norman Taurog finished filming the San Francisco sequences, the company flew back to Hollywood and moved back onto the Producers Studio lot. Danny Haller used some of his designs from *Pit and the Pendulum* (1961), including the pendulum pit and the giant blade, for Dr. Goldfoot's lair. Most of the sets, including the lab with all of its gadgetry, were built on Stages 1 and 5. AIP, always mindful of ways to publicize its films, issued a publicity release that the sets cost "more than $150,000."

Rehearsing with Susan Hart on MGM's New York Street.

On the day after the *Dr. Goldfoot* company returned from San Francisco, rioting broke out in South Los Angeles. Over the weekend, sniping and looting continued and over 500 businesses were damaged or destroyed. The rioting lasted for six days and the National Guard was called out to restore order, but before that could happen, more than 34 people died and hundreds were injured.

Then tragedy struck closer to home. A heatwave held Los Angeles in its grip and with all of the lights needed to illuminate Danny Haller's sets, the temperature inside of Stage 1 sometimes reached over 100 ° by mid-afternoon. On the afternoon of August 15, the company had just returned from lunch and Norman and I were standing on the set discussing the next setup. As we stepped away, I heard this rushing sound and then this terrible dull thump. When I looked back I saw a body on the floor in the exact spot where Norman and I had been standing a moment before. One of the electricians, a man named Roy Hicks, had passed out from the heat and fallen from a catwalk 35 feet above our heads. Everybody was ushered off the stage and an ambulance crew arrived and removed the body. It was a traumatic experience for everyone, but I realized that if Norman and I hadn't stepped away when we did, we might have been killed or injured ourselves.

On August 30, we moved over to MGM Studios' Lot 2 to shoot on their New York Street for a couple of days, then returned to Producers Studio and completed filming the various process shots for the chase sequence.

AIP went all-out to promote *Dr. Goldfoot and the Bikini Machine;* hiring an up-and-coming group known as The Supremes to sing a main title song, and even going so far as to produce a television special, *The Weird, Weird World of Dr. Goldfoot* that played in the *Shindig* spot on ABC television at 7:30 on November 18, 1965. In addition, Nicholson, Arkoff and Taurog were interviewed on the ABC-TV weekly news documentary *ABC Scope* on the subject of "The New Hollywood." A world premiere was held in San Francisco on November 10, with Vincent Price and many other cast members in attendance, and shortly after, Frankie Avalon and Susan Hart, along with Jim Nicholson and several AIP starlets, embarked on a 30-day tour of 18 cities in 13 countries to promote the film.

Howard Thompson of the *New York Times* was only mildly impressed, observing, "Occasionally it's diverting to see just how bad or unfunny a supposed laugh-package of a movie can be. Meet *Dr. Goldfoot and the Bikini Machine.* Is there anything at all funny about it? Yes—Fred Clark." *Newsweek* declared, "What could have been a fine little comedy becomes a tasteless slumgullion of self-indulgence, derivative gadgetry, anarchic plot and disjointed chases that culminate in a race between a speedboat and a cable car on the streets of Sausalito." *The Hollywood Reporter* was kinder, noting, "Some of *Goldfoot* is rather silly, but enough of it is fresh and funny to make it count. Norman Taurog has directed with a light hand and a sure pace, so that the parody doesn't bog down or lose momentum." It also congratulated Nicholson and Arkoff on their diverse casting of the bikini girls: " [W]orthy of note is the fact that the producers have made it an integrated chorus line." *Variety* singled out Susan Hart for praise, saying that she was "very good in a role which demands several dialects, human warmth and robot inanity, often in rapid sequence." They also disagreed with *Newsweek* about the chase sequence, declaring, "With Sam Leavitt's versatile Panavision-Pathecolor camera, Taurog has staged some exciting chase scenes in and around Frisco hill, unrelated to the plot but a sure attention-grabber. Taurog has been directing this type of comedy for years and he hasn't lost the touch."

AIP booked the picture into 400 holiday dates over the Thanksgiving weekend and the picture did fairly well. It was a moderate success in the United States, but did quite well in Europe, particularly in Italy. When the film was to be released in England the title had to be changed to *Dr. G and the Bikini Machine* because it turned out that there were two doctors who bore the name of Goldfoot. In 1966 AIP produced a sequel in Italy, *Dr. Goldfoot and the Girl Bombs* that had Vincent Price recreating the title role and was directed by Mario Bava, an Italian cinematographer-director who specialized in horror films.

MGM – With Elvis Once Again

After a brief return to MGM in 1963 for *It Happened at the World's Fair*, Norman Taurog moved back into an office suite in MGM's Thalberg Building in the late autumn of 1965, returning after nearly two decades to the studio where he had previously spent 13 years of his career. He must have felt a great sense of nostalgia, returning to the scene of so many of his earlier triumphs, and knowing that he would again be working with his old pal Joe Pasternak, the producer of his last film at the studio in 1951, *Rich, Young and Pretty*. The film they were about to start was another Elvis Presley saga, *Spinout* (1966), and the contrast between this project and the two films Taurog had just finished at AIP was almost incalculable. MGM, although going through some hard times, was still a first class studio and Elvis, whose film *Viva Las Vegas* (1964) with Ann-Margaret had been a big moneymaker for the studio, would receive $750,000 plus 40% of the profits for *Spinout* and for his next film, *Double Trouble* (1967). Taurog had a firm contract for two pictures, which he knew was due to the intercession of his old friend Colonel Parker. The Colonel and Taurog were contemporaries (Parker was roughly ten years younger) and he felt comfortable having Taurog direct his boy, knowing that he would look out for him.

Taurog's office was on the first floor of the studio's executive administration building, known as the Thalberg Building. It stood just outside of the studio's East Gate. A corner suite with a small dressing room and bathroom, it had a large main office that was painted white, as were all the offices in the building, with postmodern furniture and a view of the studio's main gate from one of several windows. The office came equipped with a lovely lady named Constance Bean, who would be Taurog's personal assistant for the next four years. Connie would come to adore both Norman and Sue Taurog and would often help Sue with her charitable and political endeavors. Connie was president of the Los Angeles and Hollywood chapters of "Women of the Motion Picture Industry" in 1966 and 1967 and was awarded their "Woman of the Year" award. When Connie retired, she and her husband moved to San Marcos, where she would live for over 27 years until her death on May 29, 2004.

Joe Pasternak had changed; Taurog found his old friend suffering from the neurological effects of Parkinson's disease, which caused his hands to constantly shake and caused him to walk with a shuffling gait. Joe was immensely proud of his son Michael, who was living in London and who had become famous as the disc jockey Emperor Rosko on the pirate radio station Radio Caroline, which broadcast from an old freighter anchored several miles offshore in the English Channel. Joe spoke of Michael often, and he sometimes seemed more interested in his son's exploits in swinging London than in the Elvis project he was producing.

Returning to the studio was a kick for me too; except for my brief visit with Norman on the set of *It Happened at the World's Fair*, I hadn't set foot on the lot since I had worked there as an assistant film editor in 1953 and 1954. The script for *Spinout* had been written by the team of Theodore J. Flicker and George Kirgo, and had gone through a number of revisions and title changes since they had begun work in the spring of 1965. According to Kirgo, for their first attempt to write a Presley film they based it loosely on Elvis' own life story, but the Colonel summarily rejected that idea and they were forced to choose a different approach. Each draft had a new title such as *Never Say No*, followed by *Never Say Yes*, until in frustration Kirgo and Flicker dubbed it *The Singing Race Car Driver*. At this point, Flicker left the project and moved over to Paramount Studios to write and direct a political satire (how about that, they were back in style) called *The President's Analyst* (1967) and I was assigned to work with George on another rewrite of *Spinout*. One of our biggest jobs was to choreograph the two race car sequences in detail, so that the filming could be divided between a first and second film unit.

George Kirgo was one of the funniest men I ever met. I don't think I have laughed so much in my life as I did sitting in an office with George; it's amazing that we accomplished anything, but somehow we did, and several weeks later a revised script was published. George began his writing career in 1958 with the publication of his first comic novel, *Hercules, the Big Greek Story*, which caught the attention of talk show host Jack Paar, but unfortunately very few other readers. Paar invited George onto his show and asked him why his first novel had sold so few books. George replied, "Word of mouth." The title of his next book earned George a regular spot on the *Jack Paar Show*: *How to Write Ten Different Best Sellers Now in Your Spare Time and Become the First Author on Your Block Unless There's an Author Already*

Jack Mullaney, Elvis, Deborah Walley and Jimmy Hawkins in *Spinout.*

Living on Your Block in Which Case You'll Become the Second Author on Your Block and That's Okay Too and Other Stories. George later became president of the Writers Guild (1987-1991) and had the unenviable task of presiding over the Guild's 22-week labor strike in 1988. When George died after a long illness in 2004, a huge crowd of mourners attended his memorial at the Writers Guild Theatre. Typically for a George Kirgo production, the laughs far outnumbered the tears.

The cast of characters for *Spinout* was rather extensive, which gave Norman another chance to hire actors he knew and liked. On January 14, 1966, the trades announced that Jack Mullaney and Deborah Walley had been signed to play members of Elvis' band in the film. Counting her brief bit in *Dr. Goldfoot*, this would be Deborah's third film with Norman Taurog and she adored him. "I thought he was wonderful," she told researcher Bill Bram. "He really could time the action, he had a great sense of comedy, he was a very personable guy; so working with him was fun, and he made it fun." Jimmy Hawkins, who had also appeared with Elvis in *Girl Happy*, finally went to work for Taurog as the third member of Elvis' band. Jimmy had a slightly different take on his director: " I wish I'd worked with him in his heyday," he told me. "He concentrated mostly on Elvis. He directed one of Elvis' best pictures in my opinion, *Blue Hawaii*." We began testing actresses for the remaining female roles; Warren Berlinger, a marvelously funny actor who had starred in several teenage comedies and had previously worked for Taurog in *All Hands on Deck*, stood in for Elvis during the tests. Berlinger would play Phillip, the milquetoast assistant to Carl Betz and ends up with Shelley Fabares at the fadeout.

Shelley had already co-starred with Elvis in *Girl Happy* (1965) and would appear with him again in *Clambake* (1967). Diane McBain would play the mysterious author Diana St. Clair who is stalking Elvis as the subject of her next book. Dodie Marshall had a small but notable bit as a go-go dancer who flirts with Elvis in one of the party sequences and ends up replacing Deborah Walley on the drums in the final song. She would catch the eye of Hal Wallis, who would cast her as Elvis' co-star in *Easy Come, Easy Go* (1967). Other cast members included Will Hutchins, from television's *Sugarfoot* (1957-1961), who played Lt. Tracy Richards, the policeman-gourmet chef who gives Deborah Walley an excuse to put on a dress instead of the terribly unattractive wardrobe she wears throughout most of the film. Carl Betz, who had played Shelley Fabares' father on *The Donna Reed Show* (1958-1966), would again portray her father in *Spinout.*

Other Taurog favorites were Cecil Kellaway and Una Merkel as Mr. and Mrs. Ranley, the owners of the mansion who Elvis cons into taking a second honeymoon so that he and his band can move in, Frederic Worlock as

Carl Betz with Elvis and Shelley Fabares in *Spinout.*

Elvis, Cecil Kellaway and Una Merkel at the Dodger Stadium location for *Spinout.*

their butler, Blodgett and Dave Barry as Elvis' manager. This would be Una Merkel's final film, but she would appear one last time in 1968 in an episode of the television series *I Spy* (1965-1968). All in all Merkel would appear in five films for Norman Taurog, including *The Bride Goes Wild*, *Bundle of Joy*, *Rich, Young and Pretty*, *The Fuzzy Pink Nightgown* and *Spinout.*

Elvis reported to MGM for wardrobe and music meetings on Friday, February 11. On Wednesday of the following week, he began two nights of recording the songs for the film at the Radio Recorders studios in Hollywood. I was still working with George Kirgo on the script at this time and didn't see Elvis until the following Monday, when *Spinout* began filming. My first view of Elvis was standing waist- deep in water beside a mockup of a partially submerged AC Shelby Cobra 427. We were filming the scene where Shelley Fabares has run Elvis off the road at a small bridge on Malibu Canyon near Thousand Oaks, California. Elvis looked a little pudgy and I remembered what Norman had told me about his weight problems. Elvis had a bad habit of pigging out on junk food when he was at home at Graceland, and he could put on as much as twenty-thirty pounds in a few months. According to Norman, Elvis once drove by a Winchell's Donut shop and sent one of the boys in to buy a box of a dozen assorted donuts and then ate the entire box of donuts himself. When the Colonel would notify him of his upcoming start date on a new picture, Elvis would start taking Dexedrine to suppress his appetite and go on a crash diet to lose the excess pounds. Although much has been written about Elvis' drug habit, during the five years that I worked with him I never saw him noticeably under the influence of drugs or alcohol. However, I've always believed that the drug habit began with his taking Dexedrine, an amphetamine otherwise known as uppers. He was known to have trouble sleeping, probably caused by the amphetamines, so he then took sleeping pills or downers to try to sleep. It was a vicious habit that eventually grew into greater quantities of drugs that ultimately contributed to his early death.

But on this bright day in February, Elvis was in a happy mood, even after having to totally submerge himself in the water. Norman made sure that he only needed to shoot that one time, and then we moved on to filming parts of the road race sequence with our old friends Carey Loftin and Bob Harris handling the stunts. We shot drive-bys for the race sequence for several days all over Kanin Road in Agoura and then turned it over to a second unit to complete and to film the background plates needed for the process shots. The company traveled to the Ascot Park Speedway in Gardena to film some additional car footage and some dialogue scenes with Elvis, Carl Betz, Jimmy Hawkins, Deborah Walley and Jack Mullaney.

By the time we returned to the studio we were ready to settle down to some nice quiet interior scenes, but after filming a few sequences that didn't involve Elvis, we were back on location at Dodger's Stadium to film the start of the road race with the entire cast, 12 custom racing automobiles and two hundred extras. It was a typical Southern California morning with heavy fog, which didn't make our cameraman Daniel Fapp very happy, so Norman started by shooting as many close-ups as he could until the sun began

Shelley Fabares looks down at an unhappy Elvis that she has just run off the road in *Spinout.*

to break through. Taurog managed to complete the sequence in the allotted time, in spite of the late start, and the company returned to MGM where we next moved out for several days of filming at the swimming pool on Lot 2. The pool had been the site of many of Esther Williams' swimming sequences in her films and had been dubbed the Esther Williams Pool in her honor. We were they to film a big outdoor party sequence and one of Elvis' musical numbers, "Beach Shack." It was choreographed by Jack Baker, who was making his fifth film with Taurog, and as usual the number consisted of Elvis singing to a bevy of bikini-clad beauties. For you trivia buffs, hidden somewhere in that pool sequence was actress Rita Wilson making one of her first film appearances; the same thing had happened in the *Palm Springs Weekend* pool sequence where Dallas' Linda Gray also went unrecognized.

Most of the songs in the film, including both the original title tune "Never Say Yes" and "Spinout," were disappointing, but the final melody, a rousing "I'll Be Back" by Sid Wayne and Ben Weisman and staged by Jack Baker in the big party set with future choreographer Anita Mann shaking her booty in the foreground, was an upbeat finish for the film. After seven weeks of filming, *Spinout* completed principal photography on Friday, April 8, 1966 on the process stage, and Elvis spent the next week doing publicity photos and looping his dialogue, before returning to Memphis on April 16.

As an indication of the slipping boxoffice for Presley movies, *Spinout* opened in multiple theaters in Manhattan on December 14, 1966, on a double-bill with a European adventure film called *Marco the Magnificent* that had German actor Horst Buchholz playing Marco Polo—the adventurer not the swimming pool game. The *New York Times* review duly reported, "[T]his transparent package… is neither a bargain nor a colorful Christmas bauble. Mr. Presley, to be precise, has made more than 20 films, but the minor variation this time is that he… loves his Duesenberg more than any dame, manages to sing eight songs [author's note: there were actually nine], win the big road race and remain footloose and fancy free." *Time* magazine in its November issue rather cruelly made note of the more corpulent Elvis and his new Larry Geller-coiffed hairstyle, saying, "Elvis Presley at 31 is really changing his scene. Eleven years of living high on the hawg (his income from films and royalties averages about $6,000,000 a year) has emphatically porked up his appearance. His cheeks are now so plump that he looks like a kid blowing bubble gum and his mouth is still so squiggly that it looks as if the bubble had burst. What's more, he now sports a glossy something on his summit that adds at least five inches to his altitude and looks like a swatch of hot buttered yak wool."

As usual, the Hollywood trades viewed the film with kinder eyes, with *The Hollywood Reporter* claiming, "*Spinout* is a bright collection of fair humor and good musical numbers, that looks like it should be just the Rx for

Presley fans and younger audiences." *Variety* followed up with, "*Spinout* is an entertaining Elvis Presley comedy-tuner, in which four gals compete for his attention between nine new songs." However, when the film reached England with its new title *California Holiday*, one London reviewer really went after Elvis' appearance again: "Apart from any other considerations, Elvis is now getting decidedly tubby. To be brutally frank he is becoming too old for such goings-on, and while he hasn't yet reached eligibility for the mutton-lamb comparison, he should take stock seriously of where his career is going. I can think of more careers that have been ruined by trying to repeat earlier successes, and let's face it most of his films here have played to half- empty cinemas."

Spinout would gross only $1.77 million and be ranked #57 in the boxoffice poll for the year. 1966 would also be the final year that Elvis would place among the top ten boxoffice draws in the annual movie exhibitors' poll. In spite of these dire indications, MGM decided to extend their contract with Elvis for four more films, with his fee set at $850,000 for each with profit sharing at 50%. His next film for the studio, *Double Trouble* (1967), still to be made under the old contract, would pay him $750,000 and 40% of the profits. Of the four new films, *Speedway* (1967), *Stay Away, Joe* (1968), *Live a Little, Love a Little* (1968) and *The Trouble with Girls*, Taurog would split the directing assignments with Peter Tewksbury, directing *Speedway, Live a Little* and *Double Trouble.* These films would constitute Elvis' final commitments to MGM, and after that there would be only two more independent films before he gave up on Hollywood completely and went back to live performances.

By the end of 1966, Norman and Sue Taurog's two children, both 21, had left home and married. Priscilla, the first to marry in early 1965, had already given birth to Patti Jean Keith; she would have her second daughter, Penny Sue Keith in 1968. In October of 1966, newspapers announced that Jonathan Taurog had secretly married Cindy Fairchild, "a pretty non-pro who works at MGM's 'Lab'"

Endless Nights On the Back Lot

MGM's Lot 2 and Lot 3 were famous for their vast variety of sets. You could find almost any distant location you needed, authentically recreated by MGM craftsmen over the years, and during their heyday they were in constant use. Now, in 1966, with films being shot on actual locations all over the world, sets like Lot 2's Waterfront Street and Lot 3's Dutch Street resembled a ghost town, until we arrived in the summer of 1966 to film *Double Trouble*. In February of 1966, *The Hollywood Reporter* announced that Judd Bernard and Irwin Winkler had signed a contract with MGM to produce an Elvis Presley-starring picture tentatively titled *You're Killing Me*. Production was scheduled to begin in June after Presley completed his next MGM picture *Spinout*. This was to be Bernard and Winkler's first film as producers and they had formed a production company along with another partner, Robert Chartoff, called BCW Productions. Winkler was a former William Morris agent, Bernard had been a press agent, and Chartoff a personal manager. The team would break up after *Double Trouble* and Chartoff and Winkler would go on to produce a succession of blockbuster hits including *Rocky* (1976) and all of its sequels, *Raging Bull* (1980) and *The Right Stuff* (1983).

In 1965, BCW Productions had purchased a humorous mystery story from British television writer Mark Brandel called *Somebody Is Trying to Kill Me* and hired a young writer named Jo Heims to adapt it into a screenplay that they called *You're Killing Me*. The original plan was to film it in Europe with James Coburn and Geraldine Chaplin, but Coburn decided to do *Our Man Flint* (1966) for Twentieth Century-Fox and Winkler came up with the idea of submitting the script to MGM for Elvis Presley to star. Winkler and

The permanent Dutch Street set on MGM's Lot Three.

Bernard didn't want Taurog to direct their film and fought hard for a television director named Rod Amateau. They lost their battle when MGM, with some behind-the-scenes encouragement from Colonel Parker, told them emphatically that Taurog would be the director on the film. Bernard later admitted to Elvis researcher Bill Bram that he thought Taurog was "a very good director; he knew his craft and was a pro." It must have come as a shock to poor Jo Heims to learn that her screenplay was now to become an Elvis Presley movie,(plus the fact that I was going to work with her on revising the script to fit Elvis' specifications) but she took it with good humor and we were able to work together without difficulty.

All of the action in *You're Killing Me* took place in London and Brussels, and Jo and I attempted to keep the Hitchcokian elements of the mystery plot as intact as possible, while making room for Elvis' songs and the humorous byplay that Norman liked to include. I suggested including a sequence on a fog-shrouded steamer crossing the English Channel, with several mysterious characters stalking Elvis, which was right out of one of my father's films (Dennis Hoey, who played Inspector Lestrade in the Universal *Sherlock Holmes* series). Norman liked the idea and we developed it, utilizing some of his suggestions as well. Toward the end of May, around the time we finished our work on the script, the studio announced a name change for the film from *You're Killing Me* to *Double Trouble.* While we were working together, Jo Heims would often speak about an original screenplay that she had written that she hoped would one day bring her success. A few years later she sold the script to Clint Eastwood and it became his directorial debut and a big hit called *Play Misty for Me* (1971). Tragically, Jo Heims' young life and her all-too-brief career ended when she died of cancer in 1978 at the age of 48.

Choosing the cast for *Double Trouble* was a lot of fun; since the story takes place exclusively in Europe we were able to cast the excellent character actor John Williams, who having appeared in both *Dial M for Murder* (1954) and *To Catch a Thief* (1955) helped to make the Hitchcock connection. Also cast were veteran British actors Norman Rossington and John Alderson and

Annette Day.

Australian actor Chips Rafferty. Also Maurice Marsac, Leon Askin, Stanley Adams and Walter Burke, and a young actor who would soon become associated with many of Woody Allen's films, Michael Murphy, would play one of the less obvious heavies in the film. Another import from England was sultry actress Yvonne Romain, who was married to composer Leslie Bricusse and had been appearing on American television since arriving in California. I suppose that I have to take the credit or the blame for using the Wiere Brothers as a trio of bungling detectives who think Elvis is a jewel thief.

Harry, Herbert and Sylvester Wiere owned a supper club in Hollywood, to which they had retired after years of performing in nightclubs and on the road. Their accompanist was the mother of one of my first wife's girlfriends and I suggested them to Taurog, who liked the idea perhaps a little too much. I think he let them go a bit too far over the top, but they did add some amusing moments to the Antwerp sequences.

Judd Bernard was responsible for two pieces of casting that ultimately caused us problems. The first was the hiring of a young English girl named Annette Day that Judd had spotted at her parents' antique shop in Portobello Road and decided would be perfect to play the girl that gets Elvis' character into all the trouble. Judd had been in London to meet with Hayley Mills about playing the role, but Haley wasn't available and Annette Day bore a certain resemblance to her.

The problem with Annette (through no fault of her own) was that she had never acted before in her life, and here she was co-starring with Elvis Presley. Norman got the studio to agree to a week's rehearsal to get Annette comfortable in her role and Elvis became very protective of her, running lines off stage to relax her, so that her performance would be as natural as possible. Annette was a very sweet young lady and the crew took an immediate liking to her, doing anything they could to make her feel at ease. She would arrive on the set knowing her dialogue and receptive to whatever direction Taurog might give her. In my opinion, her performance was more than acceptable, but it turned out to be her one and only screen appearance. She returned to London and today lives in Telford, West Midlands and occasionally appears at Elvis tribute events.

The second of Judd Bernard's casting choices was a British actor named Monty Landis who had played one of the minor roles in the British classic *The Mouse that Roared* (1959) and had appeared in the first Connecticut production of *Man of La Mancha*. Bernard had given Landis the impression that his role was more important than it turned out to be and he was rather unpleasant on the set. Then one night when we were filming the Antwerp carnival sequence on Lot 2, Landis made a play for one of the extras and tried to get her into his portable dressing room at the back of the set. The extra, a young girl who felt he was coming on too strong, reported it to one of the as-

Annette Day and Elvis chatting with Norman Taurog between scenes.

sistant directors, Gene De Roulle, who took it to Bernard and Irwin Winkler. I don't think Taurog even knew what had happened until the producers came to him and told him about it. Landis was fired, which wasn't a problem since most of his work had already been completed, and he wasn't missed in the rest of the film.

Elvis reported to MGM on June 27, 1967 for wardrobe fittings and music meetings and he looked terrific. He had slimmed down to a much more acceptable weight and his hair had a natural sheen and less body. The songs for *Double Trouble* were probably some of the worst selections in any of the Presley films up to that time. I heard rumors that Elvis was particularly upset with "I Love Only One Girl," which was a flat-out rip-off of the old French folk tune "Aupres de Ma Blonde," and an even worse version of the World War I era nursery rhyme "Old MacDonald" with some lame new lyrics stitched together by Randy Starr. Starr's other contribution to the soundtrack, a lugubrious ballad called "Could I Fall in Love," wasn't much of an improvement, which is perhaps why Norman staged it with Annette Day's character falling asleep at the end. From what I heard, Elvis eventually stormed out of the studio in disgust and the final recordings had to be completed a few days later on MGM's Scoring Stage.

The only part of the film that was actually shot in Europe was some second unit footage in Brussels of the truck driving along country roads and along the canals with doubles for Elvis and Annette. Merrill Pye, who had designed the wonderful art deco set for the "Begin the Beguine" number in *Broadway Melody of 1940*, designed the *Double Trouble* sets and supervised the second unit filming, including process plates to cover close shots of Elvis and Annette back at the studio. The filming schedule wasn't easy for Norman, but he never complained or slowed down; we filmed for several weeks at night on Lot 2, around an area known alternately as Copperfield Court, Wimpole Street and Waterfront Street, and then came back to film several day sequences on the same sets. Then we moved out to Lot 3 to spend several nights filming along the Salem Waterfront set. This meant that we would report to the studio at 6 pm and work until the sun came up around 5:30 the following morning. Trying to sleep during the day must have been difficult for Norman; I know it was for me. Almost immediately after we completed the night sequences we travelled to San Pedro and filmed a sequence on board an old derelict freighter, then returned to Lot 3 and filmed the last of that sequence in the big water-filled process stage tank. On top of that, my idea of the fog shrouded steamer turned out to be a problem, since the fog effect made everyone ill and we had to constantly open the big stage doors to air out the set. The big Antwerp carnival sequence, complete with dancers, acrobats and several hundred costumed extras, took several nights to film, including Alex Romero's excellent staging of the "I Love Only One Girl" number that made it look and sound far better than it was.

From the day we first met, Elvis had insisted on calling me "sir." It was in his nature to use the customary title of Mr. or Mrs. to show respect to people in authority, and it wasn't until the middle of our third film together, *Double Trouble*, that he finally started calling me Mike, even though we were almost exactly the same age (our birthdays were three months apart to the day). In all the years that I worked with him, I never heard Elvis call Norman anything but Mr. Taurog, and Taurog once described to an interviewer what happened when he asked him to stop. "You see, Mr. Taurog," Norman quoted Elvis as saying, "when I was a little boy my mother told me that any man that was even a year older than I must be called 'mister.' I have never forgotten that, and I couldn't change now." Norman went on to explain, "Calling me by my first name simply didn't come naturally to Elvis—and unless something comes naturally to him, whether it's in acting or otherwise, he can't do it." Elvis' generosity was legendary; he once gave Norman a gift of a brand new Sony video camera and recorder that had just come on the market. The gift was somewhat inappropriate, since Norman was blind in one eye and, as I was soon to discover, rapidly losing the sight in his other eye. Elvis also gifted Taurog with a brand new Cadillac sedan, which he kept for many years, having his driver Leon chauffeur him around town. Elvis gave me gifts of television sets and belt buckles, and once he gave me a watch, which he had also given to other members of the cast and crew, that he had specially designed by a jeweler in Memphis. A cross superimposed with a Star of David on its face was meant to represent universal brotherhood; Elvis had become deeply religious since his new hairdresser Larry Geller had given him several books on spiritualism. Colonel Parker didn't care for Geller and he was eventually eased out of the Presley organization by the Colonel, and Elvis' interests turned to recording an album of gospel tunes. That album, *How Great Thou Art*, would win a Grammy for Best Sacred Performance of 1967, and in its initial release would sell 200,000 copies.

Norman was no fool; he recognized the negative effect that weak, repetitive stories were having on Elvis' career. "Jack up the hat and run another Elvis under it," he used to say. We even developed an idea with a very dramatic storyline that had Elvis playing a quarterback on a professional football team and presented it to Elvis. He respectfully referred us to the Colonel who refused to read it, saying, "Give me a million dollars and you can have him and shoot the phone book, if you're crazy enough." If you think this is an exaggeration, here is another example of the Colonel's philosophy. In an interview with Michael Fessier Jr. that appeared in *Variety* on January 15, 1964, Colonel Parker told a story about a producer who came to him with a "great script that would get Elvis' career back on the right track and would cinch him an Oscar." He wanted the Colonel to trim Elvis' asking price, but the Colonel told him, "Pay us our regular fee and if Elvis gets the Oscar we'll give him his money back. " He added smugly, "We never saw him again."

The last sequence to be filmed on *Double Trouble* was the process shots of the infamous "Old MacDonald" number on the back of the truck with Elvis overcoming his aversion to the song and singing to Annette Day with genuine joy. Now that was good acting. Norman wrapped the company on the evening of August 30, 1966, and Elvis barely had time to record his loop lines and pose for publicity shots before he had to report to Paramount Studios for wardrobe fittings on what would be his last film for Hal Wallis, *Easy Come, Easy Go* (1967). Wallis, who had once said, "A Presley picture is the only sure thing in Hollywood," had come to realize that the Golden Goose had died. Wallis would soon leave Paramount for Universal, where he would spend the remaining six years of his career producing prestige films like *Anne of a Thousand Days* (1969) and *Mary, Queen of Scots* (1971). When Wallis died in 1986 his art collection would be auctioned off for $39.6 million.

The *Double Trouble* reviews were surprisingly good, and many disagreed with my judgment of the songs, such as *The Hollywood Reporter* which called the movie "the most lavishly produced Elvis Presley film since *Viva Las Vegas*. It has been briskly directed by Norman Taurog, boasts one of Presley's most tuneful and melodic scores, and again proves the singer's natural instinct for comedy." Even Howard Thompson of the *New York Times* begrudgingly complemented the film: "*Double Trouble* is pretty fair and far better than the last three Presley clunkers... At least the picture moves. Furthermore, the good tunes arrive thick and fast, and several numbers are festive and charming. El, now a personable actor with an ingratiating ease, at least has steered his movie career back on the track." Kevin Thomas in the *Los Angeles Times* agreed: "*Double Trouble* is more handsomely-mounted than most Presley pictures. The cast never left Culver City, but you would never know it, so cleverly have quaint Belgian streets and other European settings been reproduced on the back lot. Complementing the production values are the likable cast, the breezy script by Jo Heims and the deft direction of Norman Taurog, who has directed Presley six times before and, as always, gets better, more relaxed performances out of him than anyone else."

Double Trouble opened nationwide on April 5, 1967, just two weeks after *Easy Come, Easy Go,* and ended up grossing $1.6 million, which was $400,000 less than the Paramount film and $670,000 less than his previous MGM film, *Spinout.*

On May 1, 1967, roughly a month before he was due to report to MGM Studios to begin work on his next film, *Speedway*, Elvis Presley and Priscilla Beaulieu were married at the Aladdin Hotel in Las Vegas, Nevada. "I guess it was about time," Elvis told reporters. After a brief honeymoon in Palm Springs, the couple flew to Memphis and Graceland.

Presley and Sinatra

For Elvis' next picture MGM decided to go back to the proven-successful formula of *Viva Las Vegas* and pair Elvis with an established singing star. The result was *Speedway* (1968) co-starring Nancy Sinatra, who had several hit records to her credit, including "These Boots Are Made for Walkin'", "Sugar Town," and a little ditty called "Somethin' Stupid" that she recorded with a singer named Frank. Her continued collaboration with singer-songwriter Lee Hazlewood resulted in several more chart toppers, and her starring in *For Those Who Think Young* (1964) and with Peter Fonda in *The Wild Angels* (1966) helped to establish her as a credible box-office draw, and so she was signed by producer Douglas Laurence for the film. Nancy would even get her own solo, Lee Hazlewood's "Your Groovy Self," which the Colonel, desperately seeking ways to bolster sales for Elvis' albums, would include in the *Spinout* soundtrack album—making her the only other artist to ever be included on an official Presley record.

Douglas Laurence had already produced two films for MGM in partnership with director Delbert Mann and writer Dale Wasserman, *Quick Before it Melts* (1964) and *Mister Buddwing* (1966), and he had just recently completed his third film for their company and MGM, *Doctor, You've Got to Be Kidding!* (1967). Even with a cast of attractive young players like Sandra Dee, George Hamilton, Bill Bixby and Dwayne Hickman, and directed by Peter Tewksbury, it was still a perfect example of the appallingly unfunny comedies that MGM was turning out at that time. *Speedway* would be the first of three films Douglas Laurence would produce with Elvis. Laurence's background had been in show business ever since he was discharged from the U.S. Army Air Corps at the conclusion of World War II, after having flown 50 missions

Douglas Laurence with Elvis and Nancy Sinatra.

as an engineer/gunner in B-17s in Europe. Although he never spoke to me about it, I learned later that he had been shot down, taken prisoner and escaped. He must have been injured, as he was awarded the Purple Heart, as well as the Air Medal and the Distinguished Flying Cross. Doug was a fascinating guy; even though I worked closely with him for several years, I never felt that I got to know him all that well. What I did know was that he had once worked with Tommy Dorsey, Judy Garland and Rowan and Martin, had been the entertainment director at the Flamingo Hotel in Las Vegas, and knew all of the important players at MGM at that time, including the head of the studio Robert O'Brien and his number two man, Clark Ramsay. He also seemed to know a lot about Kirk Kerkorian, who would later buy the studio, not to mention half of Las Vegas, and sell off at auction all of MGM's back lots and the invaluable props and wardrobe.

The script for *Speedway* (originally called *Pot Luck*) by screenwriter Phillip Shuken wasn't all that different from *Spinout*; Elvis was once again "The Singing Race Car Driver," with the additional twist that this time he was being audited by IRS investigator Nancy Sinatra. There was as an additional subplot involving a broken-down race car driver and his brood of young kids. Shuken, a successful television writer, had also written the screenplay for *Doctor, You've Got to Be Kidding!* He unfortunately seemed to have the Presley formula down pat, so I spent just a few days working with him to incorporate Norman's notes, which didn't help much, as his screenplay left me cold. In the meantime, on May 25, 1967, Norman, Doug Laurence, a camera crew and a group of stunt men left to film the Charlotte World 600 Stock Car Race at the Charlotte Motor Speedway in Charlotte, North Carolina.

Taurog set up six cameras to film the actual race from positions around the track, as well as having a camera mounted in one of the race cars and another onboard the official pace car. The day after the race, Taurog and the MGM stunt drivers began filming several days of spinouts, crashes and rollovers, under stunt coordinator Carey Loftin's supervision, as well as background plates for process photography that would be filmed back at the studio with Elvis and the other actors portraying drivers in the Charlotte World 600.

Bob Harris, an actor-stunt man who had done stunts in several earlier films for Taurog and would play Lloyd Meadows, one of Presley's pit crew members in *Speedway*, was one of the MGM stunt drivers who went to Charlotte and doubled Elvis in several of the stunt crashes. "While we were filming the actual Charlotte World 600," he told Bill Bram in an interview, "they picked out a car that was doing pretty good and after that they used that car as Elvis' car and I flipped it, I think I turned it over." The car was a white 1967 Dodge Charger with the number 6 on the side and a double of that car was used in the stunts in Charlotte and again in Hollywood. "Norman was a gentle man," Harris continued. "He was very understanding... very patient, but very direct. He would give us rehearsals; he wasn't loud at all, or effusive. He was just a gentle, very nice person."

A local boy named Robbie Robinson was hired to be Elvis' photo double. He looked enough like Elvis that Taurog was able to get some fairly close shots of him driving the Dodge Charger that was supposed to be Elvis' car, speeding around the race track. Taurog also shot close-ups in the pit area of

(L-R) William Schallert, Carl Ballantine, Poncie Ponce, Carl Reindel, Elvis, Bill Bixby and Nancy Sinatra.

a number of the actual race car drivers seated in their cars, including Richard Petty, Buddy Baker, Cale Yarborough and Tiny Lund, and these close-ups appeared in the film's main title.

While in Charlotte, Taurog was interviewed by a reporter for the local *Gastonia Gazette* and offered this appraisal of Presley: "I've done a lot of pictures with Elvis and I feel he still has talent to give which hasn't been touched yet. To me he's a fine light comedian. He's not an actor, but a reactor. He always tackles his roles with a comedic tongue-in-cheek. I feel as he matures he could turn into a very fine character actor."

The cast of *Speedway* was quite large and included such reliables as Gale Gordon, returning once again to the Taurog stable as Internal Revenue Service chief R.W. Hepworth, William Schallert as Abel Esterlake, the widowed race car driver with four young daughters (one of whom was played by 18 month-old Patti Jean Keith Norman Taurog's first granddaughter). Another of Esterlake's daughters was played by six-year-old actress Victoria Meyerink, who would grow up to become an award-winning film producer. Also in the cast were comedian-magician Carl Ballantine as Birdie Kebner, Elvis' crew chief; and as members of his racing crew, Poncie Ponce from TV's *Hawaiian*

Eye, Carl Reindel, Harper Carter and Bob Harris. Bill Bixby played Kenny Donford, Elvis' skirt-chasing buddy and manager, a character not much different from the one he'd played in *Doctor, You've Got to Be Kidding!* Kenny has not only lost all of Elvis' prize money on the horses, but he's submitted a cockamamie tax return filled with illegal deductions that Hepworth summarily disallows, causing Elvis to owe the IRS $145,000 in back taxes. And that's where Nancy Sinatra comes in; she's there to collect.

Elvis and Nancy were old friends and they worked together beautifully. Nancy had been at McGuire Air Force Base in 1960 to greet Elvis when he returned from his stint in the Army, and had then appeared with him on her father's ABC television show *The Frank Sinatra Timex Special: Welcome Home Elvis.* Nancy was game for anything and feisty enough to stand up Elvis, who obviously enjoyed working with her. However, there was one time while we were shooting *Speedway* where things didn't go as planned. It was late in the day and we'd been working on a scene between Elvis and Nancy in a rather confined set that was supposed to be the interior of his trailer. The scene was basically an argument, but since they found each other very attractive it also had a sexual undercurrent. Elvis always had trouble playing this kind of scene; he didn't deal well with subtext, and on top of that it had been a long day and everyone was tired. Elvis kept stumbling over the same line of dialogue, and about the third time that he blew it he started to giggle. Taurog would call for another take, and the minute he said "action," Elvis would burst into laughter. His laugh was so infectious that Nancy started to laugh, and soon all of us were laughing with them; everyone, that is, but Norman Taurog, who was furious, but knew from experience that when Elvis went up like this it was hopeless to continue, and reluctantly dismissed the company. The next morning a contrite Elvis apologized to "Mr. Taurog," and we got the scene on the first take.

Elvis had arrived at MGM on Monday morning, June 19, 1967, and immediately attended a music meeting with Taurog, Douglas Laurence and Colonel Parker. From there he reported to the wardrobe department for fittings. The following two evenings were spent recording the soundtrack for the film on MGM's Orchestra Stage. Except for Nancy's song "Your Groovy Self'" which had been written by Lee Hazlewood, all of the *Speedway* songs were written by the team of Mel Glazer and Stephen Schlaks, and they were certainly a step up from *Double Trouble,* with one glaring exception, a song called "He's Your Uncle, Not Your Dad." This was a production number flat-out of a Broadway musical and had no place in an Elvis movie. Alex Romero was back with us and he choreographed it complete with a male chorus and high kicks, and Elvis and Bill Bixby did their good-natured best to keep up. Romero also choreographed a couple of energetic numbers with Elvis and Nancy in the Hangout Club, the car-themed nightclub setting that art direc-

The original car-themed nightclub in *Speedway*.

tor Leroy Coleman created for the film, and which Quentin Tarantino later "borrowed" for his film *Pulp Fiction* (1994).

On the days that a musical number was being filmed, Elvis would watch his dance-in Lance LeGault go through the routine that Romero had staged with whoever else was backing Elvis, generally a small combo or some dancing girls, and then he would step in and do it, adding his own moves. Elvis never did a lot of rehearsing beforehand, but Lance would work with the choreographer and lay out the number. If there were dance steps that Lance felt were too complicated for Elvis, he would have the choreographer adjust it to something less demanding. Elvis mostly did basic steps incorporating his karate moves, which he felt comfortable with and looked good doing. The days of the classic, hip-swiveling "Elvis the Pelvis" were long gone, which as it turned out was undoubtedly a huge mistake.

Norman had already made me aware that he was having trouble with the sight in his good eye. One day, partway through filming, he mentioned that his doctors had told him of a laser procedure that could help restore the sight in that eye, and that he was planning to fly to Denver to have the operation. He asked if I would accompany him and I readily agreed. He was thrilled that there was a chance to save his eyesight, but over the weekend Norman met with his doctors who decided that the operation wouldn't help. Just like with his other eye years before, Norman's diabetes had caused a condition called proliferative retinopathy, which had damaged the blood vessels of the retina. In addition, he was suffering from an advanced case of glaucoma. The trip was cancelled and I felt terribly sorry for Norman, for we both knew that this had been his last hope of saving his eyesight.

Leroy Coleman constructed a large replica of the pit section of the Charlotte Raceway on MGM's Lot 2 and we filmed there for several days under the hot July sun, with many of us ending up with sunburned faces. Ross Hagen, who played Elvis' Charlotte World 600 competitor Paul Dado, recalled his impression of Taurog for Bill Bram: "He was a legendary director. We always played jokes on and off the set, but when he arrived on the set you knew the 'head honcho' had arrived." A lot of attention was paid to the race sequences in *Speedway*; between the actual race footage and the process shots of Elvis and Hagen in their stock cars, we probably filmed for several weeks. Richard Farrell (brother of actress Glenda Farrell) did an excellent job of editing the footage for the maximum effect. Filming the process shots was difficult for Norman, as the flickering screen aggravated his eye condition, so he asked me to keep tabs on the action and make sure that everything was okay before he would call for the take to be printed.

Budgeted at approximately $3,000,000, *Speedway* began filming on June 26, 1967, and midway through filming, on July 12, 1967, Elvis happily announced to everyone on the set that Priscilla was expecting their first child. Filming was completed on Friday, August 18, 1967, and the following Monday Elvis recorded his replacement dialogue for the film. In the afternoon I met him out by the Esther Williams saucer tank at the back of the studio's main lot and supervised some exterior makeup tests for his next film, *Stay Away, Joe* (1968), in which he was to play a half-breed Navajo Indian. Bill Tuttle, the head of MGM's makeup department, wanted to see how the various makeups looked under natural light. I told Elvis that Doug Laurence had

Charlotte Raceway's pit section as recreated on MGM's Lot Three.

just hired me to do a rewrite on the *Stay Away, Joe* script, which was based on a humorous novel by Dan Cushman, and he was genuinely happy for me. Norman wouldn't be directing this one; that assignment would go to Peter Tewksbury.

The studio kept *Speedway* on the shelf for almost a year, and by the time it was released two more MGM Presley films had completed filming, and *Clambake* (1967) and *Stay Away, Joe* had already been released. What was the problem with *Speedway*? Elvis looked terrific, Nancy Sinatra was sexy, the songs were the best in a long time, and the race footage was beautifully staged. So what was wrong? In two words, the script. MGM was now actively trying to come up with scenarios that would give Elvis a chance to play more sophisticated characters and break the restrictive mold that had become the pattern in his films; and the plot for *Speedway* was, sorry to say, as hackneyed as any of his previous films.

Finally, on June 2, 1968, MGM sent Doug Laurence and Bill Bixby back to Charlotte, North Carolina, to attend two days of celebratory parades, complete with floats, marching bands and a drum majorette, and an evening premiere of the film at the city's Park Terrace Theatre. On June 13, 1968, *Speedway* opened in New York at the Lyric Theatre and in other neighborhood theaters, along with another MGM film, *Sol Madrid* (1967). In what would turn out to be the final *New York Times* review of an Elvis Presley film, reviewer Reneta Adler would write, " [T]his is after all, just another Presley movie which makes no great use at all of one of the most talented, important and durable performers of our time. Music, youth and customs were much changed by Elvis Presley 12 years ago; from the 28 movies he has made since he sang 'Heartbreak Hotel' you would never guess it." Kevin Thomas in the *Los Angeles Times* wrote, "*Speedway*, playing citywide, has a script that ran out of gas before Elvis Presley was born. Presley pictures can be unpretentious fun, but this one is both uninspired and too much of an imitation of too many of his previous movies." *Variety* summed it up with, "Under Norman Taurog's know-how comedy direction even some of the silliness in the Philip Shuken script gets by as entertainment, but the story lacks the legitimacy of the better Presley starrers."

As it turned out, *Speedway* barely recovered its production costs.

Last Hurrah

Burt Kennedy was originally supposed to write, direct, and produce *Stay Away, Joe* under his indie banner Brigade Productions, but on August 21, 1967, MGM announced that Douglas Laurence would be the producer of Kennedy's screenplay. By the time I was assigned as writer, the project had officially become an Elvis Presley film. I saw an opportunity to make something more than just another "Elvis movie" and tried to create a character for Elvis based in some respects on Paul Newman's character in *Hud* (1963), a conman who could talk an Eskimo into buying an ice-making machine, or a pretty girl into believing a one-night stand was an invitation to permanent bliss. It was an ambitious idea, but it didn't work out. When director Peter Tewksbury got to the location in Sedona, Arizona he threw away the script and had the cast improvise scene after scene. The energy level was terrific, but with all of the yelling, fighting and partying that went on, you couldn't understand what anybody was saying and Joe and his friends and family ended up looking like a bunch of "drunken Indians." Boy, did I miss Norman Taurog. The critics hated the film, with *The Hollywood Reporter* saying that it "moves with the boisterous vulgarity of a marathon beer bust, though its quaint and patronizing view of American Indians as brawling, balling, boozing children should rightly offend many or all." *Variety* added, "At best, film is a dim artistic accomplishment; at worst, it caters to outdated prejudice. Custer himself might be embarrassed—for the Indians." It was probably just as well that the *New York Times* had ceased to review Presley films, God know what they would have said.

While we were filming *Stay Away, Joe* in Sedona, I had a chance to meet Priscilla. She and the wives and girlfriends of the "Memphis Mafia" arrived

The talented, but wasted cast of Stay Away, Joe: (L-R) producer Douglas Laurence, Burgess Meredith, Katy Jurado, Susan Trustman, Elvis, Thomas Gomez and writer Michael Hoey. Not shown, Joan Blondell, Henry Jones, Anne Seymour and L.Q. Jones.

at the location one day, and it was an amazing sight. We all knew that Elvis, who had naturally brown hair, dyed his hair black, but it was a shock to see all of the women, including Priscilla, arrive on the set with jet-black hair. They all looked alike, and particularly in Priscilla's case, they all looked like Elvis.

While in Sedona, Doug Laurence gave me a book to read saying it was to be Elvis' next picture. The book was called *Kiss My Firm But Pliant Lips* and it was written by a guy named Dan Greenburg whose previous books had such catchy titles as *How to be a Jewish Mother* and *I Could Never Have Sex With Any Man Who Has So Little Regard for My Husband*. *Pliant Lips* had originally been set up as part of a three-picture deal at Columbia Pictures in 1965 with Ernest Pintoff set to direct and Dan Greenburg in collaboration with Pintoff to write the screenplay based on his book. The plot of *Pliant Lips* involved a meek little man—think Woody Allen—who has a traumatic relationship with a dominating temptress. Hardly the kind of material for an Elvis Presley movie. But Doug insisted that's what it was going to be, and furthermore I was going to write it and Norman Taurog would direct.

I was happy that I might have a chance to redeem myself with this new assignment, but it was going to be a challenge to bend and shape the premise to accommodate our macho hero. 1968 was a time of change; there were riots in the streets, the flower children were parading in the Haight-Ashbury district of San Francisco and The Beatles had released their soon to be legendary album *Sgt. Pepper's Lonely Hearts Club Band*. Movies with drug themes were beginning to show up in theaters; *The Trip* (1967), *Psych-Out* (1968), *Wild in the Streets* (1968), and a LSD-laced atrocity from director Otto Preminger called *Skidoo* (1968) were all released within a matter of a few months. It seemed to me that it was about time to bring Elvis up to date. Norman came up with the clever idea of taking Dan Greenburg's device of having Elvis working at two jobs simultaneously in the same building and making him a fashion photographer who has to continually sneak up and down the back stairs in order to be in two places at the same time. I based one boss on Hugh Hefner and his *Playboy* magazine, and the other on an ad agency run by a stuffy individual very much like Rudy Vallee's character in the film, *How to Succeed in Business Without Really Trying* (1967), and as it turned out, we were lucky enough to actually get Rudy Vallee to play the part. The kooky character of Bernice (who keeps changing her name to fit her mood) was Greenburg's creation, but I took advantage of her unpredictable qualities to keep Elvis' character constantly off balance; she moves him out of his apartment and into her beach house, attacks him in the shower and has her dog chase him into the sea. It was also made explicitly clear that they end up in bed together, and not just to sleep. Elvis' photo assignments allowed Taurog to stage scenes that took place on location all over Los Angeles, from the Music Center (where Elvis' father, Vernon, played a small role) and Marineland in Palos Verdes, to Malibu and a house in the Trousdale Estates section of Beverly Hills.

Both Norman and Doug Laurence agreed that we should keep our new Elvis' singing down to a minimum of three or four songs that would be integrated into the action as seamlessly as possible. With the exception of a title sequence that had Elvis driving a dune buggy all over the Malibu sands with his voice on the soundtrack singing "Wonderful World," I thought the selection of songs was pretty good. In one sequence, which was quite honestly inspired by a dance sequence I'd always admired from the MGM musical *Lili* (1953), Bernice slips Elvis a hallucinatory drug, which triggers a fantasy dream complete with a talking dog and disappearing dancers. It was choreographed by Jack Regas to the song "Edge of Reality." The big musical hit of the film was Mac Davis and Billy Strange's "A Little Less Conversation," which was staged by Jack Baker and sung by Elvis to mini-skirted Celeste Yarnall at a hip cocktail party hosted by the Hugh Hefner character, played by Don Porter. In 2003, 25 years after Elvis' death and 35 years after the film's release, a remixed

Elvis, Michelle Carey and Brutus on location in Malibu for
Live a Little, Love a Little (1968).

version of his vocal became a huge hit in Europe and was #1 in the UK for a number of weeks. The track was also used over the main title for the TV series *Las Vegas* (2003-2008) and the 2001remake of *Ocean's Eleven*. The final tune, a bossa nova by Luiz Bonfa with lyrics by Randy Starr called "Almost in Love," was one that I really liked and I fought to have it included; it showed off Elvis' skill with a love song, but failed to get much notice as a single.

When Elvis reported for work he looked terrific. There hadn't been much of a lag between finishing *Stay Away, Joe* and starting this film, so Elvis was still in good condition. In addition, he was preparing for his television special that he would tape toward the end of June and was actively trying to keep his weight under control. Elvis seemed enthusiastic with the changes to a more sophisticated storyline and he really worked hard throughout the filming, even though he had to do a lot of difficult scenes, including being chased into the surf by a growling dog. There have been a lot of stories written that the dog belonged to Elvis, but they're not true. The dog, an enormous Great Dane named Brutus, was owned by a Hollywood animal trainer who was with us on the set at all times.

Michele Carey, who played Bernice/Betty/Suzie/Alice, had made a few television appearances before she was "discovered" by Howard Hawks and cast opposite John Wayne and Robert Mitchum in *El Dorado* (1966). By the time that Doug Laurence signed her for the picture, she had appeared in a few more television shows and had a small role in *The Sweet Ride* (1968) at Twentieth Century-Fox. Carey's patchy career continued until 1982 and consisted mostly of guest star roles in television series and a few TV movies. Her final screen appearances were in a couple of low-budget horror films made in Kenya and South Africa in 1986 and 1987. Douglas Laurence would later say, "She had the requirements to be a star. . . I can only believe that she didn't make a big splash because she didn't want to."

Don Porter and Rudy Vallee were both popular character actors in the '60s; Porter, who had been a contract player at Universal in the '40s and had stared in dozens of "B" movies such as *She Wolf of London* (1946) and *Buck Privates Come Home* (1947), had worked for Taurog once before at MGM in *Mrs. O'Malley and Mr. Malone*. He had recently played Sally Field's father on the *Gidget* television series (1965-1966). Vallee had at one time been the Elvis Presley of his day in the 1920s and 1930s as Rudy Vallee and His Connecticut Yankees. When his singing career ended, he successfully built a new career playing the stuffy second lead in films like *The Palm Beach Story* (1942) and *The Bachelor and the Bobby Soxer* (1947). In 1961 he co-starred in the Broad-

Elvis and Rudy Vallee, two icons from different times.

way production of *How to Succeed in Business Without Really Trying*, which played at the 46th Street Theatre for over 1,400 performances. When the play was filmed by the Mirisch Corporation for United Artists in 1967, Vallee and his co-star Robert Morse recreated their original roles.

I happened to be in Norman's office when Rudy Vallee came in to meet with him. He was absolutely charming; he loved the script, loved the part, and he was looking forward to working with Elvis. "What a publicity coup," he proclaimed, "two idols from different eras working together for the first time." He even suggested that he could wear his own clothes in the film, thereby saving the studio the cost of purchasing a wardrobe for him. Everyone thought that would be a good idea, until we received a phone call from our costume supervisor saying that Rudy had arrived with his station wagon filled to the roof with every piece of clothing he owned and was demanding that the wardrobe department clean and repair everything. I was sent down to reason with him and come up with some sort of a compromise. I took one look at the contents of Rudy's station wagon and I could see that the phone call had not been an exaggeration. The vehicle had air horns on each of the front fenders that were at least four feet long and a license plate with the word "CROONER" printed on it. I learned later that he had petitioned the city to have the name of his street changed to Rudy Vallee Lane—how's that for an ego? Rudy quickly realized that his scam wasn't going to work, and went about selecting just the right combination of suits, shirts and ties that the stuffy head of an advertising agency would wear. That was the end of our troubles with Mr. Vallee; throughout the shoot he was always a total pro and a great asset to the film.

Other cast members included Dick Sargent, who played Harry Baby, Bernice's ex-boyfriend who can't stay away. Sargent had appeared in any number of television series and a few films such as *That Touch of Mink* (1962) and *The Private Navy of Sgt. O'Farrell* (1968), and would soon take over the role of Elizabeth Montgomery's beleaguered husband in the television series *Bewitched* from 1969 to 1972. Film veteran Sterling Holloway played Bernice's milkman who always stayed for breakfast, and former child actor Eddie Hodges (the 1960 *Huckleberry Finn*) played her delivery boy. Joan Shawlee gave a wonderful performance as the woman in a slip who has rented Elvis' old apartment and thinks he's a peeping Tom, and Ann Doran (James Dean's mother in *Rebel Without a Cause*) played the landlady. I'll bet that Elvis must have besieged her with questions about his idol James Dean.

Just before we began filming *Kiss My Firm But Pliant Lips*, the title was changed to *Live a Little, Love a Little*, which was no shorter, but at least sounded more like an Elvis Presley vehicle. And on Thursday, February 1, 1968, Priscilla Presley gave birth to a baby girl, Lisa Marie, at Baptist Hospital in Memphis. Elvis reported to MGM on March 4 to record the four songs for the picture under the supervision of Billy Strange, who had done all of the arrangements and would go on to write a terrific score for the film.

Production began on Wednesday, March 13, 1968, with the company filming runbys of Bob Harris doubling Elvis in the yellow dune buggy on Kanin Road in Malibu. This was for the main title sequence, and we also filmed close-ups of Elvis in the dune buggy. There would be no process shots in this film. When we left the studio that morning I noticed two young women standing outside the gate, waiting to catch a glimpse of Elvis as he passed by. An hour later on the location I saw the same two young women standing with a couple of Elvis' boys, who had obviously picked them up and brought them along. Our other locations included an isolated beach house in Malibu, which became Bernice's home; the *Hollywood Citizen News* building, where we filmed the obligatory fight scene with Elvis, Red and Sonny surrounded by the roaring presses; a garden apartment complex; and more driving scenes along Larchmont Boulevard in the Mid-Wilshire district.

Location filming went well; it was good to be back working with Norman Taurog again, who was up to his old tricks of inserting broad comedy touches wherever he felt the need. I have to admit that some were very funny. I could tell that Elvis was having problems with his character's relationship with his leading lady, and that was partially my fault as I never came up with a good motivation for Greg Nolan (Elvis) letting Bernice boss him around. Because he was so uncomfortable, Elvis played many of his scenes with a lot of anger, which he shouldn't have. I was hoping for more caustic wit, but Taurog never really gave him the proper guidance. The biggest problem was that for perhaps the first time Elvis was playing a character who wasn't in control of the relationship. It was a problem inherent in Dan Greenburg's book that I couldn't resolve.

We had returned to the studio and begun filming the "Edge of Reality" number, when word came down to the set that Martin Luther King Jr. had been assassinated in Memphis. We were all very upset, but Elvis seemed to take it particularly hard since it happened in his hometown. He asked for a few minutes alone in his dressing room and after he returned he was able to complete the rather complicated dance routine without any difficulty. One afternoon when we were at the studio filming the interiors of the Trousdale house, Elvis motioned me over to a section of the bedroom set which wasn't being used. He spread out a number of photographs on a bed and modestly proclaimed, "That's my baby." He was so much the typically proud father at that moment that it almost brought tears to my eyes. I never met Lisa Marie, but I have seen her performance videos and she definitely inherited her father's looks and voice.

Before *Live a Little, Love a Little* was released in October of 1968, the studio's publicity department carried out a blitz of stories about "the new Elvis Presley." Army Archerd in *Variety* devoted half of his *Just for Variety* column

Elvis and Priscilla present their new baby daughter, Lisa Marie, to the world.

to a story about the sexy elements in *Live a Little*. He even quoted both Doug Laurence and me confirming that there was no question in the film about "the Presley-Carey carryings-on." Norman Taurog's reply to Army Archerd's question, "was he trying anything new?": "There's nothing new we're using hand-held cameras, but I used them in silent two-reelers when the cameraman was Hans Koenekamp, the father of Fred, who is my cameraman on this one." Unfortunately, our attempt to modernize by using hand-held cameras, split screens, freeze frames, wipes and jump cuts didn't impress the critics, who rightly attacked the script. *Variety*: "*Live a Little, Love a Little* is Elvis Presley's 28th film. It is also one of his dimmest vehicles. Story peg—why has Michele Carey effectively kidnapped him—is sidetracked in banal plotting and trite dialogue until the answer not only doesn't matter, it is barely noted at all." *The Hollywood Reporter*: "*Live a Little, Love a Little* is Elvis in Marienbad. [It] offers a number of interesting situations and abandons nearly all. Musically anemic as well, the film has been stretched with protracting entrances and exits to just under an hour and a half. Though given the standard MGM polish by producer Douglas Laurence and director Norman Taurog, it gives too little to be critical of what it gets."

May 1, 1968, was the final day of filming, and after assistant director Al Shenberg announced, "That's a wrap!" a half-hearted party was held on the set and we all signed Norman's traditional cast and crew certificate. That would be the last time that I ever saw Elvis in person, but I did watch him later on several of his television specials. The first one, which Steve Binder directed and produced along with his partner Bob Finkel, was a huge success and revitalized Elvis' career. He was singing like he used to and obviously enjoying the hell out of it. The image of him in that black leather suit was truly iconic. I wish that could have been the image I carried in my memory, but unfortunately there would be another televised documentary called *Elvis in Concert* (1977) that followed Elvis on his final tour and showed an obviously ill Elvis who was pudgy and listless, and that would be the image that I will always remember. There was a was a close-up near the end of that special that showed a bloated Elvis standing backstage in Omaha, Nebraska, waiting to go on. His eyes were absolutely lifeless, with the fat jowls and sweat pouring off his forehead only helping to accent his ghastly appearance. This special was filmed just two months before he died unexpectedly at Graceland on August 17, 1977.

Live a Little, Love a Little's general release hardly caused a ripple at the boxoffice, with ticket sales matching the unimpressive returns of *Speedway*

Elvis watches as MGM studio head Robert O'Brien congratulates Norman Taurog on the completion of filming on *Live a Little, Love a Little*.

The bloated Elvis in concert (1977).

and *Stay Away, Joe.* Elvis would make one more film for MGM with an even lengthier title than *Live a Little.* It would be called *The Trouble with Girls (and how to get into it)* (1969), and was released by MGM on a double bill with a Japanese science-fiction film called *The Green Slime* (1969).

After having produced six films for MGM, Douglas Laurence would leave the studio and would never produce another film. Norman Taurog also finished, not with a bang, but with a whimper. After having completed his 78th feature film, won one Oscar and been nominated for another, been nominated three times for a Laurel Award and once for a Golden Lion at the Venice Film Festival, and had his personal star placed on the Walk of Fame in the heart of Hollywood, he retired to his home in Beverly Hills and never directed another film.

The Final Act

Within a year of completing *Live a Little, Love a Little*, Norman Taurog was totally blind. In spite of this he never displayed any signs of self-pity or depression; in fact he always made a point of being cheery and upbeat. Elvis would occasionally visit him whenever he was in town, and I would pick him up and take him to lunch as often as I could.

Norman's lengthy film career did not go unrecognized. On February 8, 1960, his star was placed on the Hollywood Walk of Fame at 1600 Hollywood Boulevard at the corner of Hollywood and Vine, near the star of onetime silent movie personality and later John Ford character actress Mae Marsh. There was no individual ceremony, as there would be for later recipients, but then Taurog didn't have to pay the selection fee of $30,000 to the Hollywood Chamber of Commerce, which is what current nominees are required to cough up. In 1966, based on the success of his Elvis films, Norman was nominated for a Golden Laurel Award by the Motion Picture Exhibiter Magazine, rising to fourth place behind Norman Jewison, George Cukor and David Lean. Pretty heady company, but the next year, while still nominated, he dropped to fifth place, and the following year, 1968, the year he retired, to eighth place. This was more an indication of the boxoffice returns of the Elvis films than a comment on the quality of Taurog's work. One evening in 1973 I attended a tribute for Norman that was held at the Directors Guild of America's theatre in Hollywood. His good friend director George Seaton introduced him by saying that Taurog's ability to tackle any type of film made him "the Decathlon champion of the DGA." Norman then joked, "My agents told me that if I do well here tonight they'd book me into the Desert Inn in Las Vegas." Also on the dais were one of his favorite cameramen, Joseph Ruttenberg, actress Kathryn Grayson, and Gene Reynolds. Jackie Cooper had been invited, but declined to attend, citing previous commitments. There was a screening of *Boys Town*, followed by a question and answer session with the audience. When Taurog was asked why current films lack sentimentality, his reply revealed a sense of bitterness I hadn't seen before, "It is a matter of the times," he said. "Even in everyday life, people haven't got time for you. The sentiment isn't here today. I haven't made a picture in seven years, and I have no desire to."

Norman would continue his involvement with the film students at the University of Southern California's Cinema Department, lecturing and monitoring their progress. He also continued his support of his favorite charity, the Braille Institute on Vermont Avenue in mid-town Los Angeles. He would have Leon chauffeur him to his appointments in the Cadillac that Elvis had given him. Norman served on the Board of Directors of the Braille Institute for thirteen years, and for many of those years he provided for the entertainment at the children's and adult's Christmas Shows. In 1976 Norman Taurog received the Light Award for "service to the Braille Institute and its work on behalf of the blind." The presenter was his old friend George Seaton at a banquet held at the Beverly Hills Hotel

Sue Taurog continued to be involved with political and charitable volunteering. In addition to her position as president of the Los Angeles Orphanage Guild and its association with the Maryvale Orphanage fundraising efforts, and being president of the KCET Channel 28 Women's Council, she was also active on the Harvard School Women's Committee, and headed up Disney Studio's premiere of *The Happiest Millionaire* (1967) that grossed $1 million for the California Institute of the Arts. The Board of Directors of KCET presented her with an Award of Appreciation for chairing several very successful fund-raising premieres, and the Business and Professional Women's Club of Beverly Hills named her "The 1970 Woman of Achievement." For her work in support of Richard Nixon's 1968 Presidential campaign, Sue and Norman Taurog were invited to a champagne reception at the White House that was held shortly after Nixon's inauguration. In November of 1972 Sue appeared on the speaker's platform at a rally at Ontario International Airport with the president and Mrs. Nixon, Governor Ronald Reagan and Astronaut Buzz Aldrin. She later received personally signed photographs from both President Nixon and Vice-President Spiro Agnew with thanks for her support during the second presidential campaign.

In May of 1977 Norman was dealt another blow to his health and was admitted to St. John's Hospital in Santa Monica. A circulation problem caused by his diabetes forced doctors to amputate his toes. After that Norman became more and more of a recluse and eventually he and Sue sold the Beverly Hills house and moved to a condominium in the desert community of Palm Desert. I hadn't heard from him in several months when Sue called one day to tell me that Norman was gravely ill with cancer and was at the Eisenhower Medical Center. I drove down to Rancho Mirage to see him, and when I walked into the room I was shocked to see how frail he looked. Sue said, "Norman, Mike Hoey is here," and in a weak voice he greeted me, "Hello, Mr. Holy." God bless him, he never lost his sense of humor. Norman Taurog died at the Eisenhower Medical Center on April 7, 1981 at the age of 82. His funeral was held three days later at All Saints Episcopal Church in Beverly Hills. Sue Taurog would eventually move from Palm Desert to Woodland Hills, California, where she would live until her death in 2008 at the age of 92.

Why did Elvis think so highly of Norman Taurog? Certainly their films together were not the highlights of Elvis' career, yet he happily followed Taurog's direction in nine films. My guess is that Elvis, who was a big movie fan, admired many of the stars who had appeared in Taurog's earlier films, such as Bing Crosby, Spencer Tracy, Cary Grant, Robert Taylor and Mickey Rooney, and felt safe with the man who had guided their film careers, not to mention the careers of his contemporaries Pat Boone, Eddie Fisher and Frankie Avalon. Taurog did his best to protect Elvis, perhaps too much; and if he can be faulted for anything, it would be that he relied too much on broad visual humor to liven up what he correctly perceived to be weaknesses in the scripts.

Of course Elvis went back to performing in live concerts and resuscitated his lagging career for another nine years until his death in 1977. His influence on his generation and on the generations that followed was so great that 36 years after his death, his presence is felt throughout the world. Visitors still flock to Graceland, now a museum, and to the multitude of displays and gift shops that line Elvis Presley Boulevard. Every year, on the anniversary of his death, a celebration dubbed "Elvis Week" is held in Memphis with various celebrities and former Presley associates appearing as guests at a series of events, including an Elvis Presley impersonators contest. Elvis impersonators still stalk the stages of Las Vegas nightclubs, and on January 24, 2012, the conspiracy theorists, who maintain that Elvis never died, were gifted with a two-hour movie called *Elvis Found Alive* that was released on DVD. The video contained a photograph of a man named John Burrows, who looked a bit like an elderly Elvis Presley, and a recording called "Stars and Stripes," sung by someone who sounded vaguely like Elvis, that was supposedly delivered to various radio stations across the country. The video based its specious claim that Elvis was still alive and living under an assumed name on this material, as well as a clip from a local Fox News affiliate's announcement that a half-sister of Elvis' named Eliza had come forward and according to an "expert" in Arizona, her DNA matched the man called John Burrows. It then went on to "expose" the fact that Elvis had secretly been a government agent using the name John Burrows and was now in hiding because of his prior activities. The filmmakers interviewed a man, whose face was concealed by shadows, who claimed to be Elvis and spoke in a familiar Southern drawl like so many of the Elvis impersonators. It was all pretty far-fetched, but for the conspiracists that was all the proof they needed that Elvis hadn't died. I think it was Johnny Carson who once said, "If life was fair, Elvis would be still be alive and all of the impersonators would be dead."

In truth, Elvis *will* never die, because his music lives on, and his records will continue to be sold. His films will continue to be viewed on television each year on the anniversaries of his birthday and of his death. Books will continue to be written about him. He will be remembered as the enormously talented performer he was, before the drugs and the overindulgent lifestyle brought him down.

* * *

There is a sad aftermath to this story. Some years after Norman Taurog's death all of his personally signed cast and crew certificates began showing up on eBay, along with many of his scripts, photographs and other memorabilia. Taurog's red morocco leather-bound Final Shooting Script for *The Adventures of Tom Sawyer* became available on eBay, inscribed by producer David

Photograph that appeared on eBay announcing the auction of Norman Taurog's 1931 Academy Award.

O. Selznick, "For Norman with happy memories of a nice association and with gratitude for a fine job, David S. 1938." Then a Martin D-28 guitar that Elvis Presley had given to Norman was put up for sale, and eventually even Taurog's 1931 Oscar for *Skippy* was auctioned off. How sad that someone was pillaging his personal effects.

In his comprehensive study *World Film Directors: Volume I (1890-1945)*, editor John Wakeman quotes film historian Ephraim Katz's description of Norman Taurog as, "the ideal studio director, an excellent craftsman capable of turning almost any assignment into an attractive boxoffice package. Not even the French have claimed *auteur* status for Norman Taurog. He did what he was told, but did it well enough to create—amid all the dross—ten or a dozen splendid entertainments. Many more prestigious figures achieved less." The likes of films such as *Skippy, The Adventures of Tom Sawyer, Boys Town, Broadway Melody of 1940, Young Tom Edison,* and *Room for One More* would remain a lasting legacy for a man whose 52-year career gave audiences countless hours of entertainment and who quite obviously loved making movies.

I learned a lot from Norman Taurog, more than I even realized until I too began to direct. When a problem would come up on the set, I'd frequently ask myself, "What would Norman do?" One night, when Norman and I were preparing to film *Palm Springs Weekend*, we were sitting at the bar at the Palm Springs Racquet Club and Norman started to regale me with stories about his experiences in early Hollywood. The stories were fascinating, and as I listened to marvelous anecdotes about silent screen stars Larry Semon, Oliver Hardy, Lloyd Hamilton, and later stories of W.C. Fields, Bing Crosby and Fred Astaire, it made me wish that I could have been with him in his heyday; I was jealous of Jack Mintz, who *had* been at his side during those exciting times. I loved the idea that everyone was young and just starting out and that it was a time of exhilarating experimentations. In those days nobody could tell you it couldn't be done, because nobody had done it before. Norman's recollections of early Hollywood became the inspiration for a short fantasy film that my writing partner Bruce Belland and I wrote and produced and that I directed called *Those Were the Days*. There was a character in the film, an old silent film director clearly based on Norman Taurog, who was lecturing to a USC Cinema class. I would have loved to have had Norman play the part, but unfortunately his health wouldn't allow it. I did however include clips from one of his silent two-reel comedies with Larry Semon that the cinema class is viewing, and which elicited genuine laughter from the young extras playing the students as they watched it for the first time.

Acknowledgments

Many photographs came from the author's private collection, but for others I must thank the following:

Tom Weaver, a true friend and a dedicated devotee of film history, who guided me through the lengthy development of this book, edited the final manuscript and contributed several important interviews and photographs.

Scott Gallinghouse, who once again contributed his amazing research capability and was an incalculable resource for both newspaper articles and photographs.

Film Historian Bill Bram, who kindly gave me access to his vast collection of Elvis Presley photographs and memorabilia and to various interviews in his files.

Ned Comstock, Archivist at the University of Southern California Cinematic Arts Library, for his invaluable guidance and support in accessing the Norman Taurog papers, MGM, Twentieth Century-Fox, and Joe Pasternak-Universal Pictures correspondence and production files.

Sandra Joy Aguilar, Curator and Director and Jonathon Auxier, Curator, USC School of Cinematic Arts, Warner Bros Archives, for granting access to *Room For One More*, *Onionhead* and *Palm Springs Weekend* correspondence and production files.

Jenny Romero, Department Coordinator of the Special Collections section of the Margaret Herrick Library at the Academy of Motion Picture Arts and Sciences, for allowing me access to the Norman Taurog, Samuel Goldwyn, Paramount Pictures and MGM-*The Beginning or the End* correspondence and production files.

Robert Vaughn, Librarian, Louis B. Mayer Library, American Film Institute Conservatory, for granting me access to the Jack Mintz papers.

Dr. Robert J. Kiss for locating background material and newspaper clippings that helped to explain Norman Taurog's seeming period of inactivity during 1943-1946.

In addition my personal thanks to the following:

Bob Baker
Edward Faulkner
Earl Hamner Jr.
Susan Hart
Jimmy Hawkins
Roger Mayer
Gene Reynolds

Bibliography

Astaire, Fred. *Steps in Time*. New York: Harper & Brothers, 1959

Behlmer, Rudy H. *Memo From David O. Selznick*. New York: The Viking Press, 1972

Berg, A. Scott. *Goldwyn*. New York: Riverhead Books, 1989

Bergan, Ronald. *The United Artist Story*. New York: Crown Publishing, 1986

Bingen, Steven and Stephen X. Sylvester and Michael Troyen. *MGM: Hollywood's Greatest Backlot*. Solana Beach: Santa Monica Press, 2011

Bram, Bill. *Elvis: Frame By Frame*. Livermore, CA: WingSpan Press, 2007

Brownlow, Kevin. *The Parades Gone By...* New York: Alfred A. Knopf, 1968

Brownlow, Kevin. *Hollywood: The Pioneers*. New York: Alfred A. Knopf, 1979

Chaplin, Charles. *My Autobiography*. New York: Simon and Schuster, 1964

Cooper, Jackie. *Please Don't Shoot My Dog*. New York: William Morrow and Company, 1981

Crowther, Bosley. *The Lion's Share*. New York: E.P. Dutton & Company, 1957

Curtis, James. *Spencer Tracy*. New York: Alfred A. Knopf, 2011

Custin, George F. *Twentieth Century's Fox: Darryl F. Zanuck and the Culture of Hollywood*. New York: Basic Books, A subsidiary of Perseus Books, 1997

Eames, John Douglas. *The MGM Story: The Complete History of Fifty-Seven Roaring Years*. New York: Crown Publishers, 1976

Eames, John Douglas. *The Paramount Story*. New York: Crown Publishers, 1985

Ellenberger, Allan R. *Margaret O'Brien: A Career Chronicle and Biography.* Jefferson, NC: McFarland and Company, 2000.

Finch, Christopher and Linda Rosenkrantz: *Gone Hollywood: The Movie Colony in the Golden Age.* New York: Doubleday & Company, 1979

Fleming, E.J. *The Movieland Directory.* Jefferson, NC: McFarland and Company, 2004

Fordin, Hugh. *MGM's Greatest Musicals: The Arthur Freed Unit.* New York: Da Capo Press, 1996

Frascella, Lawrence and Al Weisel. *Live Fast, Die Young: The Wild Ride of Making Rebel Without a Cause.* New York: Simon and Schuster, 2005

Fricke, James. *Judy: A Legendary Film Career.* Philadelphia, PA: Running Press, 2010

Guralnick, Peter and Ernst Jorgensen. *Elvis Day By Day: The Definitive Record of His Life and Music.* New York: Ballantine Books, 1999

Harmetz, Aljean. *The Making of the Wizard of Oz.* New York: Alfred A. Knopf. 1977

Harris, Marlys J. *The Zanucks of Hollywood: The Dark Legacy of an American Dynasty.* New York: Crown Publishers, 1989

Haver, Ronald. *David O. Selznick's Hollywood.* New York: Alfred A. Knopf, 1980

Hay, Peter. *MGM: When the Lion Roars.* Atlanta, GA: Turner Publishing, 1991

Hirschorn, Clive. *The Warner Bros. Story.* New York: Crown Publishers, 1979

Hirschorn, Clive. *The Universal Story.* New York: Crown Publishers, 1983

Jewell, Richard B. and Vernon Harbin. *The RKO Story.* New York: Crown Publishers, 1982

Lewis, Jerry. *The Total Film-Maker.* New York: Random House, 1971

Lewis, Jerry and James Kaplan. *Dean and Me (A Love Story).* New York: Random House, 2005

Lewis, Mark. *The Movie Book: The 1940's.* New York: Crescent Books, 1988

Loy, Myrna and James Kotsilibas-Davis. *Myrna Loy: Being and Becoming.* New York: Alfred A. Knopf, 1987

Macgowan, Kenneth. *Behind the Screen: The History and Techniques of the Motion Picture.* New York: Delacorte Press, 1965

Marx, Arthur. *Everybody Love Somebody Sometime (Especially Himself).* New York: Hawthorn Books, Inc. 1974

Moore, Mickey. *My Magic Carpet of Films: A Personal Journey in the Motion Picture Industry 1916-2000.* Albany, GA: BearManor Media, 2009

Parish, James Robert and Gregory Mank. *The Best of MGM The Golden Years: 1928-1959.* Westport, CT: Arlington House Publishers, 1981

Ragan, David. *Who's Who in Hollywood.* New York: Facts on File, 1992

Rainsberger, Todd. *James Wong Howe, Cinematographer.* San Diego, CA: A.S. Barnes, 1981

Rooney, Mickey. *Life is Too Short.* New York: Villard Books, 1991

Ross, Lilian. *Picture.* New York: Proscenium Publishers, 1984

Secrest, Meryle. *Somewhere For Me: A Biography of Richard Rogers.* New York: Alfred A. Knopf. 2001

Shipman, David. *Cinema: The First Hundred Years.* New York: St. Martin's Press, 1993

Simpson, Paul. *The Rough Guide to Elvis: The Man, The Music, The Movies, The Myth.* London: Penguin Books, Ltd. 2002

Silverman, Stephen M. *Dancing on the Ceiling: Stanley Donen and his Movies.* New York: Alfred A. Knopf, 1996

Thomas, Bob. *Selznick.* New York: Doubleday, 1970

Thomas, Tony and Aubrey Solomon. *The Films of 20th Century Fox: A Pictorial History.* Secaucus, NJ: Citadel Press, 1979

Tornabene, Lyn. *Long Live the King: A Biography of Clark Gable.* New York: G.P. Putnam's Sons, 1976

Tunzi, Joseph A. and Bill Bram. *Elvis in Tickle Me.* Chicago, IL: JAT Productions, 2007

Ursini, James. *Preston Sturges: An American Dreamer.* New York: Curtis Books, 1973

Wakeman, John. *World Film Directors: Volume I (1890-1945).* New York: The H.W. Wilson Company, 1987

Yudkoff, Alvin. *Gene Kelly: A Life of Dance and Dreams.* New York: Watson-Guptill Publications, 1999

Zmijewsky, Steven and Boris Zmijewsky. *Elvis: The films and career of Elvis Presley*, Secaucus, NJ: Citadel Press, 1976

Periodicals

Classic Images
Daily News
Daily Variety
The Hollywood Reporter
Los Angeles Times
The New York Times
The New Yorker
PM
Philadelphia Enquirer
New York Herald Tribune
The Hollywood Citizen
Chicago Tribune
Newsweek
Billboard
Los Angeles Herald-Examiner
Time Magazine
The Lion's Roar
New York World Telegram
New York Mirror
Motion Picture Herald
San Francisco Examiner
Saturday Evening Post

Index

CPSIA information can be obtained at www.ICGtesting.com
Printed in the USA
BVOW03s1440161113

336353BV00007B/98/P